CHARITY, PHILANT
IN AMERIC

The study of philanthropy has transcended the structure of traditional disciplines, often involving nonhistorians in historical analysis. This book presents professional historians addressing the dominant issues and theories offered to explain the history of American philanthropy and its role in American society. The essays develop and enlighten the major themes proposed by the book's editors, often taking issue with each other in the process. The overarching premise is that philanthropic activity in America has its roots in the desires of individuals to impose their visions, ideals, or conceptions of truth upon their society. To do so, they have organized in groups, frequently defining themselves and their group's role in society in the process.

Lawrence J. Friedman is Professor of History and Philanthropic Studies at Indiana University. His publications include *Identity's Architect: A Biography of Erik Erikson* (1999) and *Menninger: The Family and the Clinic* (1990).

Mark D. McGarvie is a Golieb Fellow in Legal History at the New York University School of Law. He has published in various academic and legal journals.

CHARITY, PHILANTHROPY, AND CIVILITY IN AMERICAN HISTORY

Edited by

LAWRENCE J. FRIEDMAN
Indiana University

MARK D. McGARVIE
New York University

CAMBRIDGE
UNIVERSITY PRESS

PUBLISHED BY THE PRESS SYNDICATE OF THE UNIVERSITY OF CAMBRIDGE
The Pitt Building, Trumpington Street, Cambridge, United Kingdom

CAMBRIDGE UNIVERSITY PRESS
The Edinburgh Building, Cambridge CB2 2RU, UK
40 West 20th Street, New York, NY 10011-4211, USA
10 Stamford Road, Oakleigh, Melbourne 3207, Australia
Ruiz de Alarcón 13, 28014 Madrid, Spain
Dock House, The Waterfront, Cape Town 8001, South Africa

http://www.cambridge.org

First published 2003
First paperback edition 2004

Printed in the United States of America

Typeface Garamond 11/13 pt.

A catalog record for this book is available from the British Library

Library of Congress Cataloging in Publication data is available

ISBN 0 521 81989 X hardback
ISBN 0 521 60353 6 paperback

To Eugene Tempel, Dwight Burlingame, Robert Payton, and the Indiana University Center on Philanthropy for continuous support of this venture in independent and critical scholarship.

"For behold, are we not all beggars?"
Mosiah 4:19, *The Book of Mormon*

CONTENTS

Contents

PHILANTHROPY IN AMERICA: HISTORICISM AND ITS DISCONTENTS

LAWRENCE J. FRIEDMAN

Until the last quarter of the twentieth century, philanthropy was not re-garded as a field for systematic scholarly endeavor. At the beginning of that century, programs designated as "philanthropy" often resided in American schools of social work and represented narrowly focused remedial efforts for social improvement. It was not until the early 1980s that John Gardner, the eminent public intellectual, liberal Republican, and reformer, established a functioning agency for coordination of activities and institutions that involved philanthropy – the Independent Sector (I.S.). Gardner created the I.S. to forge a self-consciousness among grant-making and voluntary organizations – a sense that they occupied a distinct third space between government and the private market economy. By 1983, the important Independent Sector Research Committee was established. Chaired by Robert Payton, formerly a U.S. ambassador and president of the Exxon Educational Foundation, and staffed by Virginia Hodgkinson (I.S. vice president for research), the committee recommended that philanthropy become an interdisciplinary research field in American higher education – that it tran-scend its origins in social work and in the pursuits of relatively autonomous scholars.

This Payton–Hodgkinson proposal became a partial reality. Although no distinctive departments of philanthropy have emerged in American colleges or universities, several research centers that focus on the third or independent nonprofit sector have come into being. Payton founded one of the largest and most active: the Center on Philanthropy at Indiana University. Two scholarly organizations for philanthropic studies have also been established – the Association for Research on Nonprofit Organizations and Voluntary Action (ARNOVA) and the International Society for Third

Sector Research (ISTR). Each organization publishes its own journal dedicated to scholarly research in the field.

In the course of the 1990s, philanthropic studies (although still heavily concentrated in the United States) spread beyond American shores. The United States became the global locus of a significant and homogeneous nonprofit sector. Indeed, scholars from many parts of the world have come to study the nonstate, nonmarket sector in their own countries and in other nations within their regions. This interest has been augmented by post–Cold War concern with the nature of "civil societies" – places of public discussion and governance that permit decided overlap between state and market forces. Independent sectors and those who study them abroad have played crucial roles in determining the shape of this overlap. In that way, these sectors and their scholars have done much to discuss and define the essentials of civil society and even the potential for the spread of democracy within particular societies and cultures in the post–Cold War world.

By the beginning of the twenty-first century, therefore, a very large body of scholarship focusing on the nature and processes of philanthropic activity has been cultivated in the nonprofit sector in America and abroad. Predictably, most of this scholarship has concentrated on the activities and especially the fundraising ventures of specific third-sector organizations. The focus has been heavily contemporary and overwhelmingly institution-based – congruent with the orientation of disciplines like sociology, economics, policy studies, and business administration.

Although some professional historians also have come to specialize in the origins and development of institutions like the Carnegie Corporation, which eventually became part of the I.S., most have looked at philanthropy more broadly (congruent with the more general and less institution-centered concerns of their discipline). They have found philanthropy within public discourse, in gift exchanges, in religious experiences (especially revivals), in reformist climates, within clinical relationships, and in other not entirely institution-bound forms.

The historian contributors to our volume all take this broader view. We consider philanthropy as a collective form of charitable giving. In our view, the giver's intent becomes an acid test to distinguish who is and who is not a philanthropist. Philanthropists intend to impose their vision of the good society through collective missionary-like (religious and secular) ventures. Whereas some of these ventures are self-reflective and deeply attentive to the concerns of the recipients, others are not. As individual charitable impulses are shaped by organizational stimulants and constraints, complex and variable philanthropic weaves result. The history of philanthropy registers these ever-changing weaves.

Our research interests and even our broad definitional perspective are not widespread, for we historians constitute a small minority within ARNOVA and ISTR. Indeed, much of the scholarship in philanthropic studies has lacked a long-term historic focus – a closely textured professional view of change over decades and centuries – that has addressed cultural, psychological, and intellectual issues in conjunction with organizational concerns. Moreover, what historical writing there has been on philanthropy by Clio's craftspeople has usually been scattered over a wide array of disconnected topics. With roughly half of her contributors drawn from professional historians, Ellen Lagemann's recent and interesting anthology, *Philanthropic Foundations: New Scholarship, New Possibilities* (1999), illustrated this disjointed quality. Cooperative, focused, and closely coordinated research efforts by those trained in the historical discipline have been almost nonexistent.

Perhaps more than scholars in any other traditional department-based discipline engaged in philanthropic studies, historians have seemed reticent to participate fully and actively in a third-sector research community. Indeed, only three of our authors – Peter Hall, David Hammack, and Kathleen McCarthy – might be regarded as philanthropy "regulars." This reticence can be explained by a disinterest of most academic historians to join in efforts that may seem to represent less than craftsman-like use of their calling. Therefore, the historical perspective in philanthropic studies has been provided by participants in other callings who have sensed its importance. Far more often than not, they have offered historical perspectives that have fallen short of deploying what we consider satisfactory evidential and methodological imperatives; they have contributed to a troublesome rendering of the past on matters philanthropic.

Stated more judgmentally, the reticence of professional historians to enter the fray in philanthropic studies for fear of connections with amateurs seems to have given no few amateurs freedom to engage the past immune from sufficient scholarly responsibility. The consequences have not been optimal, and one example should suffice. Through our self-inflicted marginality, professional historians have rarely been critical of the propensity of the amateurs to characterize philanthropy as an entirely institution-based third sector that has always existed in America with its current institutional roles. That is, the "third sector" and even philanthropy generally in 2002 has quite wrongly been portrayed in its present dimensions in the America of 1607, 1776, 1789, 1819, 1865, and 1917. Because we professional historians remain preponderantly on the sidelines, we have therefore contributed to our own discontent as we listen to public debate and see public policies being formulated on the premise that what is always was.

One of the most troublesome signs of the undeveloped state of historical scholarship on American philanthropy has been the persistence of a synthetic volume that preceded the I.S. The primary source of historic information for nonhistorian scholars and general readers on the history of American philanthropy has been Robert H. Bremner's 1960 book, *American Philanthropy*. Slightly revised in 1988, the volume was a product of a post–World War II consensus approach to the American past. A pioneering and exceedingly creative social welfare historian, Bremner assumed that Americans had always debated within the context of a general and fundamental consensus or accord on the values of liberal capitalism, political democracy, and the marketplace. To his credit, Bremner knew that philanthropy involved much more than nonprofit institutions. But he got into trouble by defining philanthropy with a vagueness that bordered on glibness, eschewing the distinctions that we make between individual charitable acts and more organized philanthropic ventures. For Bremner, philanthropy became "improvement in the quality of human life. Whatever motives animate individual philanthropists, the purpose of philanthropy itself is to promote the welfare, happiness, and culture of mankind." Bremner surveyed "voluntary activity in the fields of charity, religion, education, humanitarian reform, social service, war relief, and foreign aid." Starting with John Winthrop and William Penn, upper- and middle-class white males – especially wealthy entrepreneurs and professionals – became focal points. The 1988 revised edition did not do much to integrate the historic research since the mid-1960s on African Americans, Native Americans, Hispanics, and other ethnic groups as they pursued charity and philanthropy to voice concerns that elites ignored. What had become a vigorous and innovative area of study by the time of his second edition – the history of women and how they often resorted to charitable acts and philanthropic ventures to define themselves – was rarely evident. Nor was Bremner attentive to the clients or the subjects of reform: children, the poor, and other less-than-powerful groups that did not leave abundant written records. A considerable historical literature that located the American past in global context was rarely cited. Nor did Bremner pay much attention to the proliferation of work on philanthropy in other disciplines. A much-used source on the past for nonhistorian specialists in philanthropic studies, *American Philanthropy* rarely drew on the research of related disciplines.

Bremner's book was, therefore, a product of his time, not ours, and reflected the way most scholarly American history was written in the 1950s. Thus, *American Philanthropy* became increasingly peripheral to mainline historical scholarship as the decades progressed. As early as the late 1960s and through the 1970s, historians like David Rothman and Clifford Griffin broke from Bremner's view that philanthropists intended the well-being of society. They found increasing favor with a view that philanthropists sought to control lower-class and deviant populations to augment ruling-class profits and social stability. By the 1980s, professional historians shifted again – away from this social control perspective, but hardly back to Bremner's stress on philanthropy as good thoughts for humankind. Sincere, benevolent intentions and social control in the interests of ruling-class hegemony came increasingly to be viewed by historians like Robert Abzug and James Stewart as different, shifting, and often competing layers of motivation within most philanthropists. Unfortunately, these two post-Bremner waves of historiography were never able to provide an integrating focus to scholars in the emerging interdisciplinary field of philanthropic studies. Indeed, Bremner's book continued to be their primary reference on the past, despite the fact that the new work in the area – influenced by new concerns over popular democracy, the effects of global trade, and new experiments with civil society – substantially challenged Bremner's focus and thesis.

Bremner certainly deserves no blame for this disjunction. Part of the reprobation must be directed at professional historians, including most of the contributors to this volume. We have been so immersed in our specialized concerns that we have not undertaken broad new synthetic work concerning the history of American charity and philanthropy. Yet, our neglect eventually caught up with us. By the late 1990s, literature in diverse historical specialties that was germane to the history of philanthropy had proliferated to the point where no single historian could possibly have done a respectable job of general synthesis. Indeed, Clio's craft had split so decisively into discrete specialties that proficient up-to-date synthetic contributions might have been too much for even three of four professional historians working collectively.

In 1998, one of our authors, David Hammack, attempted a partial remedy. His *Making the Nonprofit Sector in the United States* was a rich and very useful collection of major primary documents in the history of

American philanthropy, from the English *Statute of Charitable Uses* (1601) to the U.S. Supreme Court's important 1991 decision in *Rust v. Sullivan*. Hammack included documents relevant to ethnic and racial minorities, to gender relations, and especially to religion. For his book's many and considerable strengths, however, Hammack focused exclusively on nonprofit organizations – institutions that owed their existence to the nineteenth-century imposition of a public-private sector dichotomy, with its limits on government, and its requirement for nearly the past two centuries on church-state separation. Documents carrying less institutional centrality, and perhaps more relevant to cultural, social, and intellectual history – sexuality in the gift relationship, for example, or White Citizens Council perceptions of lynching as voluntary action for the public good – were not Hammack's concerns. Nor, given his institutional focus, could he carry us far enough in fathoming how random individual charitable impulses evolved into more complex philanthropic undertakings.

A gifted historian, Hammack has readily acknowledged that the evolution of nonprofit institutions has only been part of philanthropy's historic career. Consequently, he joined us in this multiauthored enterprise. Our intentions were to identify the major themes and the dynamic academic impulses presented in the best of the recent material published on philanthropy, while offering reasons for the rejection of less meritorious work in the field. A group of academic historians with established track records from all over the United States has offered broadly interpretive essays that frequently take off upon, but sometimes take issue with, one another. These essays concern charity and philanthropy within the context of a great many periods and places in the American past. As well, American localities, religious and ethnic identities, and gender concerns have been accorded major historical relevance. This is a story of the appreciable diversity of the American population and its varied communities as they have changed over time. Unlike much scholarship on the topic, we postulate that charity and philanthropy themselves can sometimes have multiple and shifting meanings. In definition as well as in practice, it is sometimes rather challenging to determine what charity and philanthropy are not.

* * *

Let us take up this matter of definition and meaning more directly than we have. Well into the eighteenth century, philanthropy in Britain and America was a form of charity – a charitable attitude or feeling toward others that prompted benevolent behavior. In dictionary projects, Samuel

Johnson defined philanthropy as "love of mankind; good nature," whereas Noah Webster characterized it as "benevolence towards the whole human family; universal good will." Addressing the vestrymen in each parish of Virginia, Thomas Jefferson similarly insisted that philanthropy was charitable motivation that, when acted upon, provided the well intended with "the approbation of their neighbors, and the distinction which that gives them." Concerned with the charitable feeling of the virtuous individual, American Revolutionaries were not overwhelmingly attentive to distinctions between public and private sectors of society or the form of the social institutions that encouraged moral action.

Enlightenment thinkers generally saw the human being with an internal moral compass. The recognition of human goodness and reasonableness, as much as human rationality, prompted the premise that humankind could engage in self-government. For example, Adam Smith based his call for a "free market" on the human's innate sensitivity to and compassion for others. In *The Theory of Moral Sentiments*, Smith referred to "benevolence as universal" – part of what makes us human. Benevolence would curb selfish tendencies: "And hence it is that to feel much for others and little for ourselves, that to restrain our selfish [affections], and to indulge our benevolent affections, constitutes perfection of human nature; and can alone produce among mankind that harmony of sentiments and passions in which consists their whole grace and propriety."

Enlightenment figures like Webster, Jefferson, and Smith were largely thinking of individual charitable giving and assistance, all in the interests of general civility, even as they spoke of benevolent affections and sometimes invoked the term *philanthropy*. In essence, when they spoke of benevolent feelings and unselfish acts by the individual toward others, they were drawing on a long-standing tradition of individual charitable assistance as a mainstay of civil society. As Robert Gross explains in our first chapter, the charitable impulse dominated life in small communities in early modern Europe and colonial America. Through a charitable act, one person ameliorated the life of a local inhabitant less fortunate by offering something specific and temporary like a bowl of soup or a night's lodging. As life in Europe and especially early America became less communal and began to rely more on the rational dictates of law, social organization adopted a more systematic approach – organized philanthropic societies and other institutions to solve deep social problems that simply were not addressed effectively by individual charitable acts and benevolent intentions. By the mid-1800s, Gross postulates, despite a decided lag in rhetoric, the transition from individual charity to organized philanthropy to enhance civility had largely been completed. To be sure, charity still existed as a fundamental attitude and a way one person helped another with an immediate local difficulty. But the charitable impulse was being directed toward a more systematic institution-centered approach to long-term problems emerging from the new social order – organized philanthropy. Therefore, benevolence came to be equated less with the considerate feelings and charitable acts of individuals than with the actions of voluntary societies and other institutions through which citizens proceeded to shape public policy and the welfare of their more complex communities. Societies became more civil.

Authors Amanda Porterfield and G. J. Barker-Benfield (see Chapters 2 and 3) draw the chronological divide between the earlier charitable impulse of the individual and organized philanthropic institutions less sharply than Gross does in our first chapter; however, they agree with Gross that there was a significant transition. By the 1830s, Wendy Gamber maintains (see Chapter 6), the old charitable world of individuals was no longer the most central avenue for reform; philanthropy was, and it essentially assumed the form of interlocking reform societies. In this emerging nineteenth-century context, Mark McGarvie details (see Chapter 4) how distinctions between public and private institutions and between church and state became increasingly relevant to the shaping of civil society. A reconceptualization of philanthropy as institutional process deepened during the nineteenth century. By the middle decades of the twentieth century – according to chapters by Gary Hess, Claude Clegg, and Peter Hall – philanthropy largely referred to diverse practices and behaviors by individuals and groups within complex institutional structures that yielded concrete consequences. According to a recent edition of Webster's dictionary, *philanthropy* was characterized as a "service, act, gift, [or] institution" that ends up helping humankind.

This is not to say that organized philanthropy has supplanted the older tradition of individual charity. Individual charitable good feeling toward others has continued to manifest itself rather decidedly within philanthropy's institutional processes and goals. If sometimes differing in emphasis, all of our authors agree on both the chronology of the transition from charity to philanthropy in the shaping of civil society and this persisting interaction between the two. Indeed, Ruth Crocker's chapter (see Chapter 9) wonderfully underscores how, by the early twentieth century, Mrs. Olivia Sage could be both charitable and increasingly involved in philanthropic institutional processes.

Philanthropic-studies guru Robert Payton merits praise for his resolute (and decidedly Jamesian) insistence before sometimes skeptical and indifferent I.S. managers that the attitude of the individual has counted for much, even as the historic context has changed and philanthropy has been redefined. Indeed, a preponderant position in this volume is that philanthropy has had much to do with a specific person who has intended at least some measure of charitable benevolence toward others and has acted upon that intention in the interests of civil society. To a greater or lesser extent, the philanthropist has imposed his/her vision of a good society abundant with civility on others through his/her missionary spirit and has mobilized resources and institutions to effect that vision. Yet, the individual philanthropist has never, even in charity-dominated early America, been separable from the institutional context of his/her behavior. Specific Catholic and Jewish philanthropists, for example, have been difficult to identify without persisting consideration of the religious structures and institutional rituals of their faiths.

We also hold that philanthropists have never been a homogeneous lot even as they have often shared a missionary-like temperament and have been inclined to impose their vision on others. It became increasingly clear to me while we assembled *Charity, Philanthropy, and Civility in American History*, nevertheless, that a good many philanthropists have demonstrated a remarkable capacity for self-criticism. Indeed, a self-critical temperament has sometimes checked their disposition to impose their vision on others. Periodically, this predisposition even made some of them more respectful of the autonomy of those they sought to help.

The authors of this volume insist, to a person, that philanthropy has to be historicized. Breaking from pervasive practice in the general literature on philanthropy, for example, we insist that French traveler Alexis de Tocqueville's view of American associations in the 1830s (everything from Bible societies to for-profit corporations) must be distinguished sharply from Gardner's perspective on the I.S. organizational nexus of the 1980s. But historicize as we must, most of our authors portray philanthropists as missionaries with great energy and strong, intense vision. Porterfield (see Chapter 2) is particularly vocal on this count. Like all other authors, however, she sees philanthropic missionaries almost always implementing their moral visions through institutional structures. Indeed, even adjusting for changing historical context and for the process of philanthropic redefinition, *Charity, Philanthropy, and Civility in American History* holds that in the intensity of their missionary presence and their moral fervor and vision, philanthropists have distinguished themselves from others in American society. If philanthropists can be universally characterized at all, it is by the energy behind their desires to transform the insufficiently civil world that is into the world that might be. Unlike Willie Loman in *Death of a Salesman*, who was totally absorbed in his own diminishing capacity for financial gain and reputation, the philanthropist has energetically and deeply cared about the needs of others and the broader society and has sought passionately to render decisive changes.

* * *

Although we cover the full chronological sweep of American philanthropy, our story is thematically driven. First, most of our authors believe that charity and philanthropy have always involved intense preoccupations with deeply compelling visions. Portraying philanthropists as people with often inspirational visions for the "good society," our chapters explore the many, varied, and often contesting visions that have been advanced. There were marked differences over how homogeneous or diverse the "good society" was to be, how inclusive or exclusive, and what its values were to be.

Following their visions, several philanthropists tried to counter widespread policy and custom. Pursuing visions of democracy and inclusion within civil society, for example, some who felt disenfranchised sought to renegotiate pervasive, sometimes government-sanctioned, practices. Warren (see Chapter 5) explains how early nineteenth-century Indian preachers, exhorters, and translators sometimes influenced white missionary institutions and practices in ways that the missionaries had not intended – to abort white encroachments on Indian village traditions, beliefs, and hereditary leaders. Gamber (see Chapter 6) and McCarthy (see Chapter 8) explain how antebellum female reformers who lacked votes or public office attempted to use voluntary associations to steer American society away from slavery, inebriation, and intolerance of the poor, the weak, and the infirm. McCarthy carries this tradition into the early twentieth century and characterizes female philanthropic ventures of the time contributing to a national welfare state. Similarly, Stephen Whitfield (see Chapter 14) traces a Jewish reform vision, enlarging as the twentieth century progressed, that sought out integration and inclusion in mainstream American life and that eschewed communal marginality. Claude Clegg (see Chapter 16) presents civil-rights activists of the 1950s and 1960s, oftentimes excluded from the ballot box by race or age, as philanthropists who pursued a more inclusive vision of American democracy and civility.

But it was not only the disenfranchised and minority groups who invoked philanthropy to impose or share their visions of the "good society." Porterfield (see Chapter 2) describes the attempts of some within the colonial American ruling elite to impose their theocratic visions on Native Americans and European dissenters. Roy Finkenbine's discussion (see Chapter 7) of the postbellum Slater Fund, Judy Sealander's chapter on the formation of large foundations at the beginning of the twentieth century (see Chapter 10), Gary Hess's chapter (see Chapter 15) on the role of foundations during the Cold War, and Peter Hall's chapter (see Chapter 17) on the emergence of a post–World War II philanthropic-government policy elite all concern efforts of powerful ruling elements to advance their vision for change.

Yet, despite the intentions of philanthropists to impose their vision of the "good society," philanthropy has also involved reciprocity between givers and recipients of "good" qualities – our second theme. Porterfield discusses how seventeenth-century New England missionaries, while trying to impose their worldview on Indians and other "heathen," discovered that the cultures of those heathen could change them and their fundamental vision. Warren's study of the nineteenth century underscores complex multiple negotiations between missionaries stationed in the changing western borderlands and Indians who dwelled there. Gamber describes how antebellum reformers often discovered that as they shifted between optimism and anxiety, they were imposing on themselves the same requirements of piety, control, and self-determination that they required of the less fortunate. Reform changed the reformer as it changed circumstances for the "needy" recipient. Emily Rosenberg (see Chapter 11) details how American missionaries who sought to "uplift" foreign lands and peoples during the early twentieth century sometimes ended up not only empowering the recipients of their aid, but also profoundly shifting themselves toward less hierarchical worldviews and values.

Contrasting with Bremner's *American Philanthropy*, most chapters in this volume are not preoccupied with elite white male Protestants. Pertinent philanthropic actors were fringe dissenters as well as the establishment, women perhaps more than men, blacks and Native Americans as well as whites, Catholics and Jews in addition to Protestants. Without space limitations, I would add materials on Hispanics and Asian Americans, Muslims and "born again" Christians, Holocaust survivors, and gay activists. As the public intellectual, Ronald Takaki, made abundantly clear in his richly textured classic, *A Different Mirror: A History of Multicultural America*

(1993), these and many other diversities were inseparable from the evolution of American philanthropy.

There is a third persisting theme concerning ways in which philanthropy, as a form of civic action, redefined concepts of gender. For G. J. Barker-Benfield (see Chapter 3), the eighteenth-century Anglo-American concept of "sensibility" toward others was closely associated with new imperatives and opportunities for middle-class womanhood in an emerging commercial economy. Gamber emphasizes the resolve of female reformers to ward off the exploitation of women. Crocker (see Chapter 9) details how elite women like Olivia Sage found strong new voices in public benevolence. Philanthropy essentially excused or rationalized their new public roles in civil society. Mary Oates (see Chapter 13) underscores the critical historic roles of nuns and female lay parishioners in Catholic philanthropy. McCarthy describes how women (primarily though not exclusively Protestant, white, and middle class) used their voluntary associations to build a distinctive and powerful political culture. In the nineteenth century, they fashioned an infrastructure of their own in the "space" society permitted for public-private partnerships. Through that infrastructure, they offered measures that foreshadowed welfare programs of the New Deal and the Great Society. Discussions by these and other authors suggest that in forging philanthropic concepts and enterprises, many women were establishing their own identities as consequential people while they redefined the scope of female involvement in civil society.

Finkenbine's chapter illustrates a fourth pervasive theme – that the lines between ethnic and philanthropic experiences were often deeply permeable. Historically, race and ethnicity have often been superimposed on conceptions of citizenship and civility. As African Americans and other ethnic minorities engaged in philanthropy to extend their roles as citizens, they destabilized the very racial and ethnic biases inherent in citizenship, especially the premise that America was "the white man's country." The Freedmen's Bureau and postbellum enterprises for black industrial education served as clear illustrations that these biases had little connection with reality. Reconstruction-era collective activities in pursuit of social goals helped to shape African American identity. By the mid-twentieth century, Clegg explains, African Americans often built civil-rights organizations and campaigns in the "space" between government policy and their own private lives and aspirations. Of course, chapters by Oates and Whitfield (see Chapters 13 and 14) on Catholics and Jews make it abundantly clear that religious and ethnic thought and organization were inseparable from philanthropic experience.

Attentive to the variables of gender, ethnicity, and religion, several chapters underscore a fifth, if related, general theme – how philanthropists derived a sense of both empowerment and identification from their activities. They learned much about their philosophies, goals, and chosen vocations; seventeenth-century New England missionaries, for example, often derived a sense of their specialness in the course of their activities. Antebellum abolitionists conveyed a sense of belonging to a sacred vocation more devout than "temporizing" churches. Activists in female voluntary societies frequently found the strong and empowering sense of what a woman could accomplish. African Americans often found a sense of public purpose and profound ethnic pride through civil-rights ventures. Erik Erikson, the architect of the theory of psychologically and socially grounded identity, insisted throughout his life that identity involved the strong sense of connectedness to others and profound rootedness in time and place. Philanthropic goals and activities often promoted such identification and sense of roots in those who took up the cause.

A sixth theme, pressed strongly by some of our authors and not irrelevant in any chapter, concerns fluctuations in the American mix of public, private, and voluntary agencies to meet peoples' needs, and the role of law in defining the mix. During the *ancien regime* in Europe and in Colonial America, distinctions between public and private or voluntary realms and between church and state were subordinated to larger concerns over public welfare needs. Benjamin Franklin's autobiography was written late in the eighteenth century, as the mix was first beginning to change. Still, it illustrated marked public, private, and voluntary overlaps. By the early Jacksonian period, important distinctions between them were discernable, with lawyers and judges enunciating those distinctions most forcefully. Decidedly more than Europeans, American legal practitioners emphasized distinctive categories of institutions – public, private, and voluntary. They described distinctions between these institutions theoretically and perhaps somewhat technically in terms of the functions and outcomes of each. More succinctly, law, lawyers, and judges became central in shuffling and reshuffling juridical and sometimes *de facto* distinctions between public, private and voluntary agencies. McGarvie's chapter presents a new appreciation for the groundbreaking U.S. Supreme Court's decision in the *Dartmouth College* case of 1819. Speaking for the Court, Chief Justice John Marshall ruled that American law separated public and private spheres as it separated church and state; the churches could not use the state or government power to coerce behaviors. Rather, churches had to persuade citizens through proselytizing within voluntary associational ventures. Marshall also maintained the superiority of private contract rights over public interests. Social reform for the "good society," church-based or otherwise, was not to be aided by government efforts so much as by the market economy and through the efforts of "private" voluntary associations.

Based largely on the work done by McGarvie, we characterize the legal imposition of a distinction between public and private organizational activity in the early decades of the nineteenth century. That distinction was tested first through the politicization of many societies within the "Benevolent Empire" and then through far-reaching federal political and economic legislation after the Civil War. Some of our authors consider the legal distinction between public and private spheres to be exceedingly important; yet, others, like Gamber and I, do not. Why, for example, did antebellum state legislatures grant incorporation rights to several of the "private" missionary reform associations, but not to others, following the legal imposition of a public-private distinction? Something other than law may have been influential in these actions. Moreover, reliance on this perceived public-private divide historically has been used to limit the expansion of public philanthropy. On some weighty matters in this volume, therefore, readers will discover that the authors differ on important aspects of philanthropy's career.

McGarvie and I both recognize a fluidity in the legal distinction made in 1819. Justice Marshall's separation of the public realm and private voluntary ventures was revised during Reconstruction. Finkenbine (see Chapter 7) explains how new conceptions of democratic inclusion and social equality prompted the expansion of federal authority after the Civil War. Radical Republicans in the North pressed others to use law as a primary vehicle for this expansion; they applied new federal laws and national policy generally to the ex-Confederate states. But the expansion of federal authority was not long-lasting. With the overturn of federal Reconstruction in the South, an activist national government protecting the legal rights of the freedmen was abandoned. Correspondingly, some government intervention for private corporate development came to be embraced.

However, the changes brought through war and Reconstruction were shortlived. The U.S. Supreme Court and other governmental and legal authorities premised, near the end of the nineteenth century, that private corporations were basic vehicles for social improvement. Once again, law and lawyer-made public policy was delegating the pursuit of some of society's goals, at least formally, to purportedly private and voluntary spheres.

All the while, the corporate model produced private business entities with great economic and social power, at times exceeding that of state governments. As Sealander shows (see Chapter 10), the corporations established large nonprofit foundations and trusts run by a new managerial elite to pursue various ventures for society's benefit.

However, much like Reconstruction, the Great Depression and the New Deal called the existing and primarily juridical public-private-voluntary distinctions into question. Laws were passed during the 1930s allowing the federal government to assume new responsibilities in order to relieve dire economic conditions. Yet, Hammack (see Chapter 12) challenges the traditional premise that private charitable donations and voluntary organizational activities were eclipsed as the New Deal enhanced federal relief programs. America's wealthiest donors and largest foundations clung to the ambitious goals they had advanced in the 1920s – often cooperating with state and federal agencies and programs. Finally, Hall explains (see Chapter 17) how, during the post–World War II decades, the federal government devolved a good many of its functions to states and localities, which shifted many important responsibilities back to private sector (legally defined) elites. Once again, in a legalistic sense and sometimes very much in a *de facto* sense as well, the public, private, and voluntary distribution of authority was revised.

Therefore, our sixth theme underscores both change and continuity in the government, private, and voluntary mix (primarily though not exclusively through legal and public-policy measures). At no point was there anything approaching an autonomous voluntary sector. America's experiment with philanthropy, therefore, exposed the vicissitudes in the purported distinction between the public and private sectors. Indeed, the term *Independent Sector* was more the prescription of contemporary figures like Gardner and Hodgkinson than a grounded historical reality.

Our seventh theme is that American philanthropy can hardly be understood without the benefit of a complex international perspective. Barker-Benfield (see Chapter 3) characterizes the emergence of a cult of sensibility during the eighteenth century that was both British and American. Rosenberg (see Chapter 11) documents a vast array of voluntary religious organizations during the first half of the twentieth century that addressed evangelism, poverty, education, and health. America's moral "virtues" and civilities were to be exported, and no few reformers who pressed for "good works" abroad assumed that they, as well as their foreign recipients, would be beneficiaries. Hess (see Chapter 15) describes how, during the Cold

War, the Rockefeller and Ford Foundations often reflected the objectives of American foreign policy in the Third World. In a postwar version of internationalism, Foundation officials pressed for Western "democracy" and modern market-oriented economic development in Asia, Africa, and other at least economically "backward" regions. In a detailed final essay – far more than a traditional epilogue – William Cohen describes how European and American philanthropic organizations and reformers sometimes paralleled each other in striking ways; periodically, they cooperated. Even with the space constraints of this volume, the editors and authors could probably have done a good deal more to describe international contexts for American philanthropic traditions.

Bremner and his immediate postwar generation of historians embraced a premise about America's place in the family of nations that most of our authors find troublesome. Insisting that America was special and distinctive, Bremner's generation perhaps inadvertently embraced the late nineteenth-century "higher-lower" doctrine, which postulated purportedly "natural" hierarchical arrangements among humankind. Historians like Bremner and Daniel Boorstin (representatives of the "consensus" school in American historiography) sometimes characterized the United States and Americans as if they were nineteenth-century July Fourth orators; it was the Promised Land or Redeemer Nation of God's chosen people. America supposedly brought hope, democracy, and marketplace vigor to morally and politically benighted citizens of foreign countries. Bremner and his colleagues advanced this perspective (often in muted form, to be sure) without critically examining the diverse values and complex contributions of other nations and colonized peoples. The United States may have had stronger "private" and "voluntary" sectors than many other countries and a more constricted central government; however, this has been so only in degrees, and with profound changes over time in the public-private-voluntary mixes.

As a corollary, Bremner's generation assumed that much of American philanthropy and philanthropic culture was distinctive. It was unique because of the intensity of popular belief steeped in the virtues of the isolated, Adam-like individual – the mythic Kit Carson or Daniel Boone who "made it" entirely through his or her own resources. We differ in this assessment of American "national character." Contributors to *Charity, Philanthropy, and Civility in American History* find that connectedness or civic-minded reciprocity with others was generally a far stronger quality than self-help individualism. Settlement-house workers, like missionary reformers, often learned from and were changed by those they sought to help. Racial, gender, religious, and ethnic identities among philanthropists were usually closely tied to others – to fellow philanthropists and to those they sought to assist. The eighteenth-century (and even the altered nineteenth-century) cult of sensibility concerned the recognition and appreciation of the other. Indeed, our findings tend to confirm Tocqueville's observation in the 1830s that Americans saw themselves as cooperative members of groups and societies more than as isolated individuals. Much of the historic scholarship on the American West since Frederick Jackson Turner has underscored traditions of civic-minded community assistance rather than of Lone Ranger–like rugged individualism. If American philanthropic culture has been more reciprocal and connected than egoistically individualistic, assertions of American exceptionalism by Bremner, Boorstin, and others of their generation should command our skepticism. Indeed, the dual premises of individualism and exceptionalism have discounted some of the basic strengths of American philanthropy and the civilities of American society.

Although we reject the premise of a distinctive third sector in America, our eighth and final theme is that philanthropy became more structured, rationalized, and professionalized over time. This is the point of Gross's opening chapter – that, whereas seventeenth-century Americans resorted to person-to-person charitable giving, benevolent societies, which operated more systematically, had emerged by the time of Tocqueville's travels to America. Porterfield and Barker-Benfield do not entirely agree with Gross's precise chronological signposts for the transformation, but they concur in seeing a shift toward rationalization, specialization, and bureaucratization within organized institutions. Like Porterfield, Gamber emphasizes some fluidity and spontaneity in antebellum philanthropic reform societies, but she insists that by the 1850s, bureaucratic imperatives became more decided. Advancing a chronological perspective that contrasts with Gamber's, Sealander detects a crucial turning point in the early twentieth century. By then, she shows, promoters of "scientific" philanthropy created elaborate charitable foundations to promote the systematic discovery and application of knowledge. Somewhat similarly, Oates describes the increasingly bureaucratic organizational structure of Catholic Church philanthropy over the past seventy years, especially since the 1960s when the historic proclivity of American Catholics toward benevolent giving began to erode. Through his study of the cooperation of the Rockefeller and Ford Foundations with the federal government to influence the "developing world" during the Cold War, Hess reveals marked manifestations of this rationalizing and structuring trend. However, Porterfield's broad portrayal of the American missionary tradition, Crocker's on Olivia Sage, Clegg's analysis of the Civil Rights Movement, and McCarthy's work on women's benevolent societies all point to a gradual, incremental, and sometimes temporarily reversible process of systematization and rationalization – one that never eradicated older, more spontaneous, and individualized traditions of helping and giving.

* * *

The dust jacket for *Charity, Philanthropy, and Civility in American History* is the well-known 1932 photograph of the elderly John D. Rockefeller handing one of his famous dimes to a young boy, William Gebele, after Sunday church service. Since its emergence as a field two decades ago, scholarship in philanthropy and the third sector has premised that Americans and their nonprofit organizations have contributed far more than "small change" to needy people and enterprises. We draw on critical historical analysis to question that premise. We ask whether private nonprofit resources have ever been very significant, proportionate to government resources, in addressing unemployment, malnutrition, deficient health care, ghetto housing and schooling, and, more generally, class and ethnic inequality. New York public-school teacher Sara Mosle (*New York Times Magazine*, July 2, 2000) once took public heroes like Secretary of State Colin Powell at their word. Mosle assumed that as a volunteer to mentor troubled inner-city children, she and fellow philanthropists might largely substitute for government by providing more efficient and vital services. Mosle introduced the kids to Duke Ellington, Scrabble, and the Staten Island Ferry; however, she soon realized that these middle-class amenities did not alter their economically impoverished lives. Only profoundly augmented government social service expenditures could do this. Mosle was probably atypical among her midtown Manhattan neighbors. The preponderance of America's more affluent philanthropists has tended to put its spare time and financial resources into concert halls, operas, and museums – resources rarely utilized by poor people. For the most part, our authors see cogency in Teresa Odendahl's compelling evidence concerning the self-serving disposition of many of the affluent (*Charity Begins at Home: Generosity and Self-Interest Among the Philanthropic Elite* [1990]).

More explicitly, the essays in this volume carry policy implications. Most of us have been positively disposed toward research in the "new institutionalism" highlighted by scholars like Theda Skocpol and Andrew Polsky.

We are impressed by how they have considered the full range of administrative, legal, bureaucratic, and coercive systems that comprise the all-important state. We feel that government policy and appropriation, with its enormous complexities, has always been a significant factor in addressing social problems – with or without private cooperation. To call simply for the massive reduction of government effort, as President George W. Bush's frequent spokesperson on philanthropy, Marvin Olasky, has done, is to enter dangerous, untested waters in addressing the complex web of poverty and welfare policies. Olasky refers to a "tragedy of American compassion" rooted in undue reliance on government expenditures and public social services. Whether the operative slogan for reducing federal programs and directives is his father's "thousand points of light" or the current President's "compassionate conservatism," almost all our authors worry that there are troublesome consequences in precipitous reduction of the role of government. Indeed, since the 1960s, there has been compelling evidence that heavy reliance on private and nonprofit agencies for policy directives and for social capital has contributed far less to alleviating poverty and other social inequities than traditional New Deal and Great Society programs of direct assistance. Augmented poverty and lower-class misery during the Reagan years of federal-service retrenchment underscores this point.

Most of us also contend that American policymakers (unlike contemporary Germany or even post-Thatcher Britain) have often used an untenable reading of our philanthropic traditions – one that has tended to preclude economic and social equity. The United States has been comparatively unique among nations in its refusal to regulate the marketplace and to redistribute economic and social capital downward – even in the Clinton years, as the stock market broke 10,000 and new millionaires were made. Obviously, our perspective must be qualified. After all, since 1960 there has been a substantial increase in expenditures by nonprofit corporations – from 3 percent of the U.S. economy to probably more than 9 percent today. Yet, this increase may have been prompted heavily by expanded federal funding of nonprofit organizations. In brief, we do not dismiss the efficacy of FDR's New Deal programs of the 1930s. It seems increasingly plausible to argue, moreover, that Lyndon Johnson's Great Society domestic programs of the 1960s temporarily destabilized or perhaps momentarily "redefined" the fiction of a distinctive and efficacious nonprofit sector.

Congruent with "the new institutionalism" and its critical tone, those who study philanthropy and work in nonprofit organizations need to become much more hard-nosed in their historical perspectives and more dismissive of quick slogans about the inappropriateness of the state for social services. Participants in the public discussion over philanthropic policy must demonstrate precisely how much "change" (up and down) – in real dollars, concrete services, and poverty levels – has occurred in America since Parliament's two fundamental 1601 enactments: the Statute of Charitable Uses and the Elizabethan Poor Law. The matter needs to be addressed systematically, affirming the methods of those trained to research and write about the past.

In addition to our misgivings over precipitous dismissals of the roles of the state for social services, our concern with the policy implications of the historical past makes us especially concerned with the current misreadings of church–state separation in America. We find precious little justification in the judicial decisions of the early national period for federal government delegation of social service functions to church-based philanthropies. Since the U.S. Supreme Court's decision in the *Dartmouth College* case, as McGarvie's chapter attests, such a delegation has rarely been considered. If the current Bush Administration proposes government appropriations and tax benefits for church-based social services, it needs to be pressed to explain why that is not a major departure from settled constitutional policy and federal practice.

Among scholars of philanthropy over the past several decades, there have been strong financial pressures to bypass the critical spirit that inspired "the new institutionalism" in terms of both social welfare philanthropy and church-state separation. Between 1992 and 1994, the National Committee for Responsive Philanthropy reported that the twelve largest foundations on the right (ranging from Bradley and Scaife to Olin) provided roughly $200 million for conservative "think tanks" like the Heritage Foundation, the American Enterprise Institute, and the Cato Institute – centers that were committed to discrediting government, "liberating" corporations from pressing social problems, and delegating government social functions to church-based organizations. The progressive Institute for Policy Studies' annual budget would have been able to run the Heritage Foundation for only thirteen working days. By 1995–1996, the conservative (if thoughtful) Hudson Institute had more than three times the assets of the Environmental Defense Fund. Nor did the track record of large, centrist American foundations of the early and mid-1990s, like Ford, Kellogg, Pew, and Rockefeller, do much to restore even a proximate financial balance between right-wing institutions and agencies for progressive policy change.

With this transparent differential in financial resources, no few scholars of philanthropic studies learned during the 1980s and 1990s how to butter their bread. "Pay no attention to the man behind the curtain," L. Frank Baum suggested irreverently in *The Wizard of Oz*. We must be perhaps overly explicit about "the man behind" our project. The Lilly Foundation of Indianapolis provided funds for two of our grant applications, totaling approximately $70,000 and extending over the last few years. Both were awarded to us through an independent faculty selection committee within the Indiana University Center on Philanthropy. The grant applications underscored one central purpose – to replace Bremner's *American Philanthropy* with a book that reflected the research and thinking of some of the most sophisticated of the current generation of American History scholars. The directors of the Center on Philanthropy knew the nature of my previous scholarship and progressive activism. They knew that this would not be a volume echoing neoconservative or even I.S. perspectives. Neither Lilly nor the Center on Philanthropy tried to redirect us, and neither sought to peruse chapters prior to publication. From Lilly funding, each contributor received a taxable $1,500 honorarium and expenses to cover two weekends in Bloomington to help coordinate this project.

As we launched this project, Mark McGarvie and I were uninterested in stacking the deck with contributors who shared ideological proclivities. Once selected, we pressured all of them to write, revise, and revise again until their chapters exhibited state-of-the-art historical scholarship. Several enlisted contributors were dropped because their drafts were not strong; this was the most painful part of the editorial process.

A concluding confessional is in order: The more I teach and read about the history of philanthropy and participate in volunteer ventures, the more I am taken by the insights of Thomas Holmes (Secretary of the Howard Association). The preface to Holmes's *London's Underworld* (1912) is striking: "The more civilised (sic) we become, the more complex and serious will be our problems. The methods now in use for coping with some of our great evils do not lessen, but considerably increase the evils they seek to cure." Like Holmes, I assume that philanthropy has often represented a trade-off of a number of complicated and sometimes intangible variables. Sometimes the beneficiaries have gotten the worst of the deal.

Part I

GIVING AND CARING IN EARLY AMERICA, 1601–1861

Beneficence is always free, it cannot be extorted by force, the mere want of it exposes to no punishment; because the mere want of beneficence tends to do no real positive evil. . . . there is, however, another virtue of which the observance is not left to the freedom of our own wills, which may be extorted by force, and of which the violation exposes to resentment, and consequently to punishment. This virtue is justice: the violation of justice is injury – it does real and positive hurt to some particular persons, from motives which are naturally disapproved of. . . . We must always, however, carefully distinguish what is only blamable, or the proper object of disapprobation, from what force may be employed either to punish or prevent. That seems blamable which falls short of the ordinary degree of proper beneficence which experience teaches us to expect of everybody; and on the contrary, that seems praise-worthy which goes beyond it..

From Adam Smith's *Theory of Moral Sentiments*, Part II, Section i, Chapter 1, ¶3–6 (1759)

COLONIAL AMERICA THROUGH THE CREATION OF A NEW REPUBLIC

During the first 200 years of European settlements in North America, the ideas and practices of Christian charity were replaced with a pattern of philanthropy that presented a means by which philanthropic actors could participate in, reform, and enhance civilities within their societies.

Europeans became aware of the native peoples of the American continents at the same time they began to appreciate the political and economic potential in their lands. Yet, awareness of the lands' inhabitants did not stop the Spanish, Dutch, Portuguese, English, and French from claiming the lands as their own. In the providential worldview of Christian Europe at the height of the Renaissance, God's will worked to enrich and empower those who followed Him. The Native Americans presented an opportunity to convert more souls to the true faith, and simultaneously a justification – in the names of both God and monarch – for the taking of their lands. The Pope sanctioned both Spanish and French colonialism as missions of God's will, recognizing that the heathens of the New World would need to be either converted or destroyed. The Christian religion, though struggling with the repercussions of the Reformation schism, provided the dominant ideological basis for European conceptions of the ideal society throughout the colonization of the Americas in the 1500s and 1600s. As understood, consistent with Biblical prescriptions of morality, colonization was less a unilateral usurpation of dominion than a reciprocal relationship in which salvation and progress were given to the Indians in return for their lands.

Reciprocity, in the form of gift exchanges, was well known as a basis of political or military alliance among the Native Americans long before their first contacts with Europeans. They welcomed the arms, clothing, and cooking utensils of the invaders, if not their diseases and their attempts to eradicate their cultural way of life. The Native Americans' assistance to the early French, Dutch, and English settlers reflected ancient patterns of forming helpful partnerships more than an embrace of the Europeans themselves or an openness to their different values and lifestyles. The gifts of each party were frequently misperceived through the eyes of the receivers, yet Europeans and Native Americans came to depend on the exchange.

By the time of England's colonization efforts in the early 1600s, religious conflict had resulted in decades of wars that showed no signs of abating. Puritan refugees hoped to found a community of saints in their new home of Massachusetts as a model for the world of the promise offered in the fulfillment of Biblical teachings. Puritan society required the subordination of individual or selfish interests to the good of the whole. Derived from Calvinist doctrine and building on premodern conceptions of community hierarchy and deference, the Puritans created theocratic societies in which all members were expected to serve communal goals and abide by religiously inspired communal values.

The striking differences in the religious and business purposes reflected in the settlement of the Virginia and Massachusetts colonies in the early 1600s have at times obscured an appreciation of their common cultural and religious heritage. Settlers of both colonies accepted a society premised upon the assertion of Christian truths. Church and state served as a unified governing authority. New England's theocracy embodied this unity to a greater extent than did Virginia's corporate governance; yet, even in the southern colony, Christian teachings governed societal regulation of market relationships, prescriptions for personal moral conduct, social responsibilities to the poor and sick, and the education of the young. Throughout the English colonies, charity was an expression of Christian duty and social responsibility. Philanthropy, understood as a feeling of benevolence, was not a private alternative to public action but an attitude that pervaded public institutions and private initiatives in furtherance of widely shared social goals and obligations. In English Colonial America, public and private distinctions were irrelevant in the pursuit of social goals, and duties to the community were prescribed first by Christian doctrine and only secondarily by law.

Despite the Puritans' seeming concern for the lives of others, New England society exhibited tremendous harshness toward outsiders. Convinced of the certainty of their Calvinist doctrines as the one truth and of their need to establish communities predicated on that truth, New Englanders persecuted dissenters to preserve communal homogeneity. Communalism subordinated private desires to the social good in the imposition of social duties upon the wealthy and the most able. This same subordination of private rights to the public good justified intolerance of different perspectives. New England's Calvinists sought a social good at the expense of individual freedoms. Massachusetts's banishment of Ann Hutchinson and Roger Williams, flogging and hanging of Quakers, and trial of suspected witches all were attempts to preserve a community with singular values, goals, and beliefs.

In Virginia and the later Southern colonies, difference was noted less in religious belief than in race. Yet, here too, religious teachings influenced the social institutions that were built on this difference. The construction of a Southern society premised upon the paternalistic benevolence of white male masters of private households and estates recognized the Christian duty of the strong and able to care for those who were weaker because of their sex or less able because of their race. Philanthropy became the ideological justification and the societal means of social control and racial subordination.

To perpetuate the paternalistic communalism necessary to maintain slavery, the Southern states were slow to embrace the profound changes in law that accompanied the transformation of the North from rural communalism to capitalistic individualism in the eighteenth century. After the

Revolution, the Northern states used contract-law principles to privatize society. Contract law embodied the republican ideals of equality, freedom, and individual responsibility for one's life and actions. Contracts accorded each member of the society the legal right to enter into an agreement with another that would be equally binding upon both. Contract law imposed a harsh rationalism on social relationships and repudiated the colonial paradigm resting on equity, morality, deference, and communalism.

Social roles and relationships were redefined as American society adapted to this new liberal ideal. The family, rather than the community, became the primary social institution in the early republic. The law accorded women some new legal freedoms of property ownership, control of their bodies and marriage, divorce, and child custody, while it confirmed men as heads of their households. As contributing if not equal members of the family, women ensured the cleanliness and uprightness of the home, while providing for the education, moral instruction, and health of the children.

The law also redefined people's relationships to their public institutions by recognizing individual rights as superior to the public good. Governmental authority was limited to protect those rights. In the process, the colonial integration of church and state, as well as of public and private endeavors, to serve the social good was rejected for the creation of separate public and private realms in which the authority of the former was circumscribed by the law's protection of the latter.

During the 1830s, two groups of Americans that were disenfranchised in varying degrees in the early republic combined to assert their political wills in private actions. Women, unable to vote, and the clergy, stripped of its political authority during the process of disestablishing state religions, worked together under the banners of the "Benevolent Empire" to encourage moral and sympathetic social awareness to mitigate the harshness and enhance the civilities of society under liberal republicanism. Traditional teachers of morality in the homes and churches, women and the clergy advocated an alternative societal ideal in which slavery, alcoholism, disease, poverty, illiteracy, penal suffering, and crime would be eliminated through public attention to social problems. Largely unable to garner support for its programs through various state legislatures or the courts, the Benevolent Empire relied on private associational efforts to redesign the society.

The conception and role of philanthropy changed dramatically from the 1500s when it was considered charity, to the early 1800s when it was organized philanthropy. Yet, in this change, certain themes identify threads of continuity. At all times, philanthropy – whether expressed through public (state-supported) or private action – served as a means of asserting a social ideal. The European explorers sought to "Christianize and civilize" the Indians; the Puritans sought to create a "community of saints"; Southern planters sought to reestablish feudal estates on chivalric ideals of white male supremacy; and the participants in the Benevolent Empire sought to impose their own moral judgments upon their fellow citizens. Throughout these actions, so-called givers had to confront their differences with the so-called recipients. Far from a unilateral exchange, philanthropists received new cultural insights and attitudes from their beneficiaries, and the process of their interaction contributed to social change to an extent and in ways unconceived of by the philanthropists themselves. In this exchange, Americans came to new understandings of religion, race, gender, and the role of ideology or belief in their society.

During the period 1607–1861, American society rejected a communitarian social ideal and implemented a legal system respecting individual rights. Governmental authority was significantly diminished during this period, and private actions expressed the social ideals of Americans more than did governmental initiatives. Government was understood as a negative force, proscribing wrongs rather than creating rights. Its authority was consistent with Adam Smith's idea that government can place blame for injury but cannot extort benevolence. The first challenge to this system would not occur until the Civil War.

1

GIVING IN AMERICA: FROM CHARITY TO PHILANTHROPY

ROBERT A. GROSS

Americans like to think of themselves as a charitable people. We take pride in the multitude of benevolent groups constantly at work to help out the needy and uplift society, both at home and abroad. Such generosity, freely given by ordinary individuals, is commonly deemed the natural expression of democratic life. In support of this happy view, we call time and again on the Frenchman Alexis de Tocqueville, who put the voluntary association at the center of his analysis of *Democracy in America*. When he traveled throughout America in 1831, Tocqueville was astonished by the "immense assemblage of associations" in the new land:

Americans of all ages, all conditions, and all dispositions constantly form associations. They have not only commercial and manufacturing companies, in which all take part, but associations of a thousand other kinds, religious, moral, serious, futile, general or restricted, enormous or diminutive. The Americans make associations to give entertainments, to found seminaries, to build inns, to construct churches, to diffuse books, to send missionaries to the antipodes; in this manner they found hospitals, prisons, and schools. If it is proposed to inculcate some truth or to foster some feeling by the encouragement of a great example, they form a society. Wherever at the head of some new undertaking you see the government in France, or a man of rank in England, in the United States you will be sure to find an association.

This tribute to the voluntary association captures a powerful theme in American culture. As Tocqueville saw it, such organizations gave energy and purpose to citizens in a democracy. In the aristocratic Old World, the few controlled the destiny of the many; not so in the new republic across the Atlantic. Owing to their very freedom and equality, Americans could exercise power only through the combined force of numbers. Alone, a single unit in the mass, every individual felt overwhelmed; linked to like-minded others, that same person acquired immense influence to do good.

So trenchant are Tocqueville's observations that they are often taken to state timeless truths about charity, philanthropy, and voluntarism in American life. But the institutions he depicted had played little part in colonial society. The French visitor was actually witness to a new phenomenon that was remaking life, especially in the northern states, in the wake of the American Revolution: the rise of formal, voluntary associations, organized by people in towns, counties, and states to meet an extraordinary array of social, educational, religious, and cultural needs. The period from 1790 to 1840 was, as contemporaries put it, "an Age of Benevolence," which gave a distinctive form to the charitable purposes that had motivated people from the very beginnings of English settlement. Tocqueville arrived just in time to record the transformation. *Democracy in America* captures that decisive moment when an older tradition of charity gave way before a new mode of philanthropy, with enduring consequences for how we carry on our lives today.

* * *

The split between these two traditions – charity and philanthropy – forms my central theme. As I have read through the vast scholarly literature on giving in America, picking my way through numerous monographs and histories, I have been taken by the curious character of the field. For early America, we have many studies of "charity" encompassing the ideas and practices of the colonists, notably the Puritans, and tracing the concrete ways the settlers sought to express their impulse to serve others. After the Revolution, the story turns to the rise of benevolent organizations and the crusading spirit of reform, culminating in the missionary, temperance, and antislavery movements of the antebellum era. Thereafter, the tone alters, reflecting the mood of the pragmatic, efficiency-minded men and women who took over the organizations for the care of the poor and the dependent and built the major educational and cultural institutions of their day. This later narrative recounts the history of philanthropy, *not* charity; it sets forth the organization of the great foundations by Andrew Carnegie and John D. Rockefeller, traces the concurrent establishment of settlement houses by Jane Addams and others, and culminates in the establishment of the twentieth-century welfare state, where big government in tandem with the key institutions of the "non-profit sector" takes responsibility for basic social needs.

Essentially, this is a story of leaders and institutions, moving from the local to the national stage over time, with the aim of showing how "the Independent Sector" of today, the current configuration of nonprofits, came into being. It is an informative story, but along the way, I have come to feel that something essential is missing. That element is the record of "charity," the contributions of "time, talents, and treasure," to use the language of the Bible, by vast numbers of well-meaning people seeking to be of service to others and to the common good. In the movement from "charity" to "philanthropy," the contributions of America's Good Samaritans, as they were enacted in the past, disappear into the fold of large-scale, philanthropic institutions. The goal of this essay is to restore "charity" to the picture and to chart its changing relation to "philanthropy." Together, the two strains form the story of giving in America. They belong together, both in our scholarship and in everyday life.

How do I define these terms? The first in time is charity, a complex of ideas and practices rooted in Christianity, particularly in the reformed Protestantism of the English settlers; it was later reinforced by the heritage of Catholicism and Judaism brought by immigrants in the nineteenth and twentieth centuries. Charity expresses an impulse to personal service; it engages individuals in concrete, direct acts of compassion and connection to other people. To some, such as Robert Payton, the founder of the Center for Philanthropy at Indiana University, such action is synonymous with "philanthropy." But, historically, as Daniel Boorstin has noted, philanthropy represents a second mode of social service. Coined as a term in late seventeenth-century England, it became associated with the Enlightenment, for it sought to apply reason to the solution of social ills and needs. Philanthropy can take secular or religious forms. Either way, it aspires not so much to aid individuals as to reform society. Its object is the promotion of progress through the advance of knowledge. By eliminating the problems of society that beset particular persons, philanthropy aims to usher in a world where charity is uncommon – and perhaps unnecessary.

* * *

Such are the two traditions of American humanitarianism. As I have sketched them, charity and philanthropy stand at opposite poles: the one concrete and individual, the other abstract and institutional. But they need not be at odds. As dual impulses, they are the equivalent of the two commitments taken by physicians in the Hippocratic oath: One vow is to relieve pain and suffering, the other is to cure disease. We all hope that the doctor can do both, and much of the time she can, though occasionally, we know, there must be a choice between the two. Similarly, in the practical world of benevolence, the two traditions of charity and philanthropy need to heal the split that opened in the early republic and unite in a common cause.

The first tradition – charity – governed the practice of benevolence from the beginnings of English settlement in the seventeenth century down through the Revolution and Constitution. Although it was carried on in every colony, the tradition is epitomized by the New England Puritans. John Winthrop gave the best statement of that ideal in the lay sermon he preached on the eve of departure for Massachusetts Bay in 1630. Now known as "A Model of Christian Charity," the document has become a classic in American history, for it is here that Winthrop declares the purpose of the Puritan colony to be the establishment of a "City upon a Hill." That image, taken from Matthew 5:14, conjured up not a physical place but rather a spiritual ideal. It embodied a godly community, overflowing in "charity." In Winthrop's evangelical view, the Puritans would not only love and assist one another, but also do so for the right reasons. They would rise above the petty calculations and narrow self-interest that so often drive human cooperation. Even the divine command to do unto others as you would have them do unto you was insufficient motivation. In Winthrop's vision, the faithful were inspired by divine grace. Imbued with gospel love, all the participants in the Bay Colony – the investors in England, the settlers about to embark on the *Arbella*, the advance party already established on Cape Ann – would regard one another as brothers and sisters in Christ. They were to "delight in eache other, make others Condicions our owne reioyce together, mourne together, labour, and suffer together, allwayes haveing before our eyes our Commission and Community in the worke, our Community as members of the same body...." This is a spirit of mutual sacrifice in the name of Christ: "wee must be knitt together in this worke as one man, wee must entertaine each other in brother Affeccion, wee must be willing to abridge our selves of our superfluities, for the supply of others necessities...." In this perspective, charity was not restricted to giving alms to the poor. Having spurned the mercenary sale of indulgences by the Church of Rome, the Puritans revived the larger meanings of *caritas* or Christian love. It could take many forms and inspire diverse sorts. It could be simply a gift of "good advice, a kind word, or an exhortation to piety," offered by anybody to a neighbor in need. A poor man could be just as charitable as a rich one.

Such Christian charity had the potential to be a revolutionary force for equality, and some sects in the Reformation tried to take it in that direction – not the Puritans. Winthrop's vision of charity was premised on the existence of inequality; differences and distinctions among men were immutable parts of the divine order. Indeed, such diversity was essential to God's benevolent design: it simultaneously expressed the plenitude of His power as Creator and drove the creatures of His making to depend on one another. As Winthrop put it, "God almightie in his most holy and wise providence hath soe disposed of the Condicion of mankinde, as in all times some must be rich some poore, some highe and eminent in power and dignitie; others meane and in subieccion." In that condition, they must work together to get by.

That was the utopian ideal, against which any group of people – even the Puritans – was destined to fall short. Even so, in its model of interdependence, the Puritan social ethic articulated an outlook with deep roots in the medieval worldview and immediate relevance to the practice of charity in the Anglo-American world. Winthrop's generation transplanted the localist traditions of Tudor–Stuart England to the "wilderness." Every community established in the Bay Colony was obligated to take care of its own legal inhabitants. When individuals or families fell in need, they could make a rightful claim on the collectivity for relief. In New England, that entity was the town, an innovative institution of local self-governance devised by the Puritans in the New World. Elsewhere, as in New York or Virginia, it took the customary form of the parish vestry.

Whatever the aegis, aid to the needy was direct, personal, concrete. Upon hearing about an individual or family in distress, local authorities, usually called "overseers" of the poor, visited the persons, inspected their circumstances, searched for relatives or employers to help out, and – if nobody else could be found – supplied the assistance required. There were no general allotments of money to be spent as indigents desired. Instead, the poor were given appropriate quantities of food and drink – so many pounds of beef or pecks of corn, drams of rum and ounces of tea – and equivalent supplies of clothing, firewood, and other goods. This was a distribution that followed the Marxist formula quite literally: from each according to his ability, to each according to his needs. Nor was there any separation between the needy and the rest of the community. In most places, there were no formal institutions – no poorhouses, hospitals, or asylums – in which to control and to segregate the dependent and the deviant. Normally, people were cared for in families, either their own or the households of others. As with foster care today, neighbors took in the aged, the sick, the orphaned, the indigent, and the helpless, and supplied their necessities at town expense. They also imposed discipline on the unruly: it was not uncommon for towns to subject village drunkards and even common criminals to the constraints of family. That was charity, too, provided for the individual's own good. The caretakers, we may surmise, had a need for the income and for the labor such inmates provided; they were seldom far removed in social position from the unfortunates they assisted.

New Englanders did worry that generous aid to the poor might actually encourage dependence and idleness. That was, in fact, an important item in the brief English Protestants drew up against the Catholic Church. "The poor ye shall always have with ye": Jesus' dictum had been woven into the fabric of Christianity for centuries. In that faith, medieval churchmen regarded the poor as instruments of providence: their misery ordained to stir feelings of compassion, their sufferings acts of charity. To fulfill this design, the rich were enjoined to give freely to the beggar at their door. Such good works would win renown in this world and credit in the next. The trouble was that alms were bestowed indiscriminately on the virtuous and vicious alike. To the Puritans, "beggars commit sacrilege who abuse the name of Christ, and make their poverty a cloak to keep them idle." It was thus imperative to separate the worthy from the unworthy poor. The former – the aged, the widow, the orphan, the disabled – were victims of circumstances beyond their control; anyone, at any time, could suffer their fate, and they deserved the aid of the community. By contrast, the second class had brought on its plight by idleness and intemperance; it was unworthy of public support. This moral distinction, built into the English Poor Law, was carried over to Massachusetts Bay. In practice, it mattered little. For more than a century after settlement, poverty was a minor problem, handled easily among rural neighbors. Even in Boston, where the ranks of the poor swelled in a stagnant economy and it proved necessary to erect an almshouse, little effort was made to screen applicants for aid and determine the "truly needy." Ministers discouraged such inquiries on the grounds that "as riches are not evidences of God's love, so neither is poverty of his anger or hatred." Indeed, to stifle the impulse to charity was to pass up the opportunity of stewardship. The Reverend Samuel Seabury urged the Boston Episcopal Charity Society in 1788 to assist "every one who is suffering for want. And no matter how their suffering comes on them, whether by accident, by idleness, by vice – while they suffer, they are entitled to relief."

Another minister thundered at the hypocrisy of those who dared to make judgments on the poor. "What if God were to refuse His mercy to those of us who do not deserve it. . . . We deserve nothing but hell; and shall we refuse to supply the poor with a little portion of God's property in our hands of which He has made us the stewards?"

Whereas New England towns readily came to the aid of inhabitants, they were quick to discriminate between neighbors and strangers. If you had not been born and raised in town or married an inhabitant, you had no automatic right to a legal settlement – the qualification for public relief. And if you arrived as a newcomer or passed through as a transient, you were likely to be "warned out" – that is, given official notice that the town considered itself free of obligation in case you fell in need. Often people stayed for a while, even the rest of their lives; as long as they remained off the poor rolls, there was no problem. On other occasions, potential paupers were forcibly ejected from the town, whipped from place to place back to their origin. Warnings out were relatively uncommon in the seventeenth century; however, as population grew, settlement spread, and trade quickened by the mid-eighteenth century, more and more people moved about the countryside, without land or resources of their own. Towns began to cast an ever-more suspicious eye on newcomers and hastened to warn out one and all.

We have a wonderful example of how the arrangements for poor relief worked and how they broke down in the experience of John Adams, future Revolutionary and President of the United States. In March 1767, he was serving as selectman and overseer of poor for the town of Braintree and, in the course of his duties, he was summoned to look after an unfortunate man named Robert Peacock and "his poor distressed Family." There, in the final cold, raw month of the Massachusetts winter, "We found them, in one Chamber, which serves them for Kitchen, Cellar, Dining Room, Parlour, and Bedchamber. Two Beds, in one of which lay Peacock, where he told us he had lain for 7 Weeks, without going out of it farther than the Fire. He had a little Child in his Arms. Another Bed stood on one side of the Chamber where lay 3 other Children. The Mother only was up, by a fire, made of a few Chips, not larger than my Hand. The Chamber excessive cold and dirty." In the face of this misery, Adams felt the anguish of a fellow human and the stirring of compassion. "These are the Conveniences and ornaments of a Life of Poverty," he exclaimed. "These the Comforts of the Poor. This is Want. This is Poverty! These the Comforts of the needy. The Bliss of the Necessitous." But did the overseer of the poor actually do anything to assist the unhappy Peacocks? Not at all. Learning that the father and three of his children had a legal settlement in Boston, Adams hurried to the capital and informed the selectmen that Peacock was the responsibility of Boston, not Braintree. "We must be excused from any Expence for their Support."

Despite this niggardliness, Adams congratulated himself on his sensitive response to the Peacocks' plight: "When I was in that Chamber of Distress," he recorded in his diary, "I felt the Meltings of Commiseration. This Office of Overseer of the Poor leads a Man into scenes of Distress, and is a continual Exercise of the benevolent Principles in his Mind. His Compassion is constantly excited, and his Benevolence encreased." The entry encapsulates the New England tradition, as it had absorbed the legacy of Christian thought: charity was as important to the giver as to the recipient; it was central to expressing one's humanity and religious faith. But Adams's remark also reveals the incursions of change. By the mid-eighteenth century, many scions of New England, especially in the merchant class, no longer quickened with the piety of the Puritan fathers – not for them the vision of brotherly love at the heart of Winthrop's model of Christian charity. In the rising commercial ethos, charity was reduced to almsgiving. To that narrow duty the privileged were called by appeals to secular as well as religious motives. They opened their purses not only to show gratitude to God, but also to display their social station. "Gentile-deeds maketh the Gentleman," advised the Reverend Cotton Mather; the "true Lady is one who feeds the poor." Such acts afforded emotional gratification; "a Ravishing Satisfaction" lay in "relieving the Distresses of a Poor, Mean, Miserable Neighbor." John Adams even enjoyed good feelings from passing the buck.

Shorn of utopian striving, New England came to resemble the Middle Colonies and the South in its culture of charity. The characteristic gesture – aid to the poor – was a public responsibility, overseen by local authorities and financed by taxes. Inhabitants cared for the sick, the dependent, and the deviant under official supervision. Voluntary contributions played a minor part. There were, to be sure, a few charitable endowments – a fund for the purchase of Communion Silver here, a legacy for the "Silent Poor" there. Certainly, churches passed the collection plate on the Sabbath and used the donations to supplement town funds. Seldom in the eighteenth century did charity flow out of town, though many communities did send help to Boston after the great fire of 1760 and in the Revolutionary crisis of 1774–1775. As with aid to the poor, so it was with other social needs, such as education. In New England, these were public matters. Harvard and Yale Colleges, chartered by their respective colonies, received legislative grants. Every town was expected to support its own schools from taxes. Such public commitment to education was distinctive to New England; elsewhere, churches and private tutors supplied instruction. Even so, the vast complex of cultural institutions so characteristic of the region today was unknown. Outside a few large towns, private enterprise had yet to emerge as a driving cultural force.

It was in Philadelphia, the vibrant entrepôt of North American trade and the fourth largest city of the British Empire, with some 23,000 inhabitants in 1774, that the second tradition of benevolence – philanthropy – took shape. Originally connoting "love toward mankind" and, hence, synonymous with charity, philanthropy acquired a distinctive meaning in the middle decades of the eighteenth century. Then civic-minded individuals in London seized on the institutional innovation of England's commercial revolution – the joint-stock company – and put it to benevolent ends. Pooling their funds, they came together to form voluntary associations, whose purposes were defined in formal constitutions and whose officers were chosen in annual elections. The motivation was traditional, the philosophy and methods unprecedented. The organizers of London's Foundling Hospital, launched in 1739, felt an urgent need to save the lives of abandoned and illegitimate children, but not merely for the sake of charity. To raise and educate the forlorn was, without question, a worthy deed. Even more, it advanced the well-being of the nation. England's growth required an expanding population of "useful Hands" and "good and faithful Servants," insisted the "political arithmeticians" of the day. What better supply than the "poor and miserable cast-off Children" of unwed mothers, rescued from early graves? Preserving those unhappy souls would be a valuable service to public policy. So conceived, the hospital advanced the novel notion of "philanthropy": a voluntary enterprise of private persons, moved by "an Inclination to promote Publick Good." In the ensuing decades, the purposes of such ventures would alter in tune with changing ideas about public needs. By the end of the century, as the Industrial Revolution unfolded, a new breed of experts – the "political economists" – repudiated the faith in a growing population and urged a redirection of charity to produce a sober, industrious, self-reliant working class. A new set of organizations, such as the Society for the Suppression of Vice (1802), arose to promote that creed.

The spirit of philanthropy quickly crossed the Atlantic and settled in the rising centers of commerce. Nowhere was it welcomed more warmly than in Philadelphia, the adopted home of Benjamin Franklin – the secular son of the Puritans who ran away from his post as a printer's apprentice in Boston and made a fresh start in the tolerant and expansive Quaker City. There he became, in the words of Boorstin, "the patron saint of American philanthropy." Faithful to his Puritan origins, Franklin affirmed that "the most acceptable service of God is doing good to man." But he departed from tradition by embracing a secular end: practical improvement in the human condition.

Picking up on developments in London, Franklin took the lead in forming societies for the general welfare. But whereas the earliest English philanthropies were initiated from the top down by gentlemen and merchants with schemes for the lower orders, the self-made printer had a more democratic approach. He initiated a club among enterprising young mechanics and tradesmen like himself for the sake of self-improvement. The Junto, as he named it, was a multipurpose institution: a combination of debating society, reading circle, support group, and youthful chamber of commerce. It was the Rotary Club of its day, an organization with an ingenious design.

In the eighteenth century, most young men starting out in the world of crafts or trade depended for advance on the patronage and power of their betters. They were obliged to seek notice and favor from the privileged, to apply to them for access to books, information, contacts, and credit in the wider world. To the proud, ambitious Franklin, this dependence on great men – the aristocrats who were the prime forces in the society of Tocqueville's France – was a personal affront. He forged the Junto as a middle-class alternative to the elite world of patronage and power. The club would offer the means of mobility through the pursuit of knowledge, science, and the rational application of virtue to human affairs. It epitomized an Enlightened blueprint for progress.

To call such activity philanthropy may seem surprising. Were not the founders of the Junto themselves the beneficiaries? Unquestionably, but to Franklin, that posed no problem. In his sunny view, rational self-interest went hand in hand with the general good. It was thus a short step from "self-reform through voluntary mutual-benefit associations" to "voluntary associations directed to public benefit." Was Philadelphia endangered by the outbreak of fire? Franklin founded the first volunteer fire company in America. Did young men want an alternative to the paucity of reading matter and the necessity of borrowing books from the cultivated few? He launched the first subscription library on the continent, still in operation as the Library Company of Philadelphia. Such ventures were followed by his promotion of our first learned institution, the American Philosophical Society, and his sponsorship of an academy and free school for poor children that eventually grew into the University of Pennsylvania. On the eve of the Revolution, Philadelphia stood in the forefront of modern philanthropy, unmatched in its "charitable public foundations," as even John Adams had to concede.

Franklin took an equally rational, progressive approach to the poor. Unwilling to accept poverty as an immutable condition, he eschewed the spiritual satisfactions of charity and took up the challenge of philanthropy. His object was the elimination of poverty: He would help the poor to help themselves. To illustrate his plan, Franklin drew on a commonplace experience of everyday life in the eighteenth century:

Human felicity is produc'd not so much by great pieces of good fortune that seldom happen, as by little advantages that occur every day. Thus, if you teach a poor young man to shave himself, and keep his razor in order, you may contribute more to the happiness of his life than in giving him a thousand guineas. The money may be soon spent, the regret only remaining of having foolishly consumed it; but in the other case, he escapes the frequent vexation of waiting for barbers, and of their sometimes dirty fingers, offensive breaths, and dull razors; he shaves when most convenient to him, and enjoys daily the pleasure of its being done with a good instrument.

This is the approach of the modern philanthropist: inspire the poor with new hope and give them the means of self-support; through such aid, they could raise themselves to respectability. To Franklin, traditional charity – alms – was self-defeating; the money would be here today and gone tomorrow, and the poor would be as dependent as ever. By contrast, philanthropy removed the conditions it addressed; in its successful wake, charity would go out of business.

In the eighteenth century, the contest between charity and philanthropy existed only in theory. Benjamin Franklin's Philadelphia – although a fluid, commercial city – was still a small-scale, personal world, where rich and poor lived in the same neighborhoods, workers and servants ate and drank with their employers, and the recipients of charity knew their benefactors. If Franklin promoted a philanthropic goal, he could infuse it with the spirit of charity. Teaching a man how to employ and repair a razor, Franklin could enjoy an immediate relation to the object of his aid and derive direct satisfaction from the results. The practice of philanthropy was not yet an impersonal act. For Franklin's generation, charity and philanthropy could still work together in a common cause.

That was surely the expectation of the generation that succeeded Benjamin Franklin. In 1776, Thomas Paine summoned colonists to the cause of independence with the fervent declaration that "we have it in our power to begin the world over again." In the new republic, Americans of all classes moved to realize that promise. Having broken with the past and established free governments upon popular consent, they cherished the power of human agency – individual and collective – to improve self and society. Key to such change was the principle of voluntary association. "Two are better than one," announced the founders of the Concord, Massachusetts, Charitable Library Society in 1795, "and a threefold cord is not easily broken." Although that insight was not new – it had inspired the formation of diverse clubs in eighteenth-century Britain and their imitation in colonial cities – it was now regarded as an article of republican faith. The new nation thus saw the full flowering of the Age of Benevolence; voluntary associations proliferated across the landscape. Many were organized for the sheer sake of sociability, like Boston's Wednesday Evening Club. Others offered concrete benefits to participants, such as life insurance from "mutual societies" and borrowing privileges in social libraries. Although they served mainly the interests of members, such groups often professed the goal of improving society at large. The greatest wave of associations promoted charity and philanthropy together, and could be found in every substantial town, north and south – especially in New England, which overcame Philadelphia's early lead. By 1820, some two thousand benevolent institutions of all types dotted the region, from Rhode Island to Vermont: "marine societies, mechanic associations, masonic lodges, humane organizations, a dispensary, a hospital, a school for the deaf, several orphans' asylums, missionary societies, tract societies, Bible societies, Sunday schools, temperance associations, Sabbatarian groups, peace societies, and many more." An "immense assemblage of associations" occupied the social landscape well before Tocqueville arrived. Philanthropy was actually what drew the Frenchman to these shores. Commissioned by the French government, he was on a fact-finding tour of American prisons.

Two features distinguished benevolence in the early republic from its colonial antecedents. The first was the leading part played by religious groups and, in particular, evangelicals; the second, closely connected, was the active participation of women. Churches had, of course, been the major medium of charity in Christendom for centuries. In early America, their generosity was confined to the parish; Anglican vestrymen, Congregational deacons, Quaker monthly meetings all took care of their own. By contrast, the first philanthropic associations in colonial Philadelphia and its sister cities had a secular thrust. However, that was a passing stage; in the new nation, religious activists made the voluntary principle their own. Philadelphia soon had its own Bible Society to disseminate the gospel, Missionary Society to seek souls, and First Day Society to run Sunday schools. The poor were the special object of female benevolence; in 1795, Philadelphia became the home of America's first female charitable society. Launched by a group of Quaker women, the Female Society for the Relief of the Distressed offered aid to "suffering Fellow Creatures," particularly widows and orphans, of any faith, "without distinction of Nation or Colour." Funded by members' subscriptions, the group supplemented municipal relief. Participants engaged directly in charitable work, visiting the needy in their "solatary Dwellings," determining their wants, and returning with whatever was required in the way of food, clothing, firewood, bedding, or medicine. That approach was widely imitated. Evangelical Presbyterians created a Female Association for the Relief of Women and Children in 1800, combining material aid – including a "Soup House" – with spiritual blessings designed to "rouse" the poor out of "apathy and indolence" to efforts on their own behalf. Self-help was closely monitored. If a woman wanted support from the New York Society for the Relief of Poor Widows with Small Children, she better not be found begging or selling liquor, no matter how hungry her children. Only respectable measures were allowed. Aid was restricted to mothers who sent their young to school and put out the older ones to "sober virtuous families." New-model philanthropy proved a flexible vehicle for old-fashioned charity.

These various societies, made up of private individuals, had a quasipublic character. Leading philanthropists were key figures in the governing class of their communities; like New York's De Witt Clinton, who served simultaneously as city mayor and president of the Free School Society, they moved easily between official duty and charitable service. Their wives were the founders and managers of humanitarian agencies from Boston's Fatherless and Widows' Society to Petersburg, Virginia's, Female Orphan Asylum. Confident of its right to rule, the benevolent elite sought and won public money for its philanthropic ends. The New York Free School Society was funded by the city to run schools for the poor; the state legislature awarded $750 to the Society for the Relief of Poor Widows with Small Children in recognition of its "great and essential services" in sparing so many needy from "the necessity of taking refuge in the Alms House."

Charities won other public favors, such as the authority to hold fund-raising lotteries and, most important, the right to incorporate. In the early republic, that privilege was restricted to groups with a public mission, be it economic (banks, turnpikes, and canal companies), municipal (cities), or religious (churches). For charities, corporate charters proved indispensable, enabling the organizations to own real estate, make contracts, and conduct business in perpetuity, even as individual members came and went, free from liability for group debts. Unlike ordinary citizens, these eleemosynary enterprises were normally exempt from taxes. In a society built on indi-vidual property holdings – notably, farms and shops – that changed hands ceaselessly from generation to generation, incorporation was a special privi-lege, jealously guarded by state legislatures and carefully circumscribed, lest the beneficiaries grow into dangerous concentrations of wealth and power. Not surprisingly, it took political clout – connections and influence – and not just a worthy purpose to win that favor. Men like De Witt Clinton, whose public service included terms as mayor, governor, senator, and Vice President of the United States, were accustomed to getting their way. Their wives, too, maneuvered skillfully to win over politicians. Although women were denied the right to vote, the "benevolent fair" exploited their elite status and lobbied "male friends" in high places, even as they made their requests with modesty and deference, portraying charitable activity as a duty of their sex. In short, the philanthropies of the early republic were not the private entities born of the spontaneous cooperation of citizens that Tocqueville portrayed. Integrated into local governance, they constituted successful assertions of political will.

As long as philanthropy was tied to community, organized benevolence stirred few complaints. However, that partnership frayed in the decades after 1820; charities ceased to be the publicly responsive institutions they had been at the start. (McGarvie's Chapter 4 provides a possible expla-nation of this change rooted in law and culture.) Quakers, Episcopalians, Presbyterians, and others had cooperated easily in Philadelphia's pioneer philanthropies, dispensing Bibles and foodstuffs alike to the distressed. But infused with the religious zeal of the Second Great Awakening, evangelicals enlisted charity in the crusade for Christ. The "spiritual food" of the gospel was now the "one thing needful;" let others run soup kitchens for the poor. In that faith, devoted to saving starving souls, they served personal goals rather than public needs. Initially, they operated on the local level, seek-ing out the poor in their garrets and hovels, and handing out Bibles and tracts. But they soon came together in state and national organizations. The

American Bible Society (ABS) and the American Tract Society (ATS) developed into large-scale publishing enterprises, with headquarters in New York and affiliates all over the country. Employing the latest advances in printing – the stereotype plate and the steam-powered press – they turned out religious materials by the million, which were distributed by the local chapters. This was a vast undertaking, dependent on contributions both from numerous small donors and from a few very wealthy patrons. The ABS and the ATS also counted on the service of devoted volunteers to carry their publications to the far corners of the land. Eventually, such far-flung efforts demanded systematic administration. In the 1840s, the national associations rationalized the business of benevolence. They kept watch over huge sums of money through sophisticated cost-accounting; they replaced inefficient volunteers with paid agents recruited and trained for the job, and supervised them through a network of regional offices; and they relied on regular memos and reports to communicate with employees and on national magazines to publicize the cause to the public. Well in advance of the railroads, philanthropy introduced antebellum Americans to modern bureaucracy.

The formalization of benevolence was most dramatic in new arrangements for the care of the dependent and the deviant. As early as the 1780s, humanitarians pushed for an end to the harsh, humiliating punishments – whipping, branding, shaming – that early American courts inflicted on lawbreakers. Stop the barbaric abuse, they urged; confine the criminal to "penitentiaries," where they could ponder their sins and cure their souls. Incarceration was at once philanthropy and charity: it addressed a social ill at the same time it created new opportunities for personal service. Having campaigned successfully for the creation of a penitentiary, Philadelphia's Prison Society did not forget about the inmates. The evangelical physician and patriot Benjamin Rush, signer of the Declaration of Independence, visited the prisoners and sent them gifts of turkeys and watermelons, asking nothing in return "but that they should consider that God by disposing the heart of one of his creatures to shew them an act of kindness, is still their Father and Friend."

Sympathy for the outcast waned over the decades. As a national economy took shape, propelled by the turbulent force of early industrial capitalism, communities were unsettled by social and geographical mobility. An army of transients passed through cities and towns in search of work. If the propertied classes feared these strangers, they knew their own laborers little better; masters and journeymen, no longer residing under the same roof, went separate ways. The waves of change drove some into crime and threw others, disoriented, onto the streets; most of all, they swelled the ranks of the poor. In response, taxpayers hardened their hearts, tightened their purses, and blamed the needy. "In our highly favored country," declared Philadelphia's Female Hospitable Society in 1835, poverty was most of the time the outcome of "improvidence and vice." The only remedy was moral reform, best accomplished by taking the poor out of the community, putting them into the almshouse, and instilling habits of industry and self-discipline. A similar fate befell the insane, the illegitimate, and the unwed mothers, each consigned to a separate site for rehabilitation according to middle-class norms. That formidable task was no longer assigned primarily to "friendly visitors" like Benjamin Rush; instead, it belonged to a new class of professionals, who made careers through their expertise in dependent care. No matter that the results of their efforts soon proved disappointing – successful reform of the criminal, the insane, and the disorderly poor was as limited then as it is today. Nonetheless, the new philanthropic institutions reduced charity to a token act. Now, an individual could contribute funds to a house of industry for the poor or to a refuge for unwed mothers, secure that he or she would never come into contact with any of the inmates.

Not all humanitarians abandoned the field to professionals. Some evangelicals went into the slums in hopes of saving souls, only to emerge as social reformers. Having witnessed the unsanitary neighborhoods, the miserable housing, and the exploitive conditions under which the poor labored for starvation wages ten and twelve hours a day, they called for changes in society at large. The urban environment urgently needed reform; without it, the poor would remain "filthy, reckless, and vicious" as a result of "the force of circumstance over which in most cases they have no control." This impersonal analysis was a spur to new modes of philanthropy, such as campaigns for public health and model tenement houses, from the 1840s on. However, it accentuated the eclipse of face-to-face charity. With battles to be fought in the political arena, reformers concentrated on exposing urban ills in the press and winning over municipal and state lawmakers. Reform could become a full-time job.

It was in the name of charity that critics objected to the new philanthropy. Humanitarianism, it appeared, had succumbed to the very ills of modern life it hoped to cure. It was becoming an abstract, specialized affair, at odds with the personalized ethos of the small-scale community most white Americans still claimed to value. This development did not happen everywhere or all at once. It was resisted in the slaveholding South, even in such large cities as Richmond, Charleston, and New Orleans, where the urban elite cherished traditional ideals. "The whole social system," Henry Pinckney told Charleston's Methodist Benevolent Society in 1835, was "but a chain of reciprocal dependence, the poor hanging upon the rich, and the rich upon the poor."

The duty of the one was to ease distress with "employment, counsel, or gratuity" the obligation of the other to "manifest their gratitude." In this spirit, the privileged took special care to remember favorite servants in their wills. In Petersburg, Virginia, the fortunate women who controlled their own estates went out of their way to reward loyal slaves. "It is my first desire to make some comfortable provision for my servants as a just reward for their affection and fidelity," Dorothy Mitchell began her will in 1837. This "personalism," as the historian Suzanne Lebsock calls the outlook, inspired men as well. Around the same time a wealthy Quaker in Charleston, John M. Hopkins, bequeathed $13,000 in bank stock to the Ladies' Benevolent Society, on the condition that it give one particular free black woman $60 a year and distribute the remaining income for "the relief of sick and infirm poor free persons of color." Visiting the poor, nursing the sick, caring for orphans: such activities remained at the heart of Southern benevolence. Indeed, through voluntary associations, the white elite could conduct patron-client relations at a cut rate. Members of the Charleston Fuel Society were entitled to recommend recipients of firewood in the winter. Orphanages admitted white children of poor, single parents, whose applications for aid were endorsed by local citizens. Preserving racial solidarity was a key function of philanthropy in the world of white masters and black slaves. As the South Carolina novelist William Gilmore Simms advised, charity must be given with open arms and a warm heart, unlike the situation in northern cities, where "the poor are made to assemble at set places, undergo examination, and be fed on soup."

In the southern backcountry and out on the frontier, northern philanthropy was no more welcome, but for different reasons. Common white farmers cast a suspicious eye on the outside agitators from the Northeast, who arrived with arms full of Bibles and tracts, and palms open for donations. The Kentucky preacher John Taylor labored for a living on his farm and, like other rural Hard-Shell Baptists, tended his church part-time, receiving occasional contributions from his hardscrabble neighbors. When he spied the "Female Societies, Cent Societies, Mite Societies, Children's Societies, and even Negro Societies" drawing nigh, he smelled "the *New England Rat*." As he saw it, the missionaries who invaded his neighborhood were hirelings of a huge benevolent empire, intent on getting the country in its grasp. "Money is the mainspring of the vast machinery," complained others. In the words of the Baptist Elder, John Leland, "the machine is propelled by steam (money), and does not sail by the wind of heaven."

The metaphor of the machine was well chosen: it captured the identification of the national benevolent societies with economic and technological revolution. For that reason, critics arose not only in the South and on the frontier, but also in the very citadels of northern capitalism. As Ralph Waldo Emerson saw it, the new philanthropy had absorbed the basic assumptions of the new order. "The revolt against the spirit of commerce, the spirit of aristocracy, and the inveterate abuses of cities, did not appear possible to individuals"; he observed about "New England Reformers" (1844), "and to do battle against numbers they armed themselves with numbers, and against concert they relied on new concert." Huge combinations of numbers and resources in pursuit of specialized ends, benevolent societies formed the exact equivalent of the business corporation and the political party, the very institutions reformers decried. Philanthropy was part of the problem, *not* part of the solution. Its achievements were purchased at an unacceptable price: the personal charity essential to any decent community. Dr. Walter Channing, a Boston physician from an elite family, with an extensive practice among the poor, was appalled by the way the so-called respectable turned their backs on the indigent. First, they blamed the impoverished individual for his miserable condition: "The pauper is forever looked to as the active, the sole agent in the production of his own misery. He is poor – he is squalid in dress and loathsome in his whole bearing. He is dependent upon others around him for that which he should obtain for himself. . . . He is in a state of willing slavery, and so he must be a degraded being." Pulling back in horror from such creatures, the privileged retreated into the comforts of their own homes. To salve their souls, they contributed to charity, but it was a cold, impersonal act, paying the bills of conscience. Gone was the true spirit of charity – Christian love. "Exclusiveness . . . is not much disposed to go to the lower places in society. If it aims to aid Pauperism, it does so by delegation."

America did not require New England intellectuals, however learned, to discern the fatal flaw of the new philanthropy. In 1803, the Massachusetts legislature granted a corporate charter to the Boston Female Asylum, which ran an orphanage in the city. That action prompted one observer, who took the pen name of "Curtius," to send an outraged letter to the *Worcester Aegis*. An unabashed traditionalist, he objected to the effrontery of the women in going to the legislature and seeking a bill of incorporation; they had "*far out step'd the modesty* of [their] *sex.*" But his complaint went beyond misogyny. What would happen to the spirit of charity? he demanded. With the growth of organized benevolence, people gained an excuse to turn away beggars from their door; they could simply direct them to the Female Asylum and its sister institutions. If those agencies refused aid, then the unfortunates could be dismissed as "unworthy." Let them fend for themselves without troubling their betters. It was a respectable ruse that Ebenezer Scrooge would come to symbolize for the Victorian age. It was born in Boston at the very dawn of the age of the asylum.

* * *

To suggest that personal charity disappeared in the early republic would be a caricature of reality. Throughout the nineteenth century, as today, a great many men and women took responsibility for aiding the indigent and helping the needy. That was true for the middle and upper classes and perhaps even more for the laboring poor, who forged ties of mutual aid among themselves for the sake of sheer survival. Giving money never eliminated direct acts of charity. But a tension arose between the two strains of benevolence – traditional charity and modern philanthropy – that runs through American history to the present. That tension is reflected in the late nineteenth and early twentieth centuries, when Christian reformers such as Jane Addams – appalled by the dire conditions of the industrial cities – established settlement houses, and the so-called Robber Barons Andrew Carnegie and John D. Rockefeller employed their vast wealth to create the great philanthropic foundations that carry their names. In Addams's case, the establishment of Hull House in a poor neighborhood of Chicago was no impersonal act of reform. It was for her a "subjective necessity," a means for educated young men and women to feel a connection to the vital forces of their age and to gain "an outlet for that sentiment of universal brotherhood which the best spirit of our times is forcing from an emotion into a motive."

To John D. Rockefeller, the purpose of philanthropy was just the opposite: to spare him the overwhelming burden of overseeing donations to worthy causes. A devout Baptist, Rockefeller had been accustomed to tithing himself for charity from the very outset of his business career, and he continued the practice as his fortune swelled. "The good Lord gave me the money," he declared, but it poured in so fast that he could no longer intelligently direct its use. He was obliged to hire a professional adviser in philanthropy, a Baptist minister named Frederick T. Gates, who was perhaps the first professional consultant in the field of planned giving. Gates started work two years after Addams founded Hull House. Although the two were moved by very different impulses, the results of their labors had much in common: they gave rise to new professions – the social worker, the foundation executive, the development officer in the nonprofit sector – and institutions that have become a staple of our society and our histories.

Organized philanthropy never eliminates the urge to personal service. The Peace Corps and VISTA in the 1960s; Habitat for Humanity; Doctors without Borders in transnational times: the spirit of voluntarism still inspires Americans, young and old, to help people in distress, with whatever amateur or professional skills they possess. The trouble is that such charitable acts, born of the hunger for personal connection to others, have been left out of most academic accounts. That absence, I suggest, is the result of the split between charity and philanthropy that began in the early republic, was sharpened in the age of Jackson, and was intensified over time. To perpetuate that omission is to undermine the very enterprise of helping others. When scholarship focuses mainly on the institutions of philanthropy, the ideas of leaders, and the issues of public policy, it distorts the benevolent enterprise. Helping others can knit society together or pull it apart. Without a compelling social program, charity can dissipate into transient encounters between unequals. But without direct, mutual bonds between givers and recipients, philanthropy sacrifices practical effectiveness and moral purpose.

2

PROTESTANT MISSIONARIES: PIONEERS OF AMERICAN PHILANTHROPY

AMANDA PORTERFIELD

At the Indian town of Crossweeksung, in New Jersey, on August 26, 1745, the famous American missionary, David Brainerd, called together the group of Housatanic Indians he identified as "my people." Brainerd had been living at Crossweeksung for the better part of a year, devoting himself to building this congregation of "about ninety-five persons, old and young." To his attentive eye, most of these individuals showed clear signs of being "affected either with joy in Christ Jesus, or with utmost concern to obtain an interest in him." Pleased with the combination of repentance for sin and hope of salvation these Christians expressed, and with evidence of the "tender, affectionate, humble, delightful melting" they showed, Brainerd announced that he was going to leave Crossweeksung to minister to Indian bands living in an even more remote region along the Susquehanna River. "I told them I wanted the Spirit of God should go with me." To this end, Brainerd went on, "I asked them if they could not be willing to spend the remainder of the day in prayer for me that God would go with me and succeed my endeavors for the conversion of those poor souls." According to Brainerd, the congregation "cheerfully complied with the motion, and soon after I left them (it being then about an hour and a half before sunset), they began, and continued praying all night till break of day."

This event is a good example of philanthropy as a form of religious expression and, more specifically, as a form of missionary work. As this chapter will show, American Protestant missionary work provided the organizational and intellectual context out of which many other forms of American philanthropy have emerged. This chapter will also show that, gender has figured importantly in this history, with men's priorities dominating – and men's urge *to* dominate – defining missionary work until the nineteenth

49

century. Women's increasing involvement in missionary work during the nineteenth century provided justification and support for major advances in women's education, both at home and abroad. As a result, New England women emerged as donors as well as recipients of missionary benevolence, imposing their vision of a good society on others as part of the process of dedicating themselves to a lifetime of service to others. Beyond consideration of the gendered aspects of this dynamic, the chapter will show that American Protestant missionary work exemplifies the reciprocity between donor and recipient at the heart of philanthropy. In the case of David Brainerd, this reciprocity involved a life transformation for recipients, as well as a form of personal empowerment for the donor.

Fighting tuberculosis and other hardships, Brainerd dedicated the last years of his short life to the conversion of Native Americans. In turn, the people he converted dedicated considerable effort and good will in his behalf. In addition to that repayment, Brainerd became internationally famous for his efforts. With his diary almost continuously in print for two and a half centuries, evangelical Protestants have celebrated Brainerd as a model of Christian virtue. Of course, they have viewed his luminosity as a manifestation of the greater glory of God; however, at the level of human interaction, Brainerd's own status was remarkably advanced by his service to others.

This kind of reciprocity is characteristic not only of American missionary work, but also of American philanthropy more generally. Donors require recipients. The more appreciative and grateful that recipients are, the more successful donors feel. And the more visible this success, the more the donor's own status is advanced in the eyes of both peers and beneficiaries.

Like philanthropists more generally, missionaries have shown various degrees of self-consciousness about the dynamic of reciprocity. And they have shown various degrees of hesitancy about imposing their own worldview as a gift to others and requiring recipients to give up, or at least modify, their own worldview as part of the exchange. In many cases, missionaries (and philanthropists more generally) have not seemed fully aware that their service to others was dependent on and repaid by the transformation that others underwent and by the gratitude, recognition, and elevation in status that they themselves received. In many cases, missionaries and philanthropists have shown few qualms about the hierarchical relationship involved in gifts of ideas, attitudes, and behaviors that established the donor's dominance and the recipient's respectful submission.

Lack of self-criticism and unself-consciousness about the rewards and repayments involved in gift-giving is only part of American missionary history, however. In more than a few cases, missionaries and philanthropists have shown awareness and real concern about these matters. In fact, awareness of the dynamic of reciprocity figured importantly in the growth of American Protestant missions in the early nineteenth century and contributed to an egalitarian idealism about universal brother and sisterhood that inspired many missionaries and converts. Concern about imposing one's own cultural values on others altered the course of American Protestant missions in the early twentieth century. That concern contributed to the division between liberal and conservative Protestants that developed in the early twentieth century and to the departure of many religious liberals from missionary work for more secular forms of philanthropy.

To understand this complicated history, it is important to see how salient aspects of American Protestant missionary history developed from the religious worldview of the New England Puritans, and especially from their desire to be part of God's New Israel and its manifestation in North America. These Puritans carried forward plans laid down by the sixteenth-century French-born Reformer, John Calvin, for bringing the Kingdom of God to earth in the form of Christian commonwealths. These commonwealths, Puritans hoped, would extend throughout the world, encompassing all the political and economic aspects of earthly society. As part of this vision, Puritans believed, the earthly vocation of each Christian was a divine calling from God. Christian merchants, lawyers, fathers, mothers, and rulers should all be engaged in building the holy commonwealths that would bring the Kingdom of God to realization.

With its characteristic set of investments in world reform, moral status, self-criticism, and self-correction, this Calvinist tradition shaped the character of the American Puritans in the seventeenth century and contributed to the strength and resilience of the culture they planted. In the early nineteenth century, often in cooperation with Protestant evangelicals from England and Scotland, American missionaries revitalized this tradition, broadcasting Reformed theology and triggering religious and social reform movements in many corners of the globe. Many of the earliest and most influential American missionary organizations were supported by Reformed Protestant denominations with direct historical ties to Calvinist theology, including the Congregational, Presbyterian, Baptist, and Reformed churches and their various offspring. The missionary organizations established by members of those denominations provided the original backbone of the American Protestant missionary movement.

In the early twentieth century, the progressive side of this tradition of missionary activism and world reform was transmuted into scientific forms of philanthropy that helped to shape domestic and foreign policy in the United States, as well as the agendas of numerous private agencies dedicated to education and social reform. Thus, Calvinist patterns of thought and behavior proved to be relevant and adaptable to different situations and cultural contexts. They have also proved to be highly effective stimuli of social change. As the historian of Reformed Protestantism, Roland Bainton, once put it, "Calvinism has injected a spirit of vitality and drive into every area in which Calvinists have been disposed to enter. They have exhibited unceasing endeavor whether they were subdividing a continent, overthrowing a monarchy, or managing a business, or again reforming the evils of the very order which they helped to create."

* * *

The Calvinist emphasis on social responsibility and reform derived from a long-standing tradition of social concern that goes back to the prophets of ancient Israel. As Christianity developed out of Judaism during the first century of the common era, this tradition of social concern fused with profession of belief in the resurrection and messianic status of Jesus. Criticism of social decay, now linked with demand for belief in Christ, emerged as part of an apocalyptic worldview in which the Kingdom of God was expected to break into history and create a new social order. Pictured as a jeweled city of eternal life from which worldly nonbelievers would be cast out and condemned, the Kingdom of God was a source of hope for Christians persecuted by the Roman Empire.

As the Roman Church became established, apocalyptic expectation diminished as investment in an ongoing eternal heaven above this world increased. In the early fifth century, the influential theologian, Augustine of Hippo, discouraged apocalyptic ideas about the overthrow of society and focused instead on the importance of individual participation in Christ's resurrection through the sacraments of the Church, defined as the means of salvation and doorway to heaven. Only when Christ returned in the remote future, Augustine taught, would the Kingdom of God bring heaven to earth.

Expectations that the Kingdom would arrive soon, ushering in a new world on earth, became popular again during the Protestant Reformation. Calvin's idea of the Kingdom of God as a holy commonwealth – and his attempt to establish such a commonwealth in Geneva – inspired English Protestants, including those who set their sites on America as the place where God's New Israel might be planted. The need for missionary outreach not only persisted as a means of bringing souls to heaven, but also intensified as part of the pressure of wanting to participate in bringing about the Kingdom of God on earth.

As Puritans understood it, missionary outreach was a consequence of the covenant of grace between God and his saints. The covenant of grace enabled the saints to act in accordance with God's will, which included the conversion of people God had preselected for salvation. This depiction of God's relationship to mankind was complicated by the belief, held by most Puritans, that individuals did not know whether they actually participated in the covenant of grace. Overconfidence on this point was a sure sign of pride, which counted against the likelihood of one's sanctity and salvation. But Puritans *were* confident that those who had entered the covenant of grace were able to live in the world in a way that carried out God's will. Again, they could never be entirely sure that they were God's chosen people, and this uncertainty about their actual relationship to God generated considerable anxiety. However, they were strongly motivated by the hope of grace and by the desire to be part of God's historical work. If they could establish a Christian society in the wilderness of the New World that would be a light to the world and a model for others to follow, their success might confirm their own chosenness and sanctity.

In important respects, this Puritan view of a Christian society encompassed Calvin's vision of a holy commonwealth in which every aspect of social life was filled with spiritual purpose and every man pursued his vocation as a divine calling. However, the Puritan concept of the covenant of grace had the effect of heightening the anxiety involved in attempting to live a Christian life far beyond what Calvin intended. Whereas for Calvin, profession of faith, disciplined behavior, and love of the sacraments were sufficient evidence of devotion, the Puritans raised the bar of presumed election to sainthood to the impossible-to-know level of living in accord with God's will. As the Puritan tradition developed in America, strenuous self-sacrifice in the cause of missionary work was a favored means of trying to reach this bar.

* * *

Of course, not all American missionaries have been Calvinist or even Protestant. Beginning in the sixteenth century, Jesuit and Franciscan missionaries introduced Christianity to Native Americans at outposts established by French and Spanish soldiers and along their routes of exploration. Among the Iroquois, Huron, Miami, and other tribes of the eastern woodlands, Jesuits were especially successful at spreading Christian ideas. Unlike Protestant missionaries who insisted that converts abandon their old religions, Jesuits were adept at integrating traditional beliefs and practices with Christianity. Thus, Jesuits in seventeenth-century New France worked with Iroquois beliefs about dreams as messages from the spirit world, and encouraged Native Americans to dream about Jesus and Mary. This syncretic approach to Christianity laid the groundwork for new religious movements led by Native American prophets that combined resistance to Euro-American colonization with millennial themes from Christianity.

During the nineteenth century, even as Protestant evangelicalism flourished in the United States, Catholic missionary work expanded along with growing numbers of Catholic immigrants. Whereas Protestant evangelicals used the public school system, print media, and various forms of public policy to indoctrinate citizens with equations between Protestant and American values, American Catholics developed a vast alternative network of schools, hospitals, charitable organizations, devotional programs, religious orders, and communities. These agencies not only strengthened the faith that Catholics brought with them to the United States, but also extended that faith in new directions and brought many new converts into the Catholic fold. In the twentieth century, American Catholic missionary work broadened to include extensive international populations, while at the same time being no less vital or effective within the borders of the United States.

Although American Catholic missionary work functioned partly as a form of countercultural resistance to Protestant hegemony, it was also influenced by the Protestant character of American culture and its Calvinist orientation. The Calvinist emphasis on the link between personal piety and social service influenced the development of American Catholic thought, especially on its liberal, progressive side. Emphasis on the transforming power of the Holy Spirit among progressive American Catholics in the nineteenth century also worked to diminish the difference between Catholics and Protestants. This "Americanist" form of Catholicism located the transformative power of grace as much in the individual soul and its activity in the world as in the sacraments themselves.

Other religious traditions in the United States have also been influenced by the Calvinist sense of social responsibility as a manifestation of individual grace. Although their official doctrines developed in reaction to certain aspects of Calvinist theology, American Lutherans, Methodists, Latter Day Saints, and others have all been influenced by Calvinism's this-worldly orientation. NonChristian traditions – including various forms of American Judaism, Islam, Buddhism, and Hinduism – have also been affected by the pragmatism of the Calvinist strain in American culture.

* * *

Missionary outreach was one of the first reasons offered by seventeenth-century New England Puritans to justify their departure from England. An image of an Indian with the inscription "Come over and help us" underneath appeared on the official seal of the Massachusetts Bay Colony. New England did produce a few notable missionaries in the seventeenth and eighteenth centuries – David Brainerd being foremost among them, whose efforts were proudly celebrated. Interestingly enough, however, the principal effect of Puritan missionary effort and rhetoric was not Indian conversions – which, in fact, were relatively few – but rather the stabilization of Puritan culture. By emphasizing their society's God-given mission to represent the gospel in the larger world, New England's religious leaders strengthened their own hand, as fledgling colonists, with respect to both their allies and detractors in England. The sense of responsibility for carrying out a God-given mission also enabled those men to maintain firmer control than they otherwise might have had over various factions and dissidents within their own communities in New England. Thus, the vision of carrying out God's will through missionary work served the important function of justifying the legitimacy and expansion of the society that produced it.

To a large extent, the society that Puritans hoped to strengthen and expand was communal in nature. Until this form of social organization began to be replaced in the nineteenth century by a legalistic consumerist economy, virtually all areas of life in New England towns and villages were characterized by relationships of interdependency and reciprocity (McGarvie describes this change in Chapter 4.). Economic, political, and religious life involved tight-knit social relationships based on expectations of high degrees of communal self-sufficiency and interdependence among individuals.

The family was the center of economic life in colonial New England. Livestock was raised, milked, and butchered at home. Vegetables, herbs, and medicines were grown and processed there. Cloth was spun, leather was cured, and clothes were produced at home, as well as soap, candles, and even furniture. To a large extent, this high degree of self-sufficiency was limited only by the interdependence of colonial families. Jams, herbs, and venison from one family might be exchanged for cheese and butter produced by another. Harnesses might be repaired at the blacksmith's shop in exchange for the king's coin – or, if need be, for a pair of hens or labor in the smithy's garden.

Care of the sick, disabled, and indigent, along with supervision of both children and elders, operated through a similar combination of domestic self-sufficiency and interdependence. The family served as a welfare institution, both for its own members and for others in the neighborhood. Because the duties of motherhood were routinely shared, children called most of the adult women familiar to them "mother." Neighbors felt responsible for the sick and poor, not simply because compassion was a Christian virtue and not only because sufferings of one's neighbors were so present and unavoidable, but also because failure to take care of others produced ill will and resulted in lack of assistance when the donor, in turn, needed help.

Religion played a central, organizing role in Puritan society. Ministers functioned as patriarchal authorities who laid down guidelines for virtuous living. Churches were community meetinghouses where the consensual piety that legitimated social order was constantly invoked and stimulated. Of course, these communities were not without dissenters, factions, or outbreaks and undercurrents of hostility. The persistence of witchcraft accusations throughout the seventeenth and early eighteenth centuries – after these accusations had almost completely died out on the other side of the Atlantic – shows that social intercourse in Puritan communities could be highly acrimonious. Nonetheless, Puritan villages and towns were communal entities, with religion playing a central role in providing an ideal picture of how Christian society should operate. With its connections to Calvin's holy commonwealth and biblical images of the Kingdom of God, Puritans lived in the shadow of this ideal, all too aware that the imperfections in their society were legion.

* * *

The effort to convert Indians was part of the process of attempting to make amends for the failure to bring this ideal to reality. What mattered most was the triumph of God's will and the establishment of His Kingdom. Only God knew whether the Indians would be mostly converted or mostly killed off in this process. Puritans felt some responsibility to assist in the salvation of those whom God had chosen as his elect. They also felt justified in wiping out hostile Indians, and imagined their skirmishes with these people as being analogous to the battles between Israelites and Canaanites described in the Old Testament.

With regard to the dynamic of reciprocity, Native American conversions – however few in number – were important tokens of exchange within the larger enterprise of stabilizing and extending Puritan culture. As Puritans understood it, the effort exerted by their missionaries on the Indians was a means of imparting, or at least offering, the precious gift of Christ. This effort was believed to be more than fair compensation for appropriating Native American lands and ruining their cultures.

But, however aggressive and self-serving this exchange with Native Americans, Puritan religious thought also involved elements of egalitarianism and self-criticism that were rooted in the Protestant commitment to the priesthood of all believers and in the consequent emphasis – among English Protestants especially – on the need for honest assessment of one's true intentions. In small ways, at least, these elements of egalitarianism and self-criticism worked to challenge the Puritan tendency to presume they were better than Indians. To some extent, they also worked to undercut the hierarchical relationship between condescending donor and submissive recipient that missionary activity often entailed. Thus, in claiming that Native Americans were, by nature, as good if not better than the English men and women, Roger Williams appealed to the element of egalitarianism implicit in Puritan ideas about the universality of original sin and the connection between humility and the transcendent power of grace. In arguing that land should be purchased from Native Americans and not simply commandeered, Williams tried to hold his fellow Puritans to the principle that Native Americans should be treated the way the Puritans would want to be treated themselves. Although he never doubted that Christ would return to judge all mankind, Williams cautioned humility, warning his fellow Puritans that "Heaven" might be "open to Indians wild, but shut to thee."

In the eighteenth century, Jonathan Edwards, the influential New England theologian (and editor of Brainerd's *Diary*), combined this sort of commitment to moral honesty with an idealistic vision of God's work of redemption as a building whose cornerstones were prophets and church fathers and whose walls were in the process of being erected. Edwards speculated that the religious revivals known as the Great Awakening might be signs that the millennium was dawning in America and that a universal Protestant society would be constructed in the years ahead. Once the building of this Christian society was complete, he believed, Christ would return to earth as its capstone.

While Edwards's vision of the Kingdom of God was projected on a scale grand enough to encompass all the nations of the earth, it was also rooted in an ideal of Puritan community close to home. Edwards's actual experience of Puritan community was fairly traumatic – he was forced out of his Northampton parish after a vote of no confidence based on his parishioners' resentment of a tendency to high-handed authority that they perceived in him. But whatever difficulties he faced in his own parish, Edwards had a clear sense of what Puritan community should be: In his ideal picture of Christian social life, spiritual fellowship and socioeconomic interdependence existed within the framework of complete submission to divine authority.

As part of his vision of the building of the Kingdom of God, Edwards celebrated the nature of genuine benevolence as an essential expression of Christian life. According to Edwards, no one was able to truly love God or other people unless the radically transforming power of grace had intervened to liberate him from the imprisoning circle of self-love that was the root of all sin and rebellion against God. Once so liberated, Edwards believed, the individual was free to love God and to behave with the same spirit of benevolence with which he or she had been transformed. However difficult this spirit was to attain and manifest in actual practice, it stood as a standard of self-critical justice that many American Protestants admired.

Edwards's influential disciple, Samuel Hopkins, focused almost all of his concentration on disinterested benevolence as the standard of Christian virtue. He made willingness to sacrifice oneself the principle means of testing and developing it. Like Edwards, Hopkins believed that historical events were contributing to the building of a universal Protestant society and that contributing to this building was the most important work anyone could do. But Hopkins went much further than Edwards in emphasizing the need for self-sacrifice and in promoting organized missionary work as a means of achieving it. He was also more specific about the connection between particular failures of disinterested benevolence and lack of sanctity. Thus, he angered some of the merchant families in his congregation in Newport, Rhode Island, by asserting that no one who owned slaves or participated in the slave trade could be Christian.

Beginning in the early nineteenth century, enthusiasm for foreign missions caught fire among young people eager to carry forward this idealism about God's plan for world redemption and to manifest the virtue of benevolence they identified with their own hope of salvation. This missionary enthusiasm was centered in New England, where bad weather, soil depletion, industrial growth, and the decline of self-sufficient village economies created stress and instability. Whereas many young people headed west to establish new lives for themselves, others looked eastward, hoping to export their Christian faith to the most remote corners of the world. Joined by Protestant evangelicals from England, Scotland, and Europe, these energetic Americans linked their own worth as Christians to their success in building God's kingdom. They imagined themselves, their colleagues, and their converts launching the conquest of Islam in Persia, overturning "Satan's seat" in India, drawing the African descendants of Ham into the fold of Christendom, and separating illgotten children of the Church of Rome in every land from their whorish mother.

As part of their Puritan heritage, these evangelicals had an underlying concern about not being qualified to lead the way in service to God. On the one hand, this concern encouraged self-criticism and continual effort to improve oneself and one's plans. On the other hand, it helped fuel a relentless and, in more than a few cases, ultimately self-centered effort to prove one's love of God. Motivated by the effort to master anxiety about their own unworthiness, as well as by their investment in an idealistic picture of the role of divine providence in history, many nineteenth-century missionaries seemed to measure benevolence more in terms of their own heroic acts of self-sacrifice than in terms of what the people they served said they needed or wanted.

In New England, where it first developed, this nineteenth-century Protestant enthusiasm for foreign missions coincided with the stresses involved in the transition from a regional, predominantly agrarian economy characterized by face-to-face exchange and consensus to a national, industrialized, consumer-based economy. The young men and women who dedicated themselves to missionary work found an outlet for their religious idealism and for their enthusiasm about new advances in transportation, communication, and labor-saving devices. Coincidently, they also found a means of improving their own situations; because of a declining regional economy, they faced uncertain prospects at home. Their vision of God's work of redemption as a building that they were helping to construct out of souls from all over the world gave them something to do. It also joined the social stability they wanted to preserve from the past with a plan for its re-creation on a larger scale in the future.

* * *

In the eyes of impoverished young women of Puritan stock, many of whom were devoted enthusiasts of foreign missions, the need for female teachers both at home and among heathen populations abroad legitimated considerable advances in their own education. At a time when increasing numbers of young unmarried women in New England were economic burdens on their families, these advances created exciting new opportunities for personal growth and employment. But prejudice against women's education also existed as a part of conventional expectations about women's proper role in relation to men. The missionary proved her worthiness to be educated through her willingness to suffer on behalf of others. This commitment to self-sacrifice compensated for the elevation in status associated with advanced education and new opportunities for employment.

While preoccupation with self-sacrifice could function to obscure the status that missionaries gained relative to both their converts and the folks back home, it often entailed considerable sensitivity to the dynamic of reciprocity. Many nineteenth-century missionaries viewed their own willing sacrifice of comfort and health as repayment, albeit insufficient, for blessings that they themselves had received. Moreover, self-sacrifice often involved desire for genuine humility and, along with that, desire to root out and destroy the pride that set the self above others and, thus, in rebellion against God. Mystical feeling and idealistic visions of people of all cultures being one in Christ implied a kind of democracy of the spirit. Connections drawn between grace on the one hand and love and compassion for others on the other could lead to acts of genuine helpfulness.

As an important center for the advancement of both women's education and missionary training in the nineteenth century, Mount Holyoke Female Seminary (founded in 1837 and renamed Mount Holyoke College in 1888) offers a good example of how this dynamic of reciprocity actually worked. The founder of Mount Holyoke, Mary Lyon, conceptualized the spiritual integrity of her seminary in terms of an even balance between the inflow and outflow of benevolence. It was important, she believed, that the donations coming into the seminary originate in a spirit of benevolence because these donations were intended to stimulate the same spirit of benevolence in the students who benefited from them. As part of her concern for a uniform quality of benevolence flowing through the seminary, Lyon believed that the "benefactors" of the institution should be of the same "class" as the "beneficiaries."

In her strategy for attracting donors, Lyon used the concept of priming the pump of benevolence to great effect. Contributing to Mount Holyoke was a great religious opportunity, she told donors, because it would enable them to exercise their own capacity for benevolence. Their benevolence would, in turn, instill a sense of gratitude and obligation in students who knew their education was paid for by older women who had scrimped to contribute to educational opportunities that they themselves had never received. In repayment, the young women would pass on the same spirit of benevolence and the same enthusiasm for education to their students, converts, and children.

As part of a universal vision of redemption, the self-sacrificial benevolence fueled at Mount Holyoke would contribute to a great momentum of universal uplift, Lyon believed, that would "advance(e) the Redeemer's kingdom." As she wrote in an 1835 circular advertising the seminary and seeking subscriptions for its endowment, "the institution is to be founded by the combined liberality of an enlarged benevolence, which seeks the greatest good on a large scale." Invoking "those great souls . . . whose plans and works of mercy are like a broad river . . . destined to give untold blessings to . . . the world," she described her donors as Christians "advancing as fast as possible, the renovation of the whole human family."

In an effort to participate as fully as possible in this broad river of benevolence, tuition at Mount Holyoke was kept to a minimum by making students responsible for all the cooking, cleaning, and washing; by furnishing rooms with donated furniture; and by employing teachers with "so much of a missionary spirit" that they would gladly accept "only a moderate salary." Only if the expenses were reduced drastically, Lyon wrote, would "a great number, who now almost despair of ever being able to realize the object of their ardent desires," be able to receive an advanced education. In response to the complaint that Mount Holyoke's low tuition put pressure on other seminaries to reduce their fees, Lyon was quite clear about the kind of currency in which she wanted to trade. "Shall we ask for higher tuition," she responded impatiently, "at the same time that we are asking for benevolent aid?"

Mount Holyoke stood for a commitment to women's education that was grounded in a millennial vision of the future. At least in its founding, Mount Holyoke stood against the tendency toward professionalization in women's teaching that began to emerge in the United States before the Civil War and against the more encompassing tendency toward professionalization that came to dominate philanthropy and social reform at the beginning of the twentieth century. Although Mount Holyoke eventually caught up with these modernizing trends, its founding vision reflected a thoroughly religious commitment to help advance the Kingdom of God by replicating and revitalizing the interdependent, communal nature of Puritan society.

Lyon and her missionaries felt little hesitation about imposing their own worldview on others. This lack of hesitation was a function of their ignorance of and lack of respect for other cultures. It was also a function of their preoccupation with self-sacrifice and of the self-absorption involved in the endless and finally impossible task of proving to oneself and others that one's benevolence was truly disinterested.

At the same time, however, Lyon's construction of the dynamic of reciprocity in terms of self-sacrifice also carried the message that all believers and contributors to the work of redemption were on an equal footing before God. Moreover, her investment in Edwards's vision of world redemption as a building or kingdom constructed through historical time carried with it the implication that Christianity should be defined – at least in part – in terms of social reform, world peace, and women's education. Thus, God's work of redemption not only transformed Christians into spiritual brothers and sisters at the individual level, but also brought them together in the work of constructing a global social order imbued with democratic spirit, moral principle, and educated intelligence.

* * *

Toward the end of the nineteenth century, the egalitarian and progressive elements of this missionary vision of redemption developed into a social gospel in which the meaning of the Kingdom of God was translated into the terminology of social justice. This development within progressive Protestant missionary thought was the result of a variety of coinciding factors, including new forms of biblical criticism and the emergence of new theories of sociological analysis. No less important were the responses of nonwestern people to the Protestant missionary agenda. In a number of different geocultural contexts, people who had received the gift of Christ from American Protestants reciprocated with enthusiasm for the egalitarian social implications of Christian ideals, but also with resistance to other aspects of missionary preaching and to the failures of missionaries to put their preaching into practice.

As an example of selective investment in missionary preaching, Hindus in the province of Maharashtra in western India appropriated some of the social-reform ideas propounded by American and British missionaries, especially in the area of female education. Several prominent Indian leaders credited these missionaries with stimulating progressive social policies and programs that challenged some of the rigidly hierarchical and oppressive institutions of Hindu traditionalism. But only a small minority of the Indians who championed these reforms converted to Christianity. In fact, the American and British missionaries in Maharashtra stimulated a revitalization of Hinduism rather than the widespread renunciation of Hinduism for which they hoped. In response to this revitalization, missionaries were divided: Some retreated from education and social work to focus on preaching and conversion, others looked more favorably on the development of new forms of socially progressive Hinduism and tried to cooperate.

In Natal in southeast Africa, criticism of American, British, and European missionaries was more direct. Beginning in the 1860s, some African Christians called attention to the gap between what the missionaries taught about Christianity and how they actually behaved. At the American mission school at Inanda, for example, several Africans made a point of praising an American woman new to the mission who sat down to eat with them, telling her that "their best and wisest men have said that the missionaries do not know them; they keep at too great a distance." In 1869, Mbiana Ngidi, a Congregationalist minister trained by American missionaries, drew a clear distinction between what missionaries said and how they behaved. "While in the pulpit, the missionaries said 'dear friends and brethren,'" Ngidi reported. But, "as soon as they came out of the pulpit, they would not call them that because they were black, but despised them."

In 1875, an independent missionary movement led by African Christians emerged at the Methodist station of Edendale and, beginning in the 1880s, a number of independent African churches severed ties with American missionary institutions. Soon after Joseph Booth launched the Africa for Africans movement in Natal in 1897, two preachers ordained by American missionaries established the Zulu Congregational Church. After that, new African churches sprung up spontaneously, without any prior connection to mission churches. These new forms of Christian community incorporated traditional forms of African religious practice, such as divination and belief in witchcraft, that missionaries had tried to stamp out. The growth of these indigenous churches demonstrated the persisting influence and relevance of native traditions. It also demonstrated the power of Christian ideas about society and the coinciding distrust of the missionaries preaching those ideas.

* * *

The effort to reconstruct the world according to Protestant vision and values characterized a great deal of nineteenth-century American Protestant missionary work. But several countervailing factors also came into play that worked to expose the self-serving aspects of missionary philanthropy, and to turn it away from the business of destroying other religions and toward the business of constructing social conditions that facilitated health and human welfare. These critical and pragmatic developments eventually came to challenge the very idea of seeking conversions. As responses to criticism of missionary paternalism, these developments reflected the efforts made by people from many parts of the world to rescue the democratic and socially progressive concepts embedded in Protestant Christianity from western missionary control.

Although it was never fully actualized in the nineteenth century, as the examples from Maharashtra and Natal indicate, American Protestant missionary thought contained an egalitarian element rooted in the Protestant commitment to the priesthood of all believers. To greater or lesser extent, this egalitarian element worked to undercut the hierarchical relationship between donor and recipient, and provided more democratic paradigms of fellowship and sisterhood. Moreover, American missionary thought involved a strong investment in self-criticism that was rooted in the biblical concern about the need for awareness of sin and, more specifically, in the Puritan preoccupation with self-assessment. This investment in self-criticism required individuals to actively search out "prideful" motives in themselves and renounce them. Lack of awareness of the self-aggrandizing effect of equating Christianity with western culture prevailed among Protestant evangelicals through much of the nineteenth century. But once this dynamic was discovered, the code of Protestant thought made it difficult to do anything but renounce those aspects – even if that meant renouncing missionary work altogether. Finally, advances in cross-cultural studies, which in more than a few cases developed through the work of missionaries and their children, led to greater understanding and appreciation of nonwestern cultures and to growing criticism of the religious imperialism of the missionary effort.

Whereas premillennialists claimed that the Bible was divine and homogeneously inspired, anticipated a catastrophic end to history, and criticized progressives for reading into it their own optimism about the future, progressives responded to new developments in biblical criticism in a way that inspired rather than undercut greater humanitarian outreach. New developments in biblical criticism encouraged liberals to be bolder in interpreting the Bible in terms of their own ideas and values. Of course, earlier readers had also interpreted the Bible through the lens of their own ideas and values, but new theories about the Bible's multiple authorship and uneven religious quality made the process of biblical interpretation much more self-conscious. In reacting against the new liberties that liberals were taking with the Bible, fundamentalists devoted considerable effort to the attempt to uncover the literal meaning and rational structure of biblical symbols. In clarifying their differences from fundamentalists, liberals became even more self-conscious about their efforts to interpret the Bible in ethical and humanitarian terms.

Liberal interpreters of the Bible like the Baptist pastor and theologian, Walter Rauschenbusch, went beyond the Edwardsean image of God's work of redemption as a building constructed through history to an even more this-worldly depiction of the Kingdom of God as a global community ruled by justice and compassion. Concerned by the plight of the urban poor and especially by the impact of industrialization on the millions of immigrants squeezing together in New York and other American cities, Rauschenbusch very deliberately removed the Kingdom of God from its supernatural associations and made it the earthly goal to which every Christian should strive. In his culminating work, *A Theology for the Social Gospel* (1917), Rauschenbusch defined genuine spiritual life in terms of prophetic anticipation of a just and humane society and in terms of brotherhood and solidarity with people in need.

At the same time that Rauschenbusch moved toward recasting Christianity in terms of ethical commitment to brotherhood and social reform, he also worked to drive a wedge between the prophetic mentality that he identified with this ethical commitment and the established institutions and middle-class expectations he associated with mainline Protestant culture. Thus, Rauschenbusch began to separate the essence of spiritual life from the dogmas, rites, and organizational structure of Protestant churches, as well as from its associations with middle-class respectability.

These ideas had revolutionary implications for understanding the nature and purpose of missionary work. However, they were also expressions of a line of thought that missionaries themselves were pursuing and that, in fact, was a logical if not inevitable result of the kind of missionary work that concerned itself with the social conditions in which people lived. Rauschenbusch's prophet of ethical revaluation was preceded in 1893 by A. J. Gordon's concept of the missionary-as-prophet who "translates the example of Christ into the dialect of daily life, into the universal speech of pain and poverty and suffering for the sake of others."

Rauschenbusch's missionary sister, Emma Rauschenbusch Clough, was like her brother in wanting to define Christianity as a basis for social change. But in her work with Telegu women in India, she went much further than her brother in trying to disentangle Christian ethics from Western culture. While Walter's understanding of the brotherhood of man and the father-hood of God was grounded in unexamined assumptions about the superior values of Victorian family culture, Emma's exposure to Telegu culture led her toward the new science of ethnology as a means of understanding it and conveying its strengths to a Western audience. With a greater degree of cultural relativism than her brother but still not fully rid – and perhaps not fully consciousness – of her own paternalism, Emma hoped that Protes-tant missionaries might lead the way in bringing about the revitalization of Telegu culture.

While fundamentalist and other conservative missionaries and their sup-porters were focusing on apocalyptic interpretations of the Kingdom of God and striving to get the message of repentance and salvation out to as many people as possible before it was too late, more liberal mission-aries like Emma Rauschenbusch Clough were laying the groundwork to challenge the legitimacy of the very ideas of missionary evangelization and conversion. The full frontal attack on these ideas, when it finally occurred in the 1970s in attacks on American missionaries as agents of American cultural imperialism and contributors to the development of the military industrial complex, was quite dramatic. But the unraveling of progressive concepts of missionary outreach that led up to it was a long time in coming. The process of this unraveling numerous strands of religious thought and feeling that had been balled together in the nineteenth century as part of the intertwining of American evangelicalism and historical progressivism began developing independently or in new combinations with one another.

The Laymen's Report called *Re-Thinking Missions* and published in 1932 represents an important step in this process. Funded by the liberal Baptist, John D. Rockefeller, Jr., the report was based on a survey of American Protestant missionary work in India, Burma, Japan, and China conducted by a commission whose members were drawn from the major Protestant denominations. Harvard Professor William Ernest Hocking, a leading voice among liberal Protestants, chaired the commission and took primary responsibility for writing the report. In a kind of culminating expression of liberal theology, the report endorsed educational and other humanitarian efforts not only as genuine expressions of Christian love, but also as legitimate forms of Christian mission in and of themselves. In addition, the Hocking commission raised concerns about the process of explicit evangelization that was often invoked to justify education and social reform. Finally, the report argued that missionary work should contribute not to religious conflict or competition, but to better understanding of different religions around the world and to greater cooperation among people from different religious backgrounds.

For more than a century, missionary work had served as one of the principal arenas in which American investment in education, women's and children's rights, and other forms of humanitarian social reform developed. To be sure, missionary involvement in these issues was always accompanied, justified, or compromised by commitment to conversion. When Hocking and other liberals not only made conversion optional, but also even suggested that explicit evangelization could obstruct the interreligious cooperation and world understanding necessary for historical progress, liberal investment in missions became difficult to maintain. Hocking himself eventually came to question the whole concept of Christian missions. Other liberal Protestants who viewed Christian love in terms of humanitarian outreach and the advancement of world understanding also became convinced that explicit evangelization conflicted with these goals. In response to the shock and outrage that this challenge generated among the many conservatives in their ranks, Protestant denominations and mission boards reacted to the Laymen's Report with varying degrees of hostility and criticism.

Since that time, fundamentalists and evangelical conservatives have dominated American Protestant missionary work abroad. Operating more through independent missionary agencies than through cooperative or interdenominational mission boards, the institutional picture of American Protestant missionary service also became more fragmented. To some extent, this institutional disunity has obscured the underlying unity of theological and social conservatism that has come to characterize American missionary operations abroad, which have grown steadily in both personnel and financial strength. As in previous eras, enthusiasm for foreign missions generates more religious enthusiasm at home. Thus, the growing strength of the religious right within the United States is partly a result of conservative investment in missionary work abroad.

With regard to liberal influence in American Protestant missionary thought, the Laymen's Report marked both a culminating moment and the beginning of the end of liberal influence in American missionary work. It was difficult to be any more liberal in terms of respecting other religions and affirming religious pluralism without relinquishing the whole concept of Christian missions. After the publication of the Rockefeller-funded report, conservatives stepped into this breach and, to a large extent, assumed leadership of American missionary work. But the liberal Protestant commitment to humanitarian outreach and social reform did not disappear or even diminish; the liberals simply stepped out of the evangelical confines of missionary work and into new philanthropic agencies funded by the Rockefeller, Ford, and Carnegie Foundations, or into academic research in anthropology or religious studies, or into development programs funded by the U.S. government.

In many respects, the impact of these endeavors has been even greater than that of American missionary boards. The "green revolution" sponsored by the Rockefeller Foundation in Mexico and India; the cultural interchange programs sponsored by the Ford Foundation in China; and the Marshall Plan, Peace Corps, and numerous USAID programs sponsored by the U.S. government all had roots in the liberal side of the American Protestant tradition of missionary outreach. As the historian of American evangelicalism, Grant Wacker, writes, "one could argue that broad public support for humanitarian programs such as the Marshall Plan, the Peace Corps, and world famine relief marked not the demise but the consummation of the liberal search for a mandate that would respond to the deepest impulses of Christian faith while respecting the integrity of other cultures."

As Judith Sealander's article later in this volume discusses, the new form of philanthropy that developed in the United States during the early twentieth century involved strategic giving based on scientifically informed efforts to improve society. This new form of scientific philanthropy played an important role in shaping American society in the twentieth century. It was rooted, to a considerable extent, in the American Protestant tradition of missionary service.

The American pioneers of scientific philanthropy came out of a culture saturated with an energetic commitment to world reform that had its roots in Calvinism and Protestant Christianity. Several of these pioneers belonged to American Protestant denominations characterized by investment in missionary service as a principal means of carrying forward that commitment. Unlike the religious conservatives and fundamentalists of their time, these evangelists of scientific philanthropy were much less concerned with religious conversion than with improving the social conditions, educational opportunities, and medical knowledge available to people both at home and abroad. But whereas they turned away from the business of preaching repentance for sin, escape from hellfire and damnation, and acceptance of Christ as a personal savior, these liberal philanthropists were like missionaries in deriving power and prestige from their efforts to reconstruct the world, from the indebtedness and gratitude of their beneficiaries, and from the admiration and competition of their peers. In some cases at least, these philanthropists could be as aggressively evangelical as any missionary in their desire to reconstruct society according to their own values and in their tendency to equate their own values with the will of God.

The movement away from religious conversion toward scientific philanthropy did not always ensure awareness of the dynamic of reciprocity involved in outreach toward others. Nor did it always mean an end to the arrogance and condescension that earlier missionaries had sometimes displayed toward the people they intended to help. The most secular philanthropist might still use the donor role as a means of building status and influence. At the same time, however, criticism of this kind of self-service has persisted in American culture as a legacy of American missionary thought. This criticism is not simply the expression of a secular or humanistic rejection of conversion-oriented evangelization; it is also the result of the egalitarian spirit, communal idealism, and commitment to self-criticism embedded within the American Protestant missionary tradition itself.

3

THE ORIGINS OF ANGLO-AMERICAN SENSIBILITY

G. J. BARKER-BENFIELD

John Howard became known in his lifetime (1726–1790) as "the Philanthropist." His fame was as a prison reformer but he first earned this sobriquet as a Bedfordshire squire because of his benevolence to his tenants: He rebuilt their cottages, established a school for their children, and relieved their "distress." Significantly, Howard required them "on pain of summary eviction" to "shun alehouses and other low amusements" – cockfighting and gambling, for example; to attend the local church or the chapel he built for them; and to keep their noses to the grindstone. Howard prospered accordingly. Howard himself had been elevated above having to work for a living by the financial success of his father, a merchant upholsterer in London. He was named sheriff of Bedfordshire, inspected the local gaol accordingly, and thereupon devoted his life to exposure of the conditions of prisons in England and Wales, and both prisons and lazarettos (i.e., leper hospitals) in continental Europe.

Howard's efforts were the most famous of many reformers' on behalf of penal reform. Other reformers, including New Yorker Thomas Eddy, called "the American Howard," aimed to move "away from the infliction of corporal pain" (e.g., branding, whipping, nostril-slitting, and ear-cropping) and away from frequent and public executions, eventually replacing them with organized imprisonment and private executions. Saying it was "sensible" of Howard's "humanity and zeal," after he appeared before it, the British Parliament passed two penal-reform bills. In the aftermath of the American Revolution, Philadelphian Dr. Benjamin Rush said he hoped "that the time is not far away when gallows, pillory, scaffold, flogging, and wheel will, in the history of punishment, be regarded as the marks of the barbarities of centuries and countries." Two years later, the

Eighth Amendment of the U.S. Constitution forbade "cruel and unusual punishments."

Penal reform was only one of the remarkable reforms undertaken in the eighteenth and early nineteenth centuries, all of them eventually expressing the missionary impulse discussed elsewhere in this volume. They included attempts to ameliorate the cruel treatment of animals and the mistreatment of children, the sick, and the insane; to change the conditions endured by penitent prostitutes; to oppose drunkenness, dueling, wars, and imperialism, abuse of the poor, the press-gang, and injustice generally; and to end political corruption, the slave trade, slavery, and the seduction and abandonment of women. The common denominator in all of these reforms was the value reformers placed on sympathy.

In explaining why he undertook his lifelong philanthropic task, Howard recalled being a civilian captive during the war with France. "Perhaps what I suffered on this occasion increased my sympathy for the unhappy people whose case is the subject of this book." The book in question, *The State of Prisons in England and Wales* (1771), was loaded with statistics and specifications for the same "reformation" of prisoners' "manners" (replacing "dissipation and riotous amusements" with cleanliness, regular habits, and hard work) as Howard had required of his tenants, but it was also fraught with his account of his responsiveness to the sufferings of people whose material circumstances were in sharp contrast to his own. He said he was "prompted" to his task "by the sorrows of the sufferers and love to my country."

The first four words of *The State of Prisons* are "The distress of prisoners." We can list *distress* as one of a cluster of terms marking the existence of a special kind of consciousness of feelings – one's own and those of people (or animals) with whom one sympathized – a consciousness then called *sensibility*. During the eighteenth century, the expression of sensibility came to be of major importance – even a "dogma" in religion, secular philosophy, and aesthetics among the emergent middle class in Britain and America – even as it sustained the potentials for the individual expressed in Romanticism. Howard's work was emblematic of "a sentimental revolution." In Britain by the 1760s and 1770s, writes historian Paul Langford, "the primacy of an individual's feelings offered a startlingly new vision of world." It was as a result of this revolution that "a new age of philanthropy was born." The connection between sensibility and philanthropic reform was as true of American history as of British. Gordon Wood, arguing that the radicalism of the American Revolution lay in its transformation of social relations up and down the social pile (a transformation embarked upon prior to the Revolution), suggests that the "affection and fellow feeling" of "politeness, sympathy, and the new domestication of virtue," in public as well as private life, "laid the basis for all reform movements of the nineteenth century."

This chapter describes the origins and development of the ideas laid out by a series of secular and religious thinkers and their disciples; secondly, it describes the relationship of these ideas to their novel material circumstances. The conclusion illustrates that the culture of sensibility was translated into philanthropy. This story shares several themes with other chapters, among them that philanthropy was an expression of a powerful urge for social reform; indeed, from the latter eighteenth century, reform and philanthropy were nearly interchangeable. Secondly, although philanthropists' impact in alleviating suffering varied in success, their efforts helped empower individual reformers and benefited them in other ways, celebrating their rise and defining their status, but – above all – bringing them a particular kind of pleasure. This in no way is meant to cast doubt on the sincerity of most reformers. Thirdly, and by definition, the chapter places American history in a trans-Atlantic context. Lastly, it suggests that considerations of gender were vital to definitions of sensibility and their translation into philanthropy.

The terms *eighteenth century* and *Anglo-American* need to be qualified. Some ideas associated with eighteenth-century sensibility had surfaced in the writings of ancient Greeks and Romans, and in the early biographies of Christ included in the New Testament. The Renaissance courts of Italy and their successors in France and Britain created models of gentility that included elements of sensibility, still influential to the eighteenth-century bourgeoisie in Britain and America; the culture of sensibility became Victorian sentimentalism. Nor was the cultivation of sensibility confined to the Anglo-American world. There were continual feedback loops between England and the rest of Europe (particularly France) in the matter of sensibility; however, in contrast to England and America, continental Europe was largely restricted to the elite in the eighteenth century.

* * *

Following is how the third edition of the *Encyclopedia Britannica*, published in Edinburgh in 1797, opened its definition of *sensibility*:

... it is a nice and delicate perception of pleasure or pain, beauty or deformity. It is very nearly allied to taste; and, as far as it is natural, seems to depend upon the organization of the nervous system. It is capable, however, of cultivation, and is experienced in a much higher degree in civilized than in savage nations, and among persons liberally educated than among boors and illiterate mechanics.

The entry went on to explain that the detection of pleasure or pain extended to the detection of virtue and vice. In our terms, sensibility was the result of nature (it was innate) and nurture (it could be developed). Its association with class hierarchy was asserted, but clearly there were democratic potentials here because it inhered in human physiology. Asking whether sensibility "ought to be cherished or repressed" in a context where "excessive sensibility" had come under sharp attack as mere self-indulgence and fashion (an attack sharpened still further by the interpretation of the French Revolution as the overflow of popular feeling), the author of a 1795 article in *The Monthly Magazine* concluded with a resounding yes, provided it was translated into action, in "offices of humanity and kindness." Here is the connection with philanthropy (*benevolence* was another key term in the culture of sensibility), but individuals attached a wide spectrum of values to sensibility: from the fashionable to the heartfelt, from the self-indulgent to the philanthropic.

That 1797 definition's "natural" side suggested the sensibility was physiological, depending on "the nervous system." Indeed, all the words incorporating "sense," including sensibility and sentimental, referred literally to the receptivity of the senses, the material basis of consciousness in a psycho-physiological scheme that originated a century earlier. In his "Essay Concerning Human Understanding" (1690), the English philosopher, John Locke, had dismissed the notion that human beings are born with innate ideas and replaced it with the famous image of the tabula rasa or a blank page on which experience, including childhood, wrote character. The foundation of Lockean psychology was "the concept and definition of sensation." According to Locke, sensation was received by the organs and conveyed by the nerves to the brain, generating ideas, which were connected to each other by reflection and association. Scientist Isaac Newton's enormous intellectual authority provided this sensational psychology with its understanding of the specific operation of the nerves. Newton held that the nerve transmitted sense impressions by the vibrations of the "most subtle spirit," ether, inhering in all solid bodies. The speed of such neurological transmissions depended on the elasticity of the nerve, and later proponents of the cultivation of sensibility attached moral value to the "degrees" of elasticity and speed. Newton and Locke would be as influential among British-American colonists as they were in metropolitan Britain.

Locke's view of human psychology had obvious implications for child-drearing, and historians have suggested that it helped to effect a notable liberalization of family dynamics, as well as religious and political history. However, through his employment as personal physician to the first Earl of Salisbury, Locke was secretary to the Lords Proprietors of the new American colony of Carolina. He drew up Carolina's "Fundamental Constitution," which established slavery there.

As the new scheme was popularized, moreover, it was gendered. Newton had not distinguished women's nerves and brains from men's in arguing, for example, that vibrations could be excited in the brain by the power of the will and propagated thence "through the Nerves into the Muscles." However, his popularizing successors questioned the operation of the will in woman's supposedly more delicate nervous system. The view that women's nerves were more delicate than men's – making them naturally creatures of greater sensibility and less rationality – became a central convention of the eighteenth century. The refinement of the nerves was identified with a capacity for suffering and sympathy with it, a view on which middle-class women would capitalize in a range of ways, among them their suitability for certain kinds of philanthropic efforts. Eighteenth-century men cultivated a degree of sensibility too but, unlike women, their doing so was not to be at the expense of other qualities and their participation in larger and more various goals.

One major objection to Locke's view of psychology was its implication that morality was merely constructed, just as the rest of personality was. This was the objection made by Locke's pupil, the third Earl of Shaftesbury, who inherited the Carolinian Proprietorship and owned land and slaves there. Ironically, his modification of Locke's scheme eventually would supply crucial ammunition to the antislavery crusade, perhaps the most successful of philanthropic efforts expressing sensibility. While Shaftesbury retained his tutor's psychoperceptual scheme and helped popularize it, he argued (in 1711) in favor of the idea that human beings were not born as if they were blank sheets – that, in fact, a first principle was printed thereon, something that "rul'd within." Because he celebrated the existence of this inborn "moral sense," Shaftesbury has been called "the father of sentimental ethics" and "the first synthesizer of an ethic grounded in the ultimate goodness of men."

It was not Shaftesbury who originated the idea of a sympathetic moral sense, however, but a group of Anglican theologians, called the "Cambridge

Platonists." Writing from the 1660s and reacting against the atheistic and misanthropic philosophy of Thomas Hobbes, as well as the negative view of human beings – all sinners and all of them, save a remnant, rightfully going to hell – rigorously propounded by the recently successful English Puritan adherents of Calvinism, Shaftesbury's notion of an "inward eye" was adopted by a series of aestheticians and philosophers, most notably the Scottish "moral sense" school of philosophy, headed by Frances Hutcheson. The Cambridge Platonists injected their version of a moral sense into what became a wide stream of Anglo-American Protestant teaching. These overlapping lines of thought fed into the culture of sensibility.

Latitudinarians (i.e., Anglican ministers, who were the successors of the Cambridge Platonists) popularized the view that human nature was instinctively sympathetic and that passions naturally inclined people to virtuous actions. Such actions were reinforced by the pleasurable feelings they automatically brought. "There is a Delight and Joy that Accompanies doing good, there is a kind of sensuality in it." According to another minister, "when our tempers are soft and sensible and easily receive impressions, we are pain'd within, and to ease ourselves we are ready to succor them, and Nature discharging her Burden and Oppression, creates both her own pleasure and satisfaction." From the last part of the seventeenth century, the pains and pleasures of sympathy were motives for benevolence.

Hutcheson was one of the most influential of Shaftesbury's heirs because his 1725 and 1728 books became texts in American and British colleges, where ministers and other molders of belief were trained, and because his students wrote still more popular works. In Hutcheson's view, sympathy was a social force, like Newtonian gravity. James Foster, a preacher and one of Hutcheson's better known disciples (also widely admired on both sides of the Atlantic), explicated this social, communal dimension of sympathy. "The entire community of mankind is . . . one grand and vast body; [people's] dependence mutual, universal, eternal . . . a spirit of benevolence diffused through all its parts." Foster fantasized that, according to this vision, "there are no jarring or contrarieties":

The social, the divine life! Employed in the most exalted pursuits, and abounding in the purest and sweetest pleasures that human nature is capable of! . . . That this [view of mankind as a system] is a sentiment which most powerfully enforces universal benevolence and sympathy, that enlarges and raises the heart, above the influence of every earth-born passion, that inspires it with great designs of public usefulness, and gives it god-like feelings.

This social vision was posed against "the world," a notion carrying the powerful Christian connotation derived from Christ's declaration, "My kingdom is not of this world" (John 18:36). The latter was the world of politics and commerce run by those hard, unconverted men against whom proponents of the benevolence and sympathy that manifested sensibility contrasted themselves. "When man indulgences in to[o] narrow and contracted views," Foster wrote, "and acts, for himself alone, as if he was an unallied, self-sufficient, and independent frame. . . . And if [in such a "detached member"] the glowings of humanity were universally checked, and repressed . . . what could this open to our view, but one wide and general scene of distress and misery!"

God was reconceptualized in accordance with the reconceptualization of human nature. Latitudinarians continued to maintain the view that a just God had made a "general judgment of universal damnation," but they argued he was also susceptible to "the Softer dictates and Whispers of Humanity," in contrast to the "hard and cruel things" that expressed "the extremity of Justice." (We must add "humanity" to sensibility's cluster of terms.) "The universe was reasonable and ordered because God is prompted by his feelings – the original and eternal benevolence of his nature." Leading preachers of the mid-century transatlantic revivals, as well as Quakers, combined the old and new views of God, as one might expect, given the magnitude of the transformation they betokened. John Wesley, the English founder of Methodism (and sojourner in America), believed people could make successful efforts of their own for salvation. We can see the relationship here with Locke's view of psychology. A kinder God would save everyone who was thus converted, although Wesley still maintained that God would make a final judgment, sending the unconverted to Hell. Evangelical preachers of all denominations sought to break through what Wesley called his audience's "hardness of heart." That everyone was capable of conversion and that otherwise she/he would go to Hell, was a powerful combination to motivate reform and philanthropy.

There was an overlap between these psychological and religious developments and the history of the stage and of fiction, because they adopted the same assumptions and techniques as preachers (and vice versa), with the same goals of reforming their audiences. Sentimental novels were among the most effective of written popularizations of sensibility, often addressed by women authors to an increasingly literate female audience, and expressing the same wishes for reform as sermons. Wesley, who aimed to encourage literacy among his audiences – disproportionately female and working-class – abridged the sentimental novel by Henry Brooke, *The Fool of Quality* (1765–1770), and praised its capacity to invoke pleasurable pain. "The strokes are so delicately fine, the touches so easy, natural and affecting, that I know not who can survey it with tearless eyes unless he has a heart of stone." Words written, as well as spoken, had sensational effects. Harriet Beecher Stowe embodied the same values in her antislavery novel, *Uncle Tom's Cabin*, published 80 years on, and Harriet Jacobs's 1861 sentimental "slave narrative" gave her slaveowner the pseudonym "Dr. Flint."

Wesley also castigated slaveholders as stony-hearted. His views on slavery, published in 1774, were directly influenced by the recent antislavery writings of Anthony Benezet, an American Quaker and "celebrated philanthropist" (who quoted Hutcheson's opposition to slavery). From the late seventeenth century, Quakers had protested slavery and the slave trade. The Quakers had a powerful group memory of their own persecution in seventeenth-century England, which included threats of being shipped to America as slaves, although some of the earliest Quaker settlers of Pennsylvania brought slaves with them from the West Indies. One major Quaker institution was the "Meeting on Sufferings," which regularly drew up "a balance sheet of suffering" – in effect, a "litany of pain and distress" long endured by this persecuted sect, as members held fast to an "inner light" corresponding to Martin Luther's "justification by faith" and anticipating the "moral sense." The term *suffering* may be added to the very definition of sensibility, given its prominence in the experiences that culture registered; therefore, the overlap here with a formal, institutional usage is striking. It was because of Quaker activities that "a stream of . . . reforming sensibility" (in James Walvin's phrase) flowed from Philadelphia, "the intellectual heart of the North American colonies." Philadelphian Quaker antislavery arguments had a decisive influence on Britons, particularly Quakers, but Anglicans and Dissenters as well.

In reading the following quotations from Benezet's *A Caution and Warning to Great Britain and Her Colonies* (1766), we must bear in mind that one can find identical expressions of sensibility in a huge variety of written and spoken words – private letters, fiction, stories, poetry, drama, journalism, history, biography, conversation, and political thought and speeches – most of which did not address slavery. The contrast central to all of them was between those whose hearts were sensitive to the sufferings of victims and those who were unresponsive to them. Presenting "scenes" of family separation, extreme labor and physical deprivation, and vicious punishment and atrocity, Benezet asked, "Can any human heart that retains a fellow-feeling for the sufferings of mankind be unconcerned at relations of such grievous affliction?" It was a demonstration of the "laws of humanity" that Africans have "the same sensibility" as "we" do. Those who inflicted suffering had lost "the common feelings of human nature." Benezet suggested that this loss showed God's responsiveness to the "groans of the afflicted." "What greater calamity can befall any people, who have become prey to that hardness of heart . . . and insensibility to every religious impress."

Benezet asked his reader to "bring the matter home." "Home" was the location of family connections; the specific situation to which Benezet asked his readers to compare their own is enslavement's breaking of the "tender attachment" of family members, which the culture deemed the origin of "social affections." This combination of family feeling and humanity had a double significance. There was the common ground that it gave Africans and Europeans, but it also signified the existence of a kinship that transcended blood. The same point can be made of a widely distributed symbol of the antislavery movement, manufactured twenty years later: the jasper medallion made by pioneering industrialist and marketer, Josiah Wedgewood, depicting a kneeling African slave surrounded by the words "Am I Not A Man And A Brother?," which was soon followed by equivalent artifacts asking, "Am I Not A Woman And A Sister?" Such a sentiment also may be found in the Christian Bible; for example, the declaration that "God hath made of one blood all nations of men" (Acts 17:26), but it had new connotations in the eighteenth century. This medallion symbolized another aspect of sensibility: The imaginative act it called for was a reminder of the differences between sympathizer and the object of sympathy – Wedgewood's slave, chained and black, was a kneeling suppliant.

The emphasis on family ties and the prominence given to women's suffering in Benezet's pamphlet can be connected to another value typical of the culture of sensibility. That "the poor Negroes . . . are exposed naked, without any distinction of sexes, to the brutal examination of their purchasers; it is . . . another occasion of distress, especially to the females." Benezet believed such a note would ring a bell with his audience, both male and female, who would assume with him that women were particularly distressed by their bodies' public exposure and handling by men. African and European women were thus linked under a common "law of humanity," at the same time that they were distinguished from men by the gendered sensibility described previously. The calls for the separation of the sexes in

Wedgewood's medallion expressing influence of Biblical truth and women's sensitivity on the abolition movement.

prisons made by Howard, for example, and in insane asylums by American Dorothea Dix, among others, were reforms animated by the same values. Women played a crucial role in reforms, above all, in the antislavery crusade, in imperial Britain and in the United States, and here can be seen another illustration of philanthropic "reflexivity." "Behind the manifold indictments of the slave system," writes Donald Meyer, "there flickered, dim, fascinating, and horrifying, the fact of the slavery of women. Black women, but white women too."

Women of all denominations wrote religious tracts, pamphlets, missionary letters, and hymns, all promulgating sensibility. A few of them were preachers. Ministers on both sides of the Atlantic, particular those dependent on their congregations in unestablished denominations, tailored their theology to women's interests – as women came to be the majority in their congregations – a theology that increasingly was emotional rather than intellectual. Historians have referred to "the feminization of religion" at this time and in the nineteenth century, when sentimentalism became a kind of religion regardless of denominational differences.

We can link such developments to middle-class women's increasing power at home as wives and mothers, and to their related claim to moral power – even moral superiority – to men. Sensibility was itself personified and satirized as a goddess. Ultimately, the conflicts over the sexual potential for women in the culture of sensibility (which, after all, aggrandized physical responsiveness) were repressed, at least ostensibly, by the 1790s, leaving middle-class women as powerful actors in that myriad of virtuous philanthropic efforts. Yet, sexual repression could serve their interests, confirming their moral superiority and justifying their useful distancing from men.

Women's claim to moral power in the face of the suffering caused them by the actions of insensitive males was represented repeatedly by images of "virtue in distress," a weeping female personification of sensibility. Precedents here lay in the ancient stories of Christian martyrs, updated for Protestants by their sixteenth-century persecution at the hands of Catholic authorities, most notably in John Foxe's *Book of Martyrs* (1563 and 1641), which catalogued the torture and execution of English Protestants. One may see the first British North American "Indian captivity narrative," Mary Rowlandson's autobiographical and bestselling *The Sovereignty and Goodness of God* (published in Boston and London in 1682), as an adaptation of such martyrology – although, of course, authors of such narratives survived. While still adhering to Puritan Calvinism, Rowlandson's terms anticipated those soon to be popularized by the culture of sensibility. The author presented herself throughout as a figure of virtue in distress, at the mercy of Indians she presented as beasts and wolves. Meeting a sick and half-naked captive white youth the Indians had kept out in the cold, Rowlandson wrote that this "sight was enough to melt a heart of flint." She described herself bursting "into tears" when a few of her captors showed her kindness, her heart melting, and she described the affecting impression her as-yet unpublished manuscript had on its readers.

In England, the most famous and influential representations of virtue in distress were Samuel Richardson's novels, *Pamela and Clarissa* (1748), widely read on both sides of the Atlantic and inspiring a host of imitators, injecting British or American elements accordingly. In Clarissa, the well-educated and religious heroine did become a martyr, having resisted both the marriage her father attempted to force on her and the sexual advances of her hypocritical rescuer, the rake, Richard Lovelace – who traded on Clarissa's finer sensibility and who, like Rowlandson's persecutors, was depicted as a savage beast. He drugged and raped Clarissa, who – not insignificantly for us – had implemented her sensibility in her charitable acts for the "worthy" poor.

Indian captivity narratives persisted in America alongside such Americanized versions of Clarissa as Hannah Foster's *The Coquette* (1797), vehicles for the culture of sensibility. Another was the 1824 account by James Seaver, *The Life of Mary Jemison: The White Woman of the Genessee*, captured by Indians in 1755 but who subsequently chose to stay with them. Seaver connected sensibility to philanthropy, believing that such biographies as his, exciting "all the sympathies of the soul," taught "benevolence for the destitute and compassion for the helpless." He hoped that this particular "lesson of distress" would help to "increase our love of liberty; to enlarge our views of the blessings that are derived from our liberal institutions." In short, the culture of sensibility was adapted to postrevolutionary American circumstances. Such an adaptation is further illustrated by Rush's hope for the new republic:

Let it be our pride and pleasure to open new sources of wealth and happiness to our country – to lessen human misery by inviting the distressed of all nations to partake in our ample and easy means of existence . . . to protect the innocent . . . to wipe away the tears of widows and orphans – and to do every other good thing that reason, patriotism, and religion shall dictate to us.

* * *

Rush assumed that abundance would sponsor responsiveness to suffering. Adam Smith, another student of Hutcheson, had explained this relationship in *The Theory of Moral Sentiments* (1759) by describing the difference between "us" and "our" response to "our brother . . . upon the rack," our trembling and shuddering at the thought of what he felt, and the apparent imperviousness of "the savages of North America" to their own sufferings and the sufferings they inflicted on others. They had been hardened by living at and below the level of subsistence and by their physically punishing customs, including torture. Such circumstances "not only habituate [the Indian] to every sort of distress, but teach him to give way to none of the passions which that distress is apt to excite. He can expect from his countrymen no sympathy or indulgence for such weakness. Before we can feel much for others, we must in some measure be at ease ourselves." The "civilized" human beings of Smith's world lived under circumstances no longer requiring the "self-denial" required of the subsistence-tied Indians; the "general security and happiness which prevail in ages of civility and politeness afford little exercise to the contempt of danger, to patience in enduring labour, hunger, and pain."

As Smith and his contemporaries saw it, British society had passed beyond that socioeconomic stage. Modern historians have described "a consumer revolution" in Britain and its American mainland colonies during the eighteenth century, whereby increasing numbers of people bought an increasing range of "nonessential" goods; that is, goods (e.g., food, clothing, household items) intended for pleasure, not mere subsistence. Prior to this consumer revolution, most people's lives were much closer to the circumstances faced by the "savages" of North America. Subject to famine and plague; living in smoky, windowless dwellings wherein the things we associate with basic comfort (e.g., chairs, head pillow, eating and cooking utensils) did not exist, and objects of pleasure (e.g., books and musical instruments) were absent too – they worked from dawn to dusk. They faced a grim ideology of inescapable judgment after death, followed by eternal torture, some of which corresponded to the actual system of official punishment publicly meted out to the masses on earth. Within this traditional world, women and children were still worse off, because any margin was enjoyed by the men who had power over them.

The productive side of the consumer revolution was directed by a new kind of entrepreneurial capitalist male, the "self-sufficient" man criticized by Foster. Religion of the kind described previously may well have contributed to the modification of the public manners of such men; however, the urge to self-improvement, to profit from an economy they were transforming as they revolutionized agriculture – and as they appealed by new modes to ever-widening constituencies of customers – had a still more powerful effect on their manners and their personalities. Their adherence to sensibility was an outgrowth of their internalization of the profitable "Protestant ethic" – in effect, the "reformation of manners" that Howard required of his tenants and then of prison inmates.

During the mid-eighteenth century, many British and American businessmen recognized the value of cultivating a degree of sensibility as they networked. Clubs and societies had been established to encourage "mutual consideration," "mutual benevolence," and "friendly feeling" among men, generating what one club called "principles of Benevolence, Charity, and Humanity." The charity of male associations, in the words of Peter Barstow, "acted as an evangelizing means of improving the social environment, making it a better place in which to trade, sell, borrow, and lend." That men also engaged heedlessly in speculation and profiteering provided pleasure, but also continuing grist for guilt and for others' criticism of their masculine world. Foster held that "commerce . . . ought . . . to propagate benevolence and a more universal sense of morality." Smith, the best-known advocate of the view that free trade promoted "the wealth of nations," argued that history's culmination was he "who joins to the most perfect command of his own original and selfish feelings, the most exquisite sensibility to the original and sympathetic feelings of others."

In 1756, a group of Boston merchants established the Society for Encouraging Industry and Employing the Poor. "Every Man of Sense must see and . . . deplore the Calamities that must arise from increasing Poverty, Idleness, and Vice: but every Christian will feel the Miseries of such a State, almost as if they were his own." The remedy they proposed was that poor women and children be put to work manufacturing linen, which would help Massachusetts's balance of trade with Britain and lessen the tax burdens on those supporting the poor, as well as teach the latter "to become useful and valuable members of the community." One can find the same combination of sensibility and economic considerations expressed by reformers and philanthropists throughout this century and into the next. Thus, in one of the earliest of slave narratives (published in 1789), Olaudah Equiano, an Anglicized Ibo, demonstrated that he was a man of sensibility, described his conversion to Methodism, and argued for the establishment of commerce in Africa. He asserted that its inhabitants' work ethic and their capacity to produce raw materials in return for their "consumption of British manufactures" – commerce that Equiano identified with the advance of "civilization," including the abolition of slavery. Three years later, Irish reformer, Mary Burkitt, made the same case to philanthropists – although, unlike Equiano, she believed Africans' manners could use improvement:

Thy vessels crown'd with olive branches send,
And make each injure'd African thy friend:
So tides of wealth by peace and justice got,
Oh, philanthropic heart! Will be thy lot.
Plant there our colonies, and do their souls,
Declare the God who form'd this boundless whole:
Improve their manners – teach them how to live,
To them the useful lore of science give.

Evidently, such philanthropy embodied the missionary impulse illustrated by other chapters in this book.

Women were an extremely significant part of the consumption side of the consumer revolution, creating the "home demand" on which it depended. The home became the primary site for consumption and, there, women gained significant authority over the relations of new objects to the home's inhabitants, creating what we think of as domesticity. The centrality of the family and of mothers to the culture's view of the origin of social affections points to the changing styles of parenting consistent with Locke's environmental psychology. By the mid-eighteenth century, an older, patriarchal authority was giving way to a new parental ideal characterized by a more affectionate and egalitarian relationship with children. Middle-class British and American families were "sentimentalized."

The rise of the culture of sensibility not only coincided with the consumer revolution, it also coincided with Britain's coming to dominate the transatlantic slave trade. The vast majority of the slaves shipped to the Americas went to the sugar plantations of the Caribbean and Brazil, where they also produced coffee and chocolate. Sugar came to be of central importance to the new consumerism; it sweetened chocolate, coffee, and – above all – tea, served in the new china tea sets (made by Wedgewood, among others) on specially designed tables, spooned and stirred with silver utensils (or cheaper duplicates), with the ritual presided over by women. Middle-class women exerted social power for themselves and their male collaborators, helping to generate their own collectivity, as it were, in dispensing tea and sympathy, whence they brought criticism to bear on the world of unfeeling men.

In short, as commercial capitalists and then industrial capitalists helped to create prosperity by immiserating millions, they also helped to elaborate a consumer society nourishing the possibilities for the aggrandizement of the interior life, of the elevation of feelings. Sociologist Colin Campbell has traced the "autonomous hedonism" of consumer psychology back to those pleasurable feelings in doing good, sanctioned by the Cambridge Platonists as innate as well as virtuous, and eventually coming to be enjoyed for their own sake as a kind of "dream play" – perpetually regenerated by their materialization not merely in "good," but also in consumer goods, promising ever more satisfaction. Such psychology is marked by the frequency in sentimental writings of the notion of enjoying "the luxury of grief" or "indulging one's feelings." A 1770 novel declared that pity was "the greatest luxury the soul of sensibility is capable of relishing." Playwright Richard Cumberland acidly remarked that, to poets, "the slave was a mine of sentiment." Yet, the same process, revitalized by evangelical Christianity, could result in philanthropy, keeping pace with the proliferation of consumer goods now produced by the industrial revolution. Therefore, capitalists helped create the cultural basis for the criticism of and eventually crusades against the immigration they fostered.

Langford has described the relationship between entrepreneurship and reform from the other angle, calling philanthropists "entrepreneurs of charity, marketing philanthropy much as Wedgewood marketed porcelain." He provides a list of such "novel kinds of reformers . . . not great benefactors, but opinionmakers, men who sought out distress, analyzed its causes, campaigned for its alleviation, coordinated its eradication." The list includes John Howard, as well as Robert Young, founder of the Philanthropic Society, which hoped to abolish poverty.

It is crucial for our understanding of the origins of sensibility to recognize that there were striking limitations to the consumer revolution. Many people in America and Britain remained vulnerable to much of the suffering the new middle class was escaping. The contrast between the lives of the people enjoying leisure and consumerism on the one hand and those of the poor on the other was marked from the time of the culture's inception. *The Spectator* (a magazine immensely popular on both sides of the Atlantic, reprinted throughout the century) reported in 1711 that in "the same street" in London where people rolled in "luxury and power and wealth" lived "creatures" so miserable, hungry, and naked that one would have thought them "a different species." Hence, *The Spectator*'s advocacy of the establishment of charity schools, in which one can detect the fear of rebellion and, conversely, the wish for social control. But the important point for us was the value *The Spectator* placed on profound socioeconomic – and, therefore, psychological – contrast:

When we read of torments, wounds, deaths, and the like dismal accidents, our pleasure does not flow so properly from the grief which such melancholy description gives us, as from the secret comparison which we make between ourselves and the person who suffers. Such representations teach us to set a just value on our own condition, and makes us prize our good fortune, which exempts us from the like calamities.

The Spectator aggrandized "pity," love softened by a "degree of sorrow . . . a kind of pleasing anguish, as well as generous sympathy that knits mankind together," but implicit in that aggrandizement was the dependence on social distance. The pleasures *The Spectator* advocated were largely those of relief, complacency, and a sense of safety, adequately remote from a pain on which they depended for "secret comparison." They depended on it for the pain not only of their unleisured, live-in servants and of those nearby "creatures" so miserable that they seemed to be of a different species, but also of those slaves who produced the sugar for the tea with which the authors of *The Spectator* wished their magazine to be served. One of them, at least, Richard Steele, owned slaves. A major theme in British-American antislavery propaganda was the sheer material contrast between the luxurious lives of slaveholders and the lives of slaves who produced that luxury. The pleasures *The Spectator* described, very close to the pleasures of sympathy advocated in contemporary sermons, were the fruit of the contrast generated by the historical process indicated by Adam Smith in *The Theory of Moral Sentiments*. Such feelings were at the heart of the culture of sensibility.

* * *

Bourgeois Anglo-American white women were now enabled to enter a new public world of formal visits, pleasure gardens, shopping parades, assembly rooms, and theaters of the "urban renaissance" – spaces intended for the enjoyment and cultivation of new heterosocial manners, including their tasteful expressions of sensibility. Women's publication of their wishes and feelings on an unprecedented scale was a parallel development; they articulated their sense of real and potential victimization by men along with their rising expectations for pleasure and even liberty, provoking strong reaction, particularly during the upheavals of the 1790s.

Middle-class women in the eighteenth century also had been able to extend the genteel practice of aristocratic ladies making their own private charitable visits to the humble dwellings of the poor – visits recommended and publicized as part of the culture of sensibility. They argued that they could understand the sufferings of poor women and suffering generally, including a proclivity for piety. In 1784, evangelical Anglican reformer, Hannah More, yet another writer influential on both sides of the Atlantic into the nineteenth century, had defined "sensibility" as a female muse in a poem of that name, "Thou sweet precursor of the gen'rous deed." Opposing Mary Wollstonecraft's scathing attack on the gendering of sensibility in *Vindication of the Rights of Woman* (1792), More had declared that women's "hearts are naturally soft and flexible, open to impressions of love and gratitude; their feelings tender and lively; all these are favorable to the cultivation of the devotional spirit." Unequal to men in body and mind, More wrote, women were equal in evangelical Christianity. More's own contributions to philanthropy included support of Sunday schools and the writing and distribution to the poor of conservative tracts recommending self-improvement. She approvingly witnessed the creation of a new kind of philanthropy by private subscription and committee, rather than by the previous parochial endowments and "institutional chartered charity"; that is, the change described by Professor Gross in the first chapter.

The official and unofficial writings generated by philanthropists, as well as the private correspondence surrounding them, are full of the language of sensibility. Women's "peculiar texture of her mind, her strong feelings and quick sensibilities ... especially qualify her, not only to sympathize with suffering, but also to plead for the oppressed," wrote Elizabeth Heyrick, a British Quaker antislavery campaigner, in 1828. The 1833 minutes of the Society for the Relief of Poor Widows with Small Children in New York (an association typical of the gendered philanthropies of which women embarked) illustrated the same absorption of sensibility's values. Former donors to this society, fallen into poverty and therefore now recipients of its philanthropy, felt "more keenly the barbed points of poverty and want" because they had known "elegancies and were unused to grappling with adversity." This relation between material freedom from want and the greater capacity for feeling was precisely what Smith had laid out seventy years earlier. American Margaret Fuller made the same argument in her 1843 contrast between the way Indian women bore their harsh lot and the more sensitively suffering white women.

Women's leading role in the boycott of slave products – sugar above all – was another expression of gendered sensibility. It drew on widespread ambivalence by the middle class over its own habits of consumption. Reformers also directed their concern at the consumption habits of the lower classes, for which they blamed their "Misery and Poverty ... viz. Intemperance among the Men and the love of dress among the Women." Organized boycotts of sugar and other slave products awaited the 1790s, but the famous boycotts in the period of the American Revolution of tea and imported cloth marked the fact that the colonies had undergone a consumer revolution. "Male leaders needed women's cooperation to ensure that Americans would comply with the request to forgo the use of tea and luxury goods." The same was the case with the sugar "abstention" campaign, launched in Britain in 1791 because of the failure of petitions to Parliament. Burkitt declared on its behalf:

Yes, sisters, to us the task belongs,
'Tis we increase or mitigate their wrongs.
If we the produce of their toils refuse,
If we no more the blood-stain'd luxury choose
And in our brethen's sufferings hold no share.

There was an attempt to organize a similar abstention campaign in America at the same time, which did not get very far, but the subsequent campaign to urge consumers to buy only "free produce" – intended to raise money for abolition and kept alive particularly by free black women in Philadelphia and subsequently by female Quakers there – made more headway in the 1840s and 1850s.

None of this is to say that male philanthropists did not express the culture of sensibility. One final document can represent this fact. Antislavery Quaker William Allen introduced the first issue of *The Philanthropist* (1811) by describing the "Duty and Pleasure of Cultivating Benevolent Dispositions" that, as his title indicates, recapitulated one of the theological views outlined previously in this chapter. Like Benezet, Wesley, and Burkitt, Allen wished to roll away a "load of guilt and infamy . . . from our country" and he rejected the "narrow limits" of sectarianism within British Protestantism. Allen's piece perpetuated visions of class and spousal harmony, which he believed reflected the mutuality and cooperation of God's relations with his creatures in keeping with the vision Hutcheson and Foster had laid out. Even if the poor peasant could not "subscribe to public charities," he could comfort his "afflicted" wife by "a look of tenderness and sympathy" and the resultant "harmony which pervades this family" was "a fund of consolation to themselves" and "an instructive lesson to the surrounding neighborhood." The man of the "middle or superior" rank, able to donate and to serve on "committees" and personally to inspect poor neighborhoods and give them "advice," as Howard had done, carried the resultant "pleasurable feelings . . . into the bosom of his own family . . . there still farther productive of comfort and joy." Allen appealed to those who had been elevated to the "middle ranks . . . above the anxieties of poverty" and who, therefore, had "a portion of leisure at their command" wherein, by exercising benevolence, those ranks could enjoy in retrospect a rich harvest of delightful sensations." He concluded, "To a mind of sensibility, the very sight of an object it had been instrumental to relieve is a source of secret joy."

4

THE *DARTMOUTH COLLEGE* CASE AND THE LEGAL DESIGN OF CIVIL SOCIETY

MARK D. MCGARVIE

William Plumer, elected governor of New Hampshire in 1812, 1816, and 1817, wrote a series of letters to the *New Hampshire Patriot* newspaper in 1813 in which he accused the ministers then leading the current religious revivals in that state and throughout New England of participating in a reactionary plot to destroy republicanism and overturn the American Revolution. He asserted that the clergy sought "to traduce and vilify the [republican] government, to counteract and enfeeble its measures" in pursuit of its "publicly avowed object [of] a religious establishment."

Typical of many bright young men in late eighteenth-century America, Plumer turned away from Christianity in his twenty-first year after reading the rationalist literature of the Enlightenment. He came to see the Second Awakening – the religious revivals that responded to the perceived immorality of the early republic – as an ideological counter-revolution threatening the republican principles upon which the new nation was premised. His political career became a crusade to defend republicanism from the onslaughts of the evangelical Christians. As governor of New Hampshire, he played a crucial role in redefining the constitutional separation of church and state through his efforts to secularize Dartmouth College. In the process, American churches assumed new roles on the periphery of American institutional society from where they could express views and pursue social goals that dissented from policies of liberal republicanism.

* * *

The early republic was a period of contentious debate over the form of the new social institutions and the values to be embodied in and disseminated by them. As new institutions were created to reflect the ideals of the new republic, old ones had to be torn down. This involved removing the churches from their roles of public authority in the process known as "disestablishment." On the eve of the Revolution, nine of the thirteen colonies recognized established churches supported by public tax dollars. Christian leaders in all colonies contributed to the design of laws reflecting theological influences, and the churches assumed major roles in providing education, care for the needy, and the maintenance of community records. The separation of church and state involved the removal of the churches from the performance of these social functions. Moreover, as Americans came to think of themselves as a unified people, public institutions were required to reflect American values. Ultimately, law required churches – as private institutions – to divorce themselves from serving public roles.

One of the unusual characteristics of the revolutionary era, relative to the rest of American history, is the degree to which a single ideology – republicanism – dominated the political consciousness of the American people. Historian Gordon Wood has found that popular conceptions of republican self-government recognized its dependence on a virtuous citizenry. Both of the parties arising within George Washington's administration accepted the classical republican reliance upon virtue, but differed in their confidence in the degree to which the American people were possessed of virtue. The old Constitutional-era divide between federalists and antifederalists expressed itself in the 1790s as the Federalist Party of Hamilton and Adams sought to restrain the democratic excesses they perceived as emanating from the Jeffersonians in the Democratic-Republican (Republican) Party.

Different interpretations of American cultural ideals erupted after 1800 as expressed by the Second Awakening and the ascendancy of the Jeffersonians. Classical republicanism had tempered liberty with virtue, the social recognition that liberty is not license and that the good of the commonwealth required voluntary restraints. After 1800, the tenuous reliance on virtue to prevent anarchy seemed to many Federalists to have been overwhelmed by Jeffersonian liberalism. Historian Gordon Wood writes: "All they [Federalists] and their Republican successors had was the assumption, attributed in 1806 to Jefferson, 'that the public good is best promoted by the exertion of each individual seeking his own good in his own way.' " Historian Joyce Appleby recognizes this developing liberalism as the expression of Adam Smith's Enlightenment doctrine that political and economic freedoms, both naturally derived, must go hand-in-hand to realize economic efficiency and political self-determinism. In the early 1800s, Americans did their best to realize this social ideal as private pursuits tended to take priority in the national consciousness. Common-law judges used the law to redefine the roles of people in society. In the process, they helped to supplant a communitarian ideal with an individualistic one rooted in contract as an expression of legal independence and equality.

The Enlightenment encouraged people to rely on their own reason and rationality both to discern nature's laws and to apply their own judgment to create a better world. In this, humankind is the primary actor. Humanistic philosophy may conceive of God as a distant creator, rendered benign by his own unobtrusiveness – or even as an anachronism, irrelevant in a society of human construction in which The Golden Rule had come to replace the Ten Commandments as a guide to behavior. The Enlightenment engendered a republican education reflecting both the changed conception of morality from Christian piety to civic virtue and the elevation of individual over community as the primary social unit. Yet, for many, religion remained a matter beyond human reason and rationality, rooted in a mystical spiritual world that forever would exceed human comprehension. In this world, God – as a living spiritual entity – did unceasing battle with Satan for human souls. The need to design institutions to preserve public order against human tendencies to sin – incorporating the teaching of God's laws as moral absolutes – derived from these beliefs. Religiously conceived voluntary associations reflected the degree of pietistic concern – and even hostility – toward the mainstream culture. The founders of the American Tract Society in 1814, committed to publishing pamphlets and books expressing Christian doctrine and morals, conceived of secularists as "the enemy" and expressed their contest with the "satanic press" in terms of war: "there is in this direction an invasion of the private virtue and public morals of the nation, more insidious, but not less formidable, than the approach of a foreign army, with all the demoralizing influence of war."

It is precisely these conflicting views of American society that precipitated the campus eruptions of the early republic. The conflict over the teaching of the young was a battle over the vision of American society itself. Republicans sought to teach practical knowledge and a humanistic morality fitting the young for business, politics, and citizenship. Their opponents objected to the loss of deference to God, the threat to social order, and the degradation of public morals that such a humanistic curriculum promised. The contest for control of Dartmouth College that resulted in the Supreme Court decision of 1819 was, by that time, a capstone on decades of conflict over the goals of American higher education.

Several states, including Pennsylvania, Virginia, Massachusetts, New York, and Kentucky, rewrote college charters to transform formerly "private" schools into state universities. In every case, the move was prompted by legislative interests in supporting a progressive republican secular institution as opposed to one with religious affiliation. In other states, tenuous accommodations were reached as sectarian private schools, such as Yale, retained their independence only by embracing a broader curriculum and a deemphasis of religious instruction. These changes did not occur without conflict. Religious revivals, boycotts, and riots provided striking evidence of the passionate feelings held on both sides of the cultural divide.

Several conclusions can be drawn regarding higher education in this period. First, the republican enthusiasm of the Revolutionary era, transformed into liberalism by the Jeffersonian Republicans, persisted into the nineteenth century to influence the form of civil institutions, including colleges and universities under state control. These influences included the demand for religious tolerance, secular curricula, and the teaching of virtue derived from republican ideals. Second, the proliferation of competing denominations and their reaction to Enlightenment humanism expressed through the Second Awakening embodied an alternative vision of American society that contested with the dominant secular model. Third, both the advocates of republicanism and evangelicalism largely ignored distinctions between "public" and "private" in attempting to impose their ideal vision of civil society upon the whole. Consequently, the colonial model, (described by Robert Gross) of shared public and private responsibility for serving educational needs, persisted in form but not in substance. Civil society continued its reliance on the combined efforts of private and public forces to provide education; however, the resultant institutions were not products of community consensus as much as the results of an unresolved political and ideological contest. Fourth, the constitutional guarantees of the protection of contract, freedom of religion, and the separation of church and state remained muddled as various state legislatures pursued political agendas openly violative of protected rights. State legislatures consistently repudiated school and university charters to redesign educational institutions to serve political ends. Some religious bodies retained a modicum of control over their schools by accepting legislative direction in curricula and faculty appointments. Others relinquished established schools to the state and resolved to form competing schools under their control.

By the time the New Hampshire legislature attempted its takeover of Dartmouth College, the nation had grown accustomed to campus conflict.

Yet, none of the earlier conflicts were tested or resolved through the court system. The Dartmouth case, originally a battle over values and social goals, would offer a new means to resolve cultural conflict. In 1819, law would resolve the conflict – not through an assessment of the values or goals asserted by either party, but by application of contract law principles that embodied their own values.

* * *

In 1769, Dr. Eleazar Wheelock, a "new light" congregational minister, successfully chartered his New Hampshire College in the name of The Trustees of Dartmouth College. He worked through the Royal Governor of the Province of New Hampshire to obtain the charter from the British Crown. The charter confirmed the major donors as trustees and gave them the sole authority to name their successors. The future of the college was secured in perpetuity, with the charter being a grant "for us, our heirs and successors forever . . . that there shall be in the said Dartmouth College, from henceforth and forever, a body politic, consisting of trustees of said Dartmouth College."

The charter specifically provided that the trustees could manage the college as a lawful business operation. Wheelock was named president and given the authority to name his successor with concurrence by the trustees. The trustees held sole authority to elect all subsequent presidents and to remove or appoint any officer, teacher, or employee of the school. Lastly, the charter asserted that the trustees of Dartmouth College existed as an independent corporation not requiring any further "grant, license, or confirmation" to maintain its independence in the future.

In the years during and immediately after the Revolution, New Hampshire paid little attention to the small college in the mountains. Wheelock died in 1779 and was succeeded by his son John, the first lay college president in America. New Hampshire began to increase its support of the school during the late 1780s, partly in response to efforts from Vermont to induce Dartmouth to move to that state. Dartmouth received a land grant from New Hampshire of 42,000 acres in 1789, another land grant in 1807, and sporadic monetary grants in the 1790s. The only college in New Hampshire – created as a private, religiously inspired, educational corporation – received both state aid and private funds. Moreover, Dartmouth appealed to the state legislature for support of its mission to serve the state's educational needs, as did other "private" schools during this era, and willingly made concessions in curriculum in return.

Conflict came to Dartmouth in the first decade of the new century. Throughout the 1780s and 1790s, state legislatures imposed secular curricula and the teaching of a republican conception of virtue on denominationally controlled institutions. By the early 1800s, the religious counter-revolution reasserted demands for greater Christian piety in American society. Dartmouth came under attack for its religious laxity.

Undergraduate religious societies began forming on New England college campuses in the 1790s. The 1802 revival at Yale spawned increased religious enthusiasm at many schools. It is incorrect to perceive this movement just as a battle for souls; the real issues were societal, not personal, as pietistic Americans expressed reactionary displeasure at the secular humanism that had taken over governmental and educational institutions. Some went so far as to imagine the infiltration of American colleges by a conspiracy of European freethinkers influenced by French philosophers and committed to deism and anarchy. The revivals were necessary countermeasures to save young Americans from infidelity and corruption.

Campus evangelicals attacked not only the curricula and political values spawned by Enlightenment humanism, but also the carnival atmosphere of college communities. To these people, student drinking, moral decline, and rowdiness combined with irreverence to God in making campuses ill-suited to their purpose of training young men for responsible positions in church and in society.

By 1804, a sufficient number of Dartmouth's trustees had aligned themselves with the orthodox resurgence to appoint Roswell Shurtleff as Professor of Divinity. The young professor also assumed the duties of pastor in Hanover's Congregational Church. In both positions, he worked to move the community to a more vital recognition of God's place in people's lives.

Shurtleff wasted little time in addressing the religious apathy on campus, leading a revival in the winter of 1805–1806. The revival succeeded in increasing religious enthusiasm among the students, many of whom began attending Shurtleff's worship sessions in town rather than those in the campus chapel. These students' new commitment to orthodoxy expressed itself in petitions for temperance and the banishment of "treating" – ritualized drinking parties accompanying major campus events. In 1809, the trustees accepted the pietists' demands. In response, students objecting to increased restrictions rioted, holding a drunken carouse, burning outhouses, vandalizing pietists' rooms, firing guns into the night air, and spreading filth over the campus environs of their suspected enemies.

Wheelock's control over faculty appointments and campus policies had continued to decline through 1809 as four new orthodox trustees joined the board, one of whom, Charles Marsh, founded The Society for the Promotion of Temperance. Piqued at his diminishing influence, Wheelock refused to punish the rioters and blamed the pietists for precipitating the unrest. He further went on the attack, accusing the trustees of a conspiracy to turn Dartmouth into a "sectarian school." Pamphlets supporting the president lamented the campus culture, which seemingly required faculty and students to wear "their badge of orthodoxy." In response, Shurtleff and his supporters referred to the president as a "liberal" who would convert the college into "a seminary of Socinianism."

Not surprisingly, the debate at the college spilled over into the larger political arena. Congregational clergy throughout New Hampshire asked for prayers for the college as a "nursery of piety" that they hoped would not revert to its heathenish state. Newspapers took sides in editorials, addressing the issue at the college as representative of competing views of American society. The Republican editor of the *New Hampshire Patriot and State Gazette*, noting both his state's and the nation's acceptance of the Republican platform, condemned the changes at Dartmouth and encouraged "the future governance of Dartmouth College" as "a means of perpetuating the republican majority in the state."

In 1815, President Wheelock formally asked the New Hampshire legislature to investigate the college. The trustees responded on August 26, 1815, by removing him from office and replacing him with Congregationalist minister Reverend Francis Brown.

In the gubernatorial campaign of 1816, Republican candidate William Plumer made the Dartmouth College debate a campaign issue and called for legislative reform of the charter. Plumer decried the seminarian aspects of American higher education, finding the teaching of dead languages inconsistent "to the pursuits and business of this life" and the ecclesiastical emphasis of many schools "hostile to our republican system." Specifically referring to Dartmouth, he said: "When the government of our college apply (sic) to the people or the legislature for aid, they (sic) represent the college as a public institution." He promised, if elected, to have the legislature take control of Dartmouth and institute reform, emphasizing a curriculum useful in daily life, religious freedom, and open availability to rich and poor alike.

In March 1816, New Hampshire voters elected William Plumer as Governor and sent a Republican majority to the legislature. One of the first acts of the new administration was a bill restructuring Dartmouth College. In Plumer's "message to the legislature," in which he advocated reform of Dartmouth, he referred to the College's self-sustaining Board of Trustees – able to operate on its own majority unchecked by popular will – as a remnant of the Crown's authority and as "hostile to the spirit and genius of free government." The legislation, passed in 1816, was not unusual. Yet, in other instances of legislative action to govern formerly "private" schools, school trustees acceded to the legislative initiative; in New Hampshire, the legislation served as a declaration of war.

Three different legislative actions addressing Dartmouth were enacted in 1816; of these, the first is the most important. On June 27, 1816, the New Hampshire legislature passed an act entitled "An act to amend the charter, and enlarge and improve the corporation of Dartmouth College." In this statute, the legislature premised its action on state interest:

Whereas knowledge and learning, generally diffused through a community, are essential to the preservation of a free government, and extending the opportunities and advantages of education is highly conducive to promote this end, and by the constitution it is made the duty of the legislators and magistrates to cherish the interests of literature, and the sciences, and all seminaries established for their advancement – and as the college of the state may, in the opinion of the legislature, be rendered more extensively useful. . . .

The legislature then proceeded to change the corporation's name to the "Trustees of Dartmouth University," simultaneously effectuating the same change in the name of the school. The distinction between a college and a university at that time was more significant than subsequent usage of those terms may indicate. The term *university* implied a school devoted to a modern curriculum designed to prepare students for diverse roles in business, government, and the secular needs of the state. The term *college* usually referred to a cloistered academic community intended to train ministers. The name change to Dartmouth University implied substantial changes in the school's goals and methods.

The statute also increased the number of trustees by nine (from twelve to twenty-one); named the governor as the source of all new trustees and of future replacements; and created a Board of Overseers, appointed by the governor to govern the University and undertake most of the responsibilities formerly held by the trustees. In a significant change from the earlier charter, the legislature expanded the practice of religious freedom at the University. The 1769 charter prohibited discrimination against any person "of any religious denomination." Atheists, agnostics, Jews, and other nonChristians were not protected within this provision, since none of them were part of a "denomination." Reversing this policy, the 1816 law accorded "perfect freedom of religious opinion" to all officers and students.

The Trustees of the College met to respond to the legislation and on August 28, 1816, issued a resolution "refusing to accept or act under" the statute. The trustees also removed William H. Woodward from his position as secretary and treasurer of the 1769 corporation. Woodward was a Republican supporter of Wheelock and had taken possession of the corporation's records, account books, and seal. A new law of December 26, 1816, provided the legislature's response to the college trustees, setting $500 fines for anyone presuming to act as a trustee or officer of Dartmouth except as provided by law. The new university trustees reinstated Woodward in their initial meeting on February 4, 1817. Subsequently, on February 8, 1817, the college trustees sued Woodward to recover the items in his possession and to raise the issue of the legitimacy of the legislative action. The case proceeded through the court system reaching the Supreme Court in 1818. Argument began on March 10 before a packed courtroom. Daniel Webster's stirring oration on behalf of the college is generally considered the most famous in the history of oral argument before the Court. Following three days of argument, Marshall announced that the Court would postpone its decision in order to reach a consensus.

The case of *Trustees of Dartmouth College v. Woodward* is often credited with "creating" a legal right of corporations to be free from state government control, thereby enabling private enterprises to pursue charitable and business goals. Yet, the law of contracts – on which the protection of corporations was premised – was rooted both in domestic and English precedent prior to 1819, and was clearly expressed in the Constitution. Article I, Section 10, the Contract Clause of the U.S. Constitution, reads in part: "No state shall . . . pass any bill of attainder, ex post facto law, or law impairing the obligation owing to contracts." In other words, private contract rights are superior to public interests asserted by state legislatures that might be used to contravene those private contract considerations.

Just prior to the Supreme Court's decision in the *Dartmouth* case, Justice Story issued a decision in *Terrett v. Taylor*. This case provides an appreciation for the *Dartmouth* decision's implicit acceptance of churches and religious institutions as private organizations, legally distinct from the public realm despite their dedication to public service. Story specifically refers to churches as private "voluntary associations" that are required to assume the corporate form to secure their pursuit of private ends from public interference.

The *Dartmouth College* case presented an opportunity for the Court to confirm its protection of contract rights; however, the Court had already done it in an earlier case. Alternatively, the court may have seen a duty to address the issue of whether a corporate charter – which is a governmental creation – was entitled to less protection from that government than other contracts. Yet, this issue was also largely resolved in an earlier case, *Fletcher v. Peck*, because the contract in question in that case, though not a charter, was a legislative creation. The real importance of the *Dartmouth College* case, therefore, is not the pronouncement of the rule of law determining the case, but rather the reasoning articulated by the Court. This reasoning expressed the Court's perception of distinct realms of public and private action, and the role of the courts in the protection of private action from public interference. In the factual context of the case, "private" connotes a religious endeavor as much as an economic one. The *Dartmouth* case gave the Court a chance to expand on the law expressed by Story in *Terrett v. Taylor*. The college was not a church; but, it was a religiously affiliated organization addressing public needs through a private agenda. It is by calling attention to the untenable aspects of this relationship that the case influenced the development of a law of philanthropy and the design of civil society. The Court's decision confirms the constitutional separation of church and state, which implicitly recognizes the status of churches in America as private voluntary institutions able to pursue their own visions of society.

Early in his opinion, Marshall redefines the central issue in the case in terms of a public-private distinction. Resolving this issue, Marshall finds that private property, "both real and personal which had been contributed for the benefit of the college, was conveyed to and vested in, the corporate body." Further, he finds that that property was used to manage the college consistent with the intentions and parameters expressed in the corporation's charter. Reaching a tentative conclusion, based solely on the nature of the corporation's property, Marshall contends that "[i]t is then, an eleemosynary, and as far as respects its funds, a private corporation."

However, the Republicans, through attorney John Holmes, argued that a corporation's purpose – in this instance, the support of the government's interest in education – is more determinative of the corporation's nature than the source of its funds. Marshall, therefore, could not rest on his finding that "as far as respects its funds," Dartmouth was a private corporation. Recognizing Holmes's argument, he asks of Dartmouth: "Do its objects stamp on it a different character?" In answer, he responds, "No." Marshall defines public institutions not by the purposes they address, but as being part of the "civil government."

Nor does the act of incorporation subject a corporation to perpetual control by the state. Incorporation allows the new entity, as "an artificial being," "the mere creation of law," to attain "immortality" and "individuality," "properties by which a perpetual succession of many persons are considered as the same and may act as a single individual."

The fact that Dartmouth College was once perceived by the state to be an organ of public service does not create, Marshall said, a presumption that the donors to the college intended to serve the legislature's determination of the interests of the people of New Hampshire. To the contrary, the only reasonable conclusion is that they intended their gifts to address the interests and purposes of the college (as determined by the trustees consistent with the charter). To protect the property interests of the donors, as well as of the corporation, the charter cannot be subject to revision or manipulation by the state. Marshall writes: "The corporation is the assignee of their [the donors'] rights, stands in their place, and distributes their bounty, as they would themselves have distributed it, had they been immortal." The corporation, then, forms the means by which the donors addressed their goals, and is not a tool of the state legislature to be used to serve state interests. Incorporation allows many individuals to come together to exert greater influence as a group than they ever could separately, and to do so perpetually, without restrictions from government that would be equally as unlawful were they asserted against individuals. In overturning the legislative action restructuring the college, Marshall asserts that legislative perceptions of the public good cannot overcome the rights of individuals expressed in contracts.

The preceding legal argument constituted a sufficient basis for the Court, pursuant to Article 1, Section 10 of the Constitution, to void the action of the New Hampshire legislature. However, Marshall's opinion went further and, in the process, clarified the status of charitable institutions in the early republic. Language in the *Dartmouth* decision prefigures the Court's subsequent decision in *Philadelphia Baptist Association v. Hart's Executors* later the same year. In *Dartmouth College*, Marshall writes: "Charitable or public-spirited individuals, desirous of making permanent appropriations for charitable or other useful purposes, find it impossible to effect their design securely, and certainly, without an incorporation act." In this passage, Marshall articulates the basis for the doctrine that unincorporated charitable institutions are too vague to receive bequests of decedents, as their intentions cannot be given definite assurance of fulfillment without a corporate charter and an organization establishing parameters for the future use of funds. In this way, Marshall not only distinguishes private charitable corporations from state governmental offices and agencies, but also requires a legal formalization of those charities in order for them to be legally secure in the pursuit of their purposes.

After the *Dartmouth* decision, government could not rely on philanthropic associations to address public perceptions of societal needs. The public-private distinction required states to define their priorities more carefully. No longer could states delegate to private enterprises the responsibility for educating young people, caring for the poor, or creating roadways, because states could no longer exercise control over how those private entities fulfilled their duties. To continue to rely on private entities after 1819 risked creating educational, welfare, or infrastructure systems significantly at odds with legislative perceptions of the public interest. Justice Story, in his concurring opinion, provides the states with one option to use in an effort to preserve the old system of state reliance on private action to serve public needs. Recognizing charters as contracts, Story writes: "If the legislature mean to claim such an authority [to control the course of private corporations by legislative enactment], it must be reserved in the grant." Seldom, in future years, would any corporation submit to such a provision in its charter. Instead, states needed to determine those priorities and concerns that could not be entrusted to private attention, and to establish governmental funds and offices for them. Accordingly, those social needs deemed less sensitive or important were left to charitable organizations to address as they saw fit. In the process, civil society was redefined, separating governmental institutions from private charitable corporations. Religiously affiliated private associations pursuing their own goals remained viable on the institutional periphery of society. Marshall's language in the *Dartmouth* decision expresses a major change in attitude from an earlier era: "These eleemosynary institutions do not fill the place which would otherwise be occupied by government, but that which would otherwise remain vacant." In recognizing the private agendas of these associations and granting them legal protection, the Court perpetuated the debate over the values, goals, and purposes of American society.

Protestant churches were the prime beneficiaries of the Supreme Court's *Dartmouth* doctrine. As voluntary organizations protected by corporate law, their attention to societal reform after 1819 through the social gospel represented an alternative vision of American society to that presented by secular or governmental policy. As Wendy Gamber and G.J. Barker-Benfield assert in their essays, Christian communalism confronted secular libertarianism in a series of social debates. The actions of individuals to form organizations and raise funds on behalf of temperance, prison reform, abolition, women's rights, and education were protected by law. The Court ensured the rights of organizations to support minority positions that might one day become acceptable to the larger society.

More narrowly, the *Dartmouth* decision of 1819 – by preventing state control over private educational corporationsm – clearly separated public from parochial education. Yet, only a few states deemed it worthwhile to found, construct, and fund their own schools: Indiana in 1820, Alabama in 1831, and Delaware in 1833. To the degree that other states continued to rely on private institutions to meet educational needs, they did so with an explicit understanding of the limits that they had in shaping the education these schools provided. The unacceptability of these terms to state legislatures stranded many private schools. In need of money, the existing colleges turned to a traditional source of financing – to religious institutions. The multiplicity of sects or denominations in the early nineteenth century, each seeking to build its membership, used colleges not only to train clergy, but also to be competitive vehicles for its distinct religious message. The decades following the Dartmouth case witnessed an "unprecedented increase in the number of private colleges" as denominations founded new schools and took over existing ones. The development of contract law in the early republic has been credited with, in legal historian William Hurst's terms, "a release of energy," contributing to the dynamic expansion of American commercial, industrial, and economic growth. Jurgen Herbst has insightfully added that the securing of contract rights for private schools likewise spurred the competitive environment in which various denominations presented their visions of American civil society free from state interference.

* * *

The Court's decision in the *Dartmouth* case produced two immediate consequences: (1) the decision by state governments to question their financial support of institutions clearly no longer subject to public control; and

(2) the proliferation of denominationally controlled private colleges, each representing a unique alternative to both the state schools and its various denominational competitors.

The public model of higher education expressed the American republic's adoption of an Enlightenment secularism that embodied its own form of religion. This "religion of the republic" reduced Christian doctrine to its lowest common denominator – essentially a code of moral behavior expressed in The Golden Rule – and positioned God as a benevolent but uninvolved creator of natural laws. Consistent with this system of belief, public schools taught practical knowledge, framed moral teachings in the language of civic virtue, and tolerated a wide range of religious expressions. Most private schools, founded and supported by denominations, expressed alternative understandings of God and espoused different prescriptions for education and the form of American society. The real importance of the *Dartmouth* case is not simply the delineation of private and public, but also the perpetuation of the alternative visions of American society by the legal recognition of public and private spheres. The decision, then, fostered the American reliance on philanthropy noted by Alexis de Tocqueville just over a decade later. By protecting the legal right of Americans to pursue different visions of American society through memberships in smaller communities, what Tocqueville found as a uniquely American form of political expression was given life.

Gross is absolutely correct in asserting that Alexis de Tocqueville's observation of thousands of voluntary associations in Jacksonian America – each pursuing its own religious, moral, or political goal – focused attention on a relatively new phenomenon. American experiments in voluntary associations, while not rare prior to 1760, really proliferated during the Revolutionary era and the early republic. Early "charitable" organizations largely addressed either personal needs – for insurance or cultural enrichment, for example – or the provision of services unaddressed by government, such as vigilante police groups or volunteer fire departments. By the early 1800s, more organizations formed to address religious, social, and political concerns reflecting alternative visions of American society. Yet, even during this period, the growth of voluntary associations was at a rate less than half that of the period after 1820. Prior to that time, voluntary associations reflected Americans' valuation of participatory democracy or republican citizenship. After 1819, as denominations both competed for membership and recognized their public responsibilities through the programs of the social gospel, chartered voluntary associations became the only means of their survival and growth.

Recent scholarship has highlighted the role of state court judges in private law cases in influencing early national culture toward the liberal Jeffersonian ideal. Law functioned as a "semiautonomous" doctrine, imposing its own ideals and values to shape interpersonal relationships in the early republic. The functioning of the Supreme Court in public law cases was complementary to this development. The *Dartmouth College* case, by demanding formal legal structures for religious and philanthropic organizations, encouraged American culture to move from the colonial model – in which community involvement in everything from barn raisings and quilting bees to the public militia, church, and school reflected informal personal relationships – toward a modern society premised on contract and formal institutional structures. Gross also notes how the growth of formal and impersonal philanthropic associations weakened individual duties to care for neighbors and exercise one's charitable impulse in community affairs. The courts' legal requirement of formal corporate status to protect the rights of voluntary associations to be free from governmental interference succeeded in ensuring their continued existence and functional role in American society. However, it also compelled the restructuring of social relationships in accordance with the liberal ideology that elevated individual freedoms over community values. The beginning of philanthropic organizations occurred not with the funding of the large trusts at the turn of the twentieth century, but in the creation of the legal model for philanthropic pursuits during the early republic.

5

RETHINKING ASSIMILATION: AMERICAN INDIANS AND THE PRACTICE OF CHRISTIANITY, 1800–1861

STEPHEN WARREN

In March 1807, members of a sectarian religious movement known as the Shakers traveled from their settlement in southern Ohio to find American Indians with whom they shared religious ideas. After dismissing the leaders of several Indian towns, the Shakers met the Shawnee Prophet named Tenskwatawa at his village in Greenville, Ohio. Convinced that he possessed extraordinary spiritual powers, the Shakers – who believed in the primacy of the Holy Spirit in conversion – thought that they had much in common with the Greenville Indians. However, neighboring whites disliked the Shakers, rejecting their habit of speaking in tongues and other physical manifestations of the Holy Spirit. The Shakers' belief in celibacy, as well as racial and gender equality, also offended many frontier whites. Yet, aside from theological differences, the Shakers sympathized with the villagers' peripheral status, claiming that they had "suffered great persecution, both from the whites & Indians, & have all manner of evil spoken of them, as we have had, & we think by the same false spirit." The Shakers pursued relations with the Shawnee Prophet out of a conviction that both groups shared access to "good spirits" through visions.

Shakers Richard McNemar, Benjamin S. Youngs, and David Darrow were greatly impressed by the size and craftsmanship of the Prophet's Greenville community, a testament to the fact that the Shakers are better known today for their furniture than their faith. The council house alone, constructed of hewn logs and clapboards, was 150 feet in length and 34 feet wide. McNemar and his fellow travelers also noted more than "fifty-seven smoking cottages" surrounding the council house. More importantly, the Shakers believed that "the spirit we felt there brought on our minds a very striking & solemn sence of what God was doing in the earth."

Greenville's population density and the concomitant size of its structures easily outstripped the strength and size of the Shakers' settlement in Union Village.

Remarkably, the Shakers attempted to forge a religious bond with a group of American Indians who were intent on turning back the flood of white settlers pouring into the Old Northwest. When the Prophet and his brother, Tecumseh, helped create a pan-Indian confederacy, it became a major concern for both President Thomas Jefferson and William Henry Harrison, who was then territorial governor of Indiana. Indicative of nineteenth-century hostility toward Indians, Jefferson remarked that the Prophet "pretended to be in constant communication with the Great Spirit . . . and that they [Indians] must return from all the ways of the whites to the habits and opinions of their forefathers." Neighboring whites took these ideas more seriously, fearing the Prophet and Tecumseh for their repeated calls for Indian sovereignty by any means necessary. Given these sentiments, which fueled the Prophet's animus for whites, why did he and his supporters at Greenville accede to the Shakers' friendship? Certainly, the opportunity for an equal religious and material exchange with the Shakers was enticing. But on a deeper level, the Prophet's involvement with the Shakers demonstrates that "giving and getting" between Indians and whites was unavoidable in the early nineteenth century, even for the most outspoken Native critics of Americans.

Before common spiritual ground could be forged, the Shawnee Prophet forced the Shakers to declare their attitude toward his movement. Initially, Tenskwatawa expressed little interest in speaking with the Shakers because "the ministers of the white people don't believe what he says." The Shakers replied that "we are not of those kind of ministers, we are a people separated from them by the work of the *great spirit*, they count us as foolish too & speak against us." According to McNemar and his companions, the residents of Union Village and Greenville were both persecuted, and a partnership between the two like-minded communities might assist them in their shared struggle to prepare the Old Northwest for the Second Coming. The Shakers believed that they were "all brothers of one family, united to the good spirits above."

Religious convictions aside, Tenskwatawa recognized his community's need for material support. The Shakers responded with both produce and agricultural implements, angering neighboring settlers who feared that the Indians might realize their vision of freeing the Old Northwest from American control. By September 1807, the Shakers had provided a grindstone, fifty bushels of wheat and rye, and other goods, including meat and salt. They insisted that "we have sent it for the present relief of those, and those only, who love the good spirit of peace and hate the spirit of war." However, two weeks after they had met the Prophet, white American hostility toward both the Greenville community and Union Village forced the Shakers to abandon these religious and material exchanges with the Shawnee holy man.

From the time of the Europeans' first visit to the Americas, they had been part of an exchange relationship. North American Indians utilized a "gift exchange" with others to show friendship, build alliances, and address disparate needs. The early European settlers' need for food and possession of kettles, guns, and blankets sowed the first seeds of exchange. Later, European demands for pelts fueled and perpetuated the earlier alliances. In this early period of European and Indian exchanges, the reciprocity of the relationship was easy to see because of the relatively equal positions of the parties.

Prior to the War of 1812, Great Lakes tribes lived in what historian Richard White describes as a "shared world" with French, British, and, later, American colonizers. Neither Indians nor European colonizers east of the Great Lakes were able to dominate the other. As small societies, tribes formed alliances – both militaristic and peaceful – with each other and Europeans to sustain themselves against their enemies. Missionaries also established long-term contact with these alliances during the colonial period. Intertribal alliances provided Indians with the political autonomy necessary to accept or reject Christianity on their own terms. Yet, after the War removed the British from the Northwest, the Indians lost their bargaining position as potential allies and faced a stronger and more dynamic American population. Exchange between Americans and Indians would continue to be reciprocal, but on very unequal terms. For the first time, white Americans sought to give something to the Indians without expectation of return. The Indian response to this "charity" defined the philanthropic relationship between the parties as reciprocal.

* * *

Shaker assistance, motivated by spiritual affinity rather than the desire to "civilize" the Shawnees, was unlike other contemporary philanthropic efforts in the Old Northwest. Ardent nationalism coupled with an undying thirst for Indian lands overwhelmed more equitable partnerships following the American victory over the British in the War of 1812. Thereafter, missionary-driven philanthropic efforts among American Indians became increasingly one-sided, particularly between 1815 and the onset of the Civil War.

In this essay, I define *philanthropy* (consistent with Friedman's introduction) as an exchange relationship motivated by the desire to transform the recipients of the exchange according to the material and cultural ideals of the philanthropists themselves. Unlike the Shakers, most later philanthropists asserted greater controls on the distribution of resources and the ends they desired. Philanthropists reasoned that Indian people had to become mirror images of their benefactors if they were to survive. In the nineteenth century, American Indians entered into social relations with whites despite the fact that donors had little interest in providing resources that addressed Native American concerns about their own needs. By ignoring Native American perspectives, American philanthropists confidently sought the destruction of American Indians and their unique ethnic status. Philanthropists pursued assimilation, a concept based on cultural extinction, rather than mingling the two societies through intermarriage and economic integration. Philanthropists were both profoundly coercive and supremely self-confident.

Yet, American cultural chauvinism tells only half the story. It is true that after the American Revolution, the tribes examined in the following pages became dependent on the United States for support. Native peoples used the missionaries, whom they regarded as agents of assimilation, to craft enduring and distinctive responses to American cultural imperialism. This essay identifies some of the motives American Indians had for working with missionaries, government officials, and other philanthropic agents. The diversity of responses to such assimilation-centered philanthropy reveals much about the persistence of ethnic pluralism at a time when philanthropists became less interested in their recipients' needs and more interested in fulfilling their own vision of cultural and ethnic homogeneity in the United States.

Missionaries and government officials imagined Indians in surprisingly homogeneous and fixed terms. Like imaginary tourists in unknown lands, some of the most important philanthropists of the early republic had very little firsthand experience with the people they intended to assimilate. Jefferson himself never traveled west of the Appalachian Mountains. With virtually no local ethnographic knowledge to support their assumptions, philanthropists developed a cultural map of Native America, placing savagery and civilization as immutable opposites. White Americans were ill-prepared for missionary labor among American Indians because they failed to recognize Native dedication to their own cultures. Missionaries believed that the rapid assimilation of American Indians into a fixed notion of the American republic was attainable.

Concepts such as assimilation and acculturation reveal little about the cultural and regional contexts in which philanthropists engaged American Indians. Regional differences often determined Native responses to philanthropists. In Ohio, the Prophet's Shawnee rivals recruited missionaries to assist them in purchasing domesticated livestock and in growing new crops, such as wheat. The Ohio Shawnee leader, Black Beard, spoke of his people's desire to incorporate domesticated livestock into the Shawnees' subsistence cycle. He observed that the white people's "Great God" provided "plenty of tame animals that you might kill them at your doors when you pleased." Black Beard conflated religious power and economic vitality; as a result, he pursued relations with Quaker missionary William Kirk to assist them in making the economic transition.

To the south, in modern Atlanta, Georgia, on the Flint River, U.S. agent Benjamin Hawkins established a plantation, complete with slaves, designed as a model farm for the Muskogee (Creeks). Hawkins hoped that the Creeks would integrate themselves into the market economy through the intensive cultivation of cotton. But, to Hawkins's dismay, Creek leaders who amassed wealth under the new agricultural model continued to redistribute their wealth and hold their land communally. Moreover, the Creeks were ambivalent about American gender roles; some Creeks preferred to continue the practice of having their women control agriculture. Both examples demonstrate that agricultural practices (and paths to success) varied greatly across the American frontier before 1830.

The federal government became actively involved in philanthropic programs after the War of 1812, providing funds and defining the general goals of assimilation for philanthropists. The Civilization Fund, established in 1819, created a pool of $10,000 to be distributed annually to missionary societies willing to promote the education and conversion of Native American peoples. Historian William McLoughlin has argued that the fund "established a formal partnership between church and state." Missionaries were thought to be the most effective resource for the task of incorporating Native Americans into the mainstream of American life.

The cadre of Americans who set out to assimilate American Indians during the early republic did so at a time of social ferment, when social controls placed on the general population were weakening considerably.

New technology and transportation, such as the cotton gin and the canals that linked America's vast interior to the Atlantic coast, also contributed to the decline of American Indian lands east of the Mississippi. Between 1800 and 1820, the trans-Appalachian population grew from 250,000 to more than two million. Ten states joined the Union between 1792 and 1821. Historian Joyce Appleby places this rapid settlement in the context of Indian-white relations, arguing that "the yearning for economic independence among ordinary white Americans sealed the fate of dependency for Native Americans."

Ironically, philanthropists concocted coercive and limited profiles of the possibilities for "being Indian" as the possibilities for the majority of white Americans expanded significantly. Christian reformers and federal officials who sponsored missionary activities hoped to assimilate American Indians into the Jeffersonian ideal of an agrarian republic. Reservations – the diminished tribal lands created by treaties between the 1790s and the 1840s – were thought to be transitional way stations for male-oriented nuclear families that would quickly choose life on an individual land allotment over communally held reservation lands.

* * *

American Indians were far less interested in Jeffersonian agrarianism and individual land ownership than philanthropists assumed. For one, the obvious poverty of many of their white neighbors and the inaccessibility of distant markets made the yeoman ideal seem precarious and unpredictable. Boom and bust economic cycles frequently struck their white neighbors, leading many tribes to advocate for a mixed economy based on hunting and agriculture. Diminished deer and beaver populations east of the Mississippi River limited the viability of hide-hunting for the fur trade by the early decades of the nineteenth century. Communal land ownership and sharing resources became even more important as Native American communities adjusted to the reality of agriculturally focused economies. Tribes such as the Shawnees and Kickapoos effectively fought poverty caused by economic dislocation by resisting missionary demands to divide reservations into individual farms.

As economies shifted and warfare between both Indians and whites diminished, a new class of Indian leaders emerged on the reservations. Indian diplomats, noted primarily for their ability as cultural brokers, led the way in this new world. Jean Baptiste Richardville of the Miamis provides one of the best examples of this shift in leadership. Richardville, the child of a

French-Canadian trader and a prominent Miami Indian mother, was reported to be one of the wealthiest men in the state of Indiana prior to the tribe's relocation in 1838. He used his wealth to help the Miamis resist removal longer than most of their Great Lakes Indian neighbors. With Richardville's help, the Miamis formed an alliance with two local Indian traders, William G. and George W. Ewing, who then used their political clout with federal and state officials to lobby against removal. Andrew Jackson's secretary of war, John Eaton, remarked that the Miamis were "well organized in their kind of government . . . with one of the most shrewd men [Richardville] in North America at their head."

American recognition of chiefly status became essential as tribesmen evaluated their leaders' ability to negotiate with Americans. The Shawnee leader Black Hoof, like Richardville, recognized the new leadership requirements imposed on him by his kinsmen. Black Hoof made the transition from war leader to diplomat and tribal chief. He used missionary schools and agricultural assistance to secure property and status for his family. His son, also named Black Hoof, combined his hereditary right to lead with an education in Quaker schools and, following relocation, emerged as a key figure in tribal politics. Good relations with missions became especially important to the next generation of leaders who were denied the opportunity for status through warfare with Americans and other Indian tribes. Education in American schools and leadership positions in mission churches became important conduits for the retention of power for both hereditary leaders and their métis counterparts. American Indian leaders understood the intimate connection between church and state, and exploited their relationship with missionaries to assure neighboring whites of their peaceful intentions.

But missionaries also contributed to the tension, exacerbating disputes between tribal leaders or competing village chiefs, undermining tribal sovereignty in the process. From the Minnesota Ojibwe to the Cherokees of the Southeast, many missionaries allied themselves with newly converted Indians – often individuals who lacked the right to lead their people and used missions as a chance to bypass leadership requirements based on heredity. Although Christian Indians without rights to hereditary leadership made inroads among the Ojibwe, traditional leaders continued to draw support from the majority of tribesmen who remained unconvinced of the need for conversion and rejected missionary involvement in tribal politics. Throughout Indian country, a large majority stood firm against missionary domination and maintained traditional cultural practices.

However, assimilation-minded philanthropists were successful in trans-forming American Indian gender roles. Between the turn of the century and the Civil War, as Euro-American models of patriarchy took hold, Native American women experienced a substantial loss in status and power. Prior to the missionary endeavors of the early nineteenth century, Indian women were the primary agricultural producers. Among the Iroquois and Cherokees, two matrilineal societies, women organized and executed the planting, cultivation, and harvest of corn, beans, and squash. Filling such an important economic role granted women significant political power and control over land ownership. But as missionaries demanded that men become farmers and women housewives, the equilibrium between the sexes was seriously disrupted. Cherokee women increasingly conformed to the southern white culture of domesticity, becoming what historian Mary Young describes as a "mirror of the republic." Their role as powerbrokers diminished steadily as male-organized agriculture and Christianity took hold. By the time of removal in the late 1830s, relationships between men and women had changed dramatically, moving from reciprocity between the sexes to protection and even subjugation.

Missionaries thus challenged long-held assumptions about the nature of families and the relationships between kinsmen. American Indian families, and the clans of which they were a part, were already struggling as successive epidemics and warfare with colonizers reduced their numbers. Missionaries focused their attention on the individual convert, thereby placing a tremen-dous strain on kin groups within tribes. By converting and leading their families to missionary churches, some Indian women found a new path to authority. Missionaries often focused their efforts on Indian women for this reason. For example, a Shawnee woman named Sophie Bigknife was baptized and received into the membership of the Baptist church on the Shawnee reservation in 1847. Within three years of her baptism, four members of her family joined the Baptist church. Yet, female converts to evangelical denominations rarely held positions of power within the mis-sion churches. Missionaries granted supporting roles to Indian men, and as a result, Indian women exerted informal influence on the missionary enter-prise. Regardless of who held positions of authority, missionaries' exclusive attention on the Indian convert accelerated the decline of Shawnee clans.

* * *

Andrew Jackson articulated a new and brutal chapter in Indian-white re-lations and American Indian policy with the Indian Removal Act of 1830. Jackson recognized that the Cherokees and their Indian neighbors remained

Women such as Biwabikogijigokwe (Iron Sky Woman), an Ojibwe from Minnesota, played a crucial role in establishing alliances between their respective tribes and missionaries. (Rockwood Photographer, New York, ca. 1870; *Courtesy* Minnesota Historical Society.)

committed to sovereignty. Consequently, Jackson rejected Jefferson's belief that the cultural extinction of the tribes would allow for the assimilation of the Indians. Removal was the only answer to the Indians' dogged commitment to their lands and their way of life. Unlike the Jeffersonians, Jackson

OTAWA

MUSENAIKUN.

EUE KO

WLKI UKENOUMATEWIN;

KUER ANINT

OMINWAHIMOWIN NOK,

KAPWA OLEPEUMOWAT

MRTO KUER HAN;

KUER OTAWAK

OTEPAKONIKRWINIWAN.

UWI TUL

WRLTOT UHIHAK,

RNONIKOHIN

KEHIMOKOMANEWE PRPTISUN.

Nalif Wrlhikatrk.

Otawa Prptise Kukekwrwikumikof.

UHIHAK, MRSENAIKUNIKRT,

1850.

This title page of the Gospel of Luke and Ottawa law from 1850 suggests the marriage of Christianity and tribal customs in antebellum mission communities. This is one of numerous Biblical texts translated and printed in tribal languages by Baptist missionary Jotham Meeker. (*Courtesy* Kansas State Historical Society.)

and his supporters argued that a cultural and physical quarantine between Indians and whites in the West was necessary for assimilation to proceed at a slower, more deliberate pace. Jacksonians also promoted the rights of states and defended their refusal to recognize tribal sovereignty within their borders. Philanthropy remained central to the Jacksonian enterprise, albeit with a longer timetable for assimilation in a racially segregated zone where Indians and philanthropists might work together, unmolested by more troublesome Americans.

Some of the most outspoken critics of Indian removal were missionaries to the Cherokees. By remaining outside the Jacksonian ethos of white dominance and Indian dislocation, missionaries gained wide acceptance among their Indian neighbors. When Indian people chose to work with one missionary instead of another, they were, in effect, making a decision about how they wanted their people and their culture described to government officials and other Americans. Although defense of Cherokee rights in the Southeast was not universal, Baptist, Methodist, and Moravian missionaries objected to Andrew Jackson and the state of Georgia's heavy-handedness. Some missionaries went to prison for refusing to acknowledge Georgia's assertion of sovereignty over Cherokee lands and government. Jeremiah Evarts, a Baptist, traveled to Washington and lobbied against removal in an exceedingly public duel with Isaac McCoy, a Baptist missionary and defender of Jackson's removal plan.

Both the missionaries and the Cherokees themselves resisted Georgia and the Jacksonians in a highly public campaign that eventually reached the U.S. Supreme Court. In *Cherokee Nation v. Georgia* (1831), Chief Justice John Marshall defined all tribes as "domestic, dependent nations." As such, tribes had a trust relationship with the federal government. In *Worcester v. Georgia* (1832), Marshall further defined the trust relationship between the tribes and the federal branch of the U.S. government. Marshall found that the state of Georgia could not legally interfere in Cherokee government or regulate travel to and from the reservation. While Marshall's decisions define the special status between the tribes and the United States to this day, it is also true that Jackson explicitly refused to enforce Marshall's decisions. The office of the president refused to follow the Supreme Court decisions and defend Cherokee sovereignty, and continued to press for removal. The Jacksonians' hunger for Indian land, particularly in the South, proved more powerful than the resistance of Indians and missionaries.

Far from transitional way stations on the road to assimilation, tribes imagined reservations as permanent territories where the acceptance and rejection of cultural elements from American society would occur on the tribe's terms. Sovereignty thus combined the permanent recognition of tribally held territory with the more abstract recognition of tribal political jurisdiction within that territory. Some missionaries agreed with this notion of sovereignty. For example, in the 1820s, the Quakers continued to work toward the general goal of establishing Christianity among the Shawnees. However, they fought against removal by purchasing the lands surrounding the Shawnees' reservation at Wapakoneta, Ohio. This buffer-zone limited the ability of frontier whites to harass the Shawnees through the destruction of tribal property, including livestock and agricultural produce.

Tribes north and south of the Ohio River made significant adjustments to American dominance before removal as opposition to their presence mounted. American Indians challenged their detractors by lobbying for the increasingly popular idea of tribal sovereignty – a political concept with cultural pluralism, ethnic tolerance, and self-determination at its core. Some missionaries supported this ideal and defended tribal leaders, such as Jesse Bushyhead, a mixed-blood Cherokee from Tennessee. Fluent in both Cherokee and English, Bushyhead founded a Baptist church, leading a congregation of nineteen Cherokees, eleven whites, and one black slave. Bushyhead's church provided just one example of interethnic cooperation and cultural survival in a time characterized by decline and loss. Bushyhead's efforts were interrupted by the removal crisis of the 1830s, a battle the tribe lost in 1838. Sixty thousand Indians from south of the Ohio River and 10,000 more from north of the river were removed to what is now Kansas and Oklahoma.

Indian removal becomes even less justifiable in the case of several southern and northern tribes that had achieved the Jeffersonian definition of *assimilation* – if one defines the term by the acceptance of Christianity, the dependence on commercial agriculture, and the reformation of traditional governments. Tribes such as the Cherokees achieved these goals, illustrating the fact that race rather than cultural practices became the primary motive for removal. But President Jackson left no doubt that the expansion of rights and opportunities for white Americans would take precedence over tribal sovereignty. He rejected the Cherokees' plan to form an independent state in Georgia and Alabama, arguing in his first annual message to the U.S. Congress that "their [Cherokees] attempt to establish an independent government would not be countenanced by the Executive of the United States, and advised them to emigrate beyond the Mississippi or submit to the laws of the United States." Removal agents threatened tribes with the loss of sovereignty and the jurisdiction of the state. This terrified tribal leaders because Indians did not have the right to testify against whites, to hold public office, or to vote. Bereft of federal protection under Jackson, most tribes agreed to removal in order to avoid the abuses of their white neighbors.

Yet, Jackson carefully balanced such naked aggression toward the tribes with equally moralistic support for continued philanthropic efforts in the newly settled Indian Territory. Missionaries from the Old Northwest, including the noted author and speaker Isaac McCoy, advised Jackson on Indian affairs during the removal struggle. Jackson promised continued funding for philanthropic efforts west of the Mississippi where, he felt, "the benevolent may continue to teach them the arts of civilization," thereby legitimizing his removal efforts. Jackson recognized that his opponents might defeat the Indian Removal Act if justification for the measure remained based on the expansion of democracy and economic power for the rest of the country. Jackson's commitment to philanthropy gave him the political leverage necessary to defeat the opponents of the act.

* * *

Hundreds of assimilation-minded philanthropists responded to the growing missionary impulse and the benefit of government funding in the years following removal. Ironically, increased competition between missionaries limited the gains desired by politicians and reformers. Most tribes hosted more than one missionary society, thus complicating the government's goal of tribal consolidation and eventual dissolution. Village leaders formed partnerships with individual missions and used their newfound denominational identities against tribal leaders intent on centralizing power. Small numbers of Christian converts thus associated mission churches with their preremoval village identities rather than their larger tribal identities.

Nevertheless, Native American involvement with missionaries deepened after removal to the Indian Territory because of the new institutions and leadership opportunities created by the missions. Evangelical missionaries in particular established a large number of supporting roles for those interested in Christianity. Missionaries themselves recognized that the assistance of Native leaders was essential to the survival of their missions. Native preachers, exhorters, assistants, and interpreters were needed to translate the message verbally and in print. In addition, Indian families hosted religious services. Belle Greene, daughter of the Shawnee Methodist missionary Jesse

Greene, recalled that the Shawnees in attendance at their services "would arise in the congregation and testify." Another Methodist missionary remembered that the Shawnees "were especially gifted in prayer and exhortation." Hosting religious services became another avenue for enhancing one's personal and familial prestige on the reservation. Missionaries noted the active participation of Shawnee congregants and the mutual reliance such participation encouraged.

Unwittingly, Baptist and Methodist missionaries established institutions and channels of communication that provided Indians with a platform from which they could ask, answer, and argue about fundamental questions regarding their tribe's past, present, and future. Across the Indian Territory, tribesmen struggled with the impact of consolidation onto united tribal reservations. Despite shared tribal affiliations, many tribesmen were unfamiliar, even unknown, to the majority of their kinsmen after many years of separation. The institutions and rhetoric of Christianity provided channels through which strangers could communicate. In exhorting kinsmen to join the faith at a camp meeting, testifying to one's sinful existence, or even in translating a preacher's message, Christian institutions presented American Indians with a means toward national conversations.

Evangelical Christianity did not simply impose new values and institutions on a powerless people; the practice of Christianity provided Indians with a chance to live their religion in new ways. As historian David Hall writes, religion "is shaped and experienced in the interplay among venues of everyday experience . . . in the necessary and mutually transforming exchanges between religious authorities and the broader communities of practitioners." Baptists and Methodists, in particular, made numerous concessions to their congregants between 1830 and 1860, building a faith reflective of the power struggles and rhythms of Native life, even as it transformed tribal value systems.

Missionaries also sought relationships with prominent men who might lead villagers and family members to join the faith. In this way, Native American leaders acted as channels through which missionaries could reach large numbers of potential converts. For example, the Ohio Shawnee leader Blackfeather became the singlemost important supporter of the Baptist mission on the Shawnee reservation. The self-proclaimed war chief and successor of Tecumseh used Baptist religious meetings to address his kinsmen. In fact, Baptist missionaries based the success of their sermons on the emotional engagement of those in attendance. However Blackfeather's speeches, conducted after the missionaries' sermons in the Shawnee language, most likely deserve some of the credit for the attentiveness of his kinsmen.

Blackfeather achieved prominence among the Baptists even though he resisted their efforts to be baptized for more than eleven years, a tireless effort chronicled in the *American Baptist Magazine.* He refused the sacrament despite the fact that he had hosted religious meetings and spoken to his kinsmen regarding the virtues of Christianity. Prior to his conversion, Baptist missionaries were clearly pleased that a highly regarded Shawnee had expressed an interest in their message. The Baptists noted that "attention to religious worship has greatly increased since the development of Capt. Blackfeather's views." Nevertheless, by 1835, the Baptists could only boast a total of eight converts between a united Shawnee-Delaware church.

The Baptists' poor showing among Blackfeather's followers is curious and calls into question Shawnee motives for working with them. Blackfeather's sermons do not reveal Shawnee motives because they were not recorded. But a closer look at the activities of Baptist missionary Jotham Meeker partially explains the appeal of his philanthropic mission. A child of one of the missionaries recalled:

When an Indian first commenced to plow, he [Meeker] would go with him and hold the plow, and show him how to manage it. He would often go and work with an Indian for hours, and then would sit down to rest, taking that opportunity to instruct the Indian in some matter of religion or morality.

In nearly all of his activities, including the printing of Shawnee language materials, Meeker worked with the Shawnees he hoped to convert. His diary and other accounts of his life describe a man who worked more hours in the fields than the pulpit. Meeker epitomized what religious historian Edwin Gaustad describes as "the farmer-preacher," a man who "earned his living as a farmer but who – in addition – took the lead in organizing a church and proclaiming a social gospel."

Throughout the 1830s, the Shawnees continued to regard the evangelicals as more of a curiosity than a serious religious and cultural alternative to their own traditions. Blackfeather's ambivalence toward full membership in the Baptist church also indicates that many Shawnees did not regard participation in evangelical Christianity as antagonistic to Shawnee customs.

Chronic economic difficulties after removal meant that most Shawnees remained preoccupied with survival. The missionary response to such desperation often meant the difference between the success and failure of a mission. The Shawnees, for example, forced the Methodist missionaries among them to drop their demand for English-only instruction in their school and to adopt the rival Baptist translation of Shawnee into script. According to Baptist missionary Ira Blanchard, the Shawnees told the Methodist missionary that "if the books were shut out from [the Indians'] society, [the Methodists] were too." After the council's vote, the Methodists reached an agreement with the Baptists for the publication of Methodist hymns in the Shawnee language. Missionary assistance in transforming oral languages into written form was widely recognized as essential to every tribe's survival after removal. With notable exceptions – including the noted Cherokee orthographer Sequoyah – missionaries translated Native languages into written form. Such assistance provided a service to both believers and nonbelievers, many of whom recognized that illiteracy increased the chance of ill treatment from American officials and settlers alike. The "Chiefs, Counsellors, Headmen" of the Shawnees admitted as much in 1838, stating that "we have borne many impositions because we are ignorant and illiterate. This and other difficulties would not have happened . . . if we had fairly understood everything."

Frontier Methodism, with its emphasis on individual conversion and the camp meeting, also appealed to the Shawnee people. Camp meetings granted the laity significant control over the proceedings, giving those interested a more active role in Christianity. These religious events were extraordinarily egalitarian and diverse – bringing together Indians and whites united in their hope for spiritual renewal. The diversity of the crowds and the shared responsibility for their success gave those Indians who participated an unparalleled sense of connection and belonging compared with earlier missionary efforts. In fact, camp meetings and other large religious gatherings were common along the Missouri border with the Indian Territory in the 1830s and 1840s. In 1835, more than one hundred Shawnees, Delawares, and Kickapoos traveled to Arrow Rock, Missouri – the site of the Shawnees last stop on their journey westward during removal – to attend a religious meeting of the Missouri Conference. The Shawnees returned to their former homelands as part of a new Methodist community after enduring many years of exclusion and genocide at the hands of the neighboring whites. Conferences and camp meetings brought these former enemies into a Christian community that embraced both Indians and whites.

On a personal level, missionaries to the Shawnees frequently related the benefits of working with Christian tribesmen. Methodist missionary

Nathan Scarritt described his relationship with his translators, noting their divergent styles and effectiveness, and was generally untroubled by his reliance upon them. The Bible guided Scarritt's understanding of his relationship with the Shawnee interpreters. Paraphrasing Proverbs, 27:17, he wrote that "steel sharpens steel, a fire is kindled more easily from two firebrands, when brought into contact, than from either, when used separately." Interpreters were far more than figures off to the side as a white preacher dominated the crowd. Scarritt recalled that it was common for interpreters to "leave the pulpit and make [their] way through the congregation, scattering the holy fire as [they] went, until almost the entire congregation would be on its feet praising and glorifying God." A synergy existed between interpreters and missionaries in translating the Christian message. Methodist and Baptist missionaries who were not literate in the Shawnee language had to depend on the emotional responses of the audience and the reliability of their interpreters to gauge the efficacy of this shared message.

Some Native people, such as Mackinaw Boachman, moved from esteemed positions within their tribes to licensed preachers. Accounts of his identity vary somewhat, but evidence suggests that Boachman was born in Michigan, the son of a French fur trader and a Chippewa woman. His diverse ancestry is typical of most American Indian people of the Great Lakes during the early republic. Boachman's mother fled to the Potawatomis at an early age, and he remained with the tribe for the rest of his childhood. Boachman eventually went to work as a hunter and trapper with the American Fur Company – a profession that pulled him out of the Great Lakes and into the Trans-Mississippi West. Marriage into a prominent Shawnee family on the reservation ultimately led Boachman to positions of authority among both the Shawnees and the Methodists.

Boachman stood apart from the majority of the Christian Indians in the Indian Territory because he was the first to become a preacher and missionary at a time when most Indians occupied less prestigious positions in the church hierarchy. As a licensed preacher, Boachman held the same position as Nathan Scarritt by 1843. The Reverend Joab Spencer, a missionary to the Shawnees in the 1850s and 1860s, credited Boachman with "exhort[ing] his Shawnee friends to forsake paganism and become Christians." Boachman's multitribal upbringing made him particularly useful to the Methodists. His linguistic skills allowed him to preach in several Native languages. Before his death in 1848, Boachman worked as a missionary to the Potawatomis, Sacs, Chippewas, and Weas.

Those Shawnees affiliated with the Methodist mission played a crucial role in presenting and translating Methodism to American Indians beyond the reservation. Exhorters were particularly important to the success of the camp meeting, for their chief duty was to invite "sinners to enter the pen by reminding them of the prospects of hell and damnation awaiting those who failed to take the step." They were responsible for those who remained unconvinced of the need for Christian conversion. At an intertribal camp meeting in 1842, a Methodist missionary described the exhorter's role. Three Kansa Indians had continually frustrated Methodist attempts to convince them of the need for conversion. As the camp meeting wore on, however, one of their number "fell from where he was sitting . . . trembling under all the horrors of deep and pungent conviction." At this point, "Brother Fish" of the Shawnees arrived and "pointed him to Christ." Soon thereafter, the Kansa woke from his confused state and remarked that "the good Lord loves me now." Fish had done his job by leading the unconverted among them into the church. These early successes allowed the Methodists to expand their operation from their base on the Shawnee reservation to neighboring tribes, including the Kansa.

The structures and institutions established by missionaries, from gristmills to schools, acted as important sites that enabled American Indians to make sense of American culture. Indeed, as this study suggests, American Indians negotiated the terms of dependency and cultural survival with these agents of assimilation. However, there are also numerous cases of Indian cultural survival that do not involve direct missionary intervention. Between the beginning of the nineteenth century and the Civil War, American Indians reevaluated traditional rituals and considered the strengths and weaknesses of Christianity. Military defeat, economic dislocation, and the loss of territory led to hard questions about Indian identity, belief, and ritual. These questions opened the door for alternative faiths, including evangelical Christianity and its promise of salvation and deliverance. The Shawnee Prophet crafted his religious movement, blending Christian and Algonquian ideas and practices, in this cultural context of defeat and loss. The Shawnee Prophet and others like him offer intriguing examples of cultural syncretism outside philanthropic institutional boundaries.

The story of the Vermillion Kickapoos, a tribe originally from the Indiana-Illinois border, fits well within this tradition and speaks to the spiritual discontent in which a new chief, Kenekuk, rose to power. As a troubled young man, Kenekuk became an alcoholic, killed an uncle, and was banished from the tribe. After living in white settlements near his former village, Kenekuk returned home sober with a plan for the spiritual renewal of his people. Kenekuk's demand that his followers destroy their sacred bundles speaks to a level of discontent beyond material concerns and struggles for power within tribes. However, Kenekuk and his Kickapoo followers did not ask for or receive the assistance of missionaries in their fight with the federal government. Rather, Kenekuk founded a religious movement that borrowed heavily from the assimilationist ideas of the day in order to combat removal and retain the tribe's homelands. For example, Kenekuk advocated male control of farming, peace with neighboring whites, and temperance. He also demanded that his followers confess their sins and submit to whipping to gain absolution. Like many other Indian advocates of similar reforms, Kenekuk lacked a hereditary right to lead his people.

Kenekuk's reformist agenda combined elements of Kickapoo customs with many of the goals articulated by missionaries and agents before the Civil War. His independence from missionaries and government officials contributed to the tribe's prolonged resistance to land sales and individually owned allotments. Kenekuk argued that "no people owned the lands – that all was His, and not to forget to tell the white people that when we went into council." In the fall of 1832, the Vermillion Kickapoos lost their battle against removal from the Old Northwest – but removal only increased Kenekuk's power among his tribesmen. His kinsmen consulted prayer sticks engraved with traditional figures – a creative invention indicative of the religious exchange of the era – to guide them in their daily lives. The prayer sticks included engraved symbols indicative of the highly permeable spiritual border between Indians and whites and allowed the Kickapoos to craft their own unified response to American designs.

Most of their Indian neighbors were forced to abandon their reservations in Indian Territory (modern Kansas) once again and head south of the path of white settlements. But after Kenekuk's death in 1852, approximately 400 of his followers managed to resist removal by holding their reservation lands in common. Ten thousand of their emigrant Indian neighbors had succumbed to American pressure and allotted their reservations throughout the 1860s, a concession that forced them into what is now Oklahoma.

Following the Kansas-Nebraska Act and the dissolution of the Indian Territory in 1854, Indian-white relations devolved and the philanthropic dreams of those who worked with the tribes remained unrealized. Isaac

McCoy died before his dream of an Indian Canaan – a region in which assimilation could proceed slowly under the benevolent supervision of Christian missionaries – also succumbed to the renewed fury of western settlement. Indian converts and the churches of which they were a part were forced to close as white squatters besieged their reservations. More than one hundred thousand settlers crowded across the border between 1854 and 1860. In the racist and often lawless environment of "Bleeding Kansas," the practice of Christianity became an individual rather than a community affair. Christian Shawnees were not welcome in the newly established Baptist and Methodist churches of eastern Kansas. Indeed, the murders of several Shawnees, their subagent William Gay, and the Methodist missionary Thomas Johnson between 1858 and 1865 illustrate the perils faced by American Indians and their supporters on what remained of their lands.

Christian missionaries between the age of Jefferson and the Civil War were driven by the goal of assimilation: the cultural extinction of American Indians. Interracial unity would proceed peacefully, they argued, as Indian people shed their identities and integrated themselves into American life. Philanthropists assumed that Indians would gladly disavow their cultures and become Americans. Indian resilience amid such aggressive attempts at social control speaks to the vitality of Native American cultures, even after the onset of economic and political dependence on the United States.

Countless ordinary Indian women and men like Sophie Bigknife showed resilience and determination to create their own individual and familial responses to philanthropists. Well-known leaders such as Tenskwatawa and Kenekuk – architects of independent and calculated responses to American strategies – also contributed to the cultural survival of their people amid the heavy-handed techniques of most nineteenth-century philanthropists. While philanthropists sought to remake American Indians in their own image, men like Jesse Bushyhead, Mackinaw Boachman, and Kenekuk were determined to preserve their cultural identities. They crafted a response that varied according to region, denomination, and tribe. These success stories among tribes originally from east of the Mississippi River reveal the determination of a people intent on redirecting assimilationist policies and programs according to their own needs.

Future scholarship on American Indians and philanthropy should consider the Indian response to the agents and rhetoric of assimilation. Until recently, scholarly attention has focused on philanthropic donors rather than American Indians themselves. American Indians used the institutions and leadership positions created by missionaries as outlets for the expression of their unique identities. Interdenominational competition for Indian converts also ensured that tribal governments modeled after the U.S. government would not destroy previously independent Indian villages and their hereditary leaders. American Indian preachers, exhorters, and translators were often responsible for translating Christianity to their people. Scholars who focus on donors and the rhetoric of assimilation fail to notice the many instances of negotiation, compromise, and cultural survival common in this crucial period of Indian-white relations.

6

ANTEBELLUM REFORM: SALVATION, SELF-CONTROL, AND SOCIAL TRANSFORMATION

WENDY GAMBER

"God hath made man a moral free agent," Charles Grandison Finney, the nineteenth century's most famous revivalist, explained. For Finney, this belief had an important corollary. Of true Christians, he insisted, "To the universal reformation of the world they stand committed." "Moral free agents" were responsible for their personal salvation and, by extension, for their earthly behavior. But they also had a duty to remake society.

Thousands of Americans acted on these beliefs. The first half of the nineteenth century witnessed a wide ranging, varied, and creative outpouring of "enthusiasms." During the decades before the Civil War, Americans organized crusades to end poverty and drunkenness, enforce the Sunday Sabbath, abolish slavery, emancipate women, rehabilitate criminals, cure insanity, and ensure world peace. They designed and inhabited model communities. They idealized new forms of behavior. The most radical challenged the very underpinnings of racial inequality.

The creature historians call antebellum reform was a complex and contradictory phenomenon. Some movements had conservative, others radical, implications. Unable to agree on the best ways to reshape American society, reformers argued among themselves; indeed, more conservative activists often reserved their fiercest attacks for "ultras." Some reform efforts empowered women, working-class people, and African Americans; others reinforced existing ethnic, racial, class, and gender hierarchies; still others did both. Yet, almost all antebellum reformers shared certain fundamental beliefs: Almost all believed that it was possible not only to change the world, but also to perfect it. Perhaps most important – and perhaps most alien from an early twenty-first century perspective – antebellum reformers were particularly prone to taking their own advice. To be sure, by the 1850s, as reformers increasingly substituted formal political action and legal coercion for voluntary efforts, ever-widening gulfs separated activists from those whom they sought to reform. But, in its heyday, Finney's characterization of antebellum reform rang true. Like the nineteenth-century missionaries described by Amanda Porterfield, the "True Christians" who immersed themselves in numerous reform efforts saw few contradictions between philanthropy and self-improvement.

History textbooks usually describe the moral crusades of the early nineteenth century as "reforms" rather than "philanthropies." (Interestingly, reformers themselves often characterized their work as "benevolent" or "philanthropic.") Yet, philanthropy was a central feature of antebellum reform. Like the philanthropists described elsewhere in this volume, antebellum reformers saw themselves as missionaries who could remake their world; as with other philanthropists, helping others and transforming oneself (what Porterfield calls "reciprocity") were two sides of the same coin.

The discussion that follows does not pretend to offer a complete account of the myriad enthusiasms that swept the United States during the first half of the nineteenth century – an undertaking that would require a book in itself. Rather, it settles for a close analysis of two types of institutions – insane asylums and utopian communities – and two moral crusades – temperance and abolitionism. The discussion that follows is hardly exhaustive, but I hope that it suggests something of the richness and complexity of antebellum reform.

* * *

In many respects, antebellum reform did not so much represent a radical break with the past as an intensification of earlier trends. Certainly, the eighteenth-century turn toward "sensibility," described by G. J. Barker-Benfield, was a necessary precondition for nineteenth-century reform. The Second Great Awakening was a more immediate catalyst. Many reform movements could trace their origins – indirectly if not directly – to this dramatic series of religious revivals. The Second Great Awakening, a movement confined to Protestant churches, flowed across denominational lines and muddled doctrinal distinctions. Revivals (i.e., emotional affairs often presided over by flamboyant ministers, during which tearful sinners acknowledged their sins and their desires for salvation) attracted Protestants from many different sects, and those who counted themselves among the "saved" usually maintained that the particular church to which one belonged was less important than whether one embraced certain fundamental beliefs.

One of these beliefs was millennialism. Millennialists believed, quite literally, that the millennium – a thousand-year period that would precede the final judgment – was "approaching near." While they offered competing estimates as to when the millennium would arrive, they agreed that when it did, peace, justice, and righteousness would reign. Even philanthropists who worked outside the confines of mainline Protestantism – indeed, even those whose orientation was essentially secular – embraced variants of millennialism. All believed that a better world was not only possible but also inevitable.

Millennialism was not a new doctrine; however, it gained strength in the years following the American Revolution in part because it reinforced common attitudes. It seemed to confirm the notion – dear to the hearts of many Americans – that the United States had been chosen by God to fulfill a great mission. Millennialism also complemented widely shared beliefs in progress and economic development: national prosperity and technological advances, according to this line of thinking, represented evidence of God's favor. Perhaps most important, millennialism provided a justification for action. Antebellum adherents believed that people should work to realize their vision of a perfect society rather than passively waiting for the millennium to arrive. After all, Finney claimed that true Christians committed themselves to the "universal reformation of the world." As Porterfield shows, this belief prompted some Americans to dedicate their lives to foreign missions. Others, like the reformers described here, chose to work closer to home by devoting themselves to remaking American society.

At the time that many Christians embraced millennialism, they abandoned predestination, a theological doctrine that had been central to many Protestant denominations. Predestination maintained that all human beings were innately sinful and that only by the grace of God could anyone be saved; the individual could play no role in ensuring his or her salvation. Always a difficult creed to follow, predestination had been slowly crumbling since the end of the eighteenth century. But nineteenth-century theologians rejected the doctrine most forcefully, popularizing its antithesis: free will. Finney explained the concept in simple and appealing terms: "The will is free and . . . sin and holiness are voluntary acts of mind." Free will shifted the responsibility for salvation from God to the individual. It was up to the individual sinner to decide whether he or she wished to be saved; the individual, in other words, determined his or her own fate. This belief had

secular as well as religious consequences, and it served secular as well as
religious purposes.

* * *

Those who applied the notion of free will to worldly affairs believed that
one's station in life was not fixed. No longer "predestined" to remain in a
particular occupation or in a particular social class, a person (at least a man)
was "free" to rise from rags to riches. But he was also free to fall. While free
will – whether spiritual or temporal – created exciting new possibilities, it
also placed a great deal of responsibility on the individual's shoulders. It
was *your* fault, not God's will, if you failed to succeed on earth or to gain
salvation in heaven.

An emphasis on values and behavior – what nineteenth-century Americans called "character" – underlay this notion of individual responsibility.
People of "good" moral character enjoyed worldly success and attained salvation; people of "bad" moral character deserved to fail and to be damned
for eternity. Proponents of free will believed that one's character was not
fixed, that it could be changed. It was this very belief that motivated many
reform movements. Thus, reformers tended to focus on changing individual
behavior. Crusaders against poverty, for example, established almshouses
where the poor could be taught "steady habits": hard work, discipline, and
sobriety. Almshouse advocates assumed that the poor themselves bore responsibility for their plight; if only they could be taught "correct" behavior,
poverty would be eliminated.

The example of almshouses raises the question of defining the relationship between reform movements on one hand, and their larger social and
economic contexts on the other. This is an especially important issue for
the antebellum period. Americans who lived during the first half of the
nineteenth century witnessed profound economic and social transformations. Certainly, historians see urbanization; the increasing importance of
regional, national, and even international markets; early industrialization;
and – as Barker-Benfield notes – the "consumer revolution" as developments that emerged in the eighteenth century, some of them even earlier.
These transformations accelerated dramatically in the early nineteenth century. They brought unprecedented prosperity to some (especially merchant
capitalists, industrial employers, and commercial farmers), declining standards of living and the loss of economic independence to others (especially
skilled workers and self-sufficient farmers).

Noting the "fit" among the values – sobriety, discipline, delayed gratification – many nineteenth-century philanthropists advocated and the

demands of an urban, industrial society, some historians have interpreted reform movements as attempts at "social control." According to this view, reformers (most of whom were white, native-born, and middle class) disregarded the hardships caused by larger social and economic forces, opting instead to place the blame – erroneously – on individuals' moral failings. Their emphasis on discipline and sobriety served the needs of new industrial employers who wanted a stable work force; they sided with those who gained the most from what historians have called the "market revolution" against those who benefited the least.

Certainly, much evidence supports this view. It is easy to see "social control" at work when we consider the career of Neal Dow, a wealthy Portland, Maine, entrepreneur and temperance activist. In the 1830s, Dow persuaded the city's employers to deny their workers their customary morning and afternoon rum breaks, a move that no doubt increased employees' efficiency and bosses' profits. Yet, social control offers too mechanistic and too simplistic an explanation for a complex phenomenon. Such a thesis might explain the temperance crusade, but sheds little light on a movement like abolitionism, whose members not only rejected materialism, but also promoted the then-radical doctrine of racial equality. Moreover, recent scholarship suggests that previous accounts overemphasized the "middle-class" character of antebellum reform. Workers organized their own temperance societies; abolitionism attracted thousands of ordinary Americans, many of them just barely able to claim middle-class membership.

Yet, to deny the existence of any relationship between economic change and the rise of antebellum reform movements would be as erroneous as treating philanthropy as a capitalist conspiracy. It is difficult to imagine the ascendancy of such values as sobriety, discipline, and efficiency in the absence of rapid economic development; philanthropists were creatures of their time and place. Abolitionists, who saw slavery as the epitome of a corrupt market society, believed in the superiority of "free labor." Free labor exacted heavy demands, even from those whom it benefited the most. Many merchant capitalists and industrial employers lost their businesses and their fortunes during the panics that swept the nation in 1819, 1837, and 1857. Melodramatic tales of genteel families forced into poverty – a staple of antebellum popular fiction – contained more than a germ of truth. Beneath millennial optimism lay a strong undercurrent of anxiety.

The concept of self-control helps to account for both optimism and anxiety and offers a means of linking together seemingly disparate philanthropic ventures. Whether a behavior to be coercively imposed on others or a moral code rigorously imposed on oneself, self-control could be either repressive or liberating. At its most expansive, self-control meant something more like self-determination. It offered a radical faith in the possibility of individual transformation, of realizing the secular promise of free will. An unyielding faith in the virtues of self-control encouraged philanthropists to think of poverty as an individual failing, not a structural problem. It also prompted Americans to anxiously scrutinize their own behavior, to consciously subject themselves to draconian regimens and routines. However, such a faith also allowed white abolitionists to transcend, at least partially, notions of African American inferiority. Few reformers – even the most irritatingly self-righteous – were hypocrites. Whatever they expected of others, they usually expected of themselves.

* * *

Two very different kinds of institutions illustrate the tensions between optimism and anxiety, self-determination and coercion. Both physically embodied their founders' social visions. Both – albeit in very different ways – suggest the relationship between philanthropy and its larger social and economic context. Together they represent both the conservative and the radical potential of antebellum reform.

* * *

There were no insane asylums in colonial America; in fact institutions of any type were rarities. Families usually cared for mentally ill relatives; towns or counties sometimes doled out meager financial assistance to caregivers. Cities consigned insane residents not to specialized institutions, but to jails and almshouses. Local officials expressed little interest in curing the insane; rather, they were concerned primarily with protecting the larger community from people who might pose dire threats to public safety. Such arrangements were not conducive to humane treatment. Mentally ill persons might be chained in attics or jail cells or locked in sheds. Dorothea Dix, who devoted her life to improving the treatment for the insane, reported the results of a tour of Massachusetts prisons, jails, and almshouses to the state legislature in 1843:

I proceed, gentlemen . . . to call your attention to the present state of insane persons confined within this Commonwealth, in cages, closets, cellars, stalls, pens! Chained, naked, beaten with rods, and lashed into obedience . . . Lincoln. A woman in a cage. Medford. One idiotic subject chained, and one in a close stall for seventeen years. Pepperell. One often doubly chained, hand and foot . . . Granville. One often closely confined; now losing the use of his limbs from want of exercise.

By the time Dix submitted her report, conditions had already changed dramatically for a significant portion of the mentally ill population. States like Massachusetts and New York had established public asylums in the 1830s; by 1860, twenty-eight of the nation's thirty-three states had done so. Several private institutions also opened their doors.

Mental hospitals, public as well as private, were secular expressions of millennial optimism. Insane asylums, by their very nature, were coercive institutions; individuals usually did not choose to commit themselves. Daily routines evinced an obsessive concern with order and control. Yet, these very routines embodied sincere beliefs in the possibility of restoring the mentally afflicted to sanity. Just as reformers believed that poverty, drunkenness, and slavery could be eliminated, so too did the architects of asylums believe that insanity could be cured.

At the same time, asylums were firmly rooted in larger economic and social contexts. Definitions of insanity in antebellum America hardly were "objective"; indeed, they demonstrate that mental illness, like all disease, is at least partly socially constructed. Diagnoses of both symptoms and causes were inexorably linked to the changes wrought by economic development. Irrational, violent behavior characterized one as insane, but so did aversions to ambition, hard work, discipline, and order. In 1845, a New York physician listed some of the causes of insanity: poor health, religious anxiety, financial losses, political enthusiasm, and frustrated ambition. Samuel Woodward, the superintendent of the Massachusetts State Lunatic Asylum, rendered the links between insanity and market society even more explicit; he attributed mental illness to "overtrading, debt, bankruptcy, sudden reverses, and disappointed hopes."

Indeed, early mental institutions offered their inmates the equivalent of a crash course in self-control. Psychiatrists believed that the key to a cure was to remove the individual from his or her current environment; temporary residence in a "well-ordered asylum" – a microcosm of an imagined well-ordered society – would enable him or her once again to function within society. Hence, many institutions were located in rural areas away from the hustle and bustle of the city; hence, many forbade visits or even correspondence from inmates' family and friends. "Loving and tender letters containing some ill-timed news, or the melancholy tidings of sickness and death . . . may destroy weeks and months of favorable progress," one official explained.

Order was a key feature of insane asylums, if not *the* key feature. Even their architectural designs self-consciously emphasized symmetry and regularity. Order pervaded daily routines. As one physician explained, "The hours for rising, dressing, and washing... for meals, labor, occupation, amusement, walking, riding, etc., should be regulated by the most perfect precision. The utmost neatness must be observed in the dormitories; the meals must be orderly and comfortably served... The physician and assistants must make their visits at certain hours." The Pennsylvania Hospital for the Insane required patients to wake at 5:00, take their medicines at 6:00, eat breakfast at 6:30, proceed to a physical examination at 8:00, work until their 12:30 dinner, resume work until 6 o'clock tea, and retire to bed precisely at 9:30. Routines of this sort are familiar enough to anyone who has visited a prison or mental hospital today. But this enforced segmentation of time – even the use of clock time itself – was new to many Americans in the antebellum period, both those who resided inside and those who lived outside institutions. Similarly, Americans – sane or insane – had only recently become familiar with the "moral treatment" prescribed by the director of McLean Hospital: "systematic, regular employment." As the historian David J. Rothman notes, "these qualities were far more in keeping with an urban, industrial order than a local, agrarian one."

Despite draconian routines, which resembled those of newly erected factories, early insane asylums reflected a radical faith in the potential of individuals. They were guided by the premise that environment, not heredity, caused mental illness. But as the numbers of "insane" persons multiplied and as state legislatures – propelled into action by philanthropists such as Dix – began to allocate funds to build public mental hospitals, enthusiasm began to wane.

The simple difference between public and private institutions does much to explain growing pessimism. Because they catered primarily to a well-heeled clientele, private hospitals like Boston's McLean Asylum or Philadelphia's Friends' Asylum could maintain favorable doctor-patient ratios. The doctors who staffed such institutions and the patients treated in them were likely to come from similar backgrounds. The population of public institutions, on the other hand, consisted disproportionately of people dependent on the state for their care, many of whom were not only poor, but also foreign-born, most of them Irish and German. These ethnic distinctions – accentuated by differences of language and by real and perceived differences in culture – widened the gulf between patients and their physicians, who increasingly saw them as "others" thoroughly unlike themselves. As patient populations outstripped available space and funds (legislative allocations had never been generous), public institutions simply became places in which to confine mentally ill people, not cure them.

New scientific theories of "race" meshed nicely with a growing interest in genetic explanations. According to this logic, some racial and ethnic groups were simply more prone to insanity than others; of course, if insanity were an inherited condition, no treatment could cure it. By the 1850s, most public mental hospitals had become custodial institutions that exemplified the prejudices and inequalities of American society. American-born patients who paid for their care received the best treatment, followed by the nonpaying native-born, immigrants, and African Americans (who received access to public mental-health services only in the North). Public asylums quickly came to resemble the nonspecialized institutions that had so troubled Dix. Persons who applied for poor relief in California in the 1850s and 1860s, for example, who were not legal residents of the county in which they sought aid were committed to the State Hospital at Stockton. Originally intended to serve the mentally ill, it had become a de facto almshouse as well.

Yet, custodialism also triumphed simply because philanthropists' millennial expectations for wide-ranging and immediate "cures" were far too high. As rates of recidivism climbed, even the staffs of private mental hospitals tempered their initial optimism. As medical opinion shifted toward explanations based on heredity, private hospitals also began to assume custodial functions. By the 1870s, comfort – not philosophy – differentiated public mental institutions from private ones. Poor people declared insane could expect to be warehoused in overcrowded, financially strapped institutions; rich people, in relatively spacious and well-appointed ones.

* * *

At the same time that model prisons, insane asylums, and orphanages proliferated, some Americans engaged themselves in constructing their own exemplary communities. Many "utopias" were short-lived and left behind few traces of their existence; thus, we may never know their exact number. We do know that the antebellum period – especially the 1840s – represented the historical high-water mark for what one reformer termed "socialistic excitements."

Utopias were very different sorts of institutions than were asylums (although some, especially those inspired by the French socialist Charles Fourier, placed every bit as much emphasis on architecture and order). Unlike mental hospitals, utopias were voluntary communities (one reason, in fact, why many so quickly dissolved). Unlike asylums, many utopian communities drew their inspiration directly from evangelical Protestantism. They represented the aversion to mainstream culture felt by the purest of Christians. Distant from the American mainstream, they constituted one of the least popular reform movements, in part because they were associated with radical forms of social organization and behavior, in part because they required intense commitments from their inhabitants. Yet, model communities had much in common with their more conventional institutional counterparts. Both removed their inhabitants to what their founders believed was the simpler, purer atmosphere of the countryside. Both shared a belief in the possibility of individual transformation; exposure to the proper environment – whether hospital ward or Fourierist phalanx – perfected individuals and, by extension, society. Finally, both asylums and utopias exemplified similar tensions between withdrawing from the larger society and emulating it. Both highly valued self-control.

Why include insular communities in a discussion of philanthropy? The answer, in part, is that antebellum utopian experiments looked outward as well as inward. Their inhabitants saw themselves as missionaries: by providing examples of perfect communities that others could emulate, utopian societies would hasten the arrival of the millennium. George Rapp, the founder of Harmony, Pennsylvania, and New Harmony, Indiana, declared that "without doubt . . . the kingdom of Jesus Christ [is] approaching near." Inhabitants of the Oneida community in upstate New York believed that the millennium had already begun, precisely on June 1, 1847. Even more secular communities, such as Hopedale and Brook Farm, owed their creation to millennial optimism; they too saw themselves as models for a more perfect society.

Antebellum utopian communities embodied a curious paradox. On one hand, their members self-consciously withdrew from a larger society that they considered corrupt and imperfect. Many communitarian societies were just that: they eschewed economic competition and private property, central tenets of nineteenth-century American society. On the other, as we shall see, they emulated aspects of the very society they sought to reject. Two of the most successful utopian experiments, the Shaker and Oneida communities, illustrate these tensions well.

The Shakers predated the Second Great Awakening, but they experienced their greatest growth in the 1830s and 1840s. Shakers intrigued people influenced by revivals but who found conventional denominations unappealing. They also attracted Americans who had a desire to withdraw from the "world" and all it entailed: materialism, competition, sexuality. Founded by "Mother" Ann Lee, an English immigrant who died in the 1780s, the Shaker sect believed that God was both male and female. Jesus represented God's masculine side; Lee, God's feminine side. Mother Ann's birth thus marked the beginning of the millennium.

Shakers founded communities that in many respects were truly radical by the standards of the day. Believing that "temporal blessings" distracted one's thoughts from God, they held all property in common. True to their theological convictions, Shakers emphasized the spiritual equality of men and women; both sexes shared spiritual authority. The Shakers' distinguishing feature, however, was their commitment to celibacy. In keeping with Lee's "abhorrence of the fleshy cohabitation of the sexes" – a stance that likely originated in her own unhappy marriage, numerous miscarriages, and the deaths of her four young children – they rejected "animal passions." Celibacy, Shakers believed, would free them from sin and reestablish the "proper" order of God's creation – an order disrupted by sexual temptation. Mastering the libido thus offered liberation rather than repression.

Shakers devoted enormous energy to maintaining celibacy. Like asylums – albeit on a much humbler scale – they enlisted architecture in the service of their goals. Shakers housed men and women in separate living quarters; some communities even built separate male and female dormitories. Men and women ascended or descended separate stairways. They ate in the same dining rooms but sat at separate tables; they worshipped together but seated themselves on opposite sides of the meetinghouse: women on the left, men on the right. Private conversations between men and women were prohibited; even handshakes were forbidden.

Celibacy required self-control; as Shakers, saw it, male self-control in particular. "If sexual coition ceases in the male, it must cease in the female, of course," one chronicler explained. Although mainstream evangelicals stressed woman's "purer" nature, Shakers' beliefs concerning female sexuality were ambivalent; they viewed women, alternately, as victims of male vice and dangerous temptresses. However, in emphasizing male self-control, Shakers bore a surprising resemblance to their more worldly counterparts, for men who lived outside utopian communities also practiced various forms of sexual self-restraint.

As many contemporaries described it, the members of the notorious Oneida Community in upstate New York practiced "licentiousness," the polar opposite of self-control. Yet, Oneida was self-consciously a religious experiment, one that derived its beliefs from ideas with which many less radical reformers would have agreed. The problem – from their critics' point of view – was that Oneidans took these beliefs to their logical extremes. One of these doctrines was perfectionism. Revivalists like Finney preached that individuals could save themselves; in accepting Christ, they could wash away their sins. Clergy disagreed over the extent to which one could become free of sin – or "perfect" – in earthly life. They recognized that perfectionism had a subversive potential: What if those who had been saved declared themselves "perfect" and, therefore, incapable of sinning? While a student at Yale Divinity School, John Humphrey Noyes, Oneida's founder, made just such a declaration. Noyes's associates responded predictably, expelling him from the ministry and the Presbyterian Church. Hostility only strengthened his belief in perfection, which he soon applied to sexual matters. Jilted by his first love, Noyes reacted creatively, deciding that "when the will of God is done on earth as it is in heaven, there will be no marriage." For Noyes this meant abolishing monogamy among the "perfect."

Noyes put these beliefs into practice in the utopian communities he founded, first at Putney, Vermont; later at Oneida, New York. Like the Shakers, the Oneidans rejected both the ethos of competition and the institution of private property. Unlike the Shakers, the Oneidans rejected celibacy; instead, they practiced "complex marriage," which allowed any sanctified (saved) partners to engage in sexual intercourse. Despite its notoriety, complex marriage offered few attractions to the truly licentious. Oneidans believed that intercourse was a holy experience, equivalent to a sacrament. As Noyes explained, "With pure hearts and minds, we may approach the sexual union as the truest Lord's supper, as an emblem and also as a medium of the noblest worship of God and fellowship with the body of Christ." Accordingly, they subjected new converts to intense scrutiny; only those with "pure hearts and minds," not just those interested in casual sex, were allowed to join the community. Similarly, mere physical attraction or sexual desire were not valid reasons for choosing a particular partner. By the 1860s, all requests for intercourse had to be made through a neutral third party and recorded in a ledger.

Indeed, complex marriage was not for the faint of heart. Noyes's signal contribution was to separate the "amative" from the "propagative" features of sex – in modern terms, to separate sexuality from reproduction. Only the most "spiritually advanced" (and, of course, no one was more advanced in this respect than "Father" Noyes) were allowed to have children. Believing like many of his contemporaries that the expenditure of sperm was debilitating, Noyes required the men of the Oneida community to practice male continence (i.e., intercourse without ejaculation). Those who failed – called "leakers" – faced ostracism and ridicule.

On one hand, Oneida represented the radical fringe of antebellum reform; its sexual arrangements both horrified and fascinated more conventional Americans. On the other, Oneida, like the Pennsylvania Hospital for the Insane, was a "well-ordered" institution. Order and control were central features of complex marriage. As Noyes himself explained, the very essence of male continence was "self-control, and that is a virtue of universal importance." To be sure, self-control – sexual and otherwise – hardly was limited to utopian communities. Coitus interruptus and sexual abstinence within marriage, for instance, seem to have been the principal means by which nineteenth-century middle-class couples limited the size of their families, inaugurating what historians call the "demographic revolution."

* * *

The temperance crusade – the movement to eliminate the manufacture and sale of alcoholic beverages – attracted more Americans than any other reform movement. Perhaps more than any other reform movement, it exemplifies the tensions between social control and self-control, between coercion and benevolence.

Late eighteenth- and early nineteenth-century reformers took the word *temperance* literally; these mostly male, mostly elite reformers advocated drinking in moderation. By the 1830s, temperance had become a mass movement, albeit one divided into various often competing constituencies. The American Temperance Society, formed in 1826, boasted a membership of 170,000 by 1831 and claimed 2,200 local affiliates – a number that excluded hundreds of additional organizations that remained aloof from the larger national body. The goal of the temperance movement changed as its membership expanded. Fueled by millennial enthusiasm and the possibility of individual perfection, "ultras" rejected moderation in favor of "total abstinence" from all alcoholic beverages; by the late 1830s, they had prevailed. Like so many reforms, temperance had both religious and secular connotations: abstinence provided visible proof of discipline and self-control, but also of salvation.

It would be easy to caricature temperance crusaders as busybodies and do-gooders motivated by nothing more than the "mortal fear that somewhere, somehow, someone might be enjoying himself" (to recall satirist H. L. Mencken's characterization of early twentieth-century "Puritans"). But the temperance movement – at least in part – represented a rational response to a very real social problem. In the words of one historian, early nineteenth-century America was an "alcoholic republic." Americans drank at every meal, including breakfast. Workers took rum breaks at 10 A.M. and 4 P.M., the equivalent of our modern-day coffee breaks, and often many more times besides. Even businessmen stopped work at mid-morning for their "elevens." Weddings, funerals, elections, and militia practice called for drunken celebrations, which sometimes continued for days after the event.

Drinking was nothing new in the early nineteenth century; however, both the amounts of alcohol Americans consumed and their patterns of drinking had increased. According to one historian's estimate, Americans drank on average about 2 1/2 gallons of hard liquor a year in 1770; by 1830, the average American consumed more than 5 gallons annually. (Men imbibed more frequently than women. In 1830, the average adult male probably drank closer to 12 gallons of hard liquor per year.) "Binge drinking" and solitary drinking had become more common; so had alcohol-related aggression and violence. Anxiety seems to have fueled much antisocial drinking. Journeymen artisans, for whom opportunities to become master mechanics were declining, were likely to be heavy drinkers; so were factory workers, who endured long hours, unpleasant working conditions, and dull, repetitive tasks. Businessmen, anxious over the increasing frequency of unpredictable cycles of prosperity and depression, also drank, often excessively. In other words, people whose status and livelihoods were threatened by economic change resorted more often than not to drowning their sorrows. Therefore, when Americans in many walks of life joined the temperance movement, they had reasons for doing so.

The reformers of the 1830s believed in the efficacy of "moral suasion"; that is, they sought to convince people of the evils of intemperance by rational argument, not by prohibiting the consumption of alcohol. Unlike earlier temperance advocates, who merely hoped to persuade by example, they employed aggressive techniques to convert the intemperate. Traveling lecturers explained the dangers of alcoholism and extolled the virtues of sobriety. Novels, songs, and plays featured drunkards who spent their wages at saloons and grog shops, leaving their wives and children to beg or starve. *The Drunkard's Wife* and *Over-the-Hill to the Poorhouse* were the standard tropes of a thriving popular culture that dedicated itself to abstinence. Scenarios like these, however formulaic and clichéd, spoke to very real social needs.

They especially spoke to women. Concerned about poverty and abuse (what we would today call domestic violence) in their own families, as well as in other families, they joined the temperance movement in large numbers. Members of the Martha Washington Temperance Society of Hudson, New York, for example, provided assistance to the wife of "a slave to the love of strong drink." The errant spouse had neglected his family both materially and morally. He probably had abused them physically, for he was "frequently morose, unkind, and cruel."

The temperance movement was at its most coercive when it invaded the workplace. Alcohol, as we have seen, was an important part of the relaxed, irregular lifestyle that characterized the United States before the industrial revolution. Employees who drank on the job and those who took "Blue Mondays" – failing to report to work after a weekend of heavy drinking – were out of place in factories and workshops that required punctuality, sobriety, and "steady habits." Indeed, abstinence from alcoholic beverages was only the first step toward a wider transformation of character that required the internalization of discipline and self-control. It was not unusual for employers like Neal Dow, the Maine entrepreneur, and the shoe manufacturers who founded the Society in Lynn for the Promotion of Industry, Frugality and Temperance, to "encourage" their workers to sober up, often by firing those who did not. Yet, people like Dow, the members of the Lynn society, and other proponents of what the historian Paul Faler has termed "industrial morality" were not hypocrites. Certainly, they agreed that a sober workplace maximized profits, but they assiduously practiced what they preached. This too had practical benefits in the volatile economy of the early nineteenth century, where businesses suffered frequent reversals and where one's credit ratings increasingly depended on one's reputation for sobriety.

Workers who embraced total abstinence were not necessarily dupes of middle-class employers, for temperance activism could be a tool of collective and individual working-class empowerment. Many early labor leaders were temperance advocates; they argued that successful strikes required disciplined, sober strikers. Indeed, in contrast to many reform movements, temperance attracted a substantial number of working-class adherents (to be sure, most of them from the ranks of skilled and native-born workers). This is especially evident in the proliferation of Washingtonian societies (named after George Washington – hardly an exemplar of total abstinence – for patriotic reasons). Much like Alcoholics Anonymous today, Washingtonian meetings adopted a confessional style that offended middle-class temperance advocates. At the first meeting, one publicly "took the pledge" to abstain from all alcoholic beverages. Reformed drunkards offered inspirational personal testimonials. "I was a drunkard. As I was, so may you become. I went to the almshouse. I beat my wife and abused my children. I looked and felt as bad as you do. Look at me now . . . healthy, happy, and respectable . . . good clothes . . . money in my pocket. All comfortable and happy at home; no more rags and starvation there. Come and sign the pledge, as I did, and you'll be a happy man." Washingtonians who signed the pledge did not simply ape their middle-class betters; rather, their testimonials articulated the rights of working people to comfortable homes, decent clothing, and respectability. Seen in this light, Washingtonians challenged rather than bolstered the economic and social status quo.

Working-class women formed auxiliaries, named – appropriately enough – Martha Washington societies. In many respects, members of Martha Washington societies resembled their middle- and upper-class sisters, "rescuing" female inebriates and offering moral support and material assistance to the families of alcoholics. But for women "whose earthly comforts are derived mainly from the labor of their own hands," the threats of alcoholism were much more immediate. For female Washingtonians, the always murky boundaries between social control and self-control were especially thin.

The life of one individual illustrates this blurring of boundaries especially well. Sylvester Graham was born in 1794 in western Massachusetts, the youngest of seventeen children (ten the result of his father's first marriage, seven from his second). John Graham was seventy-two years old when Sylvester was born, and he died two years later. He left his forty-one-year-old wife "in a deranged state of mind" and ill-equipped to rear the seven children who remained at home. Raised by a series of foster families, Graham had little firsthand knowledge of the "homes" he would later idealize. His early career, like his childhood, was marked by instability. He became a Presbyterian minister but lost his job as pastor to a New Jersey church in 1830 because his sermons against intemperance angered his congregation (in 1830, we should recall, total abstinence was still a controversial doctrine). Yet, Graham's optimism did not flag; thwarted by conventional channels, he found new ways to spread his message. Abandoning the ministry, he served as an agent of the Pennsylvania Temperance Society, traveling throughout the urban Northeast delivering temperance lectures. Soon, he expanded into other philanthropic ventures, all of them linked to the all-important principle of self-control. He became a dedicated vegetarian, preaching the virtues of whole-wheat flour (known, even today, as "Graham flour") and his "Graham cracker."

Graham believed that meat – as well as coffee, tea, alcohol, and spicy foods – excited men's "animal" appetites. Like "Father" Noyes of Oneida, he believed that expenditure of sperm was harmful. Numerous ailments, ranging from headaches and fatigue to tuberculosis and epilepsy, resulted from too frequent emissions. True to his temperance beliefs, Graham, unlike Noyes, preached near total abstinence. His *Lectures to Young Men* advised against marriage until around age thirty, when the body was sufficiently mature to endure sexual activity. Even mature married men needed to control themselves for the good of their health. "Healthy and robust" men were to limit intercourse to once a month; sickly men, depending on their condition, should engage in sexual relations less often or not at all. To dull sexual appetites, Graham prescribed a vegetarian diet, plenty of exercise, and cold baths.

Graham's regimen was both personal and political, designed to help young men succeed in their worldly affairs and to help their (far less numerous) offspring avoid the fate he had suffered as a child. It was, of course, uniquely adapted to the demands of an industrial society and to the needs of men engaged in what the historian Charles Sellers has termed "self-making." Graham was no crank by the standards of his day; he gained a substantial following and numerous Americans adopted the "Graham system." Graham's teachings inspired "Graham boardinghouses," vegetarian societies, and even the imagination of future cereal manufacturer John Harvey Kellogg. Yet, in the end, Graham proved incapable of taking his own advice. Unable to resist the tempting and stimulating foods his skeptical wife set at the family table, he suffered a nervous breakdown, even succumbing to meat and whiskey in the last years of his life.

In a certain sense, Graham's failure reflected the larger failure of the temperance movement, specifically its practice of moral suasion. In 1851, the same year that Graham died, the Maine legislature (convinced by the indefatigable Neal Dow) passed the first in a series of state laws that prohibited the manufacture and consumption of alcoholic beverages. Subject to repeal and difficult to enforce, "Maine laws" achieved only very limited success; nevertheless, they reflected a declining faith in the abilities of individuals to reform themselves. Like the shift from reform to custodialism that characterized asylums, the turn to legal prohibition was in part a response to increasing numbers of immigrants, most of them Irish and German – people whom nativist philanthropists deemed incapable of responding to rational arguments. Yet, as was the case with asylums, the temperance movement's shifting strategy also reflected disappointment. Infused with optimism, temperance advocates expected to quickly realize their millennial vision – a nation of teetotalers. Sylvester Graham's failure to achieve self-control was emblematic of the larger failure of moral suasion.

* * *

Abolitionism, the movement to end slavery, attracted thousands of Americans, but it never gained the popularity enjoyed by the temperance movement. Indeed, although many abolitionists were also temperance activists, abolitionism fits less easily into the patterns established by other philanthropic ventures. Abolitionists expressed far less interest in controlling others than in (quite literally) liberating them. Consistent with a "free labor" ideology, many abolitionists embraced economic progress and argued that a man's ability to work provided his best opportunity to progress. Yet, many others were deeply critical of materialism and economic competition. Same common threads linked abolitionists to other reformers. Most embraced the virtues of sobriety, discipline, and self-control. Despite their hostility to "luxury," they believed in the superiority of Northern society – one governed by "free labor," not slavery. Indeed, they tended to focus their critiques of luxury and materialism on the South, which they saw as the embodiment of social evils – the ultimate evil being traffic in human flesh. Like other reformers, many abolitionists drew their inspiration from the Second Great Awakening, if only indirectly. Many were veterans of other reforms, especially the temperance movement; a previous commitment to "ultra" causes such as total abstinence was a common characteristic of many early abolitionist careers. Finally, abolitionism demonstrated the liberating possibilities of self-control. Abolitionists professed a radical belief in the abilities of all people to realize their God-given potential, regardless of their race. Indeed, William Lloyd Garrison claimed that the sobriety, diligence, and orderly behavior of the free blacks he encountered in Baltimore demonstrated the absurdity of racial prejudice.

The first organized antislavery activists hoped to gradually free slaves – usually maintaining that slaveowners should be compensated for the loss of their "property" – and send them "back" to Africa. Colonizationists advocated the same policy for free blacks. (Colonizationists ignored the troubling fact that the vast majority of nineteenth-century African Americans – slave and free – came from families that had been in America for several generations.) The American Colonization Society, founded in 1816, had an impressive list of supporters – Presidents James Madison and James Monroe, clergyman Lyman Beecher, and politician Henry Clay.

Consequently, it also had political clout. Aided by funds from the federal government, it established the first permanent settlement of freed African Americans in Liberia, on the coast of West Africa, in 1822.

Colonization attracted white Southerners as well as white Northerners. Whereas some Southerners who joined the colonization movement sincerely believed that slavery was wrong, others had less lofty motives. To the latter, colonization promised a means of eliminating or at least diminishing the free black population of the South. Slaveholders disliked free blacks because they sheltered runaways and, more important, because they furnished slaves with an example of freedom. Colonization also provided profit-minded Southerners with a means of ridding themselves of slaves who had grown too old to work. But even those colonizationists, North and South, who genuinely hated slavery believed that there was no place in American society for free African Americans, people whom they believed were destined to remain inferior to whites. Henry Clay considered free blacks "the most corrupt, depraved, and abandoned" group of people in the United States." Some colonizationists attributed "depravity" to racial inferiority; others believed prejudice would forever frustrate African Americans' struggles for equality. Colonizationists of all stripes aimed, at bottom, to remove African American people from American society. As the historian Paul Goodman explained, the American Colonization Society "crystallized what for many was latent in their thinking, that the United States was a white man's republic." Indeed, some African Americans agreed. Although they rejected arguments based on racial inferiority, they concurred with pessimistic assessments that emphasized the intransigence of white racism. Thus, throughout the antebellum period, a small but vocal segment of the black community endorsed colonization.

Until the Civil War, colonization continued to attract supporters, including Abraham Lincoln and novelist Harriet Beecher Stowe. Although it continued to be a viable movement (indeed, by the 1850s, support for colonization among African Americans, if anything, had grown), a new group of antislavery advocates emerged in the 1820s and 1830s. They opposed colonization, they called for the immediate abolition of slavery without compensation to masters; hence, they became known as "abolitionists."

Borrowing their strategy from the temperance movement, abolitionists relied on moral suasion. They hoped, in other words, to persuade Americans of the immorality of slavery. Traveling lecturers crisscrossed the northern half of the United States (after Nat Turner's unsuccessful slave rebellion in 1830, publicly promoting abolitionism in the South was next to impossible), often using the language and techniques of revivalists and temperance activists. Some of the most successful lecturers themselves were former slaves; of these, Frederick Douglass was the most famous. Abolitionists bombarded the nation with a steady stream of propaganda. They graphically depicted the physical cruelty of slavery and emphasized slavery's emotional cruelty, especially the grief inflicted on slave families.

American history textbooks typically identify William Lloyd Garrison as the founder of abolitionism; however, the first abolitionists were black, not white. Alarmed by both its pronouncements and its apparent success, free African Americans organized against the American Colonization Society. In 1817, for example, more than 3,000 free African Americans gathered in Philadelphia to protest colonization "with one long, loud tremendous no." Free people of color focused on community improvement and institution-building; as examples countering their supposed "corruption" and "depravity" multiplied, support for colonization, they believed, would wither. As the editors of *Freedom's Journal,* the nation's first black newspaper, explained, "Our vices and our degradation are ever arranged against us, but our virtues are passed over." Black opponents of colonization articulated their own response to the slavery question, one that many whites would soon follow. Again, free African Americans, not whites, organized the first societies dedicated to immediate abolition. The Massachusetts General Colored Association formed in 1826; by 1830, there were at least fifty-five black abolitionist societies in the northern United States, and probably more. These organizations advocated the immediate abolition of slavery, but they also aided fugitive slaves and championed civil rights for free people of color (even in the North, public facilities often were segregated, and most northern states denied African Americans the right to vote).

David Walker, a founder of the Massachusetts General Colored Association, forcefully voiced the views of African American abolitionists in his famous Appeal to the Colored Citizens of the World (1829). Skillfully invoking one of the nation's most sacred documents, he wrote, "All men are created equal. They are endowed by their Creator with certain inalienable rights; . . . among these are life, liberty, and the pursuit of happiness." "[T]ell us no more about colonization," he continued, "for America is as much our country as it is yours." Despite its title, Walker aimed his appeal at white citizens as well; in this, he succeeded. William Lloyd Garrison, one of the most important white figures in the abolitionist crusade, credited Walker's pamphlet and his "colored friends" with helping him to abandon colonization in favor of abolitionism.

The most famous white abolitionist and certainly one of the most dedicated and enthusiastic, Garrison had much in common with his lesser-known peers. Like Garrison, many radical white abolitionists came from evangelical and reform backgrounds; like Garrison, many took the "ultra" side in debates over total abstinence and Sunday mails. Like Garrison, many self-consciously rejected conventional careers, worried about the morality of succeeding according to the "world's common standard." "I cannot study Blackstone in order to collect debts when so many are deprived of their liberty," explained one would-be lawyer. Finally, like Garrison, most white abolitionists saw their stand against slavery and racism in Christian terms. They defined slaveholding as a sin and slaveholders as sinners; slavery could have no place in the new millennium. To be sure, they did not necessarily remain within mainstream congregations. Indeed, they often criticized church complacency on the slavery question and the racism of their members. "What's the good of a revival," Elizur Wright, Jr., asked Finney, "if white Christians will not sit next to 'Niggers'?"

Women's abolitionist activity followed similar patterns. In Rochester, New York, a hotbed of evangelical activism, African American women formed the city's first female antislavery society. The white women – in Rochester and elsewhere – who followed their example usually came from evangelical backgrounds. Many had previously been active in temperance and other philanthropic causes. Female veterans of moral reform, a crusade that aimed to eliminate prostitution, seem to have been particularly attracted to abolitionism. Concern about the sexual exploitation of women seems to have been the common link. Activists who saw prostitutes as victims of male vice easily sympathized with slave women's vulnerability to sexual abuse. Revelations about the damage slavery inflicted on families – black and white – both inspired female abolitionists and justified their actions. Drawing on their identities as actual or potential wives and mothers, abolitionist women condemned slaveholders for betraying their own marriage vows and for separating slave families. Lydia Maria Child denounced "those who sell mothers separately from their children." Or as female abolitionists in Lynn, Massachusetts, explained,

> "When woman's heart is bleeding,
> Shall woman's heart be hushed?"

As the query of the Lynn abolitionists suggested, women's antislavery work aroused considerable controversy. The issue was not women's entry into the "public" sphere. As Kathleen McCarthy's essay in this volume shows, wealthy women had been active in charitable causes since the 1790s, an undertaking that their contemporaries found perfectly respectable. Rather, the nature of female abolitionist activism, coupled with a controversial cause, provoked opposition. Female speakers aroused hostility especially when they confronted "mixed" audiences that included men as well as women. Boys threw hymn books at Ellen Smith when she lectured at a church in Maine; adults in the audience – who shouted, stamped their feet, and repeatedly slammed pew doors – did not behave much better.

Women were especially prominent in circulating antislavery petitions and collecting signatures; in this, they appear to have been more successful than were men. Indeed, the so-called "gag rule" that automatically tabled all antislavery petitions presented to Congress represented in many respects a response, not to abolitionism per se, but specifically to women's abolitionist activism. "On what other occasion, on what other great question, have females thought it their imperious duty to step forth as the asserters and champions of the great right of petition?" a Virginia congressman demanded. Petitioning was an especially controversial form of female activism because it was explicitly rather than implicitly political. As the abolitionist Angelina Grimké explained to a female audience, "Men may settle this and other questions at the ballot box, but you have no such right. It is only through our petitions that you can reach the Legislature." Abolitionist women's politicking alienated not only men, but also more conservative women as well. Petitioning, advice writer Catharine Beecher made clear, was "entirely without the female sphere of duty."

Although it was a charge leveled at both sexes, abolitionist women were particularly vulnerable to accusations that their activities promoted "amalgamation" (what today we would call *miscegenation*). Horrified at her "familiarity" with African Americans, a Leominster, Massachusetts, resident asked Frances Drake, a white activist, if she would contemplate marriage to an African American man. "Yes," she responded, "if he was just as worthy in every respect as a white man ought to be." "You can have no idea what a talk it has made over town," she wrote to an abolitionist ally.

These experiences underscore the fact that abolitionism, especially in its early years, was neither popular nor "respectable." They also point to tensions between abolitionists. Drake's passionate commitment to abolitionism allowed her to transcend racism. She considered it a "great . . . blessing . . . to pillow" the "dying head" of an African American boy whom she had nursed. Other white abolitionists, like the Leominster woman who told Drake that she could be a good abolitionist "and still not treat niggers so familiarly," were unable to endorse racial equality. This was especially true as the abolitionist movement expanded in the 1840s and 1850s in response to external political events. Mobilized by events such as the annexation of Texas, the Compromise of 1850, and the Kansas-Nebraska Act, new white converts to the abolitionist cause tended to direct their energies toward ending slavery in the South, not combating prejudice and discrimination in the nation as a whole. Early abolitionism had demanded that its white adherents do more than labor to end slavery; it had required them literally to transform themselves, to free themselves of prejudice, and – as the constitution of the New England Antislavery Society put it – to work "to improve the character and condition of the free people of color, to inform and correct public opinion in relation to their situation and rights, and obtain for them equal civil and political rights and privileges with the whites." White abolitionists, as the statements of the anonymous Leominster activists suggest, had never been entirely free from racial prejudice. But if the abolitionists of the 1830s envisioned to varying degrees a society based on racial equality, their successors – focused on reforming a recalcitrant South – embraced less lofty goals. African American abolitionists, on the other hand, continued to pursue a broader agenda that included ending discrimination as well as slavery.

Gender and politics, as well as race, divided abolitionists. In 1840, internal disagreements split the American Anti-Slavery Society (AAS) into two competing factions. One bone of contention was whether women should be full and equal partners in the abolitionist cause. Those who remained within the AAS believed that they should; other less radical members disagreed. Some abolitionists evidently worried along with their opponents about the extent to which their movement empowered women. AAS members also disagreed over whether abolitionism should be a matter for electoral politics. Garrison adamantly opposed any such move, believing that political parties were the tools of slaveholders. Accordingly, activists who remained within the AAS continued to advocate moral suasion. Their opponents formed the Liberty party, which entered candidates in the presidential race in 1840 and again in 1844. Liberty candidates attracted few votes, but they set an important precedent because they helped to bring the issue of slavery into the national political arena.

Yet, the shift to political activism had costs as well as benefits: one cost was a declining faith in the efficacy of moral suasion. Another was that it marginalized African Americans and women, both of whom were legally prevented from participating in formal politics. Many women continued to work for abolitionism, often less publicly in all-female antislavery societies.

But the experiences of marginalization and exclusion affected some radical female abolitionists, like Elizabeth Cady Stanton and Lucretia Mott, profoundly. Realizing that electoral politics had become the key to reformers' efficacy, they refocused their energies on gaining political rights for women.

* * *

By the 1850s, reformers had lost much of their energy and enthusiasm – and, with them, much of their faith in the possibility of individual transformation. "The speculative has in all things yielded to the practical," the *American Temperance Magazine* concluded in 1852. The *Magazine's* observation had relevance beyond the specific movement for which it spoke. As heredity replaced environment as the primary "cause" of insanity, asylums shifted their efforts from curing the insane to simply keeping them away from society. Utopian experiments foundered, failing in their attempts to set examples that the rest of the world would follow. Longer-lived communities, like the Shakers and the Oneidans, turned inward, evincing less interest in recruitment and more in isolation. The Oneidans embraced increasingly secular and "scientific" practices, incorporating "stirpiculture," an early form of eugenics, into their sexual practices by the late 1860s. Powerful factions of the temperance and abolitionist movements abandoned moral suasion in favor of political action, concluding – as did the *American Temperance Magazine* – that "moral suasion is moral balderdash." In short, by the 1850s, antebellum reform had lost its distinguishing feature: its implicit assumption that philanthropy and self-improvement were two sides of the same coin. Increasingly, "reformers" stood on one side of the divide, those whom they believed in need of reform on the other. Nowhere are the consequences clearer than in the brief but influential career of the U.S. Sanitary Commission, a government-sponsored association that provided food, clothing, and nurses for Civil War soldiers. Commission officials elevated organization and efficiency over benevolence; as one report proclaimed, the organization's "ultimate end is neither humanity nor charity. It is to economize for the National service the life and strength of the National soldier." The Commission's superintendent of nurses was none other than Dorothea Dix, tireless advocate for the insane. But Dix's "pathetic sympathy with human suffering" rendered her less than effective in carrying out the Sanitary Commission's bureaucratizing mission. As George Templeton Strong, the Commission's treasurer, baldly put it, she was a "philanthropic lunatic" who did the organization more harm than good. Viewed from the earlier vantage point of millennial optimism, Strong's characterization of the quintessential antebellum philanthropist is startling and unsettling. It also foreshadowed the future, for the Sanitary Commission became a model for the "scientific charity" of the late nineteenth century. As Ruth Crocker's portrait of Margaret Olivia Sage makes clear, older styles of philanthropy did not disappear entirely. But Strong's disavowal of sentimental benevolence, the sharp distinctions he rendered between benefactor and recipient – between "us" and "them" – were themes that increasingly would characterize philanthropy in the Gilded Age.

Part II

THE NATIONALIZATION AND INTERNATIONALIZATION OF AMERICAN PHILANTHROPY, 1861–1930

Russell Sage! Accumulation, with him, was not a means, but rather the sole aim of life. The notion that the social mission of wealth is philanthropy and charity was brutally caricatured by the personality of this man. Not even his own life derived any benefit from his riches, let alone the lives of others. Indeed, he serves as the most striking proof of our social insanity, which suffers thousands to starve, that a few calculating human machines may pile dividends upon dividends.

Sage was the most worthy, most consistent representative of our system of robbery and theft. Unlike the dilettante philanthropists, such as Carnegie and Rockefeller, he never feigned any hypocritical humanitarianism. In this respect, at least, Sage was superior to the Old King of Sunday School fame, and to the Homestead slavedriver, immortalized by libraries and the bloodbath of July 6, 1892. He never donned the garb of beneficence. Had he undertaken the building of the Panama Canal, for instance, he would not have called it a work of progress and civilization. His keen eye would have beheld only the long row of figures and the profits.

If an artist had suggested a great masterpiece as a memorial, Russell would have shown him the door. Why this nonsensical enthusiasm for art and science? There is only one thing of consequence in life, and that is to "earn" the highest interest on money safely invested.

He was not far from the truth, with regard to his co-gamblers, Morgan, Rockefeller, and Carnegie. Probably he suspected that their pretended interest in art and science was but a feeble attempt to quiet their consciences. At least his attitude was more frank, more honest. And he was more self-centered. He was not so stupid as Morgan, who invests fortunes in poor copies of great masters, to the amusement of European artists and art connoisseurs.

This character study of Russell Sage is, in a small measure, a portrayal of our social economy – cold, cruel, heartless; with no other purpose than the accumulation of fortunes by the few, the grinding to death of the many.

From Emma Goldman's "Russell Sage," in *Mother Earth: A Monthly Magazine Devoted to Social Science and Literature* I, 6 (August 1906):1–2.

FROM CIVIL WAR TO THE
PROGRESSIVE ERA

The Civil War presented a challenge to the rights-based construction of American society. Certainly, North and South had different economic and social systems. Yet, they also had come to accept different legal and social truths. In the North, individual rights were protected by contract law and the principles of limited government. The Republican Party's embrace of "free labor" recognized the equal rights of all men, black or white, to sell their labor on a free and open market. Contract law, not governmental action, was the basis by which that right was secured. However, at the War's end, positive governmental initiatives would be needed to impose this ideal on recalcitrant Southerners.

Actually, the reconceptualization of government as a positive force began during the War. Individual rights were subordinated to the public good in President Lincoln's suspension of the protections of *habeas corpus*, the imposition of an income tax, and the reliance on a military draft. During the War years, the government, more than private associations, sought to redesign society in accordance with certain beliefs and ideals. For a brief moment in the nineteenth century, American government became an instrument of philanthropy.

The U.S. Sanitary Commission provides an excellent example of the transformation from private to public action. During the Civil War, the Union established a bureaucracy to administer medical aid and comfort to the soldiers. The Sanitary Commission, the largest philanthropic organization in national history up to that time, had been built on nursing organizations begun by women prior to the start of the War. Crisis converted a private female organization into a public one with men at the helm. This signified another war-time change, as secular white men embraced philanthropic activity to an extent that was previously unknown. By the second half of the nineteenth century, men came to see private civil action as a means both to correct social ills and channel their social energies. Devoting themselves to "the moral equivalent of war," a new professional cadre of reformers set out to rationalize American society to the teachings of science.

The Republican Party's program for Reconstruction constituted an experiment, unique up to that time, in the use of positive government action to secure rights of citizenship and social conditions necessary for republican self-government. Constitutional and legislative enactments secured freed slaves' rights to vote, contract, and hold property. Public-sector philanthropy established bureaucracies funded by tax dollars, such as the Freedman's Bureau, to distribute former confederate property in implementing the promise of providing the former slaves with "forty acres and a mule." The federal government also used the military to secure federal rights for the former slaves in the face of recalcitrant Southerners and their state governments. Once again, historical actors pursued a conceptual social ideal through philanthropy; this one premised on creating what Eric Foner terms a "national citizenship."

By 1877, the reintegration of public and private sectors to pursue a conceived public good broke down as the Reconstruction experiment encountered traditional ideas of federalism, limited government, and private property rights. In addition, economic growth and national expansion began to consume Republican energies more than racial equality. As the federal government abandoned its foray into philanthropy, Americans once again turned to the private sector for programs to improve the living conditions of people. During the so-called "Gilded Age" of the late nineteenth century, the old corporate model was professionalized and "scientifically" adapted to more efficiently serve as a tool for social engineering.

Historian George Fredrickson asserts that the Civil War dissuaded Americans of their naive idealism. The people of the United States awakened to the realities of political corruption, urban crime, spiritual malaise, and cultural and class disparities. Perceiving both the war and the social ills of the post-War era as products of moral decline, the dissipation of masculine initiative through luxury, and rampant individualism, America's social and intellectual elites combined in advocating a reprioritization of social order, self-sacrifice, and the "strenuous life" to revitalize society. Eschewing government as, in the words of Charles Francis Adams, an "impediment to intelligent progress," American's industrial, intellectual, and spiritual leaders formed a new consensus embracing institutional order premised on scientific efficiency, martial discipline, and public service. Bankers, merchants, scientists, and farmers reenergized America in their integration of personal success with social improvement. The government's role was reduced to maintaining order by compelling submission to law and letting the private sector do what was necessary to develop the country. The post-Darwinian society adapted the scientific method to improving business procedures and managing economic growth, developing an empirical jurisprudence rooted in the realities of power and history, and reforming the civil service as an efficient disciplined corps of administrators. In the process, the success of American democracy was newly appreciated as a product of historical development and prudent management, rather than as fulfillment of any philosophical ideal.

Historian Robert Wiebe characterizes the four decades from the close of Reconstruction to the end of World War I as a "search for order." In much the same way that they experimented with new institutional forms in the early republic, Americans during the second half of the nineteenth century adopted new forms of social organization to express changing values, social concerns, doubts, and fears. Following a brief flirtation with public-sector philanthropy during the Civil War and Reconstruction, Americans again opted for limited state authority, and vested civil society with primary responsibilities for addressing the public good and upholding republican ideals. In addition, the Americans exported their model of capitalistic republicanism through American imperialism.

The pragmatic reconceptualization of democracy supported initiatives to spread the nation's political and economic systems beyond its borders. In both imperialist conquests and charitable initiatives, Americans attempted to impose their social ideal on foreign peoples. The expansion of capitalism and democracy on a world scale protected American institutions from international turmoil and extended American conceptions of order.

Yet, whereas America's intellectual and business leaders reconceived of their nation's and their personal goals on a global scale, millions of other Americans, especially after 1900, sought meaning, support, and comfort in small groups. Many people less extreme in their political views than "Red Emma" Goldman distrusted the power and motives of philanthropists like Carnegie, Rockefeller, and Sage. Voluntary organizations became a means by which Americans could escape being dominated or marginalized by large-scale or "mass" culture. Huge corporations, a national media, and the proliferation of national norms for formerly personal activities (e.g., dress and child-rearing) prompted people to reassert their own individuality and regain social intimacy through small groups. Some of these groups emphasized religious or ethnic ties; others sewing, drinking, athletics, or similar social activities. Still others used hatred and bigotry to attack the changes in their society and express the alienation they brought. By the mid-1920s, Ku Klux Klan membership was in the millions and the Black Knights numbered hundreds of thousands.

Progressivism during the first three decades of the twentieth century integrated a national longing for personal meaning and participatory democracy, a resentment toward big business, an alienation spawned by misunderstood international market forces and ideas influencing economics and social mores, and a desire for order into a pragmatic program for societal regeneration. Theodore Roosevelt's trust-busting, support of regulation, and federal purchase of land all depended on a reconceptualization of government as a force for securing the social good. America's consideration of the Progressives' agenda once again challenged the early republic's delineation of public and private spheres, and left the nation – on the threshold of the Great Depression – uncertain once more of its ideals, values, and the means to use to find them.

7

LAW, RECONSTRUCTION, AND AFRICAN AMERICAN EDUCATION IN THE POST-EMANCIPATION SOUTH

ROY E. FINKENBINE

William Hooper Councill walked a philanthropic tightrope. As principal of the Hunstville State Colored Normal and Industrial School, he – like many African American educators in the post-emancipation South – engaged in a constant search for funds to keep his fledgling institution alive. The search took various forms. Councill regularly lobbied the Alabama legislature for additional appropriations to supplement the school's meager income. In 1881, copying the successful approach of Fisk University's Jubilee Singers, he led Huntsville's student glee club on a national concert tour to raise money to purchase buildings and land. He also coaxed small contributions out of the Peabody Education Fund, an early philanthropic foundation devoted to creating a public education system throughout the southern United States. Although committed throughout his career to the primacy of the liberal arts in African American education, Councill announced in 1883 that he would open an industrial-education department at Huntsville to train students in agriculture, domestic science, and the mechanical arts. A calculated action, it was prompted by the establishment one year earlier of the John F. Slater Fund for the Education of Freedmen, a foundation dedicated to promoting the industrial-education curriculum in African American schools and colleges. Councill publicly promised to offer industrial training at Huntsville as long as the school continued to receive aid from the Slater Fund, evidence of the halfhearted nature of his commitment to black industrial education.

Slater aid to Huntsville, which continued unenthusiastically for five years, was ultimately withdrawn when Councill and his students offended the racial sensibilities of the white South. In 1887, Councill attempted to ride in the "white car" on a train traveling from Tennessee to Atlanta.

After rough treatment by the conductor, he was ejected from the car despite possessing a first-class ticket. He sought redress. In the first case decided by the Interstate Commerce Commission, the new federal agency asserted that southern railroads would be required to provide equal accommodations for black passengers. The legal victory, however, did not imply imminent social change. A second incident took place later that year when Huntsville students sat in and were ejected from the "white car" on an Alabama railroad. These events prompted Atticus G. Haygood, general agent of the Slater Fund, to terminate grants to the school. He advised Rutherford B. Hayes, the president of the foundation's board of trustees, that "we can make better use of the $600 [annually awarded to Huntsville]." The message was clear: The Slater Fund – like other philanthropic foundations working with African American education in the post-emancipation South – would not permit challenges to either its curricular preferences or to the racial practices and segregation statutes of the white South.

* * *

By the 1880s, the federal government had abandoned its attempt to integrate freed African Americans into a reconstructed South. In abdicating responsibility to charities such as the Slater Fund, the country allowed the private sector to address what had been, from 1865 to 1877, the nation's primary concern.

Reconstruction tested the legal distinction between public and private spheres created during the early republic, which is described by Mark McGarvie in his essay on the *Dartmouth College* case. The Radical Republicans reconceived government as an instrument for positively shaping post-Civil War American society. The Confiscation Act of 1862 had permitted the federal government to take possession of property in areas of the former Confederacy conquered by the Union army. At the end of 1865, Congress created the Freedmen's Bureau and authorized it to distribute selected parcels of this confiscated land to freed slaves. Within months, thousands of former slaves had been settled on small farms in Virginia, the Carolinas, Georgia, and Louisiana.

Even before the end of the War, hundreds of men and women of both races from the North traveled into Union-occupied areas of the Confederacy to assist the freed slaves in establishing homes and villages, creating schools and churches, and finding work. The Freedmen's Bureau supplemented, formalized, and rationalized this ragtag group of volunteers into a federal bureaucracy headed by General Oliver Otis Howard. One of Abraham

Lincoln's last political appointees, Howard was given broad authority to assist the former slaves in securing political rights, as well as social stature and economic independence. Senator Charles Sumner of Massachusetts even proposed making the head of the Freedmen's Bureau a cabinet-level position. Under Howard's leadership, the Bureau distributed food, clothing, fuel, and medical care to black families during their transition to a free-labor economy. It worked assiduously with missionary organizations and black parents to construct schools for black children throughout the South. The Civil Rights Act of 1866 – the forerunner of the Fourteenth Amendment – provided federal protection in both the law and the federal courts for any person, regardless of race, to pursue the economic freedom available in a capitalist society by guaranteeing legal enforcement of work and business contracts.

The Radical Republicans of the Thirty-Ninth Congress perceived their mission to be one of social reform, and sought to use the power of the federal government to achieve their goals. They were quite conscious of the novel ways in which they were using law and governmental authority. Speaking of the pending 1866 Civil Rights Bill, Senator Lot Morrill of Maine admitted that "this species of legislation is absolutely revolutionary. But are we not in the midst of revolution?"

President Andrew Johnson did not think so. In 1866, he vetoed a bill that would have extended the life of the Freedmen's Bureau, finding its "immense patronage" unconstitutional. He argued that the new federal bureaucracy being created by the Radical Republicans would override individual rights rather than protect them, warning that the use of federal power to affirmatively benefit a specific group violated "all our experience as a people." Certainly, to the extent that the Civil War resulted from unresolved questions about the places of state and national authority in the federal system, the postwar actions of Congress asserted a final answer to this constitutional issue. Johnson could veto the extension of the Freedmen's Bureau. However, the Civil Rights Act of 1866, the Fourteenth Amendment, federal supervision of southern elections, and the use of the military to protect the rights of freed slaves all constituted a new national presence in the lives of Americans.

Constitutional amendments and other legislative enactments of the Reconstruction era may have permanently altered federal and state relations; however, they also temporarily restructured the traditional division between America's public and private sectors. A group of radical reformers in Congress used government to reshape American society in conformity to a more democratic ideal. Yet, the values on which Reconstruction was based were not new. The Founding Fathers had recognized the relationship between economic independence and political self-determination – the goal of the Freedmen's Bureau. The protection of contract rights found in the Civil Rights Act of 1866 is rooted in Article I, Section 10, of the Constitution and derived from republican ideology conceiving of all people as equally competent and viable actors under the law. What was new was the positive use of government authority to secure these values. Reconstruction-era legislation broke from the existing model of the federal government as an impartial arbiter in a free commercial society. From 1865 to 1877, the Radical Republicans in Congress refused to rely on the private sector to secure the values and lifestyles necessary for democracy to succeed in all sections of the union.

Wartime has generally resulted in an increase in federal authority and responsibility. In times of peace, American society has had to decide whether to dismantle the wartime bureaucracies, redirect them, or build on their increased base of power to serve broader social goals. After the Civil War, Radical Republicans in Congress chose the third option.

Postwar attempts to restructure American society were not limited to the South. In *Reconstruction: America's Unfinished Revolution*, Eric Foner asserts that Reconstruction expressed what "was first and foremost a civic ideology grounded in a definition of American citizenship . . . possess[ing] a social and economic vision . . . derived from the free labor ideology." That ideology knew no geographic barriers. Republican Party platforms of the era encouraged the repeal of any laws anywhere in the nation that restricted African American access to restaurants, trains, or hotels, as well as voting booths and courthouses. Iowa outlawed separate-but-equal education in 1868. Five years later, the State of New York prohibited discrimination in all public facilities and took steps to integrate its schools. These were not isolated actions. As a result, an African American middle class was emerging throughout the North and South by the mid-1870s, consisting of grocers, artisans, businessmen, middling farmers, and even some doctors and lawyers.

The idea of using governmental authority to promote a new social ideal was not limited to race relations. Republican state legislatures created public parks, public-health facilities, and public-utility systems to provide gas and water. Massachusetts created a State Board of Charities, integrating the work of the public and private sectors to serve social needs. In Michigan, the state government built facilities to care for orphans, the mentally ill, and the disabled, and passed laws mandating school attendance and prohibiting cruelty to animals. Republican Governor Reuben Fenton of New York created teacher-training colleges and a public Board of Charities, secured passage of minimum housing standards, and enabled legislation making possible the creation of professional fire departments and boards of health in local jurisdictions.

By 1877, however, the Reconstruction program had lost its momentum. Numerous factors contributed to this cessation of federal initiatives. The Republican party concentrated its energies in 1868 on the unsuccessful impeachment of Democrat Andrew Johnson, fragmenting the party and diverting it from its policy goals. In addition, the party suffered from the scandals of the Grant Administration and from a backlash on the part of racists and constitutional conservatives who resented the government's initiatives. The Democratic Party built a base of support among white Southerners and Northern laborers to regain congressional seats and state offices. The Panic of 1873, a major economic depression, also diverted the concerns of Americans away from the goals of Reconstruction. Most importantly, perhaps, many in the nation redirected their attention to the West and the economic opportunities it offered. The construction of the transcontinental railroad, the pacification of the Plains Indians, and the growth of mining and ranching drew interest away from the South.

As public-sector interest in the concerns of the former slaves diminished, the private sector once again assumed a larger role. African American education emerged as a primary concern for those individuals and organizations who looked southward. There were several reasons for this development. The freedmen and freedwomen of the South viewed schooling – along with land, unfettered family lives, and the vote – as a key to defining a meaningful freedom. On the other hand, many whites, especially in the North, embraced the education of African Americans as essential to perpetuate the republic. After all, 95 percent of the former slaves were illiterate. Most lacked any working knowledge of the American political process or the economy beyond that needed to fulfill the day-to-day tasks of plantation agriculture. To many benevolent souls, schooling appeared to be the best vehicle for shaping the former slaves into productive citizens and workers in the wake of emancipation.

The Freedmen's Bureau had helped establish dozens of colleges and hundreds of elementary and secondary schools for African Americans in the South in the years after Appomattox. However, once federal enforcement abated, Southern state and local governments adopted a policy of segregation and devalued African American education, supporting limited and rudimentary training for black children. Missionary organizations stepped into the breach, especially addressing the need for black higher education. Nearly all of the colleges they supported, such as Fisk University in Nashville and Atlanta University, provided meaningful instruction, usually in a classical or liberal arts curriculum. In addition, many communities of former slaves had established their own schools, hired their own teachers, and attempted to sustain both with minimal outside support. By 1870, the freedmen had expended an estimated $1 million on the education of their children; however, poverty forced many freedmen's communities to turn to missionary organizations and local governments for assistance, often resulting in a loss of black control.

Nevertheless, African American philanthropy continued to be an important force in supporting and shaping black education in the South. Especially prominent in this regard were the African American churches, which established and maintained hundreds of secondary schools and colleges in the decades after the war. By 1915, for example, black Baptist denominations alone maintained 100 secondary schools in the region. Together with black Methodist denominations, they also established twenty-one colleges, beginning in 1878 with Lane College in Jackson, Tennessee. Relying on annual fund drives and weekly collections in the pews, African American denominations sponsored institutions of higher education as a way to train pastors and teachers, and to contribute to the social progress of the race. By creating independent schools and colleges, they also avoided the paternalism and occasional outright racism encountered in working with white missionary teachers and administrators, state and local officials, and many Northern donors.

Schools built and sustained with Northern money and controlled by white administrators often assumed a deprecatory approach toward African American education. Perceiving their students as better served by a practical education in a trade, they deemphasized the traditional curricula in the classics or the liberal arts. This reinforced social stereotypes of black people as laborers rather than thinkers. It rendered them "useful" in subordinate roles within a white-dominated society, allowing for limited integration only at certain social levels.

A significant number of African American secondary schools and colleges in the South sought to attract individual Northern contributions. Booker T. Washington, the black principal of Tuskegee Institute, confided to a friend in 1901 that "[it] is impossible for me to get the money to carry on this institution withount [*sic*] going to the North." To cover their annual operating budgets and to fund new ventures, most schools found it necessary to appeal in creative ways to the consciences of benevolent donors above the Mason-Dixon line. Pioneers in this regard were the Jubilee Singers who, between 1871 and 1878, raised desperately needed funds for Fisk University. Over time, most African American schools and colleges also developed systematic fundraising efforts. Nearly all sent written appeals to potential donors in the North. A larger number published and mailed monthly or quarterly newsletters touting their successes. The vast majority sponsored annual trips northward to personally solicit contributions from likely donors at churches, clubs, hotels, and resorts. No one, however, tapped Yankee purses more effectively than Washington. Preaching a message of racial accommodation and black self-help, and developing a sophisticated fundraising organization and extensive donor list, he expanded his annual collections from $855 in 1881, the year he founded Tuskegee, to $379,704 in 1915, the year of his death. Most of this backing came from white donors in the North. Tuskegee's own records for 1910, for example, show that only $1,203 came from blacks; less than $74 came from Southern whites.

Tuskegee was more the exception than the rule. Foundation philanthropy played an increasingly important role in the financing of black schools and colleges. In fact, the earliest substantial philanthropic foundations in the United States were those created after the war to support Southern education. The first of these, the Peabody Education Fund, was established in 1867, when Massachusetts banker and financier, George Peabody, established a $2 million endowment. Under the administration of the fund's first general agent, Barnas Sears, monies were distributed on a segregated basis; he refused support for the early efforts of Radical Republican legislators to create integrated institutions in Louisiana and South Carolina during Reconstruction. Other foundations that entered the field continued the practice. Sometimes, the agents and boards of these Northern-based foundations feared the prospect of stirring hostile opposition from white Southerners. All too often, however, their endorsement of Southern racial mores and practices reflected their own views. A case in point is the John F. Slater Fund for the Education of Freedmen (popularly known as the Slater Fund), the first philanthropic foundation to work solely in the area of African American education. The fund was created in 1882 when Connecticut industrialist John Fox Slater, donated $1 million for the education of former slaves. Under the direction of a succession of general agents, monies were distributed only to black institutions that adhered to prevailing segregation customs and statutes. And funding to these schools went only for the development and support of an industrial education curriculum, which was perceived to more adequately prepare blacks for their place in an unequal Southern society and economy.

Foundations entering the field of African American education in the early twentieth century embraced both the racial and curricular models established by the Slater Fund in the 1880s and 1890s. And, like the Slater Fund, they also adopted an increasingly "scientific" approach to giving. In the process, these foundations were able to impose their own vision of an ideal society – one in which blacks participated but only in a subordinate way.

The growing sense among many foundation officials that the needs and problems of black schooling were "too complex" to be met by the existing sources of benevolence prompted the creation in 1902 of the General Education Board (GEB), a philanthropic "trust" backed by the vast wealth of oil magnate John D. Rockefeller. Both the Peabody and Slater funds operated under its umbrella. So did several new foundations – the Jeanes Negro Rural School Fund (1907), the Phelps-Stokes Fund (1910), and the Julius Rosenwald Fund (1928) – that were established to study and support the material needs of black schools and colleges. Led by the GEB, foundation philanthropy eventually assumed the primary role in determining the direction of African American education in the South.

* * *

The Slater Fund illustrates the rise and role of foundation philanthropy in the support and shaping of African American education in the post-emancipation South. The fund was the earliest of the major foundations devoted exclusively to the education of the recently freed slaves. It was also significant for the size of its endowment: of the twenty-six foundations established in the United States before 1900, the fund was one of only ten with endowments of $1 million or more. Prior to its demise as an independent foundation in 1937, the fund distributed some $4 million to black schools and colleges; no other foundation approached this degree of support for African American education until the 1920s. Equally as important as the fund's financial presence was its contribution to the curricular direction of black schooling in the South for more than a generation. The fund performed the primary role in making industrial education a major part of the curriculum in existing African American schools and colleges in the South in the 1880s and 1890s. Beginning in 1911, it played the leading role in redirecting this curricular emphasis toward the creation and maintenance of a system of county training schools throughout the region.

Slater created the Slater Fund in 1882, when he donated $1 million "for uplifting the lately emancipated population of the Southern states, and their posterity, by conferring on them the blessings of a Christian education." He was motivated by a belief that schooling was vital if the former slaves were to become responsible participants in the political process. Convinced that support for African American education could not be expected from Southern whites, Slater undertook to address this need. He named a distinguished board of trustees to administer his endowment. The original board included a former president of the United States (Hayes), the chief justice of the U.S. Supreme Court (Morison R. Waite), the governor of Georgia (Alfred H. Colquitt), two prominent Protestant clergymen (Phillips Brooks and James P. Boyce), one of the foremost temperance advocates (William E. Dodge), two wealthy bankers (Morris K. Jesup and John A. Stewart), a university president (Daniel Coit Gilman), and Slater's son (William A. Slater). Only two members of the board were from the South. Although Slater asked that the monies of the fund be distributed "in no partisan, sectional, or sectarian spirit," he gave the members of the board the "largest liberty" in establishing policies and practices for its management and disbursement. Eager to meet their charge, the members of the board met in late 1882 to set objectives and procedures for the fund. Among their initial actions, they selected Atticus G. Haygood, a noted author, editor, clergyman, and the president of Emory College, to be their general agent. The previous year, Haygood had published *Our Brother in Black*, a prescriptive discussion of Southern race relations.

Acting on Haygood's recommendation, the members of the board quickly determined to support black industrial education, an emphasis that continued for the duration of the fund. Prior to an early board meeting, Hayes confided to his diary:

A few ideas seem to be agreed upon. Help none but those who help themselves. Educate only at schools which provide in some form for industrial education. These two points should be insisted upon. Let the normal instruction be that men must earn their own living, and that by the labor of their hands as far as may be. This is the gospel of salvation for the colored man. Let not the labor be servile, but in manly occupations like those of the carpenter, the farmer, and the blacksmith.

The board resolved in 1883 to give preferential treatment in appropriations to institutions that provided instruction in agriculture, industrial skills, and other occupations that would "enable colored youth to make a living, and to become useful citizens."

Largely due to the influence of the Slater Fund, industrial education became the dominant curriculum in many African American schools and colleges during the 1880s and 1890s. Those institutions that adopted the curriculum taught black students a variety of manual skills and occupations, including agriculture, the mechanical arts, domestic science, carpentry and other construction trades, leatherworking, and metalworking. Most of the industrial education offered by black institutions in the decades following Reconstruction would be considered low-level "vocational" training today. There was little or no industrial training in the sense of preparing students to work or assume leadership roles in modernized industries. However, to many advocates of the industrial education curriculum, such manual training was more important as a means of teaching morality and work discipline than in preparing skilled workers. Members of the Slater board believed that it would foster orderly behavior, proper work habits, and moral discipline. Their expressed desire was to form "the will into habits of industry and temperance, in the virtues of punctuality, order, and good behavior." This sounded more like training than education. By this means, black industrial education would mold blacks into "more useful members of society." It would also solve a host of social and economic problems in the South. Proponents of the curriculum believed that it would limit racial discord, develop a tractable labor force, encourage sectional harmony, attract Northern capital, and cause Southern industries and railroads to flourish. Their advocacy of black industrial education harmonized easily with the philosophy of the New South movement.

Between 1883 and 1886, the Slater board distributed more than $100,000 to black schools and colleges in the Southern states, primarily to equip and operate manual training programs. Most of the money went toward the erection of buildings for industrial training, the purchase of equipment, salaries for instructors of industrial courses, and financial assistance for students in those courses. Although Haygood noted extensive opposition to industrial education in his report to the board in 1883, by 1886, he observed that there were few black schools and colleges that did not offer it in some form. By the 1887–88 academic year, the fund was spending more than $40,000 per year to aid industrial training programs in some forty-one schools. Under Haygood's guidance, the board used the promise of Slater funds to persuade reluctant institutions to adopt the curriculum. He admitted that it was the policy of the board to "bring all the best schools into line, in industrial education," and he used his influence in the division of Slater monies to control, punish, or rebuke recalcitrant schools. As a result, a shift from liberal arts to industrial education took place at many black schools throughout the South during the 1880s. The Bureau of Education estimated that, during the 1889–90 academic year, ten thousand black students were being taught some phase of industrial education in schools or colleges aided by the Slater Fund.

The Southern agents of the Slater Fund – Haygood, a Georgian, and J. L. M. Curry, a Virginian – bore particular responsibility for its direction in the 1880s and 1890s. Both had supported slavery before the war, and an examination of their beliefs about blacks demonstrates a consistent pattern of racial stereotyping after the conflict. Haygood's numerous books, articles, and speeches betray a strong belief in black inferiority. To him, the freedmen's community appeared to be ignorant, immoral, indolent, improvident, wasteful, and given to base, instinctual desires. Even black professionals, including teachers and preachers, were not exempted from this bias. According to Haygood, blacks were by their very nature "crude," primitive, and tending toward savagery. Although he took solace in the belief that the black apprenticeship in slavery had formed a "habit of submission" and a fear of white man's vengeance" in the race, he feared that schooling blacks in the liberal arts would breed discontent among them, just as he perceived that it had among Northern urban immigrants "whose murmurings hint[ed] of suppressed earthquakes." The wrong kind of education, Haygood argued, would destroy black docility and loose black savagery upon the South. Curry shared Haygood's stereotypical view of blacks. He characterized black workers as "stupid, indolent, shiftless . . . with a low tone of morality." He asserted that blacks had "loose notions of piety and morality and with strong racial peculiarities and proclivities . . . had not outgrown the feebleness of the moral sense which is common to all primitive races." Throughout his writings and speeches, Curry stereotyped black behavior again and again as ignorant, immoral, superstitious, wasteful, and lacking in foresight. On occasion, this belief prompted him to view the moral and economic uplift of Southern blacks as "hopeless" and to even express doubts as to the feasibility industrial education for blacks.

Because they viewed African Americans as inferior and craved solutions to the race question, members of the Slater circle endorsed Southern segregation. Haygood and Curry reflected this in their administration of the fund. Both used their influence to punish principals, teachers, and schools that defied segregation practices. Often these were the same people and institutions that they rebuked for halfheartedly embracing the industrial education curriculum. The clearest example was Haygood's reaction to Councill and Huntsville; however, that was not an isolated incident. When Wilbur Thirkield, the president of Gammon Theological Seminary, denounced Southern racism in a speech in Chicago in 1890, it caused a "tremendous furor" in the Southern press. Haygood threatened to withdraw Slater Fund grants from all Methodist institutions until Thirkield apologized.

Motivated by their belief in the value of black industrial education and their endorsement of Southern racial mores and practices, circle members embraced the educational model developed by Samuel Chapman Armstrong at Hampton Institute in Virginia and copied by Washington at Tuskegee and sister institutions. Armstrong's curriculum, Hayes proclaimed, "hits the nail on the head. It solves the whole negro problem." It became clear to members of the Slater board that industrial education could inculcate blacks with proper personal discipline and moral improvement, in addition to training them in agricultural, industrial, and domestic skills. It did not challenge the underlying tenets of segregation or white supremacy; such an education could train a future generation of black leaders, fitting them "for the places they are to fill in life."

In their management and distribution of the Slater endowment in the 1880s and 1890s, the members of the Slater circle – especially the general agents – underwent a shift from an older individualistic style of charity to a newer bureaucratic and "scientific" philanthropy. This mirrored what was happening generally to American philanthropy between the Civil War and the early twentieth century. The earlier style of charity had engaged philanthropists in acts of personal benevolence, placing a premium on the relationship between the donor and the recipient. Influenced by current social science and emerging management practices, however, the newer "scientific" philanthropy emphasized businesslike methods, efficiency, centralized decision-making, and the broad application of funds to social groups to achieve social objectives. It valued the bureaucratic means by which foundations were administered, eliminating personal contact between the donor and the recipient. Cold and impersonal, it depended on orderly investigation of social problems, the gathering of facts and statistics, and a reliance on experts. Yet, both models attempted to force recipients to conform to a prevailing social ideal. Whether rooted in religion or science,

Table I. *Annual Slater Fund Appropriations to Hampton and Tuskegee Institutes, 1882–1903*

Year	Total Appropriations ($)	Hampton-Tuskegee Appropriations ($)	Hampton-Tuskegee Percentage (%)
1882–83	16,250	2,100	12.9
1883–84	17,107	1,000	5.8
1884–85	36,764	3,000	8.2
1885–86	30,000	3,900	13.0
1886–87	40,000	4,000	10.0
1887–88	45,000	4,000	8.9
1888–89	44,310	3,500	7.9
1889–90	42,910	3,500	8.2
1890–91	49,650	4,000	8.1
1891–92	45,217	3,700	8.2
1892–93	37,100	7,100	19.1
1893–94	40,000	9,000	22.5
1894–95	42,400	11,400	26.9
1895–96	38,561	11,400	29.6
1896–97	41,900	13,900	33.2
1897–98	42,500	20,000	47.1
1898–99	45,000	20,000	44.4
1899–1900	43,331	20,000	46.2
1900–01	51,800	26,000	50.2
1901–02	53,400	27,000	50.6
1902–03	53,800	27,000	50.2

Source: Dwight O. Holmes, *The Evolution of the Negro College* (College Park, MD, 1934), p. 170.

nineteenth-century philanthropy imposed a social model upon the weak, the needy, and the disadvantaged.

The major beneficiaries of this new orientation were Hampton and Tuskegee (see Table I). By 1900, these two schools received more than half of the monies awarded by the fund. In that year, Slater grants accounted for more than three fifths of Tuskegee's annual nontuition income. Viewing the Hampton-Tuskegee model of industrial education as the most appropriate for blacks throughout the South, members of the Slater circle hoped that Hampton and Tuskegee would serve as models that other Southern black colleges would emulate.

An especially close working relationship emerged between Washington and the Slater circle. Hayes thought him to be "the ablest and most useful Colored Man in the Country." Curry admired Washington's "prudence" and remarked "in twenty years laboring and associating with him under all kinds of trials and conditions, I have never heard him say or do an imprudent thing." Gilman observed that he had proper "views" on the race question. Washington constantly endeavored to assure the Slater circle of his acceptance of the status quo in Southern race relations. He noted to Curry that he believed it to be a thing that "must be lived down, not talked down." As a result, the Slater circle frequently sought his advice and tolerated his interference in their decision-making, especially on the question of concentrating appropriations on a limited number of institutions.

Because they admired Washington and his rhetoric of racial accommodation and black self-help, members of the Slater board assisted in his rise as a black leader and a symbol of the industrial education curriculum. While defiant black leaders such as Councill were cut off from the Slater largesse, funding to Tuskegee and personal assistance to Washington increased dramatically. Slater subsidies to Tuskegee nearly quadrupled between 1892–93 and 1897–98 and continued to grow. Impressed by Washington's Atlanta Exposition Speech in 1895, Gilman used his position as chief of the Exposition's Bureau of Awards to make him one of the judges. Curry used Slater monies to sponsor the Tuskegee Industrial Exhibit at the exposition because he believed it would be "stimulating to the Schools and the race." After the exposition, Slater board assistance to Washington became even more direct. Board members conceived and funded an extensive speaking tour for Washington during 1897–98, which reached black audiences in ten Southern states. In 1901, the board sponsored another Washington speaking tour of black communities in Mississippi. About that time, the board purchased and distributed ten thousand copies of Washington's book, *The Future of the American Negro,* to both black and white readers in the South. Although it cannot be determined with precision what the net impact of all this Slater assistance might have been, Washington personally credited the fund with playing a major role in redirecting African American social thought away from political solutions to industrial education. He perceived that "no single agency has accomplished more in stimulating and guiding the education of the negro along proper channels than the John F. Slater Fund."

Booker T. Washington, however, did not embody the only ideal for African Americans, especially among members of his own race. W. E. B.

Du Bois criticized Washington for his willingness to subordinate African American concerns to gain social acceptance. He argued in *The Souls of Black Folks* (1903) that, as a result, a black American lived in

...a world which yields him no true self-consciousness, but only lets him see himself through the revelation of the other world. It is a peculiar consciousness, this sense of always looking at one's self through the eyes of others, of measuring one's soul by the tape of a world that looks on in amused contempt and pity.

Throughout American history, private-sector philanthropy has been a means by which philanthropic actors could empower themselves, strive for a social ideal, and redefine themselves in society. Yet, the philanthropic relationship depends on both donor and recipient – and neither is truly a passive participant. The Slater Fund attempted to use money and the promise of incremental social gain to pacify its recipients. For many years, it succeeded.

America's acceptance of this private-sector agenda after 1877 was consistent with both the changing historical meaning of the Civil War itself and a national retreat from modernist idealism. By the 1880s, Americans sought a cultural and ideological reunion of North and South, reconceiving the bitter dispute of the 1860s in relational terms. Historian David Blight writes that "what mattered most was not the content of the cause on either side, but the acts of commitment to either cause, not ideas but the experience born of conflict over those ideas. Whoever was honest in his devotion was right." George Fredrickson places this revisionist historical memory in the context of a broader cultural malaise in the late nineteenth century. The horrible death and destruction caused by the war disabused Americans of their self-image as a chosen people and rendered idealism an irrelevant remnant of an earlier romantic age. War required the subordination of private interests to a conception of a broader public good – an exchange that Americans were no longer willing to make. Yet, anti-institutional individualism was restrained by Americans' emerging desires for order, discipline, and efficiency. Popular interpretations of the growth of scientific knowledge created a belief in evolutionary progress in which the strong must lead. Boys and young men were encouraged to pursue the "strenuous life" of Spartan discipline and martial valor. America's economic and intellectual elite were to assume the responsibility for social growth and economic prosperity. Social progress was believed to result from scientists, merchants, and bankers pursuing responsible private agendas and could only be impeded by the federal government. People in commerce, law, agriculture, and industry sought only to apply the new science of the late nineteenth century to their own fields to produce greater efficiencies. Herbert Spencer's articulation of Social Darwinism, the rise of Christian missions, and the pioneering studies of cultural anthropologists combined to provide an intellectual justification for a new model of paternalism, expressed in private philanthropic organizations representing a social and business elite.

This new ideology served to support not only the laissez-faire policies surrounding industrial expansion at home, but also a reformulated conception of American society that legitimated the conquest of the Indians in the West and imperialism abroad. God, science, and the elite worked together to realize America's national destiny at the end of the nineteenth century.

* * *

Working through the GEB, the Slater Fund and similar foundations strove to broaden their influence over African American education in the South during the early twentieth century. In 1911, acting under the direction of a new general agent, James Hardy Dillard, a Virginian, the fund began to promote the development of county training schools. These were boarding institutions for black students that were operated by local public schools districts and centrally located in the counties they served. Over the next few years, Slater monies were diverted away from existing black schools and colleges and toward the county training schools. By 1931, three quarters of the annual appropriations of the fund went toward the support of the 390 county training schools in the South. But even though the recipients had changed, the social goals of the Slater board had not. Dillard and the members of the Slater board continued to adhere to the curricular preference and racial practices of their predecessors.

The Great Depression, the growth of black higher education, National Association for the Advancement of Colored People (NAACP) court challenges, and the mechanization of cotton agriculture, which increasingly sent rural southern blacks northward, all changed the context in which the Slater Fund and similar foundations operated in the middle decades of the twentieth century. Between 1935 and 1937, county training schools throughout the South were rapidly phased out or transformed into public high schools. In 1937, the Slater endowment merged with the Jeanes Fund, the Peabody Fund, and the newly established Virginia Randolph Fund to create the Southern Education Foundation. Influenced by social changes,

Lifting or lowering the veil of ignorance? Statue of Booker T. Washington and seated slave at Tuskegee Institute, with sculptor Charles Peck. (Division of Photographs and Prints, Library of Congress.)

as well as a growing racial liberalism within both the educational and philanthropic communities in the United States, the agenda and the leadership of the foundation transformed dramatically in the post–World War II period. Eventually led by African Americans and devoted to the principle of educational equality, the foundation worked behind the scenes to help facilitate the desegregation of black higher education in the South.

Ironically, the Slater endowment was employed in the 1950s, 1960s, and 1970s to dismantle the curricular emphasis and racial practices it had once promoted.

What was the impact of foundation philanthropy in the education of African Americans in the post-emancipation South? Certainly, it can be argued, the Slater Fund and those foundations that followed it into the field of black schooling imposed on many African Americans – often against their explicit wishes – a curriculum designed to train them for political, social, and economic subservience. And they maintained that curriculum through financial enticements, threats, and punishments for more than half a century. But as Judith Sealander perceptively observed, it is possible to exaggerate the power of philanthropy for good or ill. Foundation initiatives did not automatically translate into the desired social and educational objectives when applied to individual schools and students. Nor were the foundations the only sources of funding available for the support of African American education in the South. The schools and colleges sustained by the missionary organizations and African American denominations, despite paternalism and poverty, provided meaningful training in the liberal arts for several generations of black leaders – most notably W. E. B. Du Bois, Carter G. Woodson, Thurgood Marshall, and Martin Luther King, Jr. – who challenged the existing racial prejudices and worked fervently for a more egalitarian future.

8

WOMEN AND POLITICAL CULTURE

KATHLEEN D. McCARTHY

One of the enduring questions in the field of women's studies asks how women in the United States created public roles and exercised political influence before they won the right to vote. Denied access to direct political participation at the federal level for almost a century and a half after Independence, middle- and upper-class white women nonetheless left their distinctive imprint on the country's laws and its public services. This, in turn, raises a number of related questions concerning the boundaries between "public" and "private" activities, politics, and the voluntary sphere. Are these realms genuinely separate (as McGarvie contends in his chapter) or do we need to devise new ways of thinking about government that embrace ostensibly "private" philanthropic and nonprofit initiatives more fully? Who participated and how did their contributions vary? Women's activities provide an ideal laboratory for tracing the role of philanthropy – "gifts of time, money, or material goods for public purposes" – in enabling even politically disadvantaged groups to shape American society.

Several factors are important for understanding women's philanthropic roles within the United States before 1930: (1) the extent to which service provision was historically rooted in public-private partnerships, opening an enlarged "space" for female governance; (2) the role of religious traditions in fostering social mobilization and reform, issues that are also discussed in the chapters by Amanda Porterfield, Wendy Gamber, and Emily Rosenberg; and (3) the ways in which different groups of women used their volunteer time to create "parallel power structures" to the political and for-profit sectors controlled by men, and to carve out a significant place for themselves in the public arena. This essay examines the ways in which American women used their voluntary associations to build a distinctive political culture in two periods: 1790–1860, when the infrastructure for female associationalism first emerged; and 1860–1930, when women's organizations arguably laid the groundwork for a national welfare state.

* * *

Citizenship is a social construct, not a given, and several factors contributed to the gendered visions of female citizenship in the nineteenth century. According to custom and the law, women were politically invisible, legally "covered" by their spouse's identities; the reality was often quite different. Beyond the absence of skirted citizens at the ballot box, beyond the hollow rhetoric of the "cult of domesticity," lay a teeming associational universe through which women from often very different backgrounds left their imprint on American policies, politics, and practices.

Although the Revolution spread a "contagion of liberty" that led growing ranks of American citizens into the public sphere over the course of the nineteenth century, opening the door to female participation was hardly the Founders' intent. Women were absent from the Constitution, absent from the Federalist Papers, and barred from the polls in the new republic. Instead, the opening wedge for women's roles in "nation-building" emerged from a variety of disparate factors: a tradition of public-private partnerships, religious disestablishment, an ethos of limited government, and the spiralling social needs that attended the country's growth.

Alliances between nonprofit organizations and state and local governmental bodies were deeply rooted in the American past, tracing their origins to the colonial era. A few examples suffice to illustrate this point: Benjamin Franklin helped to launch the Pennsylvania Hospital for Sick Poor in 1751 by raising funds through his newspaper to match a £2,000 challenge grant offered by the colonial assembly. Harvard began to blend endowment income and private gifts with legislative grants and tuition fees in the seventeenth century. Colonial New Yorkers conducted private subscription campaigns to augment the city's outlays for poor relief, and Virginia coupled its welfare funds with private donations funneled through the vestrymen of the Anglican Church. In each instance, public and private resources and revenues were blended in the provision of public services.

These trends were strengthened by the Revolution. Unlike its European counterparts, the American government was cast in the crucible of skeptical Enlightenment thought and tinged with a strong distrust of the corrupting influence of political power. As such, the federal government was initially designed with only limited authority, including a circumscribed capacity to tax that was echoed at the state and local levels. This, in turn, produced a political context shorn of the comprehensive civil bureaucracies that oversaw public administration in Bismark's Germany and the British Empire, producing a managerial void that was often filled by citizen groups in the United States.

While popular misgivings and scanty tax revenues limited governmental capacities to build enduring bureaucracies and deliver public services, Constitutional guarantees of the right of citizens "peaceably to assemble and to petition the Government for a redress of grievances" turned associational activities into popular entitlements. Although not initially conceived as a manifesto for voluntary associations, First Amendment assurances of the right to assemble and petition for legislative change opened opportunities for even disfranchised groups to participate in public policymaking.

Disestablishment was another important earmark of American society. Prior to the Revolution, most colonies had state-affiliated churches, ranging from the Church of England in the southern regions to Congregationalism in New England. The movement to sever these institutions from state support was spearheaded by Thomas Jefferson, who drafted the country's first disestablishment law in Virginia in 1777. The law passed eight years later, one of a string of similar acts that erased the last of the country's state churches in Massachusetts in 1833. Mark McGarvie's essay describes the social tensions attendant to this process. Beyond severing specific denominations from state support, disestablishment created a level playing field in which *all* churches became voluntary associations, competing for congregants, converts, and backers on a equal basis. Far from stilling the course of religion, Jefferson's legislation spawned a kaliedescope of sects – trends that had profound implications for the growth of American philanthropy – including the spectrum of social reform movements detailed by Gamber.

Geographical expansion played a role as well. In 1790, the United States consisted essentially of a strip settlement along the Atlantic seacoast. Seventy years later, it stretched 3,000 miles across the continent to the Pacific Ocean. This rapid growth engendered a voracious appetite for educational and welfare services in newly minted towns across the moving frontier. Since government funding for these services was limited, the need for continuing public-private partnerships added a value to women's volunteer activities that they might not have had in a more centralized political milieu or a less volatile geographical setting.

All of these factors combined to draw middle- and upper-class women into extrapolitical activities that enhanced their political and economic roles while broadening the concept of female citizenship. Prior to the introduction of Married Women's Property Acts in the mid-nineteenth century, the common-law doctrine of *femme coverte* prohibited wives from owning and alienating property in their own right. Nor did they legally control their dowries or wages. Indeed, women's legal dependency on their husbands was one of the arguments used to deny them the vote because wives were deemed incapable of acting independently from their spouses.

However, once they gathered together to form a legally chartered charitable corporation, even married women assumed a part of a collective identity that imbued them with legal prerogatives that they lacked as individuals, including the right to buy, sell, and invest property and to sign binding contracts. They gained a voice in public policy-making as well. Despite their political invisibility, the women who ran urban charities were often quite adept at lobbying for municipal appropriations for their organizations.

They also exercised significant economic roles under the mantle of what would now be termed *nonprofit entrepreneurship*. As the combined forces of industrialization and marketization gathered momentum, many middle-class white women were eased out of the paid workforce. Although opinions vary about the degree of leisure this created for them, by 1830 some of these women began to have more surplus time to contribute to voluntary activities than either their spouses or working-class women or men. In an economy of scarcity where only limited funds were available for charitable activities, volunteer labor often provided the margin that guaranteed institutional survival. The end result was a social context in which policy-making was decentralized, philanthropy was encouraged, and different groups felt entitled to contend for recognition and authority in the public arena – even women.

* * *

After the Revolution, small groups of elite women began to test the boundaries of Revolutionary egalitarianism by creating charitable institutions of their own. Prior to the war, women's public roles were limited to commercial ventures, church membership, and the charitable activities of Quaker women who cared for members of their own sect. Some women also actively participated in the commercial boycotts that immediately preceded the war, but these activities were an exception rather than the rule.

By the 1790s, however, women's charities and asylums began to appear in the larger seacoast cities like Philadelphia and New York, providing charity and employment for poor women with families and asylums for dependent children. In an era in which women often comprised the majority of the urban poor, these activities accorded women's and children's issues a place on public policy-making agendas for the first time. They also provided an alternative to publicly sponsored almshouses. Generally regarded as places of last resort, these government-run asylums housed random populations of paupers and madmen, children and adults at public expense. Overcrowding was a constant problem, adding to the dehumanizing atmosphere of this heterogeneous melange. In 1797, for example, more than eight hundred inmates crowded into New York's public almshouse, conditions that gave rise to the city's first female-controlled charity: the Society for the Relief of Poor Widows with Small Children (Widow's Society).

Founded in New York in 1797, the Widows Society provided both alms and employment for women who had lost their husbands and had two or more children in their care. Because it helped to keep women out of the public almshouse, the Society became the first female-controlled charity to be granted a New York state charter in 1802. In the colonial and early national periods, the granting of charters was a political act, decided on a case-by-case basis and sparingly allotted. These were precious documents, not only conferring collective privileges on the trustees and condoning the organization's right to own property, but also affording public recognition of the institution's civic importance in addressing public problems and reducing demands on the public till.

Organizations such as the Widows Society collected both profits and property as they matured. Popular perceptions of nonprofit organizations often frame them as wholly dependent on donations from individuals, but this is a distorted image that reflects only part of the ways in which nonprofit organizations historically operated. From their inception, female-controlled charities and asylums subsisted on a mixed portfolio of donations, investments, public allocations, and generated funds. For example, the trustees of the Widows Society lent spinning wheels to their beneficiaries and provided cloth to be sewn into bedding and clothes that were then sold. Philadelphia's Female Assistance Society created an informal factory where impoverished women made cloth, receiving part of the profits in charity and alms. Asylums for orphans, destitute children, former prostitutes, and abused and abandoned wives also used inmate labor to offset their costs, teaching what were deemed marketable skills while generating revenues for institutional support. Trustees as well as inmates took an entrepreneurial turn, making handmade household goods for sale at charity fairs, benefits, and bazaars – efforts that culminated in the million-dollar profits generated for the Union troops through Civil War Sanitary Commission Fairs.

They also received state and municipal grants and contracts for their role in the delivery of social services. Municipal and county governments in New Orleans, Philadelphia, and even Fayetteville, North Carolina, all sponsored women's charities. However, New York was the most generous patron, not only of women's groups, but also of nonprofits run by diverse religious bodies, immigrants, and (in a limited number of instances) African Americans. A few organizations received additional windfalls via state-sponsored lotteries, such as the $15,000 earmarked for the Widows Society in 1803. These practices emphasized the ties between local charities and the state and the role of private charities in reducing almshouse populations. The ability of elite white women to secure public charters and funding illustrated the ways in which at least some female citizens were able to carve out enlarged roles for themselves in the wake of the Revolution.

Questions have been raised by some historians about who benefited most from these institutions – was their appearance a sign of growing democracy or was it simply a tool for the consolidation of elite authority? Beginning in the 1960s, many scholars began to depict charities as instruments of social control, created by white male elites who sought to regulate the behavior of the poor as they lost their monopoly on local politics with the expansion of the vote. By the 1980s, women's historians began to pick up these themes as well, arguing that middle-class reformers and "benevolent ladies" strengthened class boundaries by sentimentalizing the plight of the poor, rather than combating the underlying social and economic causes of poverty.

More recently, a few scholars have begun to reconsider these arguments, stressing the social agency of the poor. Although many criticize the charitable endeavors that made moral distinctions between the "worthy" and "unworthy" poor, requiring good behavior in return for aid, they also note the ways in which recipients used these services for their own ends. By tapping into a variety of sources – earnings, loans from relatives and kin, and public and private charities – many were able to hold their families together in the face of cyclical unemployment and insufficient wages. More than simple victims, these interpretations stress the extent to which the working poor were important actors in the process of charitable exchange.

Many of the first female-controlled charities were far less moralistic and far more secular than the antebellum institutions that their daughters and granddaughters created. Life was precarious for *any* woman in this period, and even elite women could and did lose their wealth with stunning speed. As a result, the women who created early ventures like the Widows Society often demonstrated a considerable amount of sympathy – and empathy – with the people they sought to aid.

Beyond the issues of benefits and beneficiaries, the rise of women's charities in the 1790s provides a lens for reevaluating the legacy of the Revolution. Since the 1980s, the reigning interpretive paradigm has been the idea of "Republican Motherhood": the notion that women gained new status after the Revolution through their roles in training virtuous sons as future citizens. Philanthropy provides a different perspective for understanding the Revolution's impact on women's lives, one that reaches beyond the domestic sphere. The advent of chartered women's charities heralded the rise of a distinctive female political culture, providing a point of entry for at least some women into the rarified realms of public administration, public policy-making, and nonprofit business development – practices strengthened and democratized by religious imperatives.

* * *

The small amount of associational activity that began in the wake of the Revolution became a veritable flood in the nineteenth century, as religious institutions laced the country with the Bible, tract, and missionary societies of the Benevolent Empire. Beginning in the 1810s, these organizations appeared with growing frequency, providing an institutional infrastructure for grassroots mobilization, charity, faith, and reform.

Their power and popularity grew from the forces unleashed by disestablishment and from the Second Great Awakening – the waves of religious enthusiasm that began with the revivals of the 1790s and crested four decades later. Women were both major participants and major beneficiaries of these developments. Female parishioners constituted the bulk of practicing church members both before and after the Revolution. Although barred from the ministry in most denominations, and church boards of lay trustees in many, women filled the pews; raised a significant percentage of the funds for ministerial salaries, capital improvements, and missionary work; taught in the Sunday schools; and promoted denominational charities – activities that ultimately widened their access to public roles.

Protestantism – especially evangelical Protestantism – was a particularly important factor in these developments for several reasons. Unlike Catholicism, many Protestant denominations were relatively decentralized, allowing their parishioners to exercise considerable autonomy in controlling the institutions they created. Moreover, because ministers were dependent on their parishioners' good will for their appointments and their salaries (which depended in large measure on women's fundraising skills), they tended to endorse female participation in church-sponsored charities and social-reform movements. There were doctrinal issues as well. Whereas Catholicism and Anglicanism are liturgical religions that place rituals and sacraments at the heart of the religious experience, evangelical sects such as the more liberal branches of Congregationalism and Presbyterianism, Baptists, and Methodists regard the ability to read and interpret the Bible as the basis of religious practice and belief. In effect, among these denominations, literacy provided the key to personal salvation. The ability to read opened the world, enabling men and women to exchange ideas beyond their own parishes, neighborhoods, and towns – a vital prerequisite for the creation of national organizational networks like the auxiliaries of the Benevolent Empire, as well as the missionary societies described by Porterfield.

Catholics, Protestants, and Jews all developed charities and educational programs during the first half of the nineteenth century, and all of these activities were grounded, in part, in religious teachings. However, the first Jewish organizations tended to be inward-turning, designed to preserve communal rituals and to protect Jewish communities from Protestant missionary activities. As a result, Jewish women created charities and educational ventures within their own communities, but were far less prominent in the national social-reform movements spearheaded by their Protestant counterparts.

Similarly, Catholic laywomen were encouraged to confine their energies and attentions to fundraising for parish-based services. Nuns rather than laywomen managed Catholic charities and schools, while priests and bishops often oversaw the collection and distribution of their parishioners' donations. This model produced interesting results that were often quite different from Protestant practices. For example, research by Hasia Diner suggests that Irish women were very active contributors to Catholic churches, charities, and religious orders. Many were domestic servants who tended to marry later than their Protestant counterparts, if they married at all; if they remained single, they generally remained childless as well.

These women invested their earnings in savings accounts to tide them over in retirement, remittances to their families in Ireland, boat tickets for American-bound siblings and kin, and donations to the church. According to Diner, in "every city where the Irish settled . . . women contributed the vast bulk of financial support" for church-related services. Encouraged as donors rather than volunteers, Catholic laywomen were less likely to run their own charities, actively participate in national benevolent networks, lobby for charters or municipal support, or take the lead in social or political reform.

Protestant women, on the other hand, were important architects of the Benevolent Empire. Although headed by interlocking directorates of prominent, pious males, women ran many of the auxiliaries of organizations, such as the American Bible Society, the American Sunday School Union, and the American Tract Society. They also managed some of the services (e.g., as local Sunday Schools) and raised a significant portion of the funds.

Independent societies to distribute Bibles, train ministers, and conduct Sunday Schools began to appear around 1810, many of which were founded and funded by laywomen. Whereas Sunday Schools provided literacy training interlarded with Bible studies, missionary and ministerial societies sought to spread the faith by training young men to fill new pulpits on the moving frontier. The Benevolent Empire coordinated these activities into national systems of auxiliaries under the guidance of headquarters operations based in Philadelphia, Boston, and New York, raising funds, developing programs, and distributing materials through local parishes across the nation. Most of the Benevolent Empire societies had hundreds of auxiliaries by 1820, providing a national network for grassroots mobilization and reform that had the potential to reach into every town with a Protestant church. In the process, the Benevolent Empire provided the means through which growing numbers of ordinary citizens – including women – were mobilized, educated, and drawn into institutional development and social reform.

Who participated in these activities? Historian Elizabeth Fox Genovese argues that female philanthropy was primarily a Northeastern phenomenon, the province of middle- and upper-class white elites. Certainly, these were the women who populated the boards of the largest charities and who headed the most visible auxiliaries of antebellum reform groups like the American Antislavery Society and the American Female Moral Reform Society. Yet, although we lack statistical data on who participated in the

rank and file of women's auxiliaries, there is enough information to challenge Genovese's assertion.

Certainly, there were geographical differences. Although we now know
that Southern white women built many charities and asylums, and headed
significant numbers of church-related auxiliaries within the Benevolent
Empire's fold, they were far less likely to participate in social reform, run
highly capitalized charities, and secure charters (particularly if they were
free blacks); and were absolutely barred from promoting causes like abolitionism. Men rather than women controlled the wealthiest charities and
often supervised women's charities in the same way that they oversaw black
religious meetings, discouraging separatist ventures in lieu of mixed associations where men and women participated together.

Western women operated under a patchwork of differing state policies.
While Illinois's "benevolent ladies" worked with charters but without public
funds before the Civil War, California women netted substantial windfalls
from their local governments. The provision of municipal funding for
female-controlled institutions varied widely between locales. New York was
the most generous state, but Pennsylvania, Maryland, Louisiana, and even
Virginia funded selected women's charities, making regional generalizations
difficult.

Northern African American women were very active in religious and
secular charities by the 1840s, participating in abolitionist and mutual-aid
societies, literary groups, Sunday Schools, and moral reform. They also
raised funds to subsidize black newspapers such as Frederick Douglass's
influential *North Star*, helping their communities to create a distinctive
political culture of their own. Although free black women in Southern cities
had less autonomy and almost no hope of obtaining charters or municipal
funds, they were active in churches, some conducted Sunday Schools, and
a few even left sizable donations to their congregations.

Working women were also both donors and volunteers. Historian Christine Stansell painted our most compelling portrait of antebellum working-
class women's lives in *City of Women*, arguing that their neighborhoods were
bound by dense networks of mutual aid rather than formal associations.
However, work by other historians suggests that working-class women were
involved in the church, in antislavery movements, and (most obviously) in
labor reform. For example, the Lowell Female Labor Reform Association
(LFLRA) promoted legislation; coordinated statewide petition drives in
Massachusetts; and publicized the need for labor legislation in newspapers,

pamphlets, and journals during the 1840s. Although their campaign for the 10-hour day failed to yield new laws, their petition drives did produce Massachusetts' first legislative labor inquiry in 1845, forcing at least some factory owners into arbitration to reduce their employees' workdays – all of which suggests that female philanthropic activities were broadly etched in the antebellum period and fairly democratically based.

Other concepts require revision as well, particularly the centrality of the "Cult of Domesticity" in providing a rationale for antebellum female benevolence. According to this interpretation, bourgeois domesticity became one of the controlling metaphors of American society in the 1820s and 1830s. As the traditional household economy disintegrated under the combined weight of marketization and nascent industrialization, middle-class families created a distinctively private domestic sphere and a sentimental culture that celebrated the home as the empire of maternal rule. Middle-class wives were expected to be pious, virtuous, self-sacrificing, and *very* domestic, ideas used to justify their confinement in the home. Drawn from the literature and prescriptive writings in women's magazines, annuals, gift books, and advice books, this notion has been used as a catch phrase to characterize the lives of antebellum women for nearly three decades. Many historians have noted the extent to which the concept of domesticity provided a double-edged sword, legitimizing women's participation in charity and missionary work, as well as their domestic confinement. But given the substantial political and economic roles that female charity trustees, asylum directors, and Sunday School managers played in American society, this idea is far too cloying and too narrowly cast to accurately describe bourgeois womanhood as a whole.

More recent interpretations have taken a different tack, stressing women's political culture, citizenship, and nation-building activities. *Political culture* refers to the experiences and values that lead people to make political choices. In effect, it "colors a people's expectation about the realities of politics and instills in them shared expectations as to what their public life might be." This concept also provides a more encompassing definition of politics *per se*, allowing even nonelected and disfranchised citizens to be seen as political actors in their own right when their actions intersected with formal political and governmental processes. The women who built the asylums; founded the auxiliaries; and funded the spread of Catholic, Protestant, and Jewish charities also profoundly shaped the ways in which Americans perceived middle-class womanhood and women's appropriate sphere, building an edifice for charity and reform that reached into state and federal policy-making as the century progressed.

* * *

Participation in voluntary associations ultimately gave women a voice in local, state, and national legislative debates, as well as the distribution of charitable resources. Women – especially (but not exclusively) middle- and upper-class white women – used the parallel power structures that they created through their charities to influence legislation in three ways: publicity, lobbying, and the collection and filing of petitions. Through activities such as these, female auxiliaries and groups such as the American Antislavery Society, the Women's Christian Temperance Union, and the National American Women's Suffrage Association spearheaded the passage of constitutional amendments to extend the rights of citizenship to formerly enslaved black males, outlaw liquor sales, and win the vote for themselves – and they did so without direct access to the polls.

The history of these Constitutional campaigns is well known and, therefore, will not be detailed here. However, the ramifications of more recent debates about women's roles in nation-building and the rise of the modern welfare state have not been fully explored. Some of the liveliest debates in this area have centered on the work of Theda Skocpol, who contends in *Protecting Soldiers and Mothers* that women, rather than men, laid the groundwork for American welfarism. Moreover, according to Skocpol, they did so by effectively promoting the introduction of "maternalist" legislation for women and children in the 1910s and 1920s, well before the New Deal programs of the depression-riddled thirties that have traditionally been thought to mark America's experiment with a welfare state.

Women's alliances with state and federal policymakers dated from the Civil War. Northern white women played a particularly prominent role in the U.S. Sanitary Commission (USSC). Authorized by Abraham Lincoln on June 9, 1861, the USSC provided medical aid, funding, and assistance in systematizing the collection and distribution of donated supplies for the troops. The men who directed it used their authority to apply the scientific lessons learned from Florence Nightingale's nursing corps during the Crimean War. Middle- and upper-class white women, on the other hand, used their administrative and fundraising skills to coordinate more than seven thousand soldiers aid auxiliaries, collecting and distributing more than $15 million in supplies for the troops over the course of the war.

One of the USSC's most notable innovations was the Sanitary Fairs that were held in major cities between 1863 and 1865. Women's organizations had participated in quasicommercial ventures since their inception in the 1790s, and the Sanitary Fairs amplified this work tenfold. In 1863, Chicago's Northwestern Sanitary Fair raised almost $80,000 in less than a month for the troops and for battlefront hospitals. Similar initiatives were subsequently staged in Cleveland, Cincinnati, Pittsburgh, Philadelphia, Albany, Brooklyn, and New York, generating more than $2 million for Union soldiers and USSC operations by 1865.

Fundraising also provided a point of access to federal policymakers and program development for African Americans. Black women formed a variety of soldiers aid societies to aid African American soldiers, their families, and former slaves, such as the Louisville Ladies' Aid Society, which solicited donations to build a hospital and school for recently liberated Southern freedmen. Similarly, Philadelphia's Freedmen's Relief Association was created in 1865 with an ambitious pledge to support teachers and schools, send clothing and medical supplies to impoverished freedmen, and establish asylums for dependent children and the aged. Members solicited funds in their churches, sponsored fairs and sewing circles, and even established children's fundraising groups.

Many of these organizations later collaborated with the federal Freedmen's Bureau. Some African Americans taught in federally sponsored southern schools or raised funds for independent black churches and schools in liberated areas. Remarkably, many former slaves also invested their time and meager earnings in the creation and incorporation of churches and schools, establishing permanent, legal institutional bases for black communal life. In some instances, they provided matching funds for northern grants contributed by organizations such as the American Missionary Association and the Freedmen's Bureau to pay for school buildings and teachers' salaries. Although it had a troubled history in many other respects, the Freedmen's Bureau made a lasting contribution through its educational programs, coupling more than $1 million in federal funds with private donations to build the South's first formal institutions for African American education. Thirty-one Northern missionary and aid societies added another $15 million in donations between 1865 and 1870, providing instruction for more than 150,000 students in 2,700 schools taught by almost 4,000 white and black teachers, as well as laying the foundations for a string of black colleges throughout the South.

White women's fundraising and soldiers aid societies also surfaced with impressive speed in the Southern states at the beginning of the war. According to some estimates, 150 societies appeared in South Carolina alone during the first three months, and almost 1,000 were created throughout the region as a whole. Most raised funds or sewed goods for the troops from materials supplied and distributed by government officials, but a few took a more direct hand in shaping Confederate policies by subsidizing the acquisition of military equipment, including the purchase of gunboats to patrol coastal waters.

The war marked a major turning point in Southern white women's philanthropy. Historian Anne Firor Scott highlights the extent to which Southern women's activism was a product of the postwar years, a theme echoed by other authors as well. One of the leitmotivs of these studies is the extent to which women worked with their governments to create services and wield policy-making authority, heralding the advent of new forms of Southern female activism. African Americans also benefited from the newly secularized national infrastructure for social mobilization and reform that was forged in the war. Even in a racially divided South, where considerable efforts were made to dismantle the political gains won by African Americans during Reconstruction, the institutional infrastructure that began in the collaborative efforts of the missionary societies, churches, women's groups, and the Freedmen's Bureau endured, providing a base for a century-long campaign for human dignity and civil rights.

The war also added a new gendered spin to philanthropy. Many of the men who provisioned the troops and built the transportation system amassed enormous fortunes during and after the hostilities, becoming America's first generation of millionaires. The upshot was that men's and women's philanthropic styles began to move in different directions after the war. Whereas wealthy businessmen such as John D. Rockefeller and Andrew Carnegie lavished massive donations on growing crops of foundations, universities, museums, and think tanks created in the corporate image of their business ventures, women – even very wealthy women – continued to build their own organizations through an economy of time rather than cash.

Their ability to contribute time was a source of their political strength. Middle- and upper-class women, especially white women, were the only group in America's industrializing economy with sufficient leisure and financial security to embrace voluntarism as a full-time career. This vocational advantage reinforced their ability to donate large amounts of service, enhancing the importance of these donations within the arena of American governance.

The Gilded Age witnessed a remarkable expansion of national women's organizations, a few of which – like the Women's Christian Temperance Union (WCTU) – numbered more than a million members by century's end. Women's clubs also appeared in cities and towns across the nation, providing laboratories for middle-class self-education and reform. Missionary societies also expanded exponentially among both black and white women's groups, whereas African American women formed separate YWCAs and the National Association of Colored Women's Clubs. Many of their groups cast their claims for enlarged public roles in the idiom of the household, whether they used the WCTU's term *home protection* in lobbying for tighter liquor laws, or the Progressive Era motto of *municipal housekeeping*: the idea that women had a political stake in ensuring that they and their families would have clean streets and markets, clean water and milk, and access to decent educational institutions.

However, there were other ways in which they enhanced their political roles and their "nation-building" capacities through their associational activities, beyond maternal rationales. Other industrialized nations developed their welfare states around the needs of male breadwinners rather than women and children. Other than Civil War veterans' pensions, which were categorized as a military expense, the first widespread public-welfare initiatives in the United States were the forty-one state programs to provide mothers' pensions and the federal grants-in-aid for child health activities mandated by the Sheppard–Towner Act in the 1920s. The U.S. Children's Bureau (USCB), which administered the Sheppard–Towner funds, was the first national bureaucracy in any country to be created and managed almost entirely by women. Skocpol describes the organization as "an internationally distinctive maternalist welfare state" headed and administered by female professionals.

Skocpol and others have triumphantly traced these patterns to the power of women's networks. What began as isolated charitable endeavors at the threshold of the nineteenth century matured into a dense array of local, state, and national women's organizations after the Civil War. By 1900, they were "knit together in huge, nation-spanning federations, networks that paralleled the local/state/national structures of U.S. parties and government." This organizational infrastructure enabled groups like the Women's Trade Union League, women's clubs, the National Consumer's Leagues, and the National Congress of Mothers to spread ideas and marshall volunteers for lobbying efforts with impressive speed. Their numbers were impressive; for example, the National Congress (which later became the PTA) counted more than 190,000 members in thirty-seven states as of 1920.

However, just underscoring the existence of these groups falls short of explaining how they actually functioned as networks and why they were so effective as a policy-making bloc. Some scholars, such as Kathryn Kish Sklar, Seth Koven, and Sonya Michel, have concluded that the efficacy of "women's activism is inversely related to the power of the state," and that decentralized governments will produce the strongest civil societies, opening wider opportunities for public influence for women. However, this interpretation still leaves unanswered questions. For example, why were voteless women able to assume such an important policy-making role?

Philanthropic organizations also enjoyed a special status – that they operated outside the spheres of both the for-profit economy and of patronage politics reinforced their moral authority, enabling them to lobby for and implement public programs. Underscoring "the political uses of moral rhetoric," Skocpol notes that "the party-based 'corruption' that many U.S. reformers associated with the implementation of Civil War pensions prompted them to argue that the United States could not administer any new social spending programs efficiently or honestly." Because of public fears about political corruption, "adult males could not become legitimate beneficiaries of public social spending for workers." Conversely, "women's rhetoric appeared to rise above narrowly partisan considerations" by invoking symbols of motherhood and "notions of selfless morality."

Recent research suggests that women rather than men were the primary architects of the American welfare state, successfully promoting the introduction of "maternalist" legislation for mothers and children in the 1910s and 1920s, well before the New Deal programs that have traditionally been thought to mark the advent of modern American welfarism. Yet, the point that should be stressed is that women's groups were able to do so because they relied so heavily on voluntarism and, therefore, could develop even national public programs at minimal cost through what economists would term a *commodity of time* rather than money. Women's voluntary networks played an indispensable role in helping implement the work of the Children's Bureau by distributing information and literature, coordinating local meetings, and conducting research. In the process, they also reduced the need for salaried, male-controlled administrative bureaucracies.

In effect, voluntary associations were unusually influential in decentralized governmental systems such as that of the United States in this era, precisely because these countries lacked the funds to create large, permanent, public bureaucracies to administer welfare programs. Quite simply, strong governments and the elaborate bureaucratic infrastructures that support them cost money. The American government did not have a great deal of surplus cash at its disposal before the 1930s. Moreover, public sentiment militated against the expansion of government spending, particularly after the veterans' pension programs became embroiled in pork-barrel politics.

In 1915, the tab for the pension program tallied more than $6 million in the state of Massachusetts alone. By comparison, the Children's Bureau initiated its national programs with an annual budget of $26,000 in 1912. By 1915, that figure had risen to $165,000. When the Bureau was charged with the administration of the national grants-in-aid program for the Sheppard–Towner program in 1921, its annual appropriations finally topped the million-dollar mark. With that amount of money, it distributed twenty-two million pieces of literature, coordinated 183,000 health conferences, and established almost 3,000 clinics for prenatal care. It simply would not have been possible to achieve a record like this without the aid of a virtual army of unpaid workers.

Ironically, when women won the vote in 1920, much of the advantage of female moral authority was compromised because the voting returns revealed the extent to which the "female dominion" created by alliances of women reformers, professionals, and volunteers was a middle-class construct that failed to accurately represent American womanhood as a whole. Once the suffrage amendment was ratified, all of the centrifugal forces of class and kin, ethnicity, religion, and race surfaced, dissipating the political clout inherent in the power of numbers, which had traditionally given women's organizations much of their political authority.

It proved to be a precarious strategy. As it became increasingly apparent that female voters would not cast their ballots as a cohesive gender bloc after they won the vote in 1920, the political influence of women reformers waned. Federal appropriations for the Sheppard–Towner program, which was the main source of revenue for the Children's Bureau, began to be phased out in 1926. To quote Muncy, as child welfare services "slid into the mainstream of public policy, women lost their exclusive hold" on these programs, and the public dominion created by settlement-trained researchers and social workers "dissolved."

How does this analysis alter our understanding of the political roles of women's voluntary associations in the United States? Since the mid-1980s, a small but growing number of scholars have underscored the political nature of female voluntarism. One defined its primary role as gap-filling: providing services for causes and constituencies overlooked by political policymakers; another lauded its contributions as "an early warning system" that continually identified and acted on emerging needs.

Rather than simply filling gaps or identifying needs, women worked in tandem with government, blending their contributions as volunteers with public and private donations, income-generation activities, and fees-for-service to provide crucial social welfare services. The special advantage that middle-class women brought to their charities and their legislative campaigns was their ability to run these organizations primarily through an economy of time, rather than relying on large-scale public or private expenditures. This ostensibly placed them above the market place, above the political arena, and above the scramble for extensive federal funding.

In the process, their organizations became powerful political tools in the decentralized and relatively impoverished governmental milieu of the United States. The federal government was often hamstrung in the expansion of its powers to implement national welfare programs in the decades before the New Deal, which led it to forge alliances with nonprofit organizations. By the early twentieth century, philanthropic foundations had begun to create three-tier tracks of managerial elites that linked foundations, government, and academe, helping to develop and test public policies on a national scale in the early decades of the twentieth century. Similarly, women's groups that could volunteer the use of their existing local, state, and national infrastructures were ideally positioned to administer welfare initiatives on a national scale, while applying minimal pressure on the public till.

* * *

Toward the end of his treatise on democracy in the United States, Alexis de Tocqueville mused that if he were asked "to what the singular prosperity and growing strength of [the American] people ought mainly to be attributed," he would reply, "to the superiority of their women." For Tocqueville, the quintessential American woman was white, middle-class, and politically invisible. Despite his keen perception of the importance of voluntary associations in fostering American governance and American democracy, he ultimately concluded that women in this country "irrecoverably" lost their independence "in the bonds of matrimony" and, therefore, they never "take part in political life."

It was an odd omission, one that suggests that the normally canny French aristocrat fundamentally misinterpreted the extent and nature of the civil society that he sought to portray. Far from being apolitical, many middle-class housewives were deeply enmeshed in the practice of governance well before they won the right to vote. Their participation was borne of a variety of factors, not the least of which was the role of Protestantism in spreading literacy and webs of reform across the national landscape. Although the first female-controlled charities were founded and managed by female elites, by the 1810s a national infrastructure for mobilization and reform had emerged under the banner of the Benevolent Empire. Over the past two centuries, American women effectively invested their time, talents, and funds in building an array of public services. Through their philanthropic activities, black and white women – both North and South – backed their churches, founded charities and literary societies, participated in social reform movements to end slavery and extend the vote, and worked in tandem with state and federal officials over the course of the Civil War. These activities enabled at least some to win political and legal benefits for themselves, to accord women's and children's issues a prominent place on the public agenda, and to promote social change to a degree unmatched in other industrialized nations. In the process, they managed to shape American government and the American welfare state from the periphery of the political arena through the power of philanthropy.

Women played a vital role in the emergence of civil society as well. Through public-private partnerships with local, state, and federal policy-makers, philanthropy and the nonprofit sector enabled an array of groups to claim a place on the public stage. Each group used these activities and institutions in different ways, to achieve often differing ends. We are just beginning to understand the impact of philanthropy in shaping American government and American governance, efforts exemplified by the continuing history of women's compassion and generosity.

9

FROM GIFT TO FOUNDATION: THE PHILANTHROPIC LIVES OF MRS. RUSSELL SAGE

RUTH CROCKER

"Each gift is part of a system of reciprocity in which the honor of giver and recipient is involved."
Mary Douglas, "No Free Gifts." Foreword to Marcel Mauss, *The Gift: The Form and Reason for Exchange in Archaic Societies*, trans. · W. D. Halls (1950, New York: W. W. Norton, 1990 ed.).

American philanthropy at the turn of the twentieth century has its cast of colorful and eccentric characters, many of whom have found their biographers. Their lives have reached a wider reading public, and recently Ron Chernow's study of John D. Rockefeller, Sr. (Titan, 1998) became a bestseller. Such lives can instruct, amuse, and astonish us. But biography can also contribute to a scholarly history of philanthropy, providing insight into the identity and motivation of donors as they put private funds to public use, and offering a more nuanced understanding of those activities in the nonstate sector that we label – sometimes interchangeably – philanthropy, charity, and reform.

This essay uses the career of Margaret Olivia Slocum Sage (1828–1918) to examine American philanthropy during a period when huge unmet social needs coincided with and legitimized entry into the public sphere by mobilized middle- and upper-class women, and when large fortunes were being applied to public use through the new instrumentality of the foundation. Olivia Sage's career helped to define both these developments. Her philanthropic vision was shaped by a tradition of Christian stewardship and her early practice was the genteel activism of the Victorian woman of wealth, consisting of donations of volunteer time, material goods, and small amounts of money. Yet, her major philanthropy took place in the

first decades of the twentieth century, and included the establishment with
$10 million of the Russell Sage Foundation, a significant experiment in re-
organizing philanthropic knowledge and practice. This essay, from a forthcoming biography of Sage, views her complex and layered philanthropy
as a bridge between the traditional charity of gift and personal service,
and modern foundation philanthropy. Sage philanthropy was shaped by
life-cycle issues that biography can elucidate. The Victorian (for want of
a better word) benevolence occupied the decades when she was a socially
prominent New York matron (1869–1906), donating hours of volunteer
labor to a number of reform associations. The later philanthropy of money
donations coincided with the years of widowhood and old age (1906–1918).
She gave away most of her money – about $45 million (about $770 million
in current dollars) in this latter period, when she was in her eighties.[1]

Olivia Sage[2] was the philanthropic wife of multimillionaire financier
Russell Sage (1816–1906) of whom Emma Goldman wrote, "Accumulation,
with him, was not a means, but rather the sole aim of life" (quoted in this
volume, p.). Throughout the couple's thirty-seven-year marriage, Russell
Sage devoted himself mainly to two pursuits: his work on Wall Street and
his stable of fast horses, renouncing travel and other pleasures of the very
rich. He gave nothing to charity. He was a gambler whose fortune came by
chance: wealth seemed to fall into his lap despite his blatant and (to his wife)
infuriating lack of interest in religious observance. Blessed by fortune, he
felt few obligations and was unresponsive to the promptings of conscience
or the appeals of Christian stewardship.

The contrast with Olivia could not have been greater. She was the product
of an evangelical Protestant upbringing that bred a strong sense of duty and
required performance of charitable work of all kinds. Among her papers
at the Emma Willard School (her alma mater, formerly the Troy Female
Seminary) is an undated scrap of paper on which she wrote a single sentence:
"Private greifs [sic] must not stand in the way of public duties." If Olivia
were to make her mark, it would be as "Mrs. Russell Sage," the bearer
of society's moral burden and the embodiment of (naturalized) female
benevolence whose charities would give back to the nation the money that
her husband had conjured from the thin air of Wall Street.

Olivia Sage's position during these years of married life deserves a closer
look. Benevolence is not merely activity or even sensibility. Historians like

---

[1] For conversion of early twentieth-century currency, www.eh.net/ehresources/howmuch/testdollar.
[2] She never used "Margaret," preferring the name "Olivia."

Lori Ginzberg have shown that for nineteenth-century women, it was also a "subject position" that combined a desire to reform society with self-consciousness about the power to do good, which is power over others. Olivia Sage was convinced that her social standing and New England Puritan heritage entitled her to a public presence. Too old to have children and unable to spend freely because of her husband's careful regimen, she constructed an identity around benevolence. As "Mrs. Russell Sage," she became involved in the network of reform organizations sustained by women's voluntary labor and money donations described by Kathleen McCarthy in the previous chapter. She volunteered time on boards of separate women's associations such as the lady managers board of the New York Woman's Hospital, also serving as treasurer on its mixed-sex board of governors. She took an active interest in urban charities like New York's Gospel Mission. She was also keenly interested in charities that served working women and was a board member for the New York Exchange for Woman's Work, an organization designed to restore genteel but impoverished female wage-earners to economic self-sufficiency. In the 1890s, she was active in parlor suffrage and in the Woman's Municipal League, a political organization that aimed to unseat Tammany and bring more women into public life. In 1905, a reporter wrote, "She belongs to the strongly defined New York type of well-to-do committee-working church women." (But cynics claimed that she took the stance of moral leader simply because New York society would not admit her and her eccentric husband. Like the Goulds, Harrimans, Morgans, and John D. Rockefeller, Sr., the Sages were nouveaux riche outsiders to the glittering circle of Mrs. Astor's "Four Hundred," the rulers of New York society.)

There was doubtless a self-serving aspect to the kind of philanthropy that allowed middle- and upper-class white women like Olivia Sage to enjoy a more expansive public life. As ladies bountiful, they overturned some of the barriers to women's opportunities placed there by law and custom. Charitable work conferred membership in a philanthropic elite, earning in the words of Thomas Jefferson, "the approbation of their neighbors, and the distinction which that gives them" (p. 9 intra.), and it demonstrated self-sacrifice, a necessary precondition for winning esteem in this life and salvation in the next. There were benefits also to a "face-to-face charity" that allowed the donor to enjoy the personal expression of gratitude, as J. G. Barker-Benfield points out. Finally, for Sage, voluntary activity offered an escape from a dull marriage and a chance to use her considerable powers.

Olivia Sage worked to create her image as a benevolent woman. In an autobiographical sketch written for the Emma Willard School Alumnae directory, *Emma Willard and Her Pupils* (1898), whose publication she underwrote, she portrayed herself as having been committed to good works from her earliest years when, as a young girl in Syracuse, she had copied into her diary this couplet announcing the theme of a philanthropic life:

Count that day lost whose low, descending sun
Views from thy hand no worthy action done.

Perhaps she had indeed harbored such an image of herself from an early age, for an independent account of her 1847 graduation from Troy Female Seminary includes a reference to the eighteen-year-old Olivia presenting a graduation essay to the assembled audience of parents, students, and townspeople in which she praised those citizens of Troy, New York "who spend their wealth in deeds of charity."

In her only published essay, "Opportunities and Responsibilities of Leisured Women," which appeared in *North American Review* (1905), Olivia explained her belief in philanthropy as a system of reciprocity in which the poor, Indians, the heathen, working girls, and others were objects of pity and subjects for reform. "[W]oman is responsible in proportion to the wealth and time at her command," she wrote. "While one woman is working for bread and butter, the other must devote her time to the amelioration of the condition of her laboring sister. This is the moral law."

Meanwhile, she suffered silently from her husband's grim economies. With her good intentions standing unused and old age staring her in the face, she longed to put Sage's money to good use. In June 1903, as the financier approached his eighty-eighth birthday, she granted a revealing newspaper interview on the topic of marriage. "Very often . . . have I been asked what, in my opinion, is the most frequent cause of unhappy marriages," she began. "After years of observation among different sorts and conditions of people, I have come to the conclusion that the answer is: the absence of individual incomes. A wife should have an allowance," she went on, "not only a standing order at her grocer and her milliner for whatever she wants . . . but a regular cash allowance to do with as she chooses. A man can hardly realize the galling position in which thousands of wives are placed in begging their husbands for money." For example, a young friend who turned over management of her money to her husband found that she had to "scrape along on a mere pittance of pin money which she has to beg from [her husband]." The husband had reduced her to "a pauper."

"Beggar," "pauper," "pittance" – this is bitter language. The interview had turned into an embarrassing public airing of her own grievances. Olivia resented her narrow and scraping lifestyle. She was a philanthropist with nothing to spend, reduced to what I have called philanthropy as performance. By the time she gave the interview described previously, she was a celebrity, engaging in a kind of public performance of philanthropy that cost her husband nothing and that involved visiting missions (or, during the war with Spain, battleships), opening suffrage bazaars, and attending charity events.

Occasionally, she managed to persuade her husband to make a significant money donation to an institution dear to her. With extreme reluctance, Russell Sage gave $120,000 to the Emma Willard School for a new dormitory in 1893 and $50,000 to the New York Woman's Hospital in 1899.

Olivia herself also gave small gifts of money or material goods. One gift dating from 1882 is quite revealing. In that year, she sent boxes of books for the pupils of Carlisle Indian School in Carlisle, Pennsylvania. The gift expressed her hope for assimilation (known at the time as "Indian reform") and her belief that the off-reservation boarding schools would civilize and convert America's heathen. The donation helped cement her role as a patron of Carlisle and friend of principal Colonel Pratt and his family, and her membership in the philanthropic network known collectively as the "Friends of the Indian," which included many distinguished and wealthy members of the Northeastern urban elite. She also gave as an educator. She had been a teacher and governess for many years before her marriage and, in a cover letter that accompanied the gift, she inquired of the school's principal, Richard Pratt, whether the books were written at an appropriate reading level. Indian reform drew her interest for other reasons. Elsewhere I have suggested that the goal of remaking Indian work- and family-roles appealed to Sage, whose history had been marred by her father's spectacularly unsuccessful business career and who often voiced her disapproval of the system that placed white women like herself in economic dependence on men. I believe the gift to Carlisle worked in many ways at the same time, cementing the donor's identity, signaling her affiliations, and announcing her philanthropic goals.

Another gift, its acknowledgment preserved among Mrs. Sage's fundraising correspondence in the Russell Sage Foundation Papers, was a donation to the New York City Mission and Tract Society. This was a charity that Olivia had been accustomed to support with personal visits and service in her middle years. In 1905, a large tapestry that she had donated to the

Society was returned with a note from the secretary saying, "The poor with whom we work have no way of using such things to advantage." By this date, Sage evidently had few contacts with the poor and they received few donations from her, some of these comically inappropriate.

* * *

Russell Sage died in 1906, a few weeks short of his ninetieth birthday, leaving virtually everything – about $75 million (equivalent to about $1.42 billion in 2000) – to his widow. Sage philanthropy now began. A Troy, New York, newspaper commented, "In leaving his fortune to Mrs. Sage, Mr. Sage has left it to charity."

Timing was everything. It was a sad irony for Olivia Sage that the identity of benevolent lady, carefully cultivated over previous decades as I have suggested, now proved a liability. The woman who had long been known as a "philanthropist" had lived into an age when charity reformers condemned the traditional charity of gift and personal service as unscientific, even harmful. The need was for efficient administration of charitable funds, Charity Organization Society (COS) reformers insisted, for better methods and bigger plans. The organization's 1906 annual report stated: "[T]he result to the community in eliminating and diminishing some of the more important causes of pauperism is of infinitely greater value than could have been brought about by the same amount . . . of money expended for the relief of individual suffering." These reformers (we know them as the Progressives) advocated measures to end poverty, not just to ameliorate it piecemeal. They would applaud the Russell Sage Foundation and would help staff its programs and guide its grantmaking in its first two decades.

The transformed physical, demographic, and moral landscape of America after the Civil War had provided a new understanding of wealth and poverty. Fast-growing suburbs removed well-to-do people from cities and from daily contact with the poor. In novels of the period, the poor have a glimpsed-at quality: poverty is seen, if at all, in the mass and in passing. For example, in William Dean Howell's *A Hazard of New Fortunes* (1890), the middle-class hero views working-class urban life "from the Elevated." A few years later, Jacob Riis in his famous expose of New York slums, would call the poor "the other half." The struggles of the 1880s and 1890s – when the unemployed, farmers, and strikers battled class enemies in the streets – caused governments to adopt much tougher policies toward beggars. Public relief of poverty was suspended altogether in New York City, and attitudes toward charity were transformed.

The rise of new kinds of wealth, by suggesting to some a causal connection between economic success and virtue, transformed Americans' moral landscape and put traditional forms of charity on the defensive. Older conservative ideologies explained poverty as failure of will; newer ones ascribed it to blood and inheritance. But regardless of whether social theorists saw the poor as unfit in evolution's race or as victims of habits of unthrift, intemperance, and shiftlessness, they found new reasons why the charitable should not give in the same ways as before.

The most dynamic response to the needs of urban populations and arguably the most progressive, the settlement-house movement, illustrates the challenge to traditional styles of charity and *noblesse oblige* posed by a younger generation of college graduates. Settlement leaders rejected the term *charity* all together, even as they attempted to fill public needs unmet by the state, using private funds and volunteer labor. The college-educated women and men, social-gospel ministers, and experts in labor law and public health who moved into poor and immigrant neighborhoods to staff the settlement houses called themselves "neighbors," "pioneers on an urban frontier," or sometimes "social workers," but never charity workers. The movement's leaders like Jane Addams were as careful to distance their movement from the COS as from the *noblesse oblige* of their mothers' generation.

The changing valence of "charity" was also evident when Paul U. Kellogg, editor of the social work journal *Charities and the Commons*, sought a new title for his publication on the grounds that "Charities" appealed primarily to "spinsters and society ladies." His decision in 1909 to name the journal *The Survey* tells volumes about the rising prestige of empirical social science as a basis for scientific philanthropy. Progressives like Kellogg feminized the older charity (i.e., personal giving to individuals), labeling it sentimentality and contrasting it with the muscular, fact-based "scientific charity" of the male-dominated COS and the academic social sciences, entrenched in universities that excluded or marginalized women.

The campaign to curb distributive charity was not new. In hundreds of books and sociological essays published since the war and in scholarly conference papers and newspaper articles, the advocates of scientific philanthropy had announced their intention of giving the poor what they deserved, not what they asked for. Methods of measuring need and ways of helping the deserving were endlessly elaborated, and warnings of the dangers of unwise giving constantly reiterated.

The association of women with older forms of charity placed the female philanthropist in a difficult position. At the very moment Sage inherited her vast fortune and launched her philanthropy, charity reformers identified female philanthropy (i.e., rich women using their own property for their own purposes) as emotional, irrational, and disorderly.

Proof that Olivia Sage was skewered on an image of feminized benevolence of her own making came in a crisis over the begging letters. Multimillionaires attract a lot of correspondence, and the elderly widow was now receiving hundreds of appeals a day. Sometimes she brought friends into the parlor or library of her New York home to view the enormous piles of letters, accepting their expressions of horrified sympathy. In the years that followed, she attempted to negotiate between the conflicting ideals and irreconcilable practices of face-to-face charity and scientific giving.

At seventy-eight, Olivia Sage was too elderly to practice the personal charity of her middle years. Overwhelmed with the volume of letters, she turned in October 1906 to Robert W. de Forest, her husband's attorney and a family advisor. De Forest, a lifelong president of the New York COS and a prominent advocate of scientific charity, interposed the New York COS between her and the thousands of individuals appealing for help. Correspondence now at Columbia University shows how the begging letters addressed to Sage were forwarded to COS offices, where they were investigated and sorted into two categories: wants, including "personal wants, family wants, vicarious wants, and public wants"; and needs, including "means of support, aid in business, payment of debts, purchase of home, means of education, means of medical treatment," and so on. Every time the fund got down to $1,000, Sage sent a personal check for $10,000. By 1914, she was giving $10,000 every six months. Here was the new bureaucratic charity in action; its effect was to destroy the relationship at the heart of the older charity. (COS criteria for relief were shifting. Under general secretary Edward Devine, the COS had jettisoned its ban on giving money relief, and began giving cash payments to families identified by its agents as capable of achieving self-support. Funds for these small allowances or income supports still came entirely from private donors, however.)

After this, Sage gave no donations to individuals who appealed to her (relatives and friends excepted). She tried to discourage further appeals;

interviewed for a national magazine in November 1906, she stated the COS orthodoxy: "Helping the poor does not mean giving them money. In the majority of cases, that would be the very worst thing to do."

* * *

The move freed her to deal with the thousands of begging letters from institutions. There were appeals from schools and colleges, churches, hospitals, and every kind of religious, cultural, and charitable association. The years 1906–1918 were a time of intense philanthropic activity for the elderly widow. Isolated and increasingly deaf, Sage worked from her home on Fifth Avenue or, in the summer, at "Cedar Croft" in Lawrence, Long Island. With the help of secretaries Catharine Hunter and, after 1912, E. Lilian Todd, she managed to disburse about $35 million in twelve years while fending off the claims of numerous visitors and fundraisers. It was an exhausting process, and handwritten notes on the letters or their envelopes provide a glimpse of how decisions were made. Olivia's brother Joseph Jermain Slocum and her attorney Robert de Forest hovered protectively in the background. Their persistence was rewarded: de Forest obtained large sums for the COS and his alma mater, Yale University. Joseph Slocum ("Jermain") did even better, inheriting $7 million of his sister's money in 1918.

For the rest, Sage's private philanthropy was fueled by reform enthusiasm and religious conviction and aimed at human betterment. Despite or perhaps because of her narrow existence, she brought a restless, reformist spirit to the task. One commentator noted her "active intellectual life." She kept abreast of debates about education, the suffrage, and politics. She read the newspaper with an intensity remarked on by several observers, and clipped and saved articles about educational experiments and civic reform. At her summer home at Lawrence, a reporter noted downstairs "a reading room, where the leading papers of the city are spread out." As one fundraiser confided excitedly to Harvard president A. Lawrence Lowell in 1910, "She really wishes to spend it."

Correspondence documents Sage's gifts to charitable, educational, and religious organizations of all kinds, from the New York Association for the Blind to Harvard University and from the American Seamen's Friend Society to the American College for Girls, Constantinople. Many of the reform and associational connections were already in place when she began to spend. The majority of them were in New York City and state, but there were also donations to Protestant missions, mission schools, and colleges in

Persia, Turkey, Guam, and elsewhere, illustrating the internationalization of missionary philanthropy (see Chapter 11).

Three themes of Sage's extensive private philanthropy are briefly discussed here: women's advancement, civic philanthropy, and animal welfare. References to women's advancement abound in her correspondence, speeches, and letters of gift. By women's advancement, she meant that women should have access to higher education and training for paid work in areas other than teaching. She had little patience with conditions in the teaching profession, which was overcrowded and poorly paid; although she gave a great deal of money to teachers and teachers' colleges (e.g., founding a Teachers' College at Syracuse University), she also funded scholarships and supported programs of vocational and professional education, such as the New York School of Applied Design for Women and the Pennsylvania School of Horticulture for Women. Mindful of the housing needs of single working women in the city (and perhaps recalling her years in Philadelphia as a governess, living in her employer's home), she donated to institutions such as The Virginia, a hotel for working women in New York City. By the 1890s, she was a member of the New York University Women's Advisory Board (its Law Class enrolled her friend Helen Gould) and a trustee of the Emma Willard School. She became a vocal advocate of the suffrage, and funded several suffrage associations.

Sage was keenly interested in the outcome for women and men of the still supposedly experimental coeducational universities, as her correspondence with the presidents of Cornell and Syracuse shows. She also supported all-female colleges including Vassar, Bryn Mawr, and Wellesley. (Emma Willard School, no longer a college as in her young days, nevertheless received her largest donation, $1 million.) At eighty-eight, after years of being alternately bullied and cajoled by fundraisers from the men's colleges, she announced her determination not to give them any more money. In this same year, she gave $500,000 to found a woman's college, the Russell Sage College of Practical Arts in Troy, New York, with three hundred students in departments of secretarial work, household economics, and industrial arts, and a curriculum that reflected the institution's goal of training modern women to earn their livings.

Patriotism fueled her civic philanthropy, the second broad category of philanthropy to associations considered here. Among many examples was her purchase for $150,000 of Constitution Island, off West Point, for the nation in 1908. The island symbolized the nation's birth, commemorating a Revolutionary War victory over British forces on the Hudson River. But patriotism was only one factor; a quite different interest came from her desire to save the island home of Susan and Anna Warner, bestselling domestic novelists whose *The Wide, Wide World* (1850) was a sensation of her younger days when it sold more than one million copies (as many as the better known *Uncle Tom's Cabin*). The novel was a favorite of Olivia's. Now Anna Warner, the elderly surviving sister, was faced with loss of her Constitution Island home. Sage's gift saved the Warner home and thwarted plans of commercial development for the site, plans that Olivia despised. Finally, with its natural beauty, the area held happy memories of her younger days. No one reason alone can explain Olivia's gift.

Animal welfare, a third cause to which Olivia gave tens of thousands of dollars, was a lifelong enthusiasm. The humane treatment of animals had been a popular, even fashionable cause since the founding of the New York Society for the Prevention of Cruelty to Animals (NYSPCA) in 1865 brought to America the sensibility, crusading spirit, and legislative goals of the older British movement. Before she inherited her fortune, Olivia supported the society with small donations and an annual subscription. With humane reform, as with many other reform causes, she was also an enthusiastic backer of women's "parallel" or auxiliary societies. "The tender-heartedness of woman will naturally lead her to use her influence in bringing about a humane treatment of animals," she wrote in 1905. She used her public role to condemn the docking of horses and denounced the society woman for the "barbarous fashion of wearing for her adornment the plumage of small birds."

From 1906 onward, she made large donations to animal welfare organizations in New York City and beyond, without abandoning her commitment to women's separatist organizations. For example, her philanthropic donations helped the New York Women's League for Animals in its campaign to promote the humane treatment of work horses; by 1915, the League was operating watering stations throughout New York City that could accommodate as many as 2,000 horses per day. She also gave $10,000 for an animal hospital and a Westinghouse chassis for an animal ambulance.

She also funded institutions for humane education, giving generously to the National Audubon Society and to Junior Audubon Leagues. Her support for the public educational mission of the New York Zoological Society grew as her fortune did, from a modest donation of $25 in January 1906 to $1,000 in 1912. In her will she would leave $800,000 each to the Zoological Society and the New York Botanical Garden, and $1.6 million to the Museum of Natural History. She made her greatest philanthropic investment in conservation in 1911, with the purchase for the nation of Louisiana's Marsh Island, a bird sanctuary of 79,300 acres.

This was personal philanthropy that supported large projects and Progressive agendas. But there were other donations that allowed Olivia to enjoy what Porterfield calls "the rewards and repayments involved in gift-giving" (see Chapter 2). Braving de Forest's disapproval, Olivia donated generously to the Salvation Army, even though its relief-giving practices broke COS rules by giving without investigation of need and by encouraging donors to enjoy face-to-face charity. The issue had come to the fore in a discussion in the COS organ *Charities Review*, when a small charity, the Christmas Society, rented Madison Square Garden to stage a wholesale giving of gifts to poor children. Wealthy donors paid to attend, watching from the balcony as hundreds of children filed forward to receive toys and sweets. Robert de Forest expressed his bitter criticism of pandering to donors' enjoyment of charity as spectacle, praising charity that was "personal service, not mere largess," and questioned whether the children really needed the treats showered on them. The Salvation Army continued these mass distributions of relief, ignoring the critics. In December 1913, Sage was invited by Evangeline Booth to view "The distribution of four thousand baskets on Christmas morning, at 10 o'clock in the Ninth Regiment Armory, 14th Street. It will be a sight you will never forget" (emphasis in the original.)

You are also invited to attend the entertainment that will be given to 3,500 poor children and the distribution of 6,300 toys and Christmas goodies . . . special seats in the balcony will be reserved for our subscribers. The enclosed card will admit you and your friends.

Too elderly to attend, Olivia sent a money donation, and when Evangeline Booth acknowledged the gift with, "I wish so much that you could have witnessed the gratitude of the desolate and starving to whom your bounty went," she allowed Sage to enjoy vicariously the rewards of old-fashioned charity.

* * *

Foundation philanthropy had begun two decades earlier, when the Slater Fund demonstrated a new way to organize private funds to deal with public problems (Finkenbine, Chapter 7). The foundation, a trust incorporated under state or federal law and administered by trustees appointed for life, allowed the very rich to create a memorial in the shape of a perpetual fund dedicated to some charitable purpose. Some, like the Peabody founded in 1867, were devoted to a single purpose such as improving education or building model housing; others, called general-purpose foundations, defined their purposes very broadly. Historians Barry Karl and Stanley Katz have suggested that the foundations emerged to fill the gap created by the absence of national policy-making institutions. By 1906, when Sage inherited her fortune, several foundations were in existence.

Olivia Sage brought the Russell Sage Foundation into being when she sent a letter of gift dated April 19, 1907, transferring $10 million in cash and securities to a foundation, which was then incorporated under the laws of New York state. (Noting that she made this gift conditional on the Foundation being named after her husband provides a richly ironic subtext to the story.)

A general-purpose foundation, the Russell Sage Foundation exemplified the new "wholesale" philanthropy and its terms were very broadly defined. The investment income was to be applied to "the improvement of social and living conditions in the United States of America," with at least one quarter of the funds being applied to "the needs of my own city and its vicinity."

Reformers had long sought a more scientific knowledge base for philanthropy and social work. "[A] more flexible, continued medium of information is imperative to make available the underlying facts of social conditions which affect the right living and well-being of the community," Robert de Forest had written to former New York mayor Seth Low in June 1905. As Mrs. Sage's advisor, de Forest was now able to shape the Russell Sage Foundation so that it became just such a source of social knowledge. For a decade or more, the foundation was the main institutional home of the developing social sciences in America, a new setting for the study of social problems and for the dissemination of knowledge.

Without completely abandoning the older moralism, the foundation gave credence to an ecological view of poverty, seen in the work of the brilliantly innovative Pittsburgh Survey, whose experts worked to develop social knowledge for an entire industrial region. By Sealander's definition (see Chapter 10), this was large-scale fact-based philanthropy "curing evils at their source." The foundation reflected the optimism of Progressives like Sage and de Forest that social problems had environmental causes and were amenable to reform by well-trained experts armed with the facts. It sponsored empirically based studies of many aspects of urban life: work and wages, housing, child labor, industrial relations, and consumer economics, disseminating the findings through an active program of publication and public exhibits.

The Russell Sage Foundation also gave a decisive push to the professionalization of social work, a self-consciously modern, empirical practice based on "casework" that was to supplant what were seen as the emotional and disorganized efforts of charity volunteers. It funded the profession's journals – *Survey* received grants totaling an estimated $355,100 over forty years – and helped establish Schools of Philanthropy in Boston, St. Louis, New York, and Chicago for the training of "social workers" (the term was new). Foundation grants to the New York COS totaled more than $1 million in the first forty years. The result, according to historian Dawn Greeley, was that the privately funded COS became a striking example of administrative innovation, initially nurtured by private donors and later adopted by state bureaucracies.

Olivia Sage helped determine the direction the foundation took for its first two decades by her power to appoint trustees. These came from the overlapping charitable, academic, and evangelical elites. Friends wrote to invite friends. Gentlemen's clubs and faculty clubs (then the same thing), boards of mission, ladies' parlors – some of them earlier politicized by suffrage and municipal reform movements – the trustees came from these interconnected worlds. There was Daniel Coit Gilman, first president of Johns Hopkins, the newest type of research university. There were the charity experts Louisa Schuyler and Gertrude Rice, veterans of the Civil War – era Sanitary Commission and the experimental public-private State Charities Aid Association, as well as the COS. There were reforming businessmen: racial reformer Robert Ogden, Cleveland Dodge of a famously philanthropic and wealthy family, and Alfred Tredway White, the housing reformer. A number were philanthropists in their own right, notably Cleveland Dodge, Helen Gould, and Robert de Forest.

The Russell Sage Foundation, with its new institutional arrangements for the study of social problems, was Sage philanthropy's most significant achievement. In the words of social-policy historian Alice O'Connor, it institutionalized "the space, outside government and outside the academy, where reform-minded women and men could engage in social scientific exploration and have it recognized as such."

However, it is far from clear that the foundation marked a major breakthrough in the understanding of social problems. Rather, it gathered up the separate strands of postbellum reform, uniting older charitable traditions with the new social science. John Glenn, a corporate lawyer and first director and secretary of the Russell Sage Foundation – whose earlier philanthropic work had included Protestant home missions work in West Virginia – exemplifies how the foundation linked reform networks with distinct philanthropic traditions and experience. Religious antecedents went unacknowledged in the foundation's mandate and its public image – for the act of incorporation stated its purpose in broadly secular terms – but the Protestant mission background was strongly represented by Glenn and by Olivia's friend and protegee Helen Gould, as well as by Dodge. In addition, Glenn and Mary Richmond were both from a COS background, as was de Forest. Historian David Hollinger characterizes these hybrid Progressives as men and women who believed in "the moral efficacy of social science."

* * *

What was the impact of all this spending? Could philanthropy, even on this grand scale, ever result in anything more than "small change"? Robert Bremner's *American Philanthropy* (1960) is rightly taken to task in this volume for its consensus-era complacency, but the questions Bremner raised about philanthropy are still compelling four decades later. "Was the benefactor-beneficiary relationship a denial of the equality democracy implied?" he asked. "Did charity perpetuate the conditions that created poverty? Could philanthropy, tied as it was to the purse strings of the existing order, accomplish anything of importance in building a better society?" (116).

The biographer can discuss motivation and identity, but speaks with much less confidence about results. Yet, I do not believe that these questions take us beyond strictly biographical issues. In documenting the lives of individual donors, there is no escaping the need to explore the class and institutional settings that direct philanthropy into certain channels. As Nancy Hewitt reminds us, historians must concern themselves with the ways that "the forms and consequences of particular philanthropic ventures" are shaped by "gender, racial, ethnic, and class relations rooted in structures of social, political, and economic power."

In one sense, Olivia's gifts were "small change" that left her still enormously rich. This fact was stated in a frank and somewhat cynical letter dated December 1910 from Henry Lee Higginson, a trustee of the Carnegie Institution and of Harvard University, to Harvard president A. Lawrence Lowell. Assuring the president of his willingness "to get a whack at anybody," Higginson assessed the likelihood of getting some money out of Mrs. Sage:

If you care to do it, we might try it on. Mrs. Sage received from her husband
$75 million, so she can, if she wishes, build a building a week. That means certainly
$3 million a year or $60,000 a week or $9,000 a day, and [John] Cadwalader thinks
as I do . . ., that she really wishes to spend it.

Higginson was right. "If Carnegie divested himself of $100 million, he
would still have $200 million for amusement," he wrote. Similarly, a build-
ing a week was "small change" to Sage. Nor could Sage philanthropy make
a major impact on the nation's most serious problems (see Introduction).
We would hardly expect large private fortunes to be donated in ways
that are socially redistributive or politically transforming. Whether as a
wealthy Gilded Age matron or as a Progressive-era multimillionaire, Sage
inevitably benefited from her place in America's racial-ethnic and class hierarchy. When she donated volunteer hours as a participant in the postwar
Benevolent Empire, she did not envision democratic cross-class alliances,
but represented herself as "a missionary to her poorer sisters." After inheriting her fortune, she commissioned a family history – the best that
money could buy and one befitting a person about to become a benefactor of national stature – employing Henry Whittemore of Brooklyn,
"Genealogist and Compiler of Family and Other Histories," and Mary F.
Tillinghast, a New York artist (one of many women artists to enjoy her
patronage) to travel to France and England to research the genealogy of
her family and that of her husband. Their labors resulted in a large, illustrated volume bound in pale green leather with gold figuring: *A History
of the Sage and Slocum Families: The Slocum Families Showing Three Lines
of Descent from the Signers of the Mayflower Compact* (1908), featuring the
liberty-loving Miles Standish and his Puritan descendants, along with pious
Huguenots and learned Piersons. Olivia distributed the volumes to libraries
throughout the region and sent copies to her friends. Clearly, her philanthropy was an unstable mixture of breathtaking generosity and self-serving
calculation.

Others in this collection have offered a definition of the philanthropist
as an individual with a vision of a good society and an urgent wish to
bring about change. Olivia Sage had this temperament to a remarkable
degree, even in old age. She was energetic, articulate, and opinionated. She
studied reform issues in the newspapers, subscribed to the annual reports
of a number of voluntary associations, and supported woman suffrage. She
was willing to try the new institutional form of the foundation, and energy
resonates in her declaration, at the first meeting of its board of trustees,
"I am almost eighty years old, but I feel I have just begun to live!" Religion

was a central part of her life so that philanthropy, for her, was work but it was also conviction.

We can find no neat break in the history of American philanthropy between old-fashioned gifting by individuals and the beginning of the foundations. Mrs. Russell Sage, who set up one of the first modern general-purpose foundations while carrying on a remarkable personal philanthropy, offers a fascinating case of American philanthropy as it reached toward the modern yet remained grounded in the charitable ideals and language of nineteenth-century evangelicalism and *noblesse oblige*. How we characterize those ideals still remains the hardest question to answer.

10

CURING EVILS AT THEIR SOURCE:
THE ARRIVAL OF SCIENTIFIC GIVING

JUDITH SEALANDER

It was a mild evening in the spring of 1902, but Frederick Gates was not calm. Arms waving, long white hair flowly wildly, and looking every inch the Baptist minister he once was, he paced the room, ready to preach. But the elegantly paneled study of a New York City brownstone contained no pulpit, and a select congregation heard the sermon. Characteristically banging a table with the flat of his hand, he told the small group of family lawyers and business partners who were John D. Rockefeller, Sr.'s, most trusted allies that American society faced a crisis. The competitive system, he railed, was a contradiction in terms. It was not system; it was a "heap" of struggling human beings. Just this morning, Gates continued, he had talked with the agent who insured his house and declined to reinsure with him; another company offered a savings of 20 percent. The agent, "a full-grown man, cried, actually wept." He was one of the struggling "human maggots," engaged in a business in "which he is not needed, along with a dozen or two other agents, in the town of Montclair, New Jersey, crawling over each other to snatch a bite of business. . . . The competitive system is a sort of human cannibalism, by which people eat each other up, take bites out of each other's living flesh." The only formal education Frederick Gates received was at a Baptist seminary. Yet, he became Rockefeller, Sr.'s, chief philanthropic advisor and one of his most important aides, responsible for managing companies and making deals.

Social chaos threatened and, Gates announced, Rockefeller, one of America's fiercest and most successful competitors – and he would become the early century's most important philanthropist – knew it. Therefore, he decided to devote a substantial percentage of his huge fortune to a search for solutions to the problems the country faced. He did not want merely to relieve misery; he hoped to end it. Such a task required a new approach to charity. It required "scientific giving," which represented a crucial early twentieth-century development in the history of philanthropy. The words *orderly* or *systematic* could be substituted for *scientific*. What was the character of those who created scientific giving? Why did they create a new institution: the endowed charitable foundation? What motivated them? What did they accomplish of lasting importance? All these questions demand a brief review of the immense changes that had transformed early twentieth-century American society.

* * *

Between the Civil War and the beginning of the new century, the United States burst onto the world stage as a major power. Enormous growth dominated life in the victorious North. Waves of European immigrants, more than sixteen million by 1900, helped contribute to tremendous increases in population. A nation of twenty-three million in 1850 was a country with nearly eighty million residents in 1900. And many of these people crowded into newly enormous East Coast and Midwestern cities, like Chicago, New York, Detroit, or Boston. The nation's population skyrocketed; its cities burst at the seams; and its transportation systems, industrial capacity, and aggregate wealth increased at staggering rates.

So did the number of extremely rich people. The numbers of millionaires in the country catapulted from around a hundred in the late 1870s to more than forty thousand by 1916. Remarkable, too, were the size of some of the fortunes the post-war industrial boom had created. At least twenty men were millionaires many times over. In 1901, Andrew Carnegie sold his interests in the Carnegie Steel Corporation to U.S. Steel for $447 million. By the 1990s, Carnegie's windfall was worth at least $8 billion. John D. Rockefeller's fortune might have exceeded $17 billion.

This astonishing growth, however, was in no way evenly shared. Agricultural America languished; rural families worked brutally long hours, at the mercy of fluctuating international market prices for their corn, cotton, and wheat. In the South, they barely survived on cornmeal and molasses; in other regions, they ate too many meals of pancakes and flour gravy. Many people in prosperous industrial states still suffered. Coalminers supplied fuel crucial to national growth, but many lived in squalid company towns where leaky shacks lined dirt streets and dead rats regularly appeared in pump water. Even among emerging white-collar fields, as Gates knew,

LIKE FATHER LIKE SON

John D. Rockefeller, Jr.'s, views were given in an address to his men's Bible class Sunday. He advised the workers there was no better way to make money than to save it.—News Item.

Highly adverse early twentieth century portrayal of the wealth of the Rockefellers. (Courtesy of Rockefeller Archive center.)

competition was often feverish and failure common. A tiny minority of the newly very rich felt compelled to do something.

* * *

Scientific philanthropists, first and foremost, were not typical. Indeed, in the early twentieth century, as in any age, the vast majority of the nation's

Can You Beat It?   ( )   By Maurice Ketten

1912 Characterization of Andrew Carnegie from the New Year *World*. (Courtesy of Rockefeller Archive Center.)

very wealthy continued to behave as they always had. They gave away little during their lifetimes. Only a minority gave, and usually just to local causes: they personally distributed funds to help orphans, build schools, buy paintings for museums, and subsidize orchestras.

Only a few owners of the huge new fortunes created by nineteenth-century industrial development began to rethink the purposes of charity itself. Philanthropy should seek causes and cures. It should find a remedy for a disease, rather than build a hospital to treat its victims. It should root out the reasons for poverty, not give alms to the impoverished. It should expand knowledge and deal in new ideas, ones perhaps initially too risky for government officials or private organizations dependent on public approval to embrace.

Frederick Gates, Rockefeller, Sr.'s, principal advisor on philanthropic giving, insisted that to be "scientific," philanthropy had to deal in wholesale, not retail, giving. Sears-Roebuck Company founder Julius Rosenwald used the same phrase. "I made my money in retail trade – but when it comes to philanthropy, I'm preferably a wholesaler." Indeed, he argued that the only people who could actually make a success of what he called "freelance charity – direct customer-to-customer giving" – were the poor. "When Mrs. Levy gives Mrs. Lewis a little from her meager family store to help out because Lewis is unemployed, Mrs. Lewis accepts the gift with the knowledge that the tables may be turned at any time."

This tiny group, who wanted to use their wealth to rethink and remake society – not just relieve its ills and beautify its public places – were not members of long-established wealthy families; a few were close relatives of the person who had made the family fortune. Olivia Sage, the richest woman in America in the early twentieth century, inherited her money from her skin-flint husband, Russell, who made a killing as a railroad speculator but loathed spending a penny, especially if it went to charity. In her eighties, his widow (as Ruth Crocker's chapter illustrates) enjoyed posthumous revenge, giving away his millions. Edward Harkness created the Commonwealth Fund to distribute much of the fortune his father amassed, but did not share as a Standard Oil founding partner. Elizabeth Milbank Anderson spent money accumulated by her father, Jeremiah Milbank, a Connecticut grocer who, with Gail Borden, sold a new product (canned evaporated milk) to the Union Army.

Heirs played a role, but the most influential scientific philanthropists of the early twentieth century were the self-made men who created the initial fortunes. In their memoirs and remembrances, they usually credited good luck or chance with their immense financial successes. Several were young men during the Civil War and were able to manipulate war-time circumstances to their own enormous advantage.

Only twenty-one in 1861, John D. Rockefeller, Sr., for instance, hired a substitute to fight for him, as was perfectly legal. He correctly calculated that war would inflate prices for wholesale foodstuffs and, with borrowed money, built a hugely successful trade in cornmeal, salt, and cured meat.

He then turned the wealth he had made from barrels of pork into an empire based on barrels of oil.

Others were too young to enjoy the war-time bonanza. Julius Rosenwald was born in 1862. But, as a native of Springfield, Illinois, he spent his early childhood listening to the speakers who made Lincoln's former house in town a stop on national memorial tours. By the time he was ten, young Rosenwald decided to make money from the circumstance, writing and selling pamphlets describing the Lincoln assassination in all its grisly detail. By the time he was twenty, he had joined forces with Richard Sears, who sold watches through the mail and used the name of one of his employees, A. C. Roebuck, to imply that his business was a well-financed partnership. The Sears-Rosenwald partnership was not a fiction; indeed, Rosenwald, with other scientific philanthropists, had an uncommon ability to seize opportunity. The small Sears-Roebuck Watch and Jewelry Company became mammoth Sears-Roebuck, supplier of everything from a watch to a seersucker suit to a tractor to a build-it-yourself house kit – complete with plans, lumber, carpet, and nails.

These scientific philanthropists, unlike many others of the newly rich, studied society closely, understood the dangers posed by the industrial revolution that had created their fortunes, and worried publicly about the dangers. They and their advisers fretted that the age promised opportunity and prophesied.

Their tremendous size made the new national corporations efficient and economically powerful. U.S. Steel owned coal and iron mines, limestone quarries, and railroads, as well as coke ovens and furnaces. It controlled all aspects of its product's creation and sale, as did Standard Oil, with its own wells, pipelines, tanks, and fleets of oceangoing ships. Scientific philanthropists argued that if business had expanded, so too should the scale of giving. Without big solutions to its many problems, a society in rapid transition could explode. Endowing a museum, building a library, expanding a hospital, or giving a worthy widow her due were no longer enough.

These philanthropists and their advisors decided to tackle big problems in bold ways, dealing with them "wholesale." The dynamics of business organizations were changing rapidly, the divisions between public and private responsibilities were not clearly defined, and the phrase "the nonprofit sector" did not yet exist.

* * *

Most of the charitable rich in the early twentieth century did not use the services of advisors. Rather, they gave directly to recipients and relied heavily on the advice of family and friends. They themselves delivered the check for a new hospital wing; they personally posed with the paintings donated to a local museum. However, by the Great Crash of 1929, the incorporated philanthropic foundation – the new institution that employed Gates and other managers – had begun to make an impact. Some 150 foundations existed, structured on corporate models with boards of trustees, public charters, annual reports, and managerial staffs. Scientific philanthropy was foundation philanthropy, but not all foundation philanthropy was scientific. The creators of foundations used these institutions as buffers between themselves and the beneficiaries of their largesse. Philanthropists begun to find the business of giving away money to be draining work. Once they acquired reputations for charity, they found themselves trailed in the streets by supplicants touting good causes. Strangers hounded them on trains and in church. The daily mail brought hundreds of letters begging for help.

Foundations could organize giving through established procedures, thereby relieving their creators of these burdens. But most of the foundations that existed in the early twentieth century still exercised traditional distributive charity. More than a third were community chests, organized to help groups within a city coordinate aid to the poor, the sick, or the arts. Most others had very specific purposes: helping Swedish teachers study in the United States, establishing homes for aged musicians, giving vocational training to white orphan boys from Pennsylvania.

Only eight creators of foundations established institutions that fully embodied scientific philanthropy and embraced very general goals for shaping society: Andrew Carnegie, John D. Rockefeller, Sr., John D. Rockefeller, Jr., Edward Harkness, Olivia Sage, Julius Rosenwald, Elizabeth Milbank Anderson, and Edward Filene. In complexity, size, and assets, the groups of foundations created by the two Rockefellers and Carnegie dwarfed the others. In influence, the Rockefeller institutions were scientific philanthropy's clear leaders. By 1929, John D. Rockefeller and his son had contributed at least $600 million to a group of independently endowed foundations. The Rockefeller Foundation, although chartered in 1913, did not assume its role as the umbrella organization under which most Rockefeller philanthropic efforts sheltered until a major internal reorganization in 1928–1929 merged many projects. Before then, the General Education Board (GEB), the International Health and Education Boards, the Laura Spelman Rockefeller Memorial, the Bureau of Social Hygiene, and the Rockefeller Institute for Medical Research operated as separate entities, although all had broadly stated purposes: to encourage research into and diffusion of ideas that would potentially improve society and increase the well-being of mankind.

By the time of his death in 1919, Andrew Carnegie had given the bulk of his fortune, some $350 million, to his network of philanthropies: most importantly, the Carnegie Corporation, the Carnegie Foundation for the Advancement of Teaching, the Carnegie Hero Fund, and the Carnegie Endowment for International Peace. The Carnegie foundations and Carnegie himself straddled the worlds of traditional and scientific philanthropy. "Merry Andrew," ebullient and opinionated, made good press copy and, when in 1889, "Wealth," his essay on the obligations of the rich, appeared in the widely circulated magazine the *North American Review*, it drew attention. "Wealth" argued that a rich person had three choices: he could give his money to his family, bequeath it in his will to good causes, or use it during his lifetime to improve society. Only the third option was really acceptable. Each generation should create its own great fortunes from scratch; indeed, inherited wealth was a social and personal curse. Instead, the wealthy should give away their assets. Carnegie, never bashful, offered seven specific suggestions: millionaires should (1) found universities, (2) build libraries, (3) build hospitals, (4) build parks, (5) build concert halls, (6) build swimming pools and public baths, and (7) build community churches.

Many scholars of philanthropy have unwisely overemphasized the importance of what soon became known as the "Gospel of Wealth." Contemporaries did not; at the time, Carnegie's proposal was roundly criticized. Church officials, for instance, could hardly believe that their institutions were last in line – behind swimming pools – and that, even worse, Carnegie had urged that religious giving be nondenominational. More to the point, those able to be more objective argued that much of Carnegie's advice was not particularly new.

Significantly, not a single other major philanthropist of the early twentieth century took Carnegie's advice to heart. Nobody else gave everything away to philanthropy during his own lifetime. John D. Rockefeller, Sr., divided his massive fortune between his charities and his only son. Others gave generously but made sure that the bulk of their fortunes remained in family hands. The real architects of scientific giving, such as Frederick Gates and Julius Rosenwald, urged that philanthropy never trade in "retail." Privately, Gates fumed that Carnegie gave philanthropically so that he could see his name blazed in stone all over the country.

Indeed, much of Carnegie's vast donations was encumbered during his lifetime and for almost a generation after by the great amounts spent on construction of the libraries and concert halls he loved. The free concert halls introduced classical music to tens of thousands of Americans, even if listeners in attendance might have preferred less emphasis on pieces for pipe organs, Carnegie's favorite. The libraries opened a world of books to many more. These were worthwhile but highly traditional charity projects. However, Carnegie institutions were also especially influential in raising the bar for college and professional training standards. Moreover, one could scarcely argue that Carnegie's Endowment for International Peace, on which he spent tens of millions, did not embrace a "wholesale" idea: research to "hasten the abolition of war."

Carnegie's foundations, then, were a bridge between distributive charity and scientific giving. The Rockefellers and their allies extended the road beyond. Given their much smaller capital funds (ranging from ten to thirty million dollars), the Russell Sage Foundation, and the Rosenwald, Milbank Memorial, and Twentieth Century funds – all established between 1905 and 1917 – advocated more specific purposes. But they, too, dealt in "wholesale," not "retail." The Russell Sage Foundation sought "the improvement of social and living conditions in the United States" and focussed on research in the areas of child welfare, industrial relations, and city planning. The Rosenwald Fund's chief concern was the improvement of American race relations, whereas the Milbank and Commonwealth Funds concentrated on promoting new ideas about public health. Finally, department-store owner Edward Filene's Twentieth Century Fund sought ways to improve workplace relations between labor and management.

All of these goals were daunting. This fact prompts a question: What motivated the founders to establish foundations that attempted to accomplish these goals?

* * *

Tax advantage, a reason frequently cited as a motivation for late twentieth-century philanthropy, played no real role in scientific giving. Before 1932, custom duties remained the primary source of federal revenues, and the arms of state and municipal revenue officials were not very long. Although the Sixteenth Amendment, ratified in 1913, allowed the federal government to tax income, it exercised the privilege with caution. In the wake of massive and nationally coordinated spending to finance American involvement in World War I, Congress – frightened at the specter of excessive state centralization – actually lowered tax rates during the 1920s. Most Americans paid no income tax, and taxes on property were generally modest. Andrew

Carnegie, John D. Rockefeller, and thousands of other newlyminted very rich Americans did not have to worry about the taxman, certainly not before the advent of the New Deal. Only with the passage of the Federal Tax Act of 1935 did extremely wealthy individuals have a real financial incentive to establish tax-exempt incorporated philanthropies.

The rich in the early twentieth century could spend their money as they pleased. Two faiths motivated a tiny elite to try to remake society through scientific philanthropy: one in God, the other in system. Frederick Gates insisted," To care for the hungry, thirsty, naked, shelterless, imprisoned was not merely the first element of godliness; it was the whole thing." Gates, like the Rockefellers, was a Baptist. Unlike his patrons, who remained pillars of their church, he gradually came to believe in his own nondenominational version of Christianity in which he "served humanity in the spirit of Jesus." But whether they called themselves Baptists, Presbyterians, Catholics, or Jews, scientific philanthropists and their aides wholeheartedly embraced a version of the Social Gospel, even if they did not specifically employ the phrase.

The Social Gospel movement countered another philosophy popular in the late nineteenth century: Social Darwinism, whose advocates argued that human societies passed through the same stages of competition for survival that Charles Darwin had described for populations of finches on the Galapagos Islands in *On the Origins of Species.* In organized societies, too, the fittest would compete, adapt, and prevail. Interference with this natural law was at the best unwise, at the worst dangerous. Social Gospelers argued that people should not live by the laws of the jungle; rather, they should strive for a higher standard and care for those less fortunate. The religious should not retreat from the evils of the world. True godliness required that believers actively combat society's problems.

A story told by Walter Rauschenbush clearly illustrated the ideas of the Social Gospel. Rauschenbush, a theology professor who also preached to the poor on New York's East Side, had as a parishioner an elderly street laborer. One day a street car ran the man down, injuring his leg. His daughter and Rauschenbush searched frantically among New York's charity hospitals, only to find later that three had rejected the shabby old man. Meanwhile, gangrene set in and the man died. An agent for the streetcar company promptly visited the family, offered a $100 settlement, and warned that if the family sued for a higher amount, the company would be happy to continue the case in court indefinitely. The daughter took the

$100 – brought, as usual, in the form of one hundred single dollar bills, "to make the amount look like vast wealth to a poor person." Rauschenbush concluded, "The officers of the hospitals and the officers of the street railway company were not bad men. But the impression remained that our social machinery is almost as blindly cruel as its steel machinery, and that it runs over the life of a poor man with scarcely a quiver."

The fear that they were shirking their moral duty if they did not try to improve society inspired men like Rockefeller and women like Sage. Such a belief linked scientific philanthropy with another phenomenon associated with Progressive reform: the settlement-house movement. Indeed, an educated, socially concerned woman like Olivia Sage might well have volunteered in such an institution had she been a member of the middle class, not a multimillionaire. Many of the staff members employed by the Russell Sage Foundation and other reform-minded national philanthropies did have settlement-work backgrounds.

Settlement houses were the brick and stone embodiment of the Social Gospel. In dozens of the country's biggest cities, middle-class female activists created "settlements": sturdy multistory and multipurpose buildings, usually located right in the heart of urban slums. Within their walls, a wide variety of programs sought to help the poor.

Visitors to Chicago's Hull House, for instance, described constant activity. Founded by two women, Jane Addams and Ellen Starr, Hull House echoed with recitations by immigrants learning English, toddlers' songs, the sounds of folk-dancing. In the basement of the block-long, red-brick building, new arrivals to the city found a huge kitchen equipped for "American" cooking and a public bath.

Not all settlements were as large or as influential as Hull House, but each promoted moral reform at the same time it championed social engineering. A settlement-sponsored penny savings bank helped the urban poor prepare for crises; it also provided machinery that promoted thrift. Free steambaths soothed the soul; they also preached the dogma of cleanliness. These kinds of dual agendas characterized scientific philanthropy as well.

If fear of God motivated scientific philanthropy, so too did belief in system. John D. Rockefeller, Sr., was the brilliant architect of an oil monopoly that controlled every aspect of the business – from wellhead to retail outlet. In similar ways, Andrew Carnegie restructured the steel industry and Julius Rosenwald reinvented the conduct of national retail trade. A buoyant faith that social machinery could be improved by the same big reordering processes spurred them all. Some Social Gospelers who listened to Rauschenbush's story would have wanted to give the bereaved family more money or add beds to a charity hospital. The Milbank or Commonwealth funds would have wanted to investigate health-care delivery systems within an entire community. The Rockefeller Institute of Medicine would have set a team of researchers to work looking for methods to prevent the spread of gangrene. The Sage Foundation would have begun research into city-street grids, hoping for new ideas to improve safety for pedestrians. The Twentieth Century Fund would have wanted to investigate the workmen's compensation laws of New York State. The founders and staffs of all these institutions would have said that although industrialization caused huge problems, it also offered unprecedented opportunities. Vast wealth was, according to Frederick Gates, a "Gulliver." The author of *Gulliver's Travels*, he said, could think of nothing else for the Lilliputians to do but ask Gulliver to fight their battles. So they put glasses on Gulliver to prevent the enemy from shooting tiny arrows into his eyes, and declared war on their neighbors. But what if Gulliver had been put to "far higher uses than mere destruction of enemies?" That question raises another – the final and most important one to ask about early twentieth-century scientific philanthropy: What were its legacies?

* * *

Andrew Carnegie thought he could systematize solutions to war. The Charter of the Carnegie Endowment for International Peace specified that once permanent peace prevailed worldwide, the foundation could use remaining funds to attack other significant problems. Its efforts obviously failed. Nonetheless, World War I left American territory unscathed and America itself an economic colossus. The carnage that shattered faith among European intellectuals did not deter scientific philanthropists' belief that solutions to even the most apparently intractable social problems could be found. However, the onset of a terrible depression that hit the United States harder than other industrial nations marked the end of an era, not just in American politics and culture, but also in the history of American philanthropy.

The Endowment for Peace (established in 1910) continued to work full-tilt throughout the 1920s, commissioning hundreds of scholars to engage in a massive study of World War I. By the end of the decade, 240 monographs extensively analyzing every aspect of the war's origins and outcomes had appeared. They were a weighty testament – even as memories of the conflict remained vivid – to scientific philanthropy belief that if only enough facts were unearthed, if only root causes were explored, a solution to warfare could be found.

Scientific philanthropy did not end wars among great powers. Indeed, critics accused foundations of building dangerously powerful cultural empires that controlled not just the production and distribution of essential materials, like oil or steel, but also the production and dissemination of ideas.

There is no question that the actions of private foundations were not subject to a majority vote of the American people. The founders of scientific philanthropy cared deeply about democracy, but they were not democrats. They saw no reason to give their own employees a significant voice. Rockefeller, Sr., and Carnegie opposed independent unions; some of the era's bloodiest strikes occurred at companies they owned. What could only be labeled all-out class warfare occurred in the coalfields of Colorado in 1913 and 1914, when the United Mine Workers tried to organize Colorado Fuel and Iron, a Rockefeller subsidiary. Mine owners dug trenches, installed searchlights, and brought in private armies, supplemented by the Colorado governor's compliant decision to send National Guardsmen to protect company property. Strikers, in turn, got their own guns. Disaster was inevitable when the miners' wives and children got caught in the crossfire of a firefight between strikers and guardsmen, burning to death in an underground pit in which they were hiding. The "Ludlow Massacre" became for many a searing image of injustice.

Therefore, the accomplishments of scientific philanthropy must be framed within this context. They were top-down reforms, and those meant to benefit were generally not consulted. A private memorandum in the files of the Russell Sage Foundation outlining plans for the future was illustrative:

The Russell Sage Foundation cannot become partisan. (It cannot) advocate one side or the other of views which are in controversy between people. It must exercise a judicial impartiality which will command the respect and confidence of people.

After circulating among several foundation officers, three handwritten entries had significantly altered the document's tone. The foundation should not take sides when "good" people disagreed, and it needed to command the respect and confidence of "right-minded" people.

But arguing that foundations were not democratically run slays a straw man; they never pretended to be. Moreover, to achieve success in a truly pluralistic society with divided centers of power, foundation ideas had to win relatively broad support. Long-time president of the Carnegie Corporation, Alan Pifer, was right when he wrote, "Foundations have a restricted ability to lead change but an unusual capacity to help it along." Between 1900 and 1930, scientific giving very significantly "helped along" change in three areas: American education, medicine, and the promotion of social science.

* * *

Three examples demonstrate the broad-ranging impact scientific giving had on the structure of American education. They also illustrate the fact that when foundation ideas were too far ahead of popular sentiment, achievements were muted. Foundation support spurred improved professional standards and training programs, helped create world-class universities, and – with much less success – sought to improve the education of neglected minorities, especially African Americans.

Until the late nineteenth century, there existed no widely observed standards for entrance into most American professions. Worth remembering is the fact that during the 1830s, many state legislatures banned examinations or licensing as undemocratic. As late as the end of the century, some of that old bad odor still clung to the notion of a need for exclusivity or special preparation for any occupation. Indeed, the numbers of physicians, lawyers, and engineers who trained at any college declined after the Civil War.

Scientific philanthropy played a large role in upgrading and standardizing training for many professions, among them social work, engineering, and the law. Most significantly, however, it was an important engine pushing for higher standards for medical education. Health care was primed for major change. The late nineteenth century's bacteriological revolution dramatically altered attitudes about disease and treatment. By the 1880s, the germ theory had won widespread acceptance, but American physicians lagged behind their European counterparts.

As late as 1900, Americans who wanted to learn about the newest medical theories and techniques still studied in Europe. The average physician's income and status were modest; skilled workers in the nation's booming factories often made a better and more secure living. The country's many medical schools were almost all proprietary; that is, they were for-profit operations owned by the faculty. Entrance requirements, when they existed at all, were minimal. Some schools did not even ask that a prospective candidate have a high school certificate. The vast majority of doctors did not belong to the American Medical Association (AMA). However, the AMA, in concert with the Carnegie Foundation for the Advancement of Teaching and the GEB, transformed requirements for the practice of medicine in the United States. AMA members generally were younger and far better educated than the average American doctor, and they were determined to upgrade professional standards. In 1904, the organization's leaders successfully urged the Carnegie Foundation to undertake a study of medical education in America. Abraham Flexner, the young director of a private school for boys in Kentucky who had caught Carnegie Foundation president Henry Pritchett's eye, visited all 160 medical schools in the country. His analysis, published in 1910 as the Foundation's "Bulletin Number Four" but usually called the Flexner Report, condemned most as hopeless. All but thirty should be shut down; those remaining should be reformed. Medical schools should have a four-year curriculum, with two years of classwork based on laboratory science and two years of work in hospital wards – but in hospitals approved by and connected to medical schools. Medical schools themselves should be parts of larger universities and should require all applicants to have finished at least two years of undergraduate college courses. These schools should be in big cities so that aspiring doctors would see patients with a wide variety of illnesses, but there should be no more than one medical school for a particular city or region. Finally, medical schools should specialize, their choices dominated by their locations. A medical school in Louisiana, for instance, should develop special expertise in diseases more common in the South, such as pellagra or hookworm.

Despite cries of East Coast arrogance from owners of proprietary schools, the educational coup triggered by the Flexner Report was a stunning success. The American public was willing to raise the bar for medical training. Most proprietary schools had little influence or money; although they greatly outnumbered Flexner's model, the Johns Hopkins University Medical School, they did not have its clout. Moreover, the poor and recent immigrants – Americans most likely to go to the least well-trained doctors – were also the least able to organize and be heard. Finally, throughout the 1910s and 1920s, the GEB gave more than $154 million to the few dozen medical schools Flexner deemed worthy of resuscitation and rebuilding. The money, not surprisingly, came with strings: a willingness to comply with the recommendations of the Flexner Report.

By 1930, professional medical training had been revolutionized. Per capita, the nation produced far fewer physicians who studied at a more limited number of medical schools. Physician's fees and status had begun to rise measurably. By 1915, only ninety-five schools were still open, and the number continued to drop throughout the next decade. Physicians became a better educated group, whose members were more likely to be white and male. In 1910, Abraham Flexner had urged that the country's three medical schools for women be closed. Women had, he argued, plenty of opportunities to study alongside men in the better schools, though "they show increasing disinclination to do so." He had little patience for the arguments of those who warned that closing marginal schools would close medicine to poor boys and members of minorities, and opposed offering fellowships solely on the basis of financial need. No one, he insisted, had the right to become a doctor.

Flexner soon traded work with the Carnegie Foundation for service at Rockefeller philanthropies, most notably the GEB. There he continued to promote the philosophy that grounded his views on medical education. Foundations should selectively improve only a restricted number of good schools, making them models for American educators to follow. Flexner's ideas worked best at the college level, where scientific giving helped shatter the reputation of American universities as inferior to European rivals by creating in short order a group of world-class American universities.

The University of Chicago provided a case in point. Founded in 1891, it quickly gained a reputation as a notable center for academic research. Chicago's young president was a Baptist theologian and Old Testament scholar. Nonetheless, William Rainey Harper had no intention of leading a quiet, religious institution. Rather, he used Rockefeller support to raid universities throughout America and Europe, seeking the biggest names and brightest minds. Harper's promises of extra money for research, a reduced teaching load, and funds for travel proved seductive. Within a few years, the University of Chicago boasted a world-class faculty, several of whom became leaders of new disciplines.

At the University of Chicago and other universities that were the recipients of largesse from Rockefeller or Carnegie philanthropies, money had strings attached. University administrations and curricula had to be modernized and systematized. Even at elite established universities like Yale or Columbia, entrance standards had been only loosely enforced before the early twentieth century. By 1930, a foundation model was in place: students at universities should have completed not less than four years of high school work.

Moreover, foundations demanded that to receive grants, universities accept corporate accounting techniques. The GEB carefully scrutinized the business management practices of all applicants. The middle managers of Standard Oil were responsible for the mountains of paperwork that tracked the monopoly's many assets. The GEB expected that college officers adopt similar, if simplified, tracking systems. No longer could they confuse terms like *assets, income, capital, investments,* or *current funds.* For instance, college presidents frequently listed a verbal pledge from a potential donor as an asset in their pleas for help. They soon learned that the accountants who kept the books for the Carnegie Foundation or the GEB would tolerate no such fuzziness.

If scientific giving demanded updated processes for admission of students and administration of educational institutions, it also fostered modernized curricula. At the end of the nineteenth century, American colleges still emphasized subjects that had not changed much for centuries. Students at liberal arts schools read Greek and Latin, discussed philosophy, and studied theology. By 1930, the "elective system," required at the University of Chicago, was widespread. Undergraduates spent their first two years taking a wide range of required courses in the humanities and biological, physical, and social sciences. During this time, they also experimented with a specialization, choosing three courses in a subject area, either a traditional one like philosophy or literature or one pioneered by some of their professors like psychology or sociology. Students then spent their final years working more intensively in this chosen area.

The Chicago model was enormously influential. As higher education itself became big business in coming decades, it adopted the elective system initially sponsored by foundations. Here, as in professional training, scientific philanthropy helped along a change generally supported by a population that wanted college education to provide students with job-oriented practical skills.

The Rosenwald Fund's efforts to promote improved education for black children, however, had only mixed success. The fund promoted "equal schools for all," but Americans were not ready. Between 1917 and 1928, it contributed more than $18 million toward the construction of four thousand schools for black children scattered over fourteen Southern states. Julius Rosenwald had decided that genuine social change demanded cooperative efforts with state education departments. And, in contrast to the two examples already examined, the Rosenwald Fund focussed on public, not private, education.

By 1930, more than half a million rural black children studied in clean, comfortable, one- to six-room schoolhouses. The creation of a network of modern schools where none had previously existed was a monumental achievement. However, Julius Rosenwald was no more interested than was Frederick Gates in spending money on buildings alone: he wanted the Rosenwald schools to create a revolution in public funding for education, to "shame" public officials into spending equal, even if separate, amounts for the education of black and white people. That big idea did not have even a remote chance of acceptance in early twentieth-century America; it would be decades before equal funding for education would even become stated policy, much less a reality. Julius Rosenwald's hopes for race relations were decades ahead of those shared by most of his fellow citizens; however, the idea that disease could be conquered was one whose time had come.

* * *

The early twentieth-century partnership between philanthropy and medicine was an extraordinarily productive one, both in the areas of pure medical research and in the promotion of public-health practice. The Rockefeller Institute for Medical Research (RIMR), founded in 1901, was the first American institution devoted entirely to pure research in medicine, and soon became one of the world's preeminent biomedical research centers. There is delicious irony in the fact that its founder nourished a lifelong suspicion of new medical techniques. For decades, Rockefeller, Sr.'s, own personal physician was a poorly trained homeopath named Hamilton Biggar, who became the oilman's confidante, golf partner, and constant traveling companion, as well as his doctor. In keeping with Baptist beliefs, Senior neither smoked nor drank alcohol, but he was a lifelong addict of home remedies and quack potions. This did not stop him from giving millions to cutting-edge medical research, at a time when a few German universities dominated the field.

Simon Flexner, a young Baltimore pathologist and Abraham Flexner's brother, agreed to direct the RIMR, and soon assembled an international group of talented scientists. Rockefeller's wealth infused a discipline just maturing and full of opportunities for discoveries, and the institute became a magnet for scientists from all over the world who wanted to investigate chemical processes common to diseases, the functions of skin and other tissues, and the problem of hemorrhage, among other topics. In 1965, the Institute became Rockefeller University – a rarified institution offering only Ph.D.s and research fellowships – but remained the institutional home of many of the world's most promising scientists.

Scientific philanthropy's promotion of new medical ideas involved support for public-health campaigns, as well as pure research in laboratories. The Commonwealth and Milbank Funds, as well as the Rockefeller-supported International Health Board, championed educational campaigns to rid the nation of "filth" diseases, such as hookworm infestation, diarrhea, diphtheria, and enteritis, all easily spread in unsanitary environments.

By the early twentieth century, most states had established departments of health with subordinate county and local health officers; however, in reality, they were usually staffed by volunteers or a few underpaid and poorly trained physicians. The infusion of foundation money breathed life into departments and boards of public health.

Rockefeller-funded health officers fanned throughout the American South, spreading the gospel of hookworm treatment and prevention. They dimmed the lights in local libraries or post offices and gave illustrated slide lectures featuring frighteningly enlarged drawings of hookworms and other parasites. They distributed plans for sanitary fly-proof privies and offered wire screening to install in doors and windows. They passed out bottles of thymol pills.

In New York state, the Milbank Memorial Fund sponsored "health demonstrations" in New York City, as well as in Syracuse and in upstate, rural Cattaraugus County. The Fund enabled these areas to set up tuberculosis and well-baby clinics, to send nurses into the schools to teach children about nutrition and sanitation inspectors into streets and alleys, and to hold spring and fall clean-up weeks. Disgruntled local physicians, worried about the competition, scoffed that the Milbank demonstrators had descended in a "Big Way" and had begun to "examine everybody, no matter whose patient he was, for tuberculosis, diphtheria, flat feet, and impacted molars. They cleaned up the milk and harassed the schoolchildren." Clearly, a public-health agenda was more controversial than pure research conducted in state-of-the-art laboratories. But foundation-sponsored public-health advocacy got results as well, principally because all the foundations interested in public-health work realized that they had to "sell" local public officials.

In areas where foundation-supported health demonstrations occurred, rates of fecal and insect-borne diseases often dropped dramatically. Education played a role, probably a greater one than drug treatments, because the public had to understand how to use the drugs effectively. Moreover, all the medicine and health education in the world would have meant relatively little had local politicians not joined the crusade, passing and then

enforcing statutes that gave health officers the power to shut down unsanitary restaurant kitchens, clean up filthy alleys, fine homeowners with
polluted privies, and demand that schoolchildren be vaccinated against
communicable diseases.

Public-health advocacy by scientific philanthropy was closely coupled
with its promotion of social science disciplines and social science technique.
Here, too, early twentieth-century scientific giving had a lasting impact.

* * *

Not surprisingly, the universities upon which scientific philanthropy showered money were champions of educational modernization. The Social
Gospel demanded that good Christians not closet themselves, but rather
go into their communities. According to the creed of educational modernization, scholars should study society rather than Greek. Within an
amazingly short period – just a decade or two – and largely spurred by the
deep pockets of the Carnegie and Rockefeller philanthropies, universities
like North Carolina, Yale, Columbia, Harvard, Stanford, and especially
Chicago encouraged new fields of study such as sociology, psychology, and
anthropology to sprout, grow, and become established.

Foundation sponsorship of sociology provides an example paralleled by
the rise to academic and general acceptance of other new disciplines. In the
late nineteenth century, something called sociology or "social science" was
taught in a few colleges and universities, but usually in place of a course on
moral philosophy. The professors of these courses, almost all philosophers,
were interested in questions that could be called quasitheological: Did
society have the same obligations to help a sick person lying in the road as
did the person who found him? What was the ideal relationship between
organizations and individuals? By the onset of the Great Depression, the
field had been transformed.

Sociologists at the University of Chicago and at the other elite
universities that created the discipline did not sit around debating the
nature of a perfect society. They were too busy conducting interviews,
passing out questionnaires, accumulating statistics, and producing charts
and tables. They believed that society's machinery, like that of a steel mill,
could be disassembled, examined, and eventually understood. They and
their foundation patrons wanted practical applications, not theory.

Wesley Mitchell, one of a first generation of graduate students in sociology at the University of Chicago, was firmly convinced that "It is not lack
of will that impedes progress. It is lack of knowledge." Mitchell and his

classmates did not lack the will. At Chicago, this group included a number of women who would play prominent roles in the new field, especially as criminologists working in another early twentieth-century institution – the juvenile court – or as leaders of the professionalization of social work. At other schools, female graduate students and faculty members were not made so welcome; however, throughout the country, "sociological" investigations of all types boomed, a great number of them financed by scientific philanthropy. Among the tools used to probe beneath society's layers for the "knowledge" that would buttress reform, none was more popular than the social survey.

* * *

The social survey enjoyed its heyday between 1905 and 1930. Its popularity waned by the middle of the century, though not the idea that generated it: to understand society, we must measure it. Efforts to size each other up have preoccupied Americans ever since.

No subject was too small for a survey, or too large. In 1915, the city of Cleveland successfully petitioned the Carnegie Corporation for help conducting a survey of its residents' lawn-watering practices. In 1929, the Rockefeller Foundation provided a $600,000 grant to President Herbert Hoover's Research Committee on Social Trends so they could complete their task: the compilation of a complete database on all aspects of national life.

In between these two extremes, surveys ranged over all sorts of topics; some were national. With supplemental financing from the Carnegie Corporation, then Secretary of Commerce Herbert Hoover, himself a quintessential believer in the tenets of scientific philanthropy, sponsored huge surveys on big subjects. One undertaken in 1925–1926, for example, employed hundreds of researchers and attempted to uncover all bases for "waste" in American society.

Other surveys concentrated on particular regions or cities. The Russell Sage Foundation's Pittsburgh Survey, begun in 1907, established the standard for the municipal survey: a careful block-by-block scrutiny of all aspects of urban life – from the wages and hours of steelworkers to the number of tuberculosis cases in city hospitals to the square acreage of park land per resident. After its sponsorship of the famous Pittsburgh study, the Foundation's Department of Surveys went on to initiate more than 140 other surveys in the years before 1930. Many examined the state of schooling in both rural and urban areas of the country and, with graphic maps and charts, railed against "rich towns" like Greenwich, Connecticut, that tolerated "poor schools." In a symbolic move that signified the importance attached to the technique, the journal *Charities and the Commons* changed its name to *The Survey*. With help from the Russell Sage Foundation, *The Survey* became the unofficial national organ for the new profession of social work.

In November 1932, the proofs for the 1,568-page *Report of the Committee on Social Trends* were finally ready. The several hundred researchers who had labored under the direction of University of Chicago sociologist William Ogburn and University of North Carolina sociologist Howard Odum had done their work well. Their massive study, accompanied by tens of thousands of pages of charts, tables, interview transcripts, and survey results, did take the country's pulse. Divided into three parts – America's material heritage, its human resources, and its social organization – the report contained many remarkably accurate predictions. America's native-born population would continue its long decline. As a result, at some future point, the country might again loosen its restrictions against immigration. The divorce rate would climb, but the highly likely prospect of divorce would not deter the nation's citizens from marrying and remarrying. The United States would lead the world in decades to come in genetic discoveries that would transform medicine.

However, Odum glumly and accurately concluded, "Social science is no help in getting elected." The *Report*, which New Deal administrators at all levels could have read with profit, soon disappeared, forgotten on the shelves of libraries. It was too closely identified with the disgraced Herbert Hoover.

* * *

As the Great Depression deepened, Odum was one of many Americans who concluded that "lack of knowledge" was not the only impediment to social progress. By the end of the New Deal, government played a more important role in the lives of ordinary Americans. Divisions between public and private arenas had once again shifted. A new group of philanthropies, dominated by the Ford Foundation, had emerged; an era in philanthropy was over. Most of the founders of the first foundations were dead, and many of their younger advisers had departed philanthropy for other work. Early twentieth-century scientific giving, buoyed by an optimistic faith in the possibilities of system and driven by religious principle, had ended.

Beardsley Ruml, the psychologist who headed the Laura Spelman Rockefeller Memorial during its glory years in the 1920s, symbolized the changing of the guard. First an adviser to James Angell, President of the Carnegie Corporation, and just twenty-six years old when he received the chance to supervise the granting of tens of millions of Rockefeller dollars, Ruml in 1929 returned to academic life as a dean at the University of Chicago. Soon he took on other careers: Chief Executive Officer of Macy's Department Stores and then head of the New York Federal Reserve Bank. Ruml, even in his last incarnation as a powerful banker, never possessed a pinstriped soul. He remained a flamboyant raconteur, a chain-smoker, a student of the best scotch, a dandy who favored appropriately oversized pink corduroy trousers in off hours. He spent a lifetime as a big man, with big ideas.

At age fifty-six in 1952 after he had enjoyed at least five different and nationally noted careers, Ruml decided to retire and reflect. One subject that interested him was the history of philanthropy. Having been present when Frederick Gates delivered fiery orations about saving society from chaos, and when Andrew Carnegie announced his intention to end warfare forever, Ruml concluded that foundations and foundation leaders had "become colorless by comparison." He mused:

My guess is that the trustees and officers of the great foundations, particularly the officers, never having made large sums of money themselves, and for the most part having no intimate contact with anyone who ever did, are not well prepared for the efficient use of money in the grand manner.

Many of the ideas of early twentieth-century scientific philanthropists were grand, and also grandiose. Their certain faith that society could be improved through the systematic discovery and application of knowledge now seems naive. But Beardsley Ruml was right: "We can learn much studying their thinking." They certainly left a legacy worth pondering.

11

MISSIONS TO THE WORLD:
PHILANTHROPY ABROAD

EMILY S. ROSENBERG

In 1900, John R. Mott, a leader in the YMCA's foreign missionary work and head of its Student Volunteer Movement (SVM), exhorted American youth to "evangelize the world in this generation." The most prominent missionary statesman of the early twentieth century, Mott was responding to the sense of both crisis and opportunity that had, for the previous twenty years, spread within American Protestantism. At an earlier Young Men's Christian Association (YMCA) student conference in Northfield, Massachusetts, in 1886, Arthur Pierson had provided the outlines for Mott's appeal as he launched an emotional plea for students to volunteer as missionaries, particularly in China. Native religious traditions were in decline in foreign lands, Pierson proclaimed, and God was thus preparing the world for the imprint of "true" salvation. It was imperative for young Americans to seize this critical moment to spread Anglo-Saxon Protestant Christianity around the world. Mixing a faith in history as linear progress with a foreboding about a *fin de siècle* crisis, Pierson, Mott, and others suggested that if this generation of Christians did not act quickly, millions of people would be condemned to degradation and ignorance. Personal Christian conversion, carried out by cadres of dedicated Americans on an international scale, would put the entire globe onto the path of progress and civilization. Inspired by such messages, nearly 10,000 youthful Americans traveled as missionaries to Asia and other lands. Between 1890 and 1920, the international YMCA, as well as other mission organizations, established a global presence.

The efforts of missionary leaders such as Pierson and Mott emphasize the thematic connections between philanthropy at home and abroad.

Charitable missions to the world extended abroad the various domestic discourses of promoting social betterment that are examined elsewhere in this volume. International activities such as the SVM were initially rooted in this Christian evangelism, but many gradually developed a more secular, professional-scientific cast, from which emerged models for the greater governmental involvement in philanthropy that would occur after World War II. This essay surveys several efforts that exemplified this shift: the YMCA, the Women's Christian Temperance Union (WCTU), African American educational reformers, relief agencies and the Red Cross, the Carnegie Endowment for International Peace, and the Rockefeller Foundation's campaigns to combat disease and hunger.

In examining the changing character of international philanthropy, this essay seeks to avoid older frameworks that presented philanthropists either as beneficent agents of uplift or as instruments of U.S. imperial power and capitalist hegemony. Recent scholarship suggests that meanings and impacts of international/ intercultural interactions can hardly be described according to generalized and globalized claims regarding either intent or effect. The disparity between intent and effect, as well as the reciprocity of philanthropic relationships, has been artfully described in Stephen Warren's chapter on the American Indians. Characterizations of philanthropy need to be shaped with a sensitivity to the diversity of undertakings and within the context of discrete, localized interactions and understandings. Thus, this essay tries to stress the multiplicity of meanings within American traditions of international philanthropy and seeks to emphasize not only the power represented by philanthropic gifts, but also the reciprocal agency that recipients could exercise upon the plans and strategies of donors.

As the following cases illustrate, international philanthropies – in the variety of forms surveyed here – also displayed discursive complexity. They often accentuated a *difference* between philanthropist and recipient, rescuer and needy, affluent and dependent; this difference could reinforce American feelings of exceptionalism and superiority. Yet, these philanthropic traditions also often took shape within discourses of the *universality* of human experience, emphasizing respect for cultural variety. This universalism could suggest less hierarchy, sometimes diminishing the relevance of national borders and sometimes enlarging the space within which philanthropic recipients could themselves shape outcomes. Far from being univocal, in short, philanthropic efforts often both inscripted *and* erased difference; they often claimed both special national virtues *and* a larger universalized vision.

* * *

The YMCA's turn-of-the-century missionary movement, particularly the SVM, illustrates these themes. Influenced by Dwight Moody, the evangelistic fervor of the early twentieth-century missionary movement identified the American nation with Protestant Christianity, but also with a universalistic future toward which all humankind would progress. It thus contained, simultaneously, affirmations of universalistic internationalism mixed together with assumptions of American exceptionalism and envisioned a particular Anglo-Saxon–based Protestantism as setting the ultimate cultural pattern for a common future. The tensions associated with these often-conflicting goals surfaced especially over the issue of indigenous leadership. An 1889 resolution set local control as the goal for foreign YMCAs, yet conformity to American priorities was also expected. Indigenous chapters in most countries initially tried to reconcile Christianity with nationalism, but increasingly tilted toward their own nationalistic agendas.

Beset by the tensions of particularism and universalism, and embedded in a wide variety of localized political dynamics that made setting an overall policy difficult, the YMCA's missionary goal – the evangelization of the world in one generation – rather quickly lost its power to inspire, and leaders developed diverse agendas. Some American leaders held strictly to older evangelical goals that emphasized personal salvation; others, affected by their experience overseas, veered in the direction of supporting liberal reform agendas that emphasized social change. Still others, such as Sherwood Eddy, began to advocate mixing Christianity with socialism. In some places, American Y leaders came to adopt an almost anti-American tone, fiercely advocating for localized control. In other places, such as in Russia during 1918–1919 when the Y carried on extensive anti-Bolshevik campaigns, they became virtual instruments of U.S. government policy. Overall, however, during the 1920s and especially during the economic dislocations of the 1930s, YMCA missionaries became less concerned with promoting individual salvation than with reforming societies through various kinds of social science applications. With this more secular, scientific emphasis, reinforced by the growing influence of local converts, the Y's foreign branches expanded rapidly, reaching their greatest strength during the late 1920s.

New foreign leadership often tailored the Y's Christianity to their own local circumstances, and they too devised a wide variety of platforms. During the 1920s in Eastern Europe, the locally controlled Y offered a "program adapted to a Catholic environment." Chinese Christian leaders similarly ignored the early emphasis on personal salvation and tried to overlay Christianity on Confucian tradition in order to create an ethic favoring public service and liberal theology. Foreign leaders who accepted the Protestant Christianity of the YMCA shaped their own organizations in various ways – sometimes embracing modernization and even nationalism as a protest against traditional ruling elites, sometimes confirming an outsider, marginalized status in their own culture. Y membership had many meanings, depending on time, place, and the highly specific reciprocal relationships between Americans and indigenous members.

*   *   *

The idea that Christian virtues could be spread around the world in a single generation often had strongly gendered manifestations. One of the largest transnational women's movements from the 1880s to the 1920s, closely related to the missionary effort, was international temperance reform. Temperance reform, spearheaded by the WCTU headed by Frances Willard, claimed a million followers in forty countries at its peak in 1927. Some temperance activists left remarkable if little remembered records: in 1884, Mary Clement Leavitt, a fifty-four-year-old Boston schoolteacher and mother of three, undertook an eight-year global journey on behalf of the WCTU. Traveling over five continents to establish WCTU chapters, Leavitt enrolled half a million women in her crusade – and she was not alone. According to the historian Ian Tyrell, the WCTU sent out thirty-eight global missionaries to recruit women into reform causes.

Influenced by Social Darwinist notions of Anglo-Saxon superiority, Frances Willard concentrated on spreading her organization to England, where she lived from 1892 to 1896. Leaders of the WCTU hoped that an Anglo-American–led crusade could reach much of the rest of the world through a reformed imperialism that would emphasize the causes of women's emancipation, temperance, and anti-prostitution. Like many other missionary and philanthropic efforts, the WCTU held an ambivalent stance toward imperialism: It harshly critiqued imperial states for their economic exploitation, including the peddling of opium and alcohol in their colonies. Yet, the organization surely gained influence from Anglo-America's growing imperial power. In fact, the WCTU faired poorly in areas outside the

Anglo-American cultural empire and enjoyed its greatest success in Britain's colonies and ex-colonies.

WCTU activists claimed that Christianity should not only save souls, but also should work to improve social conditions, especially for women. They traced the economic deprivation, sexual exploitation, and physical abuse that afflicted women all around the world to male drinking and drug abuse. They also believed that the United States was superior in its drinking habits to most of the rest of the world and, therefore, that American women owed a special duty to women worldwide to spread the doctrine of temperance. In fact, throughout the nineteenth century, temperance crusades *had* greatly lowered the consumption of alcohol in the United States. The WCTU was also active in peace work generally, opposing antilabor violence, lynching, prizefighting, and cruelty to animals. Peace and social justice in all areas, activists believed, would advance in step with women's rights and temperance. The WCTU was also an early pioneer of international relief efforts, organizing aid to Armenia in the 1880s, long before the better known relief efforts of the World War I period.

WCTU advocates based their arguments on notions of biological essentialism: that women, in their roles as mothers, were "natural" homemakers and peacemakers. In their view, the nation state was thoroughly implicated in a system of male militarism and profit-making and women, therefore, needed to take the lead in forging transnational grassroots pressure to foster morality and justice. As mothers of the human race, in effect, women were the custodians of social mores internationally; as at home; they would work for temperance, religion, social justice, relief, and peace. Such beliefs assumed the existence of a kind of "natural" international sorority of women waiting to embrace a universalized value system consonant with that of the American middle class. The WCTU's efforts to globalize its purity crusade and to urge women to use their "natural" housekeeping talents internationally bore similarity to many of the efforts spearheaded by Christian missionary women at the turn of the century. (At that time, up to 60 percent of American missionaries in China were women.)

As in American domestic life, these discourses of "social housekeeping" contained mixed messages. They might empower women by stressing literacy, economic security, and escape from some traditional customs. By embracing gender-based internationalism, women of the WCTU forged a tradition of transnational obligation and activity. Many current nongovernmental organizations (NGOs) that specialize in human rights, relief, and peace work can trace their roots to these women who dreamed that the whole world should be cared for as though it were their own family. Yet, discourses of social housekeeping might also prove disempowering, by reinforcing Victorian notions of natural gender distinctions and by projecting a sense of imperial duty. By essentializing women's roles and emphasizing their own special benevolence, reformist crusaders could reinforce the social structures grounded in gender and racial difference that helped perpetuate women's marginalization in civic life. As with the YMCA, the WCTU's impact had considerable local variation, often shaped less by American reformers than by those they had enlisted to their cause and by the intercultural negotiations that took place between both groups.

* * *

The close connection between missionary faiths and ideas of Social Darwinism highlights the issue of race in early philanthropic movements. Early in the century, both white and African American missionary groups formulated the burden of philanthropic duty in terms of uplifting darker races by introducing them to "civilization" and salvation. But there were sharp differences in the way that discourses of race and civilization were articulated within each group.

Most missionaries were white and, in line with the racial science of the day, most at least initially socialized only with other whites, feared miscegenation, and built their mission upon the bedrock of racial hierarchy and paternalism. Racial difference, in these cases, reinforced a sense of cultural superiority. America's foreign mission movement, in its heyday between 1880 and 1930, comprised perhaps the largest benevolent organization in the nation's history: it involved tens of thousands of Americans who went abroad and millions who supported these efforts through local churches. For most, there was a close and inevitable identification between American Christianity and Anglo-Saxon racial virtues. As Arthur T. Pierson wrote in 1886, "While God permitted Protestant England to plant an empire toward the sunrise, the Pilgrims were driven to these shores to sow the seeds of a Christian republic beside the setting sun. . . . [T]he providence of God . . . settled the question that in both hemispheres the cross, and not the crescent nor crucifix, was to be dominant."

African American leaders generally shared the desire to spread "civilization" and uplift, but formulated these doctrines in a way that projected racial solidarity with Africa rather than Anglo-Saxon superiority and paternalism toward nonwhite races.

As early as 1825, the American Board of Commissioners for Foreign Missions of the Congregational Church opened the first American mission in Africa. During the late nineteenth and early twentieth centuries, a number of African American graduates of congregationally affiliated colleges were dispatched to various mission stations there. Other denominations followed, especially the African Methodist Episcopal Church (AME), one of the most prominent African American faiths, which had especially close ties to South Africa. More than one hundred African American missionaries went to Africa between 1877 and 1900. These African American missionaries often reported that Africans were attracted less to their religion than to the prospect of obtaining an education. Mission schools thus became the center of their efforts. Most African American missionaries shared the view that they needed to "civilize" the "Dark Continent" and were especially appalled by polygamy and the "degraded condition" of African women who did agricultural labor. They tried to inculcate "Christian" values, including ones involving gender roles, but often complained that African women, in the words of one, "do not appreciate our pity, or even desire to live different lives." At the same time, many missionaries came to admire and appreciate attributes of the various African cultures with which they came in contact. Some, such as William Sheppard in the Congo, became important voices decrying the consequences of imperialism. Sheppard inverted Western discourses about the "Dark Continent," writing about the advanced African kingdoms that western practices of slave-trading, forced labor, and economic exploitation had destroyed.

Colonial powers became increasingly uneasy about African American missionary efforts, which they believed modeled the capability of challenging white authority and stimulated Africans' discontent with the status quo. In 1915, South Africa banned people of color, including missionaries, from coming into the country. After World War I, most European governments similarly banned African Americans as a danger to the maintenance of colonial order.

Although philanthropic interest in educational reform in Africa continued, it shifted in more secularized directions. The Phelps–Stokes Fund, which promoted Booker T. Washington's Tuskegee model of industrial education in the United States, became active in Africa. Well-publicized Phelps–Stokes commissions on African education in 1921–1922 and 1923–1924, chaired by Thomas Jesse Jones, issued reports that provided a rationale for industrial education in Africa. These reports were strongly backed and promoted by the British colonial office. The fund subsequently convened conferences and worked with two influential individuals in early twentieth-century Africa: John Dube, president in 1912 of the South African Native National Congress (later the African National Congress), and James Aggrey of the Gold Coast, who lionized Booker T. Washington's educational and economic development theories.

The efforts by the Phelps-Stokes Fund – picked up in even more substantial ways by the Carnegie Foundation in the 1920s and 1930s – meant multiple things to their various advocates. No doubt, many British colonial officials and foundation supporters promoted Tuskegee-style education for Africans, partly to build a conservative alternative to the Pan-African movements headed by Marcus Garvey and W. E. B. DuBois. Some conservatives maintained that Tuskegee's model would help maximize the economic contribution of black people while minimizing their political power. But, within the African context, the Tuskegee model had – from early in the century – also been championed by people concerned with the cultural independence and the political and economic development of black Africa. In this sense, Tuskegee-style schools could represent a practical and grassroots strategy of racial solidarity and empowerment. Industrial-education advocates such as John Dube, for example, envisioned this model as a developmental tool that might build Pan-African nationalism. The activities of foundations and African American reformers thus mingled with local responses to leave a variety of legacies that could both reinforce and undercut the racial politics of colonialism.

* * *

The missionary-based philanthropic impulses of the early twentieth century discussed so far generally had little direct relationship to government policy. Presidents and Secretaries of State might endorse church-based efforts to spread American values and acknowledge that their activities could bring economic or geopolitical advantages. They often denounced indigenous attacks against missionaries and, as in China, warned that American citizens must be protected. But American missionaries were in no way representatives of state policy and occasionally opposed their government's foreign policy.

Relief efforts directed at emergencies in foreign lands similarly began as organized responses with little connection to the state. A famine in Russia in 1891 touched off the first national-scale campaign to relieve foreign suffering. In this case, farm-state interests united with private philanthropists to raise public awareness about Russia's plight and to appeal for contributions of grain. Leaders of this aid effort tried but failed to get Congress to ship grain at public expense, and Russian relief remained a wholly private effort. Still, this effort raised the idea that international assistance was not just the provenance of missionaries and of secular organizations, and that government might play some role.

World War I encouraged further secularization and professionalization in America's international relief efforts. After the German invasion of Belgium in 1919, Herbert Hoover became Commissioner of Belgium Relief, a semiofficial body that directed food supplies to Belgium and France. The campaign to aid Belgium demonstrated the enormous potential of private assistance, and dozens of special nationally or ethnically based organizations mobilized to send aid to most every group in Europe or the Mediterranean area that was afflicted by the war. Dozens of church-related agencies (e.g., the American Friends Service Committee, formed in 1917), trade unions, and a variety of ad hoc groups also became conduits for private war relief. In addition, the newly formed Rockefeller Foundation's War Relief Commission spent millions of dollars on supplies and on antityphus campaigns in nations associated with the United States in the war.

At the end of the war, Congress appropriated $100 million for foreign relief, and Hoover became head of the American Relief Administration (ARA) to distribute it. Although public-sector participation in postwar relief was short-lived, Hoover adroitly reshaped the ARA into a private charitable organization and continued rapidly moving food and medical supplies to Central Europe and into the newly created Soviet Union. "Bread is mightier than the sword," said one of Hoover's assistants, acknowledging the way in which privatized aid continued to serve governmental policy goals by working on behalf of postwar stabilization.

By the end of World War I, the idea of providing American money, food, medicine, and other supplies in response to foreign emergencies had become well entrenched. Philanthropists conducted fund-raising appeals around one crisis after another: the plight of Armenians, the Japanese earthquakes of 1923–1924, the severe droughts in China, and the Japanese invasion in the mid-1930s. Historian Merle Curti estimates that, between 1919 and 1939, private philanthropic giving to various international causes reached nearly $1.3 billion. Professionally run organizations, such as the International Rescue Committee (1933) and Save the Children Foundation (1938), formed to respond to the international emergencies of the 1930s. After the renewal of war in Europe in 1939, Americans again mobilized to provide war relief there. Within the first year of American neutrality, more than

350 war-relief agencies registered under the requirements of Congress's neutrality legislation.

Once the United States entered the war, President Franklin Roosevelt created a War Relief Control Board that provided oversight and encouraged mergers of charitable efforts to make sure that private philanthropies worked in harmony with each other and with the overall war effort. United China Relief, for example, was formed in 1941 to centralize and coordinate the activities of eight different agencies that were providing humanitarian assistance to China. In 1945, voluntary agencies sent nearly $250 million worth of money and donations-in-kind abroad.

The International Red Cross became the principal agency involved in relief. Founded in Switzerland during the late 1850s, the Red Cross initially cared for the wounded during wartime. An American branch, organized in 1887, served service personnel in Cuba during the War of 1898 and became a semiofficial agency through a congressionally granted charter and subsidies in 1905. During World War I, the role of the Red Cross expanded. Red Cross officials in Russia, for example, spent millions of dollars trying to keep Russia in the war against Germany by supporting non-Bolshevik groups and sending aid, including whole hospitals. Leaders of the American Red Cross (ARC) also expected to parlay wartime cooperation into a reorganization of the international agency. They hoped that a revamped body, led by the ARC and guided by scientific experts, would not restrict itself to wartime emergencies, but would become a world health organization dealing broadly with public-health issues, such as sanitation and epidemic disease. Although this larger vision encountered considerable opposition, both at home and abroad, Red Cross societies still continued to coordinate international disaster relief. During the Japanese earthquakes, for example, President Calvin Coolidge requested Americans to channel all of their donated food and medicine through the Red Cross and, in contrast to the case of the Russian famine thirty years earlier, ordered the Pacific Fleet to deliver the supplies. The American Red Cross, unlike other philanthropies, had a semiofficial status as the international relief arm of the U.S. government.

Although most international relief efforts were orchestrated by private philanthropic organizations and donors before World War II, Americans then had begun to understand how foreign assistance – organized along a professional and scientific model – could build markets and secure strategic gains for the nation, as well as express humanitarian concerns. The growing number of agencies engaged in relief work, especially during the world wars, pointed the way toward the spectacular growth of relief and rescue-related NGOs that would become so important a part of international life in the period after 1945. They also provided organizational precedents for the ever-larger involvement of new U.S. governmental or UN agencies, such as Agency for International Development and the World Health Organization, that were formed after World War II.

Relief efforts, like other philanthropic impulses, were built on contradictory imagery. Although usually cast in apolitical terms, emergency assistance efforts invariably became entangled in politics – both international politics and those of the relief bureaucracies themselves, as the ARC exemplified. Moreover, the discourses of relief, by highlighting suffering and famine elsewhere, underscored America's own presumed well-being and abundance, reinforcing a gulf of difference between Americans and others. Visions of disaster, disease, and hunger – shaped for maximum dramatic impact – invariably cast foreign lands as stage sets for American rescue missions, even as they also purveyed the ideal of a common, interconnected humanity. The increasingly professionalized and scientific organizations of relief workers, like those of the religious missionaries, simultaneously projected both difference and universalism.

* * *

Andrew Carnegie, who sold his steel business in 1901 to dedicate himself to charities, was instrumental in bringing a professionalized and scientific cast to peace causes. To counteract what he saw as the nefarious glorification of military heroism, Carnegie first began endowing "Hero Funds" in several nations to honor ordinary civilians who saved the lives of others. Then, alarmed by the rapidly escalating arms race in Europe in the first decade of the twentieth century, Carnegie decided to enlarge and institutionalize his global educational campaign to reduce jingoism and militarism. In 1910, he established his Carnegie Endowment for International Peace. The Endowment's vision involved linking international elites to promote the "scientific" study of the causes of war, aid in the development of international law, and cultivate "friendly feelings" between the inhabitants of different nations. Guided before World War I by the former Secretary of State, Elihu Root, and the educator, Nicholas Murray Butler, the Endowment sponsored scholar exchanges in Europe, Latin America, and Japan; subsidized peace and international law societies in the United States and Europe; and supported ecumenical efforts to enlist churches worldwide in promoting peace. These initiatives, Carnegie hoped, would enhance international understanding, curb militarism, and build mechanisms for the peaceful settlement of disputes.

Rededicated to its mission after the carnage of World War I, the Carnegie Endowment continued in the interwar period its scientific and legalistic approach to the promotion of peace through international law and scholarly exchanges. It funded a 152-volume series of studies on the economic and social history of World War I, compiled by a broad range of international scholars under the supervision of James T. Shotwell at Columbia University. Its extensive publication program also underwrote a series called "Classics of International Law" and issued other collections of reports and judicial decisions. Along with the Rockefeller Foundation, it supported the prominent Institute of Pacific Relations, formed by YMCA representatives in 1925 as a nondenominational international educational and scientific body. It also continued to sponsor scholarly exchanges of visiting "Carnegie Professors," established and stocked libraries around the world, and occasionally provided research services on disarmament to governmental agencies.

Cultural exchange, like so many other philanthropic impulses, became part of the formal apparatus of governmental policy in the second half of the twentieth century. Although the Carnegie Endowment's efforts continued after World War II, U.S. government agencies (e.g., the Commission on Educational Exchange, which administered the Fulbright Scholars Program, and the U.S. Information Agency) increasingly became the dominant players in promoting a new "cultural diplomacy" designed to link intellectuals who would promote American values.

* * *

The Rockefeller Institute for Medical Research was founded in 1901 in the context of Ida Tarbell's exposés of the exploitive practices of the Standard Oil Trust. At a time when the Rockefeller name had become virtually synonymous with "trusts" and "robber barons," Frederick T. Gates, a Baptist minister who was John D. Rockefeller, Jr.'s, close adviser, pressed for the establishment of a Christian-inspired reform program. He exhorted Rockefeller to aid people not as isolated groups separated behind national boundaries, but as members of a common humanity. Gates convinced Rockefeller that "disease is the supreme ill of human life, and it is the main source of . . . poverty, crime, ignorance, vice, inefficiency, hereditary taint, and many other evils." To concentrate on fighting disease, the Rockefeller Sanitary Commission was founded in 1909 to eradicate hookworm from the southern United States. In 1910, Rockefeller then asked Congress to incorporate the Rockefeller Foundation to promote the well-being of Americans, as well as "mankind throughout the world." Rockefeller's initiatives were thus shaped within universalistic assumptions rooted in Christianity and reinforced by what his advisers regarded as the borderless nature of scientific discovery. The Rockefeller Foundation exemplified the same trends seen in many other philanthropic organizations – a growing secular and scientific emphasis, the development of models that would later be adapted to governmental efforts, and the reciprocal interplay between donors' objectives and recipients' goals.

The success of the Rockefeller Sanitary Commission led to creation of its International Health Board (IHB) (later, the International Health Division) in 1913 to carry the antihookworm campaign to the one billion people who lived in fifty-two countries afflicted by the disease. The campaign lasted thirty-eight years and, between 1913 and 1950, allocated $100 million to health activities, broadening to include malaria and twenty-two other diseases or health problems. A special yellow-fever commission, formed in 1915, waged campaigns against the mosquito and successfully developed a vaccine. The foundation trained and employed cadres of young public-health professionals worldwide, whose work would have impact for a generation and beyond. It built institutes of public health in approximately two dozen cities throughout the world to train new health-care workers and conduct research, and it helped establish women's colleges in China, India, and Japan. During these years, hookworm and the other public-health threats were drastically reduced. The health campaigns, based on the model of the Sanitary Commission, tried to work in partnership with indigenous organizations and governments so that these local entities could, in time, assume the direction and expense of the programs.

The Rockefeller Foundation developed a special interest in China. Its China Medical Board, which became an independent institution in 1928, supported the Peking Union Medical College (PUMC), which became the premier health center in China. In 1935, the foundation launched a grassroots initiative to take health care, training, and community development into rural villages in China, relying on midwives and other paramedics to bring basic care to peasants whose lives had remained unaffected by an elite research institution such as PUMC. Using the China model, the foundation also promoted medical education elsewhere, directing grants to large institutions in Beirut, Hong Kong, Singapore, Bangkok, and other locations. It also supported development of localized low-cost health services at the village level, especially in a campaign on islands in the South Seas.

The initial emphasis in the fight against disease gradually shifted from treating individuals to improving general sanitary conditions. The IHB, collaborating with local entities, helped establish a model and infrastructure for rural health service. This outreach was shaped not only in accordance with the foundation's medical models, but also often in terms of the knowledge that local participants brought to bear and of the purposes they chose to make of Rockefeller money and support. Two cases illustrate the reciprocal interaction between the international foundation and local circumstance.

In many countries of Latin America, alliances among the foundation, local vanguards of public-health reformers, and expanding national states shaped the public-health and social-welfare infrastructure. In Costa Rica, research and treatment of hookworm disease had actually preceded the Rockefeller Foundation's involvement in 1914. Foundation staff did not introduce new knowledge and techniques so much as they provided the resources for public-health activists who wanted to centralize agencies into a national department of health and develop a national network of public education focused on hygiene. The Rockefeller campaign in Brazil, begun in 1916, followed a similar pattern. To facilitate the government's extension of greater authority over provincial areas and keep ports free of quarantine, Brazilian leaders welcomed the foundation's assistance in spreading their public-health programs.

Rockefeller's IHB chose the British colony of Ceylon (Sri Lanka), a plantation-based economic crossroads and a Buddhist center, as a demonstration site for eradication of hookworm in the East. Begun in 1916, the project had some initial success on plantations, but the reinfection rate was so high that a stringent policy of forcing large planters to improve overall sanitary conditions seemed necessary. When the planters resisted adopting costly health requirements, however, the IHB officials switched course. They embarked on educational campaigns directly in villages and schools, encouraged creation of sanitary departments in provincial governments, and provided training for native herbal doctors. They broadened the focus beyond hookworm to encompass a comprehensive, grassroots public-health campaign aimed at preventing a wide range of infectious diseases. This foundation effort was shaped, from the mid-1920s on, in collaboration with a new generation of local leaders, who advocated involving government directly in health and education in the countryside, especially sponsoring mass vaccinations and maternity and child welfare services. This switch from a curative to a preventive emphasis, devised within a dynamic of cooperation between the foundation and local communities, brought a revolution in health that, in time, raised life expectancy and lowered mortality rates in Ceylon to levels comparable to those in Western Europe.

Although such outreach efforts were important parts of Rockefeller funding until the early 1930s, the health division gradually passed support onto the host states themselves, shifting more of their funding dollars to research taking place in prestigious universities, mostly in the developed world.

Building on the models of its sanitation and health programs, however, the Rockefeller Foundation also turned its attention to a related global problem: hunger. The Foundation's interest in agricultural reform was long-standing: Before World War I, it had collaborated with the U.S. Department of Agriculture to create scientific demonstration farms in the United States, a program that provided models for the U.S. Agriculture Department's Extension Service. To duplicate this domestic practice worldwide in the mid-1920s, the foundation made a number of grants to agricultural colleges abroad and awarded fellowships to international students wishing to study agricultural science in the United States. In the mid-1930s, paralleling its efforts to promote basic health services at the village level in China and elsewhere, it funded a million-dollar demonstration project to train rural community workers to spread agricultural reform. China had become almost synonymous with famine, stemming from the persistence of traditional low-yield agricultural practices. When the program collapsed during the chaotic conditions associated with World War II and the subsequent civil war in China, the Foundation switched its attention to Mexico. There, it and the Mexican government began a collaboration to improve yields of corn and wheat by developing high-yield hybrids that were resistant to drought and diseases. This "green revolution" quickly became a global crusade, as the Foundation focused also on rice and other crops. It assumed the scale and style of the Foundation's public-health campaigns of the pre–World War II era by building on international and local collaborations and spreading technical training and scientific research. It also sparked controversy because it fostered large-scale agriculture, placed small-scale farmers at a disadvantage, and necessitated large applications of often-imported fertilizers and often-scarce water supplies. The Foundation's emphasis on science and expertise at times facilitated the ideas of advancement propounded by some local recipients, but it also sometimes clashed with perceived local needs, provoking controversy and backlash.

* * *

The historian Akira Iriye has suggested that America's most significant contribution to the twentieth century has been the global spread of the type of transnational nongovernmental organizations profiled in this essay. Some conclusions emerge from surveying the philanthropic impulses in such groups.

First, in all sectors of philanthropy – missions, relief, peace work, health – the religious impulse that had initially shaped visions of charity and reform gave way to a secularized emphasis on uplift through science and technology. This shift toward scientific philanthropy is also developed more fully in chapters by Porterfield and Sealander earlier in this volume. The career of Roger Sherman Greene of the Rockefeller Foundation's China Medical Board typified this shift. Greene had come from a missionary family, and his brother wrote him that his medical work was an apt "continuation of the missionary tradition to the fourth generation of our family." But Greene himself was highly critical of the older tradition that, in his view, justified educational and medical services "merely as baits to catch people so they can be preached to." He insisted that improving human services through scientific applications, especially in medicine, should become the primary way of changing lives.

Second, although the national government had little direct involvement in international philanthropy before World War II, the early programs that spread religion, temperance, education, relief, scholarly collaboration, and medical and agricultural science did establish precedents for government's greater role after World War II. Private philanthropies experimented with many of the techniques that would characterize later governmental programs of foreign assistance and cultural exchange. New foreign policy agendas for the post–World War II period, as Gary Hess's essay illustrates, (Chapter 15), would seize on the advantages to the state of spreading American-based science and expertise.

Finally, international philanthropic impulses display such striking diversity that they fit uneasily into those familiar and overgeneralized interpretations that celebrate American expansionism as "progress" or that decry it as "imperialism." Any assessment of either the goals or the effects of philanthropy depends on specific contexts, and can be framed within a multiplicity of meanings and interpretive narratives. As the cases examined in this essay suggest, philanthropy could be imperious, expressing chauvinism, special destiny, and cultural difference; but it could also build transnational networks of people whose efforts at change came to redefine the boundaries of national loyalties and to exalt a more universal ideal. It often arose as an expression of racial and cultural superiority; but it could also provide resources that recipients could appropriate for their own purposes and empowerment so as to undermine hierarchies of race and culture. It could promote top-down control, elevating culturally bound notions of "salvation" or "expertise"; yet, its local impacts also varied widely, as recipients exerted their own agency to amend, react against, or simply ignore attempts at centralized control. It tended to preserve the status quo by promoting conservative views of social relationships (e.g., gender, race, class); yet, by its inevitable interventions in settled ways, it could also have surprising and disruptive consequences. Most important, philanthropy often bore these seemingly opposing characteristics simultaneously, depending on the position and perspective of the observer, or on which facets of the intercultural exchanges were emphasized and which were obscured. Terms such as *international philanthropy*, *globalization*, and *imperialism* may, in this sense, signify the identical sets of exchanges, narrated and understood from different perspectives and in different contexts.

Part III

PHILANTHROPIC
RECONSTRUCTIONS, 1930–2001

Because of our poverty, we did occasionally feel that we were born "on the wrong side of the railroad tracks." We had only a small tree at Christmas time and the Presbyterian Home Mission sent a Christmas box each year. It was filled with secondhand clothing which we resented. One year when I was in my teens a beautiful coat with a big patch on the right elbow arrived. I liked the coat, but my pride was too great to put it on.

Ever since then, Christmas has seemed to me to be a grubby occasion. For many it is the time to give "welfare" to the people, although welfare should be of concern 365 days a year. I always felt Christmas ought to be the special occasion for expressing one's admiration, respect, affection, or love for a particular person. A Christmas gift should be, I thought, a highly individual expression of interest or concern. An apple might serve the end. The ideal gift, however, would be one that the donor had created – like a book or a slingshot or something else resulting from his own efforts. Kloochman Rock near Yakima, that rises to a sheer height of eight hundred feet, has on its ledges a rare species of penstemon. One of these flowers – tenderly collected and carefully pressed – would make a Christmas gift unequaled.

As I look back, I feel that the patched coat that came from Philadelphia or New York was a perversion of Christmas. The donor gained merit by his generosity in disposing of his cast-off clothing. This charity was the beginning of the end of personal relations. It was a miniature of the foreign aid program of the United States in the post–World War II years – a project designed essentially for the welfare of the United States, as evidenced by the fact that out of every five dollars we advanced, we received four back in the form of interest, repayment of principal, or dollars expended here.

Whatever the merits of that patched coat, it transformed Christmas into something offensive to me. Christmas eventually became a virtual monopoly of the Establishment whereby retail sales mounted. It almost seemed as if it were the duty of all Americans – measured by the GNP – to give at Christmas freely and fully. It mattered not whether the gift was cigars, lingerie, neckties, or booze – so long as one spent money. As the years passed, I came to hate the holiday more and more.

From William O. Douglas, *Go East Young Man*

FROM DEPRESSION TO THE PRESENT

The Great Depression prompted many Americans to question the fundamental principles of limited government on which their social system seemed to be based. New Deal legislation provided another opportunity for the United States to embrace governmental philanthropy. The government stepped in to provide jobs; rebuild a national infrastructure; and alleviate pain, suffering, and starvation. Yet, the Supreme Court's condemnations of early New Deal legislation indicates the extent to which traditional republican principles were rooted in law as well as public belief. Traditional conceptions of constitutional law restrained legislative initiatives, even when those initiatives were overwhelmingly supported by the American people. A constitutional crisis, greater than any in United States history other than Civil War, led to Franklin D. Roosevelt's attempt to control the Supreme Court so as to redesign American society. Although his Court-packing scheme failed, the Court eventually adopted a model of bifurcated review of legislative infringements on personal rights that upheld subsequent New Deal legislation – The new model still relied on a "strict scrutiny" standard in reviewing legislation that impinged upon civil rights; however, the Court granted deference to Congress to impose regulatory or redistributive programs that might interfere with an individual's "liberty of contract." The Supreme Court of the 1930s and 1940s essentially read the contract clause – so central to the jurisprudence of the Marshall Court – out of existence. The changes in constitutional law resulted in an unprecedented growth of government before and during the war.

From the 1930s through the 1970s, the United States again experimented with an active positivist government. In the post-war and Cold War years, a limited welfare state was built on wage and labor laws, equal employment legislation, affirmative action and other limitations on management rights in the workplace, Medicare, Social Security, and a variety of federally financed redistributive initiatives. During the 1960s, government sought to foster private philanthropic activity under public umbrellas. The creation of the Peace Corps and the Office of Economic Opportunity presented federal programs that allowed primarily young Americans to expend their energies in channeled pursuits of perceived national goals.

Many thought that government programs did not "go far enough" in redesigning American society. Large popular movements criticizing persistent racism, lack of opportunities for women, and American imperialism – most visibly its involvement in Vietnam – expressed new conceptions of an ideal American society. Throughout the nation, a new group of philanthropic activists sought to change society through nonviolent revolution.

When Richard Nixon said that "we are all Keynesians now," recognizing the necessity of government spending to the American economy, many perceived it as emblematic of even conservative Americans' commitment to the activist or New Deal style of government. Yet, once again, the long-term effects of this activist experiment were diminished by the reassertion of individual rights as a barrier to governmental action during the Reagan, Bush, and Clinton administrations. From the 1980s to the present, business was reconceived from a source of social ills to a potential tool for social progress. This is not to say that the activist state of the Roosevelt and Truman years has gone away. Rather, reflective of Eisenhower's greatest fears, the government has become a partner with business in a new system in which both rely on each other to address social needs.

Policymakers move freely from governmental positions to jobs in large philanthropic trusts and corporations, and back again. Recently, President George W. Bush has even called on some of the nation's largest nonprofit corporations – the churches – to openly assume responsibility for what had been government programs in providing care for the poor and education. The old colonial model of integrated church and state and overlap between public and private spheres, diminished in the Revolution and its after-math, has resurfaced in the twenty-first century. The American under-standing of philanthropy is once again in a state of flux – and the old private versus public debate continues to rage.

In this environment, Americans are once again turning to small groups to respond to their fear, distrust, and anger of and with the alliance of large government and corporations. Decades of urban growth have moderated as more families, retirees, and young people are moving to smaller com-munities. Church attendance is up, as is participation in club sports and social events. The reemphasis on family is evident from the recognition of "soccer moms" as a voting bloc. Even computerized "chat rooms" or "mes-sage boards" can ironically provide a sense of community from the privacy of one's home.

Many of these "communities" have come about as voice-pieces for spe-cial interests. Groups as disparate as local militia organizations, Mothers Against Drunk Driving (MADD), antiabortionists, the National Rifle

Association (NRA), and the Gay and Lesbian Alliance may be the most visible "philanthropic" movements of the late twentieth and early twenty-first centuries. Once again, Americans are seeking affiliation with others of like sentiment to attempt to impose their different versions of an ideal on the larger society.

12

FAILURE AND RESILIENCE: PUSHING THE LIMITS IN DEPRESSION AND WARTIME

DAVID C. HAMMACK

In October 1929, trustees of University Hospitals (UH), the great teaching and research medical center in Cleveland, Ohio, celebrated the recent opening of a new Institute of Pathology, largely paid for by grants from the General Education Board (GEB), a leading Rockefeller-supported philanthropy. UH trustees looked forward to the completion, within a year, of Lakeside Hospital, the centerpiece that would certify their medical center as one of America's largest and most modern. However, the Great Crash intervened. Ceilings in the old Lakeside Hospital building were literally falling, but many of those who had promised donations to the new Lakeside lost so much in the Crash that they were unable to keep their promises.

By 1931, UH faced still more serious problems. The new Lakeside had opened at last, but revenues were far lower than anticipated. With a third of Cleveland's labor force out of work for more than a year, many hospital fees went unpaid. Other sources of hospital income also dried up. The Community Chest had been paying for most charity hospital care in Cleveland, but it raised much less in 1931 than it had in 1929, even as it tried to aid the unemployed. Western Reserve University's income was down too, due to the stock market crash and to student inability to pay tuition: Western Reserve had to withhold its usual $100,000 payment for using UH as the prime teaching unit for its medical school. In October 1931, Samuel Mather – the steel magnate who was the leading donor to UH, the Community Chest, and Western Reserve University – died.

UH's trustees responded by making some tough decisions. They shut down whole floors in their new complex. They asked, "Shall we continue to render an unlimited amount of free service . . . or shall we make an effort to limit the number of patients accepted for care to a figure consistent with our financial limitations and needs for teaching purposes?" Without abandoning free care, they decided that they must work above all to build for Cleveland one of the world's leading medical research and teaching centers. Limiting free care to the amount provided by the Community Chest, they introduced a means test, raised clinic fees, and added new charges for X-rays and prescription drugs. They consolidated kitchens and shifted pre- and post-natal "field nursing" to the separate Visiting Nurse Association. They laid off nurses and other employees, reduced the numbers of interns and residents, and cut salaries across the board. In 1933, they even invaded the hospital's endowment, selling bonds into a bad market.

At the same time, UH took several key steps to maintain its position as a scientific institution of international standing. Assistant Director of Administration John Mannix, who would go on to help create the national Blue Cross hospital insurance movement, introduced a "flat-rate" scheme under which patients who paid cash in advance were charged a fixed fee per day, regardless of the services they used. To attract paying patients, UH invested in "an organized publicity and educational program." Even at the bottom of the Depression, UH trustees competed for top-flight doctors and scientists. When their surgeon-in-chief resigned to return to Harvard Medical School in 1932, they "canvassed the entire country" for a replacement. The "financial question" of paying the new surgeon the trustees vowed to answer through personal donations.

These strong actions began to pay off as early as 1934. New insurance schemes and a revived economy increased the number of paying patients. UH did not "lose sight of the fact that . . . it was in support of a program of teaching and research and care of a certain number of indigent sick that the community gave several million dollars a few years ago." But it did transfer many of the sick poor to public hospitals, and it insisted that government agencies pay for services provided to wards of the state. Then, during World War II, UH was granted the honor of providing the first American medical unit in World War II, presenting it with a personnel crisis even while introducing federal funding for some of the hospital's activities.

In the face of depression and war, America's wealthiest donors maintained the new patterns of giving they had established during the 1920s. In the North, Midwest, and West, donors and foundations had already reduced their involvement with Protestant missions. Working closely with Herbert Hoover's Department of Commerce, they had been seeking instead to use private associations – as well as private hospitals and universities – to advance a new mission: setting new national standards for health, welfare, and education. Aided by wealthy donors, the nation's hospitals, colleges, universities, and arts organizations – and the professional associations that served them – recovered quite quickly from the harsh impact of the Great Depression. Through the New Deal and World War II, they worked effectively to advance the agenda set in the 1920s.

* * *

Poor people did not recover quickly. The Depression experience of ordinary workers can be seen in the following table:

*Unemployed as Percent of Nonfarm
Labor Force 1925–1947*

Year	% Unemployed
1925	5.4
1927	5.4
1929	5.3
1931	25.2
1933	37.6
1935	30.2
1937	21.3
1939	25.2
1941	14.4
1943	2.7
1945	2.7
1947	5.4

Source: Bureau of the Census, *Historical Statistics of the United States, Colonial Times to 1970* (Washington, DC: U.S. Printing Office, 1975), p. 126.

Lack of work during the Great Depression forced many people to limit their gifts to labor and homemade goods; the Depression often destroyed people's ability to give in any way except to members of their own families. The Depression forced many people to share, even as it deprived them of the ability to be "charitable," if charity is defined as free-will giving to strangers.

In Appalachia, in the deeply impoverished South, and in the mountain Southwest – regions where cash incomes were often less than $200 a year – as many as 40 percent of all families took out-of-work relatives into their homes. Poor women everywhere "got along" by helping one another with gifts of food and clothing, by exchanging care of children and the sick, and by providing small "loans" for rent or for an essential taxi.

Most people gave through their churches. Low pay and intermittent work cut deeply into family incomes during the Depression, wrote one analyst, "forc[ing] most men to withdraw from their unions, lodges, and sometimes even from their churches." As early as 1931, the Federal Council of Churches was calling not for charity, but for legislation. The churches, it said, must "insist upon the creation of an industrial society which shall have as its purpose economic security and freedom for the masses of mankind, 'even these least, my brethren.'"

Weakened by a decline that dated to the late nineteenth century, religious charity proved far too weak to respond to the emergency. In St. Louis, the German St. Vincent's Orphanage lost more than a third of its donors in a single year. Church membership actually grew through the Depression; it increased 14 percent between 1926 and 1935, another 14 percent between 1935 and 1945, then a full 20 percent between 1945 and 1950. Similarly, the YMCA reached record membership in the mid-1930s. However, despite larger memberships, church and YMCA incomes fell sharply, by as much as two fifths between 1929 and 1935. They did not recover until after World War II.

Religious workers – church pastors, teaching nuns, missionaries, and others – endured exceptionally hard times in the 1930s. The Catholic Church had pushed with great success to build its system of parochial and diocesan schools in the 1920s, only to see building funds dry up and one student in ten leave Catholic elementary schools during the 1930s. A possibly apocryphal story held that two teaching nuns in one hard-hit Midwestern town stoically continued to teach despite a complete lack of pay, and starved to death. "Never in the history of the Catholic school system have the pastors of the diocese, the teaching priests, brothers, and sisters, and the people of the Archdiocese been called upon to make greater sacrifices," Chicago's Catholic school superintendent wrote in 1931. Everywhere, Catholic teachers accepted subsistence wages, while out-of-work parishoners donated the labor to maintain school facilities.

Worst hit were the poorest. In the Chicago area, parochial school enrollment in the poorest city and suburban neighborhoods declined by more than twenty-five thousand, as penniless parents withdrew children they could not properly clothe and refrained from having more children. At the bottom of the Depression, the Salvation Army found itself providing shelter to one fifth of America's homeless. However, the Salvation Army had always relied for funds on small gifts of money and used goods from poor people, and on the sale of refurbished secondhand goods in poor neighborhoods. In the depths of the Depression, many poor people had no money to spare. They used their clothing and household equipment until it was thoroughly worn out, and they simply could not afford secondhand goods. Starved for funds as its relief expenses multiplied seven times, the Salvation Army often found itself unable to pay either its mortgages or its full-time workers.

African Americans suffered most of all. Northern antiblack "race riots" and Southern lynch mobs had driven segregation to its peak in the 1920s; the 1930s saw little relief. Segregation meant the exclusion of African Americans from education, training, and skilled jobs. It was not a surprise that African American unemployment rates ran at double those of white Americans, or that African Americans relied even more than poor whites on the mutual support of family and friends. In cities like Chicago, Cleveland, and New York, as many as half of all African American men were unable to find work throughout the Depression – even as Southern cotton farmers faced near starvation. In Texas, county relief officials treated African Americans and Mexican Americans as though they were not really citizens, often rejecting their relief applications out of hand.

Segregation also meant the exclusion of African Americans and other people of color from "white" YMCAs and YWCAs, from "white" libraries, from "white" hospitals. While some African Americans worked through the National Association for the Advancement of Colored People (NAACP) to break down the barriers of segregation, others devoted great effort to building schools, hospitals, welfare agencies, and recreation centers for the black community. Among those who made the most important contributions were the families of black students and patients who paid what they could, and the black teachers and nurses who continued to work for tiny salaries.

Taking the view that African Americans needed better facilities "now," before the great day of integration arrived, Chicago's Rosenwald Fund and a small group of Northern foundations made substantial grants to build community centers and hospitals in many segregated communities. These grants went to organizations in the North as well as the South through the

1920s and 1930s. But when hard times deprived many African Americans of their ability to contribute to the operating expenses of these institutions, or even to pay small hospital or tuition charges, that strategy seemed as futile as the effort to overcome segregation itself. Late in the 1930s, the Phelps-Stokes Fund and the Carnegie Foundation encouraged W. E. B. DuBois to seek funds for an African American encyclopedia project, only to deny the request. Leaders of African American institutions had to struggle against defeatism and against an angry radicalism born of exclusion and frustration, even as they continued to seek donations from wealthy whites.

Middle-income "white" Americans were also hit hard by the Great Depression, but they had more resources of all kinds to fall back on, and by 1935 many were on the way to recovery. The initial blow was hard. As the leader of the American City Bureau, a major fund-raising organization, put it in November 1932, "thousands upon thousands of good, public-spirited, civic-minded citizens, who have been giving generously for many years, have now exhausted their last reserves and simply do not have the money. The old family homestead is mortgaged up to the eaves, the family Ford is about to fall apart, Mary and John cannot go to college, and the grocer must be paid."

Many middle-income Americans had relied on mutual-benefit associations, mutual savings banks, and mutual insurance companies. Some of those associations were hit hard by the Crash and many, especially those that were poorly managed, closed. Altogether, they lost a fifth of their revenues and were forced to lay off 8 percent of their staffs by 1935. These losses devastated families that had expected mutual-benefit association aid in the early Depression. However, thanks in part to New Deal legislation that created such new agencies as the Federal Savings and Loan Insurance Corporation, many mutuals – especially savings banks and insurance companies – recovered quickly in the late 1930s, and by 1940 they were growing rapidly.

* * *

The Great Depression posed a challenge that proved far too great for American philanthropy. Historically, relief for the poor and the unemployed had come from families and local governments, with significant supplements from private charity. Herbert Hoover greatly feared that federal provision of relief funds would serve as a "dangerous precedent" that would dry up private charity, launch a disastrous dependence on the dole, and "end . . . the wonderful activity of the Red Cross." Hoover gave much of his own salary to relief organizations and persuaded fifty well-known Americans, including humorist Will Rogers, to aid a special Red Cross campaign. Leading rallies with the comment "Well, folks . . . glad you are starving, otherwise I would never have met you," Rogers helped raise $250,000. Thomas Edison contributed his eighty-third birthday cake, which brought $107 at auction. These sums hardly began to address the need in 1931.

The Red Cross drive did raise $10 million and massive special Community Chest efforts in 1930 and 1931 also brought in exceptionally large sums. But the need was simply too great; by late 1931, private welfare federations everywhere were turning to government solutions – first to the states but soon to the federal government. In 1932, Edward Ryerson, a leading Chicago steelman and philanthropist, obtained $12 million from the Illinois state government for unemployment relief in Chicago. When that ran out, he went to President Hoover. "It was a curious thing for me to do," he said. "I was bitterly opposed to federal funds at that time. But I realized the problem was beyond the scope of local government." Ryerson had already accepted the fact that it was also beyond the scope of private philanthropy.

The New Deal had other impacts. It provided a welcome new source of money for the unemployed and of security for middle-class savings and mortgages. Yet, when Federal Emergency Relief Administrator Harry Hopkins ruled in 1935 that "Grants of Federal Emergency Relief Funds are to be administered by public agencies," he was also denying federal funds to private agencies that had traditionally obtained funds from local governments. Many private welfare workers had to accept the more secure employment of county welfare departments. In 1940, one YMCA leader complained that key New Dealers were out to displace private charities. "Many jobs that, in former years, were done with pretty good efficiency among the soldiers and sailors, by the Salvation Army, the YMCA, the YWCA, the Knights of Columbus, etc.," he wrote, would, if these New Dealers had their way, "be assigned to the WPA and the NYA."

Philanthropists and their organizations, especially the new foundations and federated fund-raising agencies like the Community Chest, strongly resisted the expansion of federal authority. Some New Deal agencies did threaten to displace private charities, especially in the welfare and youth-serving fields. But Roosevelt himself, very much like Hoover, thought it essential to maintain as wide a scope as possible for private initiative and private nonprofit organizations, and several New Deal policies advanced those purposes. When the Social Security Act of 1935 provided immediate streams of federal funds for the elderly and disabled, private nursing homes not only survived, but also actually began to expand. Many nursing homes were then, as now, run as for-profit businesses. Yet, a good deal of federal old-age assistance money did make its way to nonprofit homes for the elderly, stimulating religious communities and other sponsors to seek and obtain significant private donations.

Indirectly, Franklin D. Roosevelt's federal government also gave a major boost to another middle-class charitable activity, the March of Dimes. One of the pioneer nonsectarian, mass-based health charities, the March of Dimes sought to raise significant amounts of money through small donations from many individuals. Because it used its funds to care for those – like Franklin D. Roosevelt – who were afflicted by polio and to seek medical ways to prevent or cure the disease, the March of Dimes was closely associated with the President. FDR allowed the March of Dimes to recruit local postmasters as organizers of its door-to-door campaigns, and he also allowed the March to hold special fund-raising dances on his birthday. With his support, the March of Dimes showed that middle- and lower-income Americans could support a major private charitable effort, even during the Great Depression.

In yet another indication of middle-class resiliency (and self-support) during the Depression, enrollment in Catholic schools in the better-off neighborhoods of Chicago and other midwestern and eastern cities never declined during the 1930s. Catholics in southwest Chicago's upscale Beverly area, for example, built two new Catholic schools in the mid-1930s.

By the 1930s, the Catholic Church faced a very big fund-raising challenge. In addition to its traditional commitments to hospitals, the relief and job-training activities of the Society of St. Vincent de Paul, orphanages, and the elderly, it now sought money both for a very large school system and for such new agencies as the Catholic Youth Organization. Seeking all possible means of meeting these commitments, Catholic fund-raisers who had remained aloof from the Community Chest movement during the 1920s were already beginning to embrace regional nonsectarian fund-raising as "a modern, cooperative plan of securing money." In Cleveland, a leader in community-wide fund-raising, the Community Chest, provided 90 percent of all donations to Catholic welfare agencies by 1930. Catholic bishops in many other communities embraced the Community Chest during the 1930s. Faced with the terrible challenges of the Great Depression, many Catholic leaders also dropped their opposition to federal funds in this decade. But they never abandoned their insistence on approaches to funding that allowed their institutions to remain independent of federal control.

* * *

The 1930s and 1940s presented many Americans, however poor or rich, with extraordinary opportunities and challenges for philanthropy abroad. Among the traditional objects of charity recognized in the Elizabethan Statute of Charitable Uses of 1601, the founding legal document for American philanthropy, was the ransoming of prisoners. The rise of totalitarian and nationalistic states in Asia and in Europe and the widespread conflicts of World War II created vast numbers of hostages. Throughout Asia, Protestant and Catholic missionaries and international public-health and social-aid workers found themselves at risk in the face of Japanese expansion, the collapse of European colonial regimes, the rise of nationalism, and internal conflict in many nations. The Nazis sought to eliminate all Jews and all Gypsies from the face of Europe. Nazis also subordinated Slavs and other groups. As they moved into a full-scale war, Nazis seized control of Catholic and Protestant institutions as well. Nazi and Japanese expansion created millions of refugees; their ultimate defeat created millions more. A few fortunate refugee scientists and scholars found opportunities at The Institute for Advanced Study in Princeton, New Jersey (founded in 1930 by the Bamberger family) and, with funds from the Rockefeller Foundation and a few other philanthropies, at other research centers, universities, and colleges. But American philanthropy had many more opportunities to ransom prisoners during the 1930s and 1940s than it could possibly engage.

American Jewish organizations faced an especially devastating challenge. To take a single dramatic example: American Jews provided as much as 80 percent of the funds for the Organization for Rehabilitation through Training (ORT), which provided technical education to Jews excluded from state schools in eastern and central Europe. In 1939, ORT agreed with the National Council of Trades Unions in Poland to fund training for thirty thousand Polish Jewish workers. To carry out this program and similar plans in Hungary, Romania, Latvia, Germany, France, and other countries, ORT budgeted $1,475,000 for 1940. In July 1940, Poland's Nazi Governor-General disbanded all organizations, non-Jewish as well as Jewish. ORT's programs were placed under the controllers of the official ghettos of Warsaw and other Polish cities, where all Jews who had not been sent to concentration camps had been forced to move. ORT now trained factory workers and organized children to plant gardens, creating "green corners" in the ghetto. The Nazis killed all ORT leaders in Warsaw in 1943, a few months before the total destruction of the Warsaw ghetto. It became almost impossible to move funds into Romania in 1941, although an ORT school in Bucharest continued to teach radio technology right through the war. By 1944, millions had been murdered, fighting in central Europe was at its peak, and ORT could find use for only $653,000.

Three quarters of the Jews in France did survive the Holocaust. The courage and resourcefulness of Jewish organizations in France, together with the support of some French gentiles, was the key to their survival. But American Jews provided important funds; the largest share came through the American Joint Distribution Committee, which channeled money raised by Jewish communities throughout the United States to Jewish organizations abroad. Annual Joint Distribution Committee contributions in France averaged $138,000 in the early 1930s, more than $700,000 at the beginning of the war, and nearly $2 million in the mid-1940s. These funds supported rescue work of all kinds, including the support of more than ten thousand Jewish children who were taken in, at enormous risk, by non-Jewish French families and institutions, including Catholic and Protestant orphanages.

Protestant, Catholic, and nonsectarian international charities also faced enormous challenges during the 1930s and 1940s. The Great Depression and the rapidity of violent change abroad combined to make it very difficult for Americans to respond. In mid-1940, a seasoned YMCA leader asserted that it would require more effort to raise $193,000 for prisoners of war "than it took to raise many millions" during World War I.

The best estimates suggest that American philanthropies sent about $310 million abroad in 1930, and $160 million in 1935, and $180 million in 1940. Amounts did rise rapidly during and immediately after the war, to $470 million in 1945 and $650 million in 1946, then remained in the $450 million to $550 million range through the 1950s. Expressed in terms of income, total private American contributions abroad fell from about one third of 1 percent of total national income in the very early 1930s to one fifth of 1 percent in the later 1930s, and one seventh of 1 percent during the war. They rebounded to about one third of 1 percent at the end of the war, then fell back to only one eighth of 1 percent of national income late in the 1950s.

Great efforts were devoted to raising these funds, and many international fund-raising campaigns were highly publicized. To this day, American families speak of sending "CARE" packages not only to distressed people abroad, but also to their own children who are away at school. During World War II, a National War Fund raised several hundred million dollars through what War Fund president Winthrop W. Aldrich called "a comprehensive federation of war-related agencies" based on local Community Chests and the Red Cross. Reviewing appeals made for specific wartime agencies, War Fund campaign chairman (and leading Connecticut Republican) Prescott Bush asserted that "the strongest single appeal was of course that of the USO," which aided servicemen and women. But "War Prisoners Aid pulled strongly, and so did United Seaman's Service." He added that "foreign relief agencies for perfectly natural reasons, found the strength of their appeals in proportion to localized sympathies and traditional interests" deriving from specific ethnic and religious ties.

Prescott Bush also noted that "public confusion arising from continuous front-page publicity" on efforts to establish the United Nations Relief and Reconstruction Agency (UNRRA) created difficulties for the War Fund campaign, as people asked what part of the War Fund budget "had to do with foreign relief." In fact, War Fund leaders strongly supported the development of a federal tax-supported foreign aid program. During World War II, private gifts made a critical difference to the people and organizations that received them. Yet it seems likely that – with some notable exceptions – American gifts abroad were more important as a means to mobilizing opinion within the United States than in meeting international needs. In the longer term, World War II established a new American tradition of federal government funds for international relief, administered through organizations that reflected religious sponsorship, such as the American Friends Service Committee, World Vision, World Concern, and – largest of all – Catholic Relief Services.

* * *

In the 1920s, the leaders of American philanthropy had taken on a new overriding mission: to use private institutions to develop a national capacity to employ science for the public good and for national defense. In Europe, Japan, and China, this was a challenge for national governments. In the United States, the very limited power of the federal government left private philanthropists to find ways to build science in the universities, place the professions on a universalistic scientific basis, and develop scientifically competent leaders and managers for industry and the professions. As a group, the largest private donors lacked the capacity – even if they had had the will – to overcome the segregationist states-rights tradition in the American South. Although they were mostly Protestant by descent, they also had no desire to join a campaign to suppress Catholic institutions across the North or to challenge Catholic opposition to strong government controls. Making a virtue of necessity, they argued instead that private universities, hospitals, and other institutions could provide multiple perspectives and nurture excellence in many localities. Independent private institutions could, in effect, serve as the basis of powerful national networks devoted to scientific standards that would benefit everyone. Herbert Hoover fully shared this view and, in an approach identified by historian Ellis W. Hawley, used the information-gathering, convening, and regulatory capacities of the federal government to advance the "Associative State" during the 1920s. American philanthropy held to this course through the desperate years of depression and war.

American philanthropy had already reduced its traditional support for religion and personal charity, so that the crisis in religious funding and in private poor relief during the Great Depression was no surprise. Faced with economic collapse, many private donors abandoned their long-standing opposition to federal funding and embraced New Deal programs of federal unemployment relief, aid to the blind and disabled, and old-age insurance. During World War II, important donors also concluded that only the federal government could find sufficient resources for scientific research, the rapid expansion of the hospital system, and an effective foreign aid program. Yet, in key ways, American philanthropy successfully resisted the permanent expansion of federal power.

Nationally, the most influential big foundations – Rockefeller, Carnegie, Russell Sage, Rosenwald, Kellogg, the Commonwealth Fund, and a few others – had committed themselves in the early 1920s to scientific and medical research and to efforts to place the health-care, education, and social-service professions on a scientific nonsectarian basis. Many of them also sought, as historian Steven C. Wheatley has put it, to "organize and support systems for the training of elites of esoteric expertise." The approach that won their support was to promote "a national hierarchy of institutions that would channel individual ambition by assigning positions according to universal rational criteria." Private support and professional evaluation, not federal decisions, would shape this hierarchy.

The big donors frankly sought government support for their agenda. During the 1920s, they had won Secretary of Commerce Hoover's endorsement for the privately funded National Bureau of Economic Research and his active effort to expand the federal role in information-gathering and in backing the standard-setting activities of private associations. When he became President, Hoover agreed to request the massive foundation-sponsored volume, *Recent Social Trends*, designed to advance higher national standards for social work, education, and health. Like Hoover, Franklin D. Roosevelt also turned to foundations, especially the big national foundations, as he worked to mobilize private solutions for public problems in the 1920s and 1930s.

After the Community Chest failed to raise sufficient private money to relieve distress at the beginning of the Great Depression, major donors redoubled their commitment to the national agenda they had developed during the 1920s. They encouraged governments to support medical centers, research institutes, universities, public schools, and public-health programs. Carnegie, Rockefeller, and other like-minded foundations supported colleges that attracted paying students. Kellogg, the Commonwealth Fund, and the March of Dimes promoted the development of private health insurance to provide a steady income to the new medical centers. Many foundations encouraged smaller donors to join them in advancing medical centers, scientific research institutes, college alumni funds, local Community Chests, and such national health charities as the Red Cross and the March of Dimes.

Research universities and liberal arts colleges attracted notable donations right through the Depression although, like all American institutions, they lost some ground early on. Annual gifts and grants to American colleges and universities maintained a steady level in 1930 and 1931, fell briefly between 1932 and 1935, then resumed their rise. Colleges and universities prospered during and after the war, with annual donations rising from $75 million in 1939 to more than $100 million in 1950, then to well over $200 million by 1959. Student enrollment also rose steadily.

Many colleges did suffer in the mid-1930s from a decline in the value of their endowments and from the students' inability to pay fees; private colleges, like hospitals, always drew far more income from fees than from gifts. Colleges did much better, however, than churches and social service agencies. Many big donors had come to believe that the nation would benefit greatly from the discoveries of university research, from university-based medical and law schools, and from graduates of selective liberal arts colleges. These beliefs led to big donations, not only to Harvard, Yale, Columbia, and Princeton, but also to Cornell; Carnegie Tech; Western Reserve; Chicago; Northwestern; Duke; Caltech; the Universities of Michigan, Iowa, Wisconsin, California, and Texas; Amherst; Williams;

Smith; Swarthmore; Kenyon; and many other institutions as well. Faculty donations of patents beginning in the 1930s created the significant Wisconsin Alumni Research Foundation and contributed to the University of Michigan's Rackham Funds.

Hospitals and medical centers received an even more notable flow of gifts during the 1930s and 1940s. Donations to these institutions had run at about the same level as donations to universities until the late 1930s, and early in the Depression their income fell somewhat. But after 1940, private donations to hospitals rose to two or three times as much as private donations to colleges and universities. Federal support for medical research also expanded rapidly. Nearly all Americans had become convinced that modern hospitals offered important benefits. During World War II, the Lanham Act provided federal funds for the construction of nonprofit hospitals near military bases – and introduced a federal approach to health-care planning. In 1946, the Hill–Burton Act reduced the federal role in health planning, while increasing the flow of federal construction funds to "community" hospitals, especially in small towns. Hill–Burton grants covered only a third of construction costs. In this case, federal aid *increased* opportunities for private giving.

American industrialists and financiers had assembled some astonishing collections of European and modern art by 1929; during the 1930s, many of those collections were donated to museums, transforming several American museums "from provincial catchalls" into great showplaces comparable to the best in Europe. Some of the museums derived support from government, but most American museums were private and independent and, in every case, private donors shaped their collections. Nationally, Paul Mellon's 1937 gift of a hundred important old masters paintings to the National Gallery of the Smithsonian Institution (he insisted it not be named after him) led the way. The National Gallery soon attracted the Kress, Widener, and Dale collections, as well as Lessing Rosenwald's extraordinary print collection. The (private) Metropolitan Museum of Art in New York gained the medieval Cloisters and other big collections during the 1930s.

However, it was the actions of a few prominent women that made New York one of the world's leading centers of modern art during the 1930s. Abby Aldrich Rockefeller (Mrs. John D., Jr.), Lillie P. Bliss, and Mrs. Cornelius J. Sullivan, who had established the Museum of Modern Art in 1929, moved it into a permanent building on Rockefeller-donated land in 1939. The Modern was joined in 1931 by the Whitney Museum of American Art, created by Gertrude Vanderbilt Whitney, and the Solomon R. Guggenheim Museum, organized by Hilla Rebay in the mid-1930s.

Two of the biggest museum donations of the thirties sought to reassert what their donors took to be traditional American values in the face of Depression-era challenges. Henry Ford began Greenfield Village, near Ford headquarters in Dearborn, Michigan, in 1929, and opened it to 234,000 visitors in 1934; by 1940, attendance had almost tripled. Greenfield Village assembled the small buildings of American farmers and craftsmen, and celebrated trial-and-error inventors such as Edison, the Wright Brothers, and Ford himself. Its Industrial Museum offered a vision of industrial progress through comprehensive collections of tools and industrial products. Responding to criticisms of corporations and demands for big government during the Depression, Ford's collaborator, William Symonds, said that "a significant lesson of the Village" was that self-reliant Americans had once "looked to themselves for a means of livelihood rather than to an employer."

John D. Rockefeller, Jr., started work on Colonial Williamsburg in 1928; by the mid-1930s, he had invested nearly $80 million in the project. His aim was, as historian Michael Wallace has noted, to establish a "shrine of the American faith," specifically emphasizing "opportunity, individual liberties, self-government, the integrity of the individual, and responsible leadership." Although Rockefeller emphasized the re-creation of the entire environment of the 1770s and 1780s, the Colonial Williamsburg of the 1930s, 1940s, and 1950s omitted reference to slaves or to poor white farmers. In the 1940s and 1950s, Colonial Williamsburg frequently provided a showplace of American values for foreign heads of state. Other museums and cultural centers also served as centers for civic celebration. Perhaps this role helped arts organizations nearly double their income from donations during World War II.

During the 1920s, several leading foundations had launched efforts to make health care, research, college teaching, and social work into scientific professions attractive to highly able and ambitious people regardless of religious or ethnic background. These foundation efforts were never entirely free of the bias brought by white Protestant leaders, and despite Carnegie support for Gunnar Myrdal's *An American Dilemma*, the influential and critical study of American racism, they failed to end the racist exclusion of people of color from professional and scientific opportunities. However, foundations did take some effective action to reduce discrimination against Catholics and Jews in major institutions. In these spheres, as in higher education and medicine, the private philanthropy of the 1930s and 1940s accentuated the initiatives of the 1920s.

During the 1920s, for example, the Russell Sage Foundation invested heavily in voluntary efforts to establish national standards for social work in government, as well as in private agencies. At its New York City building, the Russell Sage Foundation housed most national associations of social workers and regularly hosted national conferences on social policy and social work procedure. These associations embraced most Protestant, Jewish, and nonsectarian social service professionals, and worked to develop relationships with their Catholic and Southern counterparts. Russell Sage leaders also managed the production of *Recent Social Trends* for President Hoover. When private philanthropy proved inadequate to the challenge of the Depression, Russell Sage leaders stubbornly sought to preserve roles for private charity, despite the New Deal expansion of government. The foundation's extraordinary social-research library collected and published the most comprehensive information on foundations in an effort to promote responsible philanthropy. After 1947, this activity would become the core of the Foundation Center Library.

The Russell Sage Foundation devoted two floors of its building and about a quarter of its resources in the 1920s to the production of the ambitious and comprehensive *Regional Plan of New York and Environs*. It also sponsored an expensive effort to establish a continuing association of business and civic leaders from three states to revise the plan and work with state and local governments to implement it. When the Depression made it impossible for the Regional Plan Association to sustain itself, the foundation maintained its subsidies right through World War II. Russell Sage's role as national coordinator of social services was unique, but local foundations in Philadelphia, Washington, DC, Virginia, California, and other areas sought to duplicate its regional planning work.

After World War II, other important foundations shaped their own programs to take advantage of government programs – and to shape those programs in ways compatible both with a traditional American preference for local control and self-help, and with Catholic aspirations for government aid to Catholic hospitals and colleges. The W. K. Kellogg Foundation, for example, worked hard, through the 1930s and 1940s and after, to introduce high standards in locally controlled (and usually tax-supported) public health, education, and other community- and youth-development programs in grain-growing country areas of Michigan and other states. The Children's Fund of Michigan carried out a similar campaign to improve access to modern medicine for all children in its state. Kellogg also worked to expand the services of state university extension offices. Both foundations were following the example of Andrew Carnegie, who had made his gifts to public libraries contingent on the enactment of permanent special taxes. Like Carnegie, they pushed decentralized, local, and voluntary programs that depended on payments from their clients and that voluntarily agreed to meet high standards.

Meanwhile, other foundations had quietly helped sustain the Community Chest movement through the Depression and World War II by making some of their grants through their local Chests. The National War Fund carefully nurtured the local Community Chests that actually carried out its campaigns. To the surprise of those who thought that the federal government had entirely usurped the social assistance field, the Community Chests, like the Community Foundations, survived the 1930s and 1940s to play increasingly important roles in postwar America.

One of the most far-reaching efforts of the big foundations in the 1930s and 1940s was the creation of the Educational Testing Service. The Carnegie Foundation for the Advancement of Teaching had supported test-development efforts in the 1920s. It increased its support during the 1930s, as test-makers refined their techniques. It supported those who believed that effective, objective, and fair tests could be introduced into college admissions – and that college testing could be combined with effective marketing. One study showed, for example, that thousands of very able high school graduates in Ohio were not going to college, yet colleges lacked an effective means of identifying promising candidates to fill empty seats in their classes.

Through the 1930s, Carnegie leaders worked successfully to bring elite selective colleges and both private and state universities together in support of a national set of examinations for admission to college and to graduate and professional schools. One key motive was to expand the pools of applicants to the most selective schools to include young people of all religious faiths and all regions of the country. The ultimate aim was to attract as much talent as possible into the national system of science-based professions. A subordinate purpose was to relieve universities of the necessity of administering their own tests – and of defending those tests to disappointed applicants. Standardized testing had its critics in the 1930s, as it does today. However, it provides one of the best examples of the many ways in which the big foundations defined purposes for themselves in the 1920s, then stubbornly and effectively held to those purposes in the face of depression and war. After World War II, the GI Bill, which paid tuition for veterans at any college they chose to attend – including Catholic and Jewish colleges and Protestant divinity schools – provided the type of federal support that Carnegie officials and other big donors had sought.

* * *

In the face of depression and war, America's wealthiest donors maintained the new patterns of giving they had established during the 1920s. Only through their devotion to individual responsibility and self-help and to what they viewed as universal values did Northern, Midwestern, and Western donors and foundations retain a tincture of the Protestant commitment that had shaped the work of their predecessors. Their new mission was to promote science, scientific standards, and professional values, as well as opportunity and personal responsibility. Working closely with Herbert Hoover and less directly with Franklin D. Roosevelt, they sought, with considerable success, to win federal support and then federal funds for their campaign – and to limit the power of federal regulations and of federal officials. They favored hospitals, colleges, universities, and arts organizations; with their aid, these organizations recovered quite quickly from the harsh impact of the Great Depression and did quite well during World War II. Big donors also worked effectively to increase federal funding in these fields, while minimizing federal controls. America's biggest donors had significantly reduced their support for Protestant churches and for direct aid to the poor by the 1920s; these institutions declined during the 1930s. When they reemerged after World War II, Protestant institutions found themselves relying, like their Catholic counterparts, on smaller donations from large numbers of people. Protestant colleges and hospitals, like Catholic colleges and hospitals, also benefited from the GI Bill and from other new federal programs.

American philanthropy failed to respond effectively to the Great Depression, and it played a distinctly minor role during World War II. However, American philanthropy proved exceptionally resilient; despite the challenges of depression and war, the United States entered the postwar period with a strong nonprofit sector powerfully organized to advance agendas set by private philanthropists in the early 1920s.

13

FAITH AND GOOD WORKS:
CATHOLIC GIVING AND TAKING

MARY J. OATES

Enthusiastic commitment to hundreds of church charitable institutions, hospitals, and schools distinguished nineteenth- and early twentieth-century Catholic communities, urban and rural, across America. By the early twentieth century, however, church leaders had begun to view small, locally financed, benevolent institutions as an inefficient way to allocate charity resources and an obstacle to their efforts to collaborate effectively with government agencies and mainstream charitable groups. These opposing perspectives set the stage for bitter struggles between the church hierarchy and grassroots parishioners in the 1930s and 1940s. The St. Louis, Missouri, archives of the School Sisters of Notre Dame contains a detailed firsthand chronicle of one such controversy over the fate of an Illinois orphanage.

In 1851, German Catholics in Quincy, Illinois, established a lay benevolent association, Saint Aloysius Orphan Society, to finance a parish home for children orphaned in the wake of a recent cholera epidemic. Local citizens, Protestant as well as Catholic, had ever since paid monthly subscription dues, contributed to collections, and conducted a variety of benefit picnics and fairs to support this ethnic orphanage. School Sisters of Notre Dame, members of a religious sisterhood with German roots, contributed their labor to care for the orphans, and many lay volunteers provided the institution with auxiliary services and in-kind gifts. Supported by this division of labor, the orphanage prospered.

Nearly a century later, in June 1944, James Griffin, bishop of Springfield, Illinois, dispatched the priest-director of his diocesan charitable bureau to pay a "friendly visit" to assess the condition of Saint Aloysius Orphanage. After hearing his director's report, and despite the fact that the orphanage was financially solvent and had never asked for or received funds from the diocese, Bishop Griffin determined to close the institution immediately and divert the property to another use. In July, he asked the orphanage's lay board of directors to sign over its building and land to Quincy College, a local Catholic men's college, which needed a science building.

In August 1944, the Orphan Society directors called a meeting of the society to consider the bishop's directive. Quincy College supporters – alerted to the meeting's purpose – turned out in numbers, but because there had been no prior announcement of an agenda, local community attendance was low. Those present voted to sell the orphanage to the college for $1. Quincy citizens greeted the news of this "secret" August meeting with indignation. They denounced the vote as invalid because Saint Aloysius Orphan Society was a corporation under Illinois law and disposition of its property required a two-thirds vote of the membership. To placate rising community anger, society officers called a special meeting in December 1944 to hear from the full membership. With deep emotion, parishioners eloquently testified how, until the present, the German community of Quincy had faithfully honored the sacred promise made to God by their forebears nearly a century before always to maintain the orphanage. When the society took the official vote on the bishop's request in January 1945, two thirds of the membership voted to keep the orphanage open.

However, this apparently conclusive vote did not end the dispute. Key actors in the destiny of the orphanage were the School Sisters of Notre Dame, who were heavily subsidizing it through their contributed services. Despite their indispensable role in the institution's life, these women en- joyed neither voice nor vote in the struggle over its future. Bishop Griffin, furious that lay parishioners had voted to defy his wishes and intent on closing the orphanage, now made use of his ultimate weapon – his ec- clesiastical authority over religious sisters working within his diocese. In February 1945, he ordered the School Sisters of Notre Dame to leave the Quincy orphanage "as soon as possible." Orphan Society directors – who had not foreseen this move – were aghast, because without the sisters' con- tributed labor, the institution would immediately fall into serious debt. A delegation traveled to Springfield to beg Bishop Griffin to reconsider his action but he refused, and Saint Aloysius Orphanage soon closed.

A small protest by two of the orphanage's lay volunteers symbolized the collective sorrow of the Catholics of Quincy. According to the sister- annalist, after dark, on March 10, 1945, these young women "managed, all by themselves, to get a high ladder in place inside the front entrance and scrape off with the aid of a razor-blade, the name ORPHANAGE, from the top glass transom. They felt it was no longer an orphanage, and never could pretend to be one; the name 'St. Aloysius' still holds good, nevertheless." The bishop's decision similarly confounded the School Sisters of Notre Dame. "With our feeble minds," the sister-annalist concluded sadly, "we cannot at present understand the reason for which St. Aloysius Orphanage was closed after nearly eighty years of fruitful labor."

The chronicle of the demise of this Illinois children's home is representative of the experiences of numerous small Catholic charitable institutions nationwide before 1950. Not only does it demonstrate the very different perspectives that prevailed within the church community about how best to allocate benevolent resources, it also reveals how bishops were able to compel church members, lay and religious, to accept a bureaucratic model of philanthropy. A more progressive approach, they promised parishioners, would permit Catholic charity to reach more people in need and guarantee that those aided received higher quality service.

* * *

Nineteenth-century Catholics and Protestants agreed that true Christian stewards generously and steadfastly shared their talents and material resources to benefit society. Protestants, however, believed that they would be saved through faith, and that their acts of benevolence served to reveal the depth of their faith. Catholics, on the other hand, held that their salvation rested on good works as well as on faith, and that charity was a religious duty incumbent on all believers. The Catholic Church also strongly emphasized that collective giving was preferable to independent charity because special spiritual benefits accrued to those who united with fellow believers in acts of charity. Papal teaching consistently emphasized the "social bond of charity" that joined congregants of every social class. One outcome of this attention to the importance of communal good works was that the church owned and administered, as well as financed, its charities. In contrast, by the early twentieth century, a majority of benevolent enterprises originally founded by Protestant churches had evolved into independent private agencies, generously supported – but not usually managed – by the denominations themselves.

Three distinctive spiritual values have traditionally characterized Catholic philanthropy. The first and perhaps most enduring is the understanding that voluntary service is an integral component of religious giving. That is, giving money alone does not permit one fully to satisfy the charitable mandate. The truly religious donor, whether poor or rich, also gives in direct personal ways. A second highly honored value is that anonymous giving exemplifies the religious ideal. Those who contribute primarily in expectation of public awards and acclaim are really no different from those who give only through bequests. Although the poor and needy benefit from their donations, neither type of giver has made any real personal sacrifice on their behalf. The third traditional value that distinguishes Catholic benevolence is its insistence that the needs of the poor take priority among the church's good works. Pope John Paul II reaffirmed this essential teaching in his 1991 encyclical, *Centesimus Annus*, when he reminded Catholics that the "preferential option for the poor" is "a special form of primacy in the exercise of Christian charity."

* * *

The religious tensions between Catholics and non-Catholics that marked nineteenth-century America fostered the development of a Catholic philanthropic enterprise that operated in virtual isolation from organized charities of other churches. Growing ethnic diversity within the church membership after 1840 considerably reinforced this separatist mentality. Like the Germans who settled in Quincy, Illinois, in this era, immigrants preferred to live in ethnic neighborhoods and to concentrate on charitable works that addressed the needs of members of their own groups. The provision of ethnically homogeneous orphanages, hospitals, and schools seemed to them to be the best way to preserve and pass on their culture and language, as well as their faith. As a result, church charities of the nineteenth century tended to be local, ethnic, and highly autonomous in character. Once an institution was established, even the local bishop had little control over its internal finances and operations. Occasional efforts by clergy to promote inter-ethnic collaboration were largely unsuccessful; parishioners remained tenaciously committed to their favorite ethnic charities.

Until the end of the nineteenth century, Catholic benevolent strategies changed little. Because most congregants were poor and working class, they recognized early on that only by pooling small but numerous individual donations could they address important social problems successfully. Typically, with the approval and support of their pastor, a group of laity took the initiative by forming a benevolent society whose members pledged to establish and maintain an institution devoted to a particular charitable work.

Financial concerns do much to explain the peculiar Catholic predilection for institutions. Although its monetary assets were limited, the church by mid-nineteenth century already possessed rich and growing labor resources, represented most importantly by the contributed services of members of religious orders (most of them women). Clergy and laity alike concurred that the best way to deploy this valuable labor was to establish charitable institutions where sisters could care for relatively large numbers of persons at one time. Not surprisingly, securing the services of religious sisters for their proposed institution was the first priority of a benevolent society's founding board of directors.

Each orphanage, reform school, home for the elderly poor, or hospital had its own benevolent society, open to both sexes; a subscription society, usually headed by men; and a ladies' auxiliary. Donations to the institution were used for current operating costs, which included a small annual stipend to cover the sisters' living expenses. In addition to paying yearly dues for membership in the institution's benevolent association, local parishioners contributed to special parish collections for the purchase of land, buildings, and furnishings. In return for their generosity, an institution's supporters received rich spiritual benefits and assurance of perpetual remembrance in the daily prayers of the sisters and those in their charge.

For a charitable institution to continue to prosper, it had to develop a substantial cadre of loyal friends who were emotionally and financially invested in it. Thus, benevolent society officers, sisters, and clergy offered varied opportunities for parishioners of every social class to contribute voluntary service, as well as money, to the cause. They invited prominent men to join the institution's board of directors and to represent it in public forums. These men offered free legal, medical, and financial services to benefit the sisters and their charges. Middle-class women assumed less public but very highly respected roles as valued partners with the sisters in their diverse duties. Working-class parishioners contributed their labor to keep the physical plant and grounds in good condition and responded generously to occasional calls for basic provisions or for emergency assistance.

Whereas nineteenth-century bishops promoted the cause of charity in frequent and stirring sermons, by personally attending many charity events, and by aiding an institution in crisis, few had the means to give financial support to institutions on a regular basis. Instead, local pastors and parishioners assumed full responsibility for raising the funds needed for operating expenses of the charities. This was a neverending, time-consuming, and, at times, onerous obligation.

Preferred fund-raising strategies varied by gender. An annual, week-long charity fair, conducted by the ladies' auxiliary and supported by citizens of all faiths, was a major source of institutional revenue. Women also conducted lotteries, euchres, and bazaars throughout the year to generate additional funds. These diverse events were extremely popular, not least because they allowed people of all ages to engage themselves for a small fee to a good cause. Laymen generally preferred to raise money through subscription societies. Society members would make great efforts – through leaflets, mail campaigns, and personal invitations – to recruit new members so that funds raised for the institution from subscription dues would increase significantly from year to year.

The institutional approach to philanthropy reflected an ingenious division of labor between the laity and the religious orders, as well as an efficient way to allocate limited monetary resources. Through it, a working-class church was able to reach out to thousands of needy persons and to address a wide range of social problems. By 1900, the Catholic Church was supporting more than eight hundred charitable institutions and educating approximately one million children in tuition-free parochial schools across the country. At this time, most clergy and laity judged the institutional approach to be the optimal way for Catholics to address major social needs. They believed that other approaches, like the "outdoor relief" strategy favored by mainstream groups – which required relatively more money and less labor – would seriously restrict the scale and scope of their collective benevolence.

The highly decentralized style of Catholic giving fostered intense competition rather than cooperation among the many charitable institutions. This unfortunate propensity was reinforced by the sisterhoods managing them. Religious orders, at this time, vigilantly guarded their organizational autonomy and rarely shared either professional expertise or resources with "outside" groups, even with other sisterhoods engaged in the same benevolent work. Therefore, as charitable institutions grew in number, local citizens – especially those in urban parishes – found themselves beleaguered by institutional appeals.

* * *

At the turn of the twentieth century, a growing number of bishops had determined to curb the independence of local charitable institutions. The traditional separatist approach to benevolence seemed to them both inefficient and arbitrary. Charities whose benevolent services had broad emotional appeal, such as foundling homes, easily raised funds (often more than they needed) and benefited from an abundance of voluntary service.

On the other hand, public response to charities that addressed less popular but conceivably more imperative social needs was often indifferent, with the result that these institutions had to struggle to survive.

Progressive clergy and lay charity leaders agreed with bishops that the time was ripe for fundamental changes in the church's philanthropic sector. A lessening of anti-Catholic hostility, the movement to treat the field of social work as a profession, and the steady advance of more Catholics to middle-class status combined to offer an environment conducive to radical reform. Attacks by mainstream proponents of "scientific charity" helped to fuel the movement. As a result of its proclivity for charity institutions, these critics charged, the Catholic Church was ignoring grave systemic social problems in favor of simply providing relief. As long as it continued on this path, the church – despite its immense membership – would never play a leadership role in the intensifying national battles over civil rights, labor rights, and social welfare legislation.

Several large urban dioceses launched the reform movement by introducing a new bureaucratic structure – the diocesan charitable bureau – to tighten episcopal control over benevolent institutions and agencies within a diocese. Priests, appointed by and reporting directly to local bishops, headed the new bureaus, and clergy and wealthy laymen comprised their boards of directors. Bureau officers set policies and procedures for diocesan charities and hired professional social workers to ensure that all institutions conformed to them. Prior to World War I, only five dioceses in the nation had functioning charitable bureaus; by 1930, their number had increased sixfold, with other dioceses following suit at a rapid pace.

Bishops were also seeking ways to rationalize charity fund-raising. By the 1930s, complaints were mounting from local businesses and congregants about endless solicitations from charitable institutions. Wealthy laity were particularly embarrassed by "outmoded" Catholic money-raising strategies. They condemned lotteries as a form of gambling and contended that the many garish charity fairs were seriously harming the church's image. If bishops would simply adopt the progressive fund-raising techniques that were proving so successful in mainstream philanthropic circles, they could quickly put all the charitable institutions on a firm financial footing.

With strong support from prominent laity and many clergy, bishops across the country moved quickly to centralize charity fund-raising within their dioceses. They immediately outlawed most charity events intended to benefit individual institutions and asked Catholics instead to support diocesan charities by contributing to a single annual charity collection.

Every parish in the diocese participated in the special "Charity Sunday" collection. Each pastor remitted his congregation's donation directly to diocesan headquarters, and the bishop and his advisers then distributed the pooled funds among the various charities of the diocese. This consolidated approach, parishioners were advised, would reduce pressure on institutional boards of directors to raise funds, and it would also benefit local citizens by putting an end to a continuing stream of charity appeals throughout the year.

Lay supporters of the various charities, as well as the religious sisters who managed them, regarded the new approach with considerable unease. They recognized that the survival of any charitable institution would henceforth depend almost entirely on the size of the financial allotment diocesan officials decided to give it. They also realized that by so firmly concentrating control over charity fund-raising at the central level, bishops were drastically curbing the autonomy of religious sisterhoods, as well as lay boards of directors, over the charitable institutions they supported and subsidized.

*　*　*

The early twentieth-century movement to consolidate charity organization and fund-raising had its roots not only in a conviction that the traditional decentralized approach was inefficient, but also in a growing desire among church leaders to collaborate meaningfully with government and civic organizations in social welfare activities. Unless bishops were able to monitor and control charitable services and fund-raising within their own dioceses, they could never stand together as the American Catholic hierarchy to present a cohesive "Catholic position" in public debates about social priorities, welfare policies, and reform legislation.

Two important national organizations, founded in 1910 and 1917, respectively, gave considerable impetus to the charity-reform movement. The National Conference of Catholic Charities, now Catholic Charities USA, quickly became the leading forum for diocesan charity officials and social workers, clerical and lay. The National Catholic War Council, renamed the National Catholic Welfare Conference in 1923, served a similar function for the nation's bishops.

Modest formal cooperation with extra-church charitable agencies had begun with the introduction of Community Chests in local communities across the nation after World War I. While Chest funds permitted Catholic charities to offer more and better care, some Catholics were ambivalent from the start about accepting external funds. Dependence on such funding, they

Rev. William Kerby, Bishop Thomas Shahan, and Rev. John O'Grady, founders of the National Conference of Catholic Charities, Washington, DC c. 1910. (Archives, Catholic Charities USA, Alexandria, Virginia.)

argued, could compromise church control over the priorities and policies of its benevolent sector and weaken grassroots commitment to religious giving. The unusual economic distress of the 1930s pushed such reservations to the background.

The impact of the Great Depression on the church's charity organization was, indeed, enormous. Most Catholics lived in or near major urban centers, which were hardest hit by sustained unemployment. While the national unemployment rate in 1932 averaged 25 percent, larger industrial cities reported rates ranging from 50 to 80 percent. Thanks to the recent reorganization of diocesan charities, the church was in a better position to mobilize its substantial benevolent reserves quickly and efficiently. However, all charities, religious and secular, soon realized that private resources alone could never properly address the unprecedented crisis.

Catholics, for the most part, approved cooperative efforts between church and government agencies in addressing social needs. But if church charities were to benefit from public funds, they had to meet externally imposed eligibility criteria and standards. Directors of the diocesan charitable bureaus, therefore, replaced their volunteer staffs with paid professional social workers who would make certain that the charitable institutions qualified for public funding.

Before the 1930s, church leaders (with few exceptions) had staunchly defended *laissez-faire* economics, arguing that free markets would, over time, result in improved employment opportunities and living standards for all. The pervasive economic distress of the Depression quickly changed this perspective. For the first time, Catholic bishops lobbied vigorously for social welfare programs and spoke out publicly in favor of more federal relief programs and reform legislation. A few mainstream charity leaders of the day read "politicking" in this new public stance. For example, Chicago charity leaders disparaged Cardinal George Mundelein's frequent endorsements of New Deal programs as nothing but a thinly veiled attempt to gain preferred treatment for local Catholic charities.

* * *

By the 1940s and 1950s, Catholics were joining the ranks of the middle and upper-middle classes at a very rapid rate. However, their acceptance of the church's bureaucratic approach in charity endeavors was far from unanimous. Like the Catholics of Quincy, Illinois, who were still faithfully supporting Saint Aloysius Orphanage in the mid-1940s, local communities across the country remained committed to the traditionally decentralized, more personal style of benevolence. In other quarters, opposition to public funding of church charities was mounting. The Catholic Worker Movement, founded in 1934 in New York City by Dorothy Day and Peter Maurin, is the best known and most radical of several important lay movements that bluntly challenged the church's acceptance of government funding, as well as its bureaucratic charity structure. Although never numerous, Catholic Workers and their supporters were well-educated, articulate, and influential. In books, newspapers, and speeches, they called on Catholics to return to traditional benevolent values, especially the obligation of each individual to assist the poor directly and personally. Catholic Workers – all volunteers – established Houses of Hospitality in the nation's largest cities, where they lived with the poor and shared their spiritual and material resources with them. They relied for support wholly on the goodwill of the public, neither seeking nor accepting funds from government agencies or from diocesan charitable bureaus.

Charity reformers and church officials of the 1930s and 1940s did not take warnings seriously that a bureaucratic charity structure and dependence on government funds would inevitably weaken grassroots commitment to church charities. Because private social agencies were eligible to apply for public funds and service contracts, bishops believed that they had an obligation to make sure that Catholic charities received their fair share. While they conceded, in principle, that acceptance of government funds might prompt parishioners to cut their donations to church charities, the idea of a widespread decline in giving seemed to them preposterous.

In 1960, government funds accounted for only about 15 percent of Catholic charity budgets nationwide; by 1984, this figure had soared to more than 50 percent. During this period, there were a few indications of a shift in Catholic philanthropic values. Parishioners questioned publicly whether the church's charities really needed their donations as much as worthy mainstream charities that were not receiving any government funds. Others, including some professional staff members in church charitable bureaus and agencies, charged that rising levels of government funding were noticeably undermining the religious identity of Catholic charities and compromising the church's willingness to take strong advocacy positions in controversial areas of social policy.

* * *

An outstanding feature of Catholic philanthropy has long been its disproportionately heavy involvement of women. Laywomen of the nineteenth and early twentieth centuries had traditionally worked through female benevolent societies and ladies' auxiliaries attached to the church's many charitable institutions. By the 1940s, however, bishops were insisting that local female benevolent societies direct their efforts away from individual charitable institutions in order to focus on fund-raising to benefit diocesan projects. At this time, bishops refused to appoint women to positions on diocesan charitable bureau boards, and bureau directors were replacing female volunteers with paid social workers. Thus, the new episcopal directives would, inevitably, greatly reduce the autonomy of women's benevolent societies and restrict opportunities for voluntary service. Not surprisingly, women's interest in joining benevolent societies soon dropped off sharply, and this trend has not appreciably reversed.

Although laywomen's societies historically played important roles in Protestant benevolence, mainstream churches had no real parallel for the Catholic sisterhoods that provided the labor force for most charitable institutions and parochial schools. Religious sisters, popularly called nuns, lived in celibate communities and consecrated their lives to the church and its works through public vows. Their numbers grew rapidly as European orders sent sisters to work as missionaries to assist millions of poor immigrants. Most of them were Irish and German Catholics who arrived in America in the 1840s and 1850s. Although sisters numbered only about 2,000 in 1850, convent life soon attracted many American women and, by 1890, their ranks had risen sixteen-fold. In 1920, the nation's 90,000 nuns already far outnumbered clergy and religious brothers combined. The development of hundreds of women's religious orders, most of them highly specialized in a particular type of social service or in education, was a phenomenon that marked the Catholic Church until the mid-1960s, when total membership peaked at more than 200,000. Catholics had always taken exceptional pride in the distinctively garbed nuns, seeing in them a collective, public witness to the social commitment and generosity of the entire church community.

Twentieth-century reforms in charitable organization and fund-raising profoundly affected sisterhoods. However, a decline in their memberships did not set in as early as was the case with the laywomen's benevolent societies. Sisterhoods specializing in the management of social institutions – such as orphanages, hospitals, and homes for the elderly – were the first affected. These groups saw their formerly extensive authority dissolve as bureau directors and lay social workers assumed supervisory roles over their institutions and challenged their professional decisions.

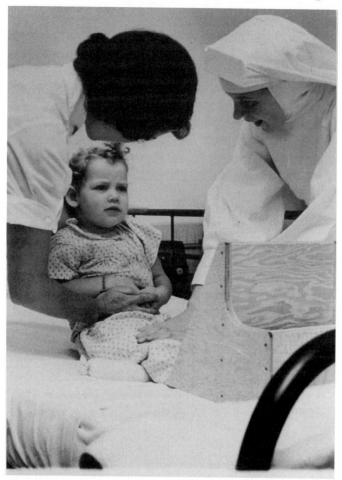

Nurses and patient, Kennedy Memorial Hospital for Children, Brighton, Massachusetts, 1955. (Archives, THE PILOT, Boston, Massachusetts.)

By the 1930s, however, more than two thirds of American sisters were not working in hospitals and social service institutions, but rather in parochial schools. For 150 years, Catholic parishes had voluntarily established and supported schools in order to provide a values-based education for local children. Because a majority of students came from poor, immigrant, and working-class families, parishioners considered the financing of "free" schools to be a pivotal philanthropic work. In 1884, however, at the Third Plenary Council of Baltimore, the national hierarchy decreed that every parish open a school as soon as possible. Although that mandate was never accomplished, the number of schools and their enrollments expanded greatly after 1890.

Unlike most charitable institutions, parochial schools received neither public funds nor a share in diocesan charity collections. Their financing continued to be the full responsibility of local parishes. A church that was heavily poor and working class until the mid-twentieth century was able to develop a national network of private schools only because members of sisterhoods provided their free services as faculty members. Thousands of sisters viewed their work as educators of poor and working-class children in parochial schools to be a compelling response to the church's benevolent call for a preferential option for the poor.

After World War II, upwardly mobile middle-class Catholics migrated in growing numbers from crowded city parishes to the suburbs. There they built many more parochial schools and looked to sisterhoods to provide free faculties for them, just as they had for older city schools. Demand for sister-teachers – always high – rose tremendously at this time, prompting bishops and clergy to advise young women considering convent life to give preference to teaching orders. Two million children were attending church schools in the late 1940s; within two decades, total school enrollment exceeded 5.7 million.

As a result of these important socioeconomic and geographical shifts within the Catholic community, American nuns in the 1960s were heavily concentrated in the nation's more than 13,000 parochial schools. By this time, however, these women had begun to have serious misgivings about a new trend in the benevolent focus of teaching sisterhoods. In particular, they questioned why – unlike earlier generations of sisters who had taught mainly children from poor and working-class families – they found themselves subsidizing the education of suburban middle-class students.

Given the phenomenal growth of sisterhoods in the twentieth century, it is not surprising that bishops, clergy, and laity took it for granted that the church's many charities and schools would continue to benefit from the contributed services of sisters. However, contrary to all expectations, an abrupt downturn in the number of applicants to sisterhoods commenced in the 1960s. At the same time, thousands of nuns left their orders. Between the mid-1960s and 1990, the number of nuns in America declined by nearly 50 percent. Although the reasons for the sudden decline in sisterhoods are complex and not entirely understood, the unexpected loss of this invaluable resource forced the issue of Catholic giving to center stage in dioceses and parishes across the country.

Sts. Peter and Paul Parochial School children, Bronx, New York, 1992.

All social agencies and hospitals of the 1970s and 1980s felt the financial impact of the shortage of sisters, but the institutions most adversely affected were parochial schools, especially those in poor, inner-city parishes. These parishes had always had to struggle to finance schools, even when sisters were staffing them. Now, with rising faculty costs and declining parish memberships, inner-city schools – in much higher proportions than suburban parish schools – had to close their doors. Ironically, in this period, applications for admission to inner-city schools from minority populations (most of them non-Catholic) expanded greatly. Minority enrollments in parochial schools averaged about 20 percent nationally in 1984, but urban schools were reporting far higher proportions; for example, 74 percent in Newark, 65 percent in Los Angeles, 58 percent in Detroit, and 55 percent in New York.

* * *

In contrast to donations from upper-class Catholics, which – although individually large – represented only a small fraction of total contributions in the 1940s, the modest contributions of millions of working and middle-class congregants were collectively very large. In the 1950s, however, as the number of very wealthy parishioners began to rise steadily and significantly, bishops and clergy sought ways to strengthen the loyalties of this group to the church's benevolent sector.

The call of early twentieth-century bishops for all parishioners to contribute to charity through annual diocesan-wide collections accorded with the church's traditional emphasis on the spiritual merits of anonymous giving. However, after 1950, many very rich Catholics had little enthusiasm for giving anonymously, especially for projects that the hierarchy rather than they themselves identified as worthy of support. They preferred to give publicly and to designate their gifts. In return for major financial gifts, they thought it entirely appropriate that the church publicize and reward their benevolence with coveted papal titles and other high ecclesiastical honors.

Fearing that church needs would suffer if they rebuffed such expectations from this rapidly growing and powerful segment of parishioners, bishops and clergy preached less often about the religious merits of anonymous giving. They justified the bestowal of public honors on major financial donors by contending that it was a splendid way to inspire observers of every social class to give more generously themselves. Many grassroots laity, however, saw the expansion of the practice to be a troubling sign that secular values were threatening the traditional democratic spirit of Catholic philanthropy.

Until the 1950s, Catholics continued to frown on the practice of building charitable endowments. In their view, funds were never sufficient to address current social needs; it was wrong to set money aside for future good works at the expense of the poor. They preferred to use their collective resources to open new institutions rather than to endow existing ones. Clergy and laity alike condemned as weak in faith those cautious parishioners who urged that charity projects be postponed until funds for their support were in hand. Most subscribed instead to an 1835 maxim of Catherine McAuley, founder of the Sisters of Mercy: "The poor need your help today, not next week."

The experiences of the 1930s led a few charity leaders to suggest that Catholics build endowments for their charitable institutions, but these proposals garnered little support before the 1950s. Boston's Archbishop Richard Cushing spoke for most Catholics when he counseled the staff of his charitable bureau in 1944: "All money given for charity in the Archdiocese should be used as it comes along, without undue preoccupation with possible depressions or other future contingencies. Contrary practices ... may be good business; they are not, however, good charity. Money given for charity should be used and used immediately – for charity. The Archdiocese is big enough and generous enough to take care of crises should crises come."

In the next decade, as their socioeconomic status rose, Catholics gradually enlarged the definition and scope of their religious benevolence. For example, in sharp contrast to affluent parishioners of the past, wealthy laity now began to make very significant gifts to Catholic colleges and universities. Because they served middle- and upper-class populations, earlier generations of rich Catholics (with few exceptions) did not view gifts to these institutions to be charity, in the strict sense of the word. Although a few prominent Catholic donors still hold this view, most wealthy parishioners see in the work of these institutions a major contribution of the church to American society.

Another recent initiative in church philanthropy is the development since the 1950s of Catholic charitable foundations. Currently numbering about three hundred, most are small – making about $500,000 in grants annually – and focused on local projects that serve the poor. In 1976, a group of individuals and foundations joined to establish Foundations and Donors Interested in Catholic Activities, Inc. (FADICA). The forty-five foundations and two individuals that comprise FADICA today support a variety of diocesan programs, schools, and charitable agencies, and sponsor influential national forums and philanthropic research projects. This pioneering organization is generating much fruitful debate about the current state of American Catholic giving and about how to make philanthropy a more effective agent in advancing the church's mission.

* * *

Over the past two centuries, American Catholics have faced critical challenges in carrying out their corporate philanthropy. Evolving political and social circumstances, as well as the nation's dominant civic, religious, and cultural traditions and values, have shaped their benevolent focus and style in lasting ways. Since 1930, they have moved rapidly from the margins into mainstream American society, and from a position of strict separatism in philanthropic expression to extensive collaboration with their fellow Americans. These transitions have allowed them to use their formidable monetary and labor resources more effectively and efficiently for the common good.

Mary J. Oates

Although the American Catholic community has traditionally been very generous, its reputation for benevolence has faded somewhat in recent years. Among religious denominations, the Catholic Church currently ranks near the top in the average household income of its members. Yet, relative to income, individual contributions to the church have fallen steadily since the mid-1960s. Nor does the record of Catholic giving today compare favorably with giving by members of other religious denominations. Although there is no consensus on what has led to this slump, one contributing factor is that American Catholics still have little say in how their financial contributions in annual, diocesan-wide campaigns for the support of the church and its charities are distributed. Another explanatory factor is that parishioners have little opportunity for direct involvement in the church's charities.

Several recent developments, however, augur well for the church's philanthropic sector. More laity, women as well as men, are assuming positions of leadership in the church's national charity organizations, diocesan chanceries, charitable bureaus, and school departments. At the grassroots level, outreach projects are beginning to link the nation's 19,000 parishes with local diocesan charity offices as well as with such major national organizations and programs as Catholic Relief Services and the bishops' Campaign for Human Development. Stewardship, sacrificial giving, and tithing programs are spreading vigorously at the parish level.

Groups of laity across the country have also begun to develop radical "new" approaches that allow them once again to honor traditional values in a personal way. One outstanding example is the movement to support charitable institutions by building endowments for them. The endowment approach, looked upon with such disfavor by Catholics a half-century ago, is now generating enthusiastic response. Its most attractive feature is that it permits donors of every social class to choose the particular charitable work they wish to support.

The movement to build endowments for parochial schools in inner-city neighborhoods is exemplary of the power of this approach. Donors to this cause are able to target their gifts, contribute anonymously and locally, and demonstrate a preferential option for the poor. By building these institutional endowments, parishioners are not only guaranteeing the financial stability and quality of inner-city schools and other church charities. Equally important, they are also notably widening opportunities for voluntary service in a variety of benevolent enterprises.

Although the church's philanthropic sector today differs in important respects from that of the nineteenth and much of the twentieth century, America's sixty million Catholics – by reclaiming and abiding by the distinctive spiritual vision and values that have guided their philanthropy for more than 200 years – will continue to contribute in dynamic and powerful ways to advancing the social and spiritual welfare of all persons in need.

14

IN DEFENSE OF DIVERSITY: JEWISH THOUGHT FROM ASSIMILATIONISM TO CULTURAL PLURALISM

STEPHEN J. WHITFIELD

No ethnic minority has taken the responsibilities of philanthropy more seriously than has the Jews, whose proportion of the American population in the twentieth century barely rose above 3 percent. Yet, their generosity has been striking. By the mid-1970s, nearly half a billion dollars was being raised annually by the United Jewish Appeal (UJA) (the leading communal charitable agency), local federations, and Israel Bonds. In 1972, the Red Cross raised $132 million from all Americans, including, of course, Jews. (The UJA itself had been reconstituted on the eve of World War II, during which annual drives produced between fifteen and twenty million dollars.) The annual budget of the UJA has been about a third of the size of the United Way (to which Jews – it must be noted again – also contribute). In 1983, the *Wall Street Journal* reported that "the UJA raises more money each year than the American Cancer Society, the American Heart Association, the Muscular Dystrophy Association, the March of Dimes, and National Easter Seal Society *combined*." In 1994, the UJA had become, according to the *Chronicle of Philanthropy*, the fourth largest charity in the United States.

Yet, if present trends continue, even the UJA and the local federations may soon be outspent within the community. Private and family foundations have begun to complement the communal infrastructure, especially for educational and cultural projects.

The Harry and Jeanette Weinberg Foundation of Baltimore, the Charles H. Revson Foundation of New York, the Wexner Foundation of Columbus, and others add up to perhaps thirty "mega-foundations," according to the executive vice president of the UJA, Rabbi Brian Lurie. They will soon be disbursing more wealth to assorted Jewish causes than Lurie's own mammoth charitable organization. The Bible claims that David, a future king, picked up a stone and hurled it lethally at Goliath. Many a Jewish fund-raiser succeeded in something as remarkable: picking up a stone and squeezing it hard enough to draw blood. But the story of communal self-help – of ensuring that a tiny minority not be dependent on the kindness of strangers – should not be confined to the efforts to maintain Jewish welfare itself.

Wealthy individual Jews have also made substantial donations to general causes (including political candidates and campaigns). To cite only one example, the largest gift in the history of public education was the half billion dollars provided by media baron Walter Annenberg. Nor do many American cities and towns brandish a cultural life that does not rely heavily on the generosity and commitment of their local Jewish citizens. Indeed, the culture of an entire region – the South – was noticeably elevated by the Rosenwald Fund of Chicago in particular. To account for such generosity requires historical investigation, although almost no scholars of American Jewry have ever undertaken it. Religion constitutes only a partial explanation, because few of the most conspicuous philanthropists have been observant or were aware of the intricacies of obligation that Jewish legal codes dictated. Some residual effects of such teachings as Moses Maimonides' medieval rules of the degrees of charity might be detected, but such vestiges are not a sufficient explanation. Fearful memories of communal vulnerability and a corresponding gratitude for the opportunities that the New World has offered are undoubtedly part of the equation. These impulses are manifestations of what Samuel Johnson called "love of mankind; good nature" – his definition of philanthropy. But if intellectual historians can find their *raison d'être* in Yogi Berra's definition of baseball ("90 percent of this game is half mental"), then a theory to warrant communal vitality and the strength of the nonprofit sector of Jewish collectivity also must be considered. That is the purpose of this chapter.

Virtually at the dawn of the twentieth century, three models of Jewish identity were formulated; all three would be fulfilled, modified, and revised down to the present. Mary Antin, Louis D. Brandeis, and Horace M. Kallen envisioned the meaning of the national experiment, specified the place of their own minority within the United States, and thus bestowed upon future generations of Jews the only serious options that the New World presented: assimilationism, Zionism, and cultural pluralism. The first two models were either enfeebling or inadequate; the third became the implicit warrant for the type of philanthropy in which American Jewry has been engaged. Indeed, Kallen's theory warranted the sort of communal life that has been conducted for the twentieth century, within which humanitarianism has been encouraged and has often been exhibited. The bulk of this essay, therefore, is devoted to an assessment of his enunciation of cultural pluralism.

* * *

Assimilation was a condition that many Jews – especially in the twentieth century – lived out, seeking integration and normality instead of a fragile marginality. Assimilationism was a *program* that Mary Antin advocated. Her roots were in Polotzk, Russia (near Vitebsk). But her legs took her to Boston, where she offered a deliberate response to the promise of American life with an autobiography dedicated to Josephine Lazarus – the sister of the first American Jew whom Ralph Waldo Emerson ever knew, and whose 1883 sonnet welcomed "the wretched refuse of your teeming shore." Antin's *The Promised Land* (1912) evokes the ordeal of pogroms and desperation in the Tsarist Pale of Settlement, where "Passover was celebrated in tears . . . In the story of the Exodus, we would have read a chapter of current history, only for us there was no deliverer and no promised land." At the end of the seder, instead of "Next year in Jerusalem," it was "Next year – in America!" The promised land was not to be located in historic Palestine but in the United States, where a liberal democratic polity, a secular system of public education, and an expanding capitalist economy would bring redemption. The opportunities of a free society could be expected to terminate a long history of persecution; integration could be achieved so successfully, she implied, that the United States harbored no Exile.

The Promised Land was perhaps the most endearing and influential – if indirect – case for frictionless integration into a hospitable society, and its author was one of more than twenty-three million immigrants who came ashore from 1880 until 1920 (though many returned to their native lands). It was her account – more than any other – of how she had been "remade" into an American that became a publishing sensation. In this autobiography, the distance from the Pale of Settlement to the hospitality of New England was mostly psychological, as a new identity was formed: "All the processes of uprooting, transportation, replanting, acclimatization, and development took place in my own soul." The consequence was gratitude for civic inclusion, though Professor Barrett Wendell of Harvard privately complained of Antin's "irritating habit of describing herself and her people as Americans" – a term to be reserved for those like his wife whose ancestors had landed three centuries earlier. *The Promised Land* could nevertheless be read as a membership application – a desire to belong to "one united people," as John Jay put it in *The Federalist*, "a people descended from the same ancestors." (Never mind that Jay's own grandfather had been a Huguenot immigrant or that his mother's stock was Dutch.) Her book confirmed the faith that homogenization would be the source of national strength, that minorities would surrender their particularist allegiances for the sake of the common weal.

A collection of Antin's letters, *From Plotzk to Boston*, had been published as early as 1899, when she was still a teenager, with an introduction by Israel Zangwill, a British Jew, whose melodrama, *The Melting-Pot*, became a hit in 1908. It was hailed by Theodore Roosevelt as "a great play" because of its optimistic faith in the fusion of nationalities into a stronger nation. A better America would result from the admixture of peoples from the Old World with those who had crossed the Atlantic earlier. The xenophobia and bigotry that had wracked Europe would dissipate in the irenic atmosphere of the New World, but the price would be the abandonment of former identities for the sake of amalgamation. That is why *The Melting-Pot* was subjected to sharp criticism from the outset by Rabbi Judah L. Magnes of New York's Temple Emanuel. Zangwill's protagonist wished to compose a New World symphony that would merge the music of the past into something novel. But Magnes used the metaphor of the orchestra for his own ends, insisting that the distinctive sounds of the instruments not be lost or blurred if the right harmonies were to be achieved. He read Zangwill's melodrama as "preaching suicide to us." For if "all men will give up the particular traditions of their own history and be formed into a new people of freedom," Magnes inferred, then "Americanization means just what Mr. Zangwill has the courage to say it means: dejudaization."

Differences should not be exaggerated, however. Both Magnes and Zang-will were Zionists, though from different motives. Even the ardently Zionist rabbi, Stephen S. Wise, considered Zangwill among the "truly noble and faithful sons" of their people. But although Zangwill was hostile to the Jewish faith (and married outside it when exogamy was still very rare), he seems not to imagined the utter disappearance of the Jewish people. In his play, the protagonist David Quixano describes himself to an antiSemite as "a Jew who knows that your Pilgrim Fathers came straight out of his Old Testament" and that his fellow immigrants are contributing more to "the glory of this great commonwealth than some of you sons of the soil." A reading of *The Melting-Pot* as invoking a durable ethnicity needs to be cut only a little slack. In a 1914 afterword to the play, Zangwill became a little obsessed with racialism, and argued that Jewry is "the toughest of all the white elements that have been poured into the American crucible, the race having, by its unique experience of several thousand years of exposure to alien majorities, developed a salamandrine power of survival." It should be added that Zangwill could not envision merging with blacks, whose genotype would be stable.

Antin had imagined an accommodation to the hegemonic culture of the Anglo-Saxon and Protestant majority; Zangwill had believed that a new nationality would be forged from the disparate groups who constituted American society. The distinction is not insignificant. But both generally championed an assimilationism that granted little legitimation to a viable Jewish community, or to the educational and charitable institutions upon which such a minority would depend. Without a memory of its own, American Jewry would be deprived of a future, had the views of Antin and Zangwill been uncontested.

A formal rebuttal was not long in coming and, indeed, was expressed only three years after the publication of *The Promised Land*. Louis Brandeis's lecture on "Zionism and Patriotism" made him the nation's most vocal prophet of Jewish nationalism. "The people's attorney" argued that far from contradicting American political values (including the formation of a more perfect union), Zionism would make Jews into better Americans precisely because their commitment to democracy would be solidified. Instead of suffering from the anguish of dual loyalty, American Zionists would find reinforcement, since the goal of building up a homeland for persecuted Jews in Palestine would help fulfill the historic American mission of serving as a city upon a hill. Amnesiacs do not make good citizens; but, democracies flourish when common purposes are found, solidarity is achieved, face-to-face organizational life can improve social welfare that the curse of bigness threatens to undermine. Brandeis grasped the psychological necessity of Zionism for his fellow Jews, suspended between the assurances of traditional piety to which they could not return and the anomie that modernization portended. But he had no knowledge of Judaism, and no interest in promoting its values through institutional practice other than in Zionism. Nor did he reflect in any systematic way on how the collective life of minorities could be harmonized with the rest of the nation.

That was the task of Horace Meyer Kallen, the most incisive of all the Jewish writers on the topic of how such groups might be accommodated themselves. No one pondered more resonantly the destiny of Jews in an open society (or granted them vindication for their communal and philanthropic energies). No thinker stated more cogently how a liberal democracy could both sustain and be reinforced by Jewish communal continuity. Oddly enough, there is still no scholarly (or even unscholarly) biography of Kallen, although the influences that shaped him are evident enough.

The son of an Orthodox rabbi, Kallen was born in Berenstadt, in the polyglot Silesia of Wilhelmine Germany, in 1882. Five years later, the family came to Boston (in the wake of the Irish accession to urban power); in 1900, he was admitted to Harvard College, from which he graduated *magna cum laude* only three years later. Three professors exerted particular influence upon him. Barrett Wendell was a literary historian with an impeccable Yankee pedigree; however, by underscoring the Old Testament basis of American civilization, he stirred Kallen's interest in his own ethnic origins. William James was the proponent of "a pluralistic universe" who later directed Kallen's dissertation on the nature of truth and gave his protégé an unfinished volume, *Some Problems in Philosophy* (1912), to edit. As for the remote George Santayana, who never surrendered his Spanish passport, Kallen claimed to have "loved him dearly.... In certain respects, he did more for my mind than even William James. But James was always comrade as well as teacher; and although in my generation I was probably closer to Santayana than anybody, there was an unbridgeable barrier."

Actively promoting Jewish culture (in the version that he called "Hebraism"), Kallen helped to establish the Menorah Society in 1906 at Harvard, from which he received his doctorate two years later. He did postgraduate work at Princeton, Oxford, and the Sorbonne, and also lectured in philosophy at Harvard from 1908 until 1911. For the next seven years, Kallen served as an instructor of philosophy and psychology at the University of Wisconsin in Madison. But he was most fully associated with the New School for Social Research, which he helped to found in New York City in 1919 and where he would teach for the next fifty-one years. Until officially retiring in 1970, he held the rank of research professor of social philosophy, and had also served as dean of the graduate faculty in political and social science from 1944 until 1946. The New School long emphasized adult education; one of Kallen's books, *The Education of Free Men* (1949), reflected that lifelong interest. In 1926, two years after the publication of his most cogent reflections on *e pluribus unum*, the collection of essays entitled *Culture and Democracy in the United States*, he married Rachel Oatman Van Arsdale; they had a son and a daughter. The family lived in Oneonta, New York, although Kallen died in Palm Beach, Florida, at the age of ninety-one. The combination of "philosophical integrity, impeccable academic credentials, felicitous advocacy, and [a] passionately American outlook," historian Moses Rischin concluded, enabled him "to play a singularly creative role" in clarifying ethnic enigmas.

Although Kallen considered Antin's model of "Americanization" demeaning as well as undemocratic, here too the ideological chasm should not be exaggerated. Like Zangwill, she managed to be both an assimilationist who had married outside the faith (and did not raise her children as Jews) *and* a Zionist. When Kallen invited her to lecture at the University of Wisconsin in the summer of 1917, Antin replied: "I still thrill over the idea of the university going to the people and I haven't gotten over that phase of my appreciation of things American." But she hoped to "use the occasion to advantage for the Zionist cause." To be sure, Antin was an ardent Republican. In 1912, she backed the anti–Bull Mooser Theodore Roosevelt (to whom Zangwill had dedicated *The Melting-Pot*). She also supported Charles Evans Hughes in 1916. Kallen was a Wilsonian Democrat despite the President's 1915 proviso that "a man who thinks of himself as belonging to a particular national group... has not yet become an American." Nevertheless, "on the subject of Americanism," she wrote Kallen, "I thought you and I... had approximately the same ideas.... I still think that we are somewhere near the same camp on that subject." Antin added: "Now let me fall back for comfort on the knowledge that we still have one great cause in common, namely Zionism."

That was the most significant ingredient in Kallen's version of Jewish culture or "Hebraism." He was converted to Zionism in 1903, and praised the struggle for national restoration as a modern form of the mission of his own ethnic group, as a reinforcement of the Jews' own distinctive identity. Zionism represented a vibrant substitute for the religious faith that the acids of skepticism and the scruples of pragmatism had eroded. Although Kallen was a tribune and a polemicist, he was at least as important in facilitating Brandeis's own conversion to the general outlines of cultural pluralism and then to a vigorous career as a Zionist activist. By showing the attorney how the organization for national redemption in the Near East could make Jews better Americans, Kallen inducted Brandeis into his historic role as perhaps the most admired and important American Jew of the century.

Kallen was barely less of a secularist than Brandeis was. Cherishing the mosaic of American society, Kallen did not adhere to the Mosaic law: his work showed more than a tincture of anticlericalism; he discarded the Old World Orthodoxy into which he had been born. But he also disliked Reform Judaism, because historical roots were severed, he claimed, when rationalist dogmas displaced experience. The notion of the Chosen People was rejected as well. In his work, Judaism was collapsed into a modernized – perhaps even enfeebled – variant of the religious civilization that had become outmoded. A participant in organized Jewish life, Kallen served as national vicepresident of the American Jewish Congress, which sought to democratize communal affairs and to challenge the American Jewish Committee formed by patricians "afraid of having their 'Americanism' impugned." He eventually earned the B'nai B'rith's Harold M. Weisberg Memorial Award for a "lifetime of creative contributions to Jewish thought." Indeed, Kallen decided to move to New York City because of its acquiescence in what Henry James (himself an Irish immigrant's grandson) called the "Hebrew conquest." In New York, the "polycentric ideal for America" necessary "to sustain the Jews' pride and creativity" would flourish.

Kallen was to devote much of his energy not only to showing the compatibility of Jewishness with citizenship, but also to reconciling the general phenomenon of ethnicity with democracy. Both, he believed, placed a supreme value upon the ideal of freedom. At the December 1914 meeting of the American Philosophical Association, he first addressed the topic of "Democracy and the Melting Pot" and later insisted that his "ideas regarding cultural pluralism have a strictly American derivation. They developed as a kind of pluralistic social philosophy and psychology from the pragmatism of William James, the courses in the literary history of America given by Barrett Wendell, and my readings in American writers and poets," like Jefferson and Whitman. "This pluralism has an entirely different philosophical and political intention than the isolationist type which developed as a projection of nationalist movements in Europe."

As a Jamesian, he was more eager to validate the Many than to envision the One, and called for a society bound into a federation of ethnic groups. Irreversible data of birth could be converted into opportunities for self-realization; ancestry would be honored as a means of revitalizing democratic possibility. Kallen's first serious effort to theorize resistance to the ideal of assimilation was published early in 1915 in two successive issues of *The Nation*. In "Democracy Versus the Melting Pot: A Study of American Nationality," he asserted that "men may change their clothes, their politics, their wives, their religions, their philosophies, to a greater or lesser extent; they cannot change their grandfathers. Jews or Poles or Anglo-Saxons, in order to cease being Jews or Poles or Anglo-Saxons, would have to cease to be." No wonder then that Kallen was fond of the metaphor of the orchestra, in which "each ethnic group may be the natural instrument" contributing to the overall harmony and balance of the symphony. Each instrument realizes itself more fully in the society than it can by "segregation and isolation." Ethnicity, therefore, need not be dismissed as parochial strutting nor as an alibi for obscurantism, but could instead promote national loyalty and cohesiveness by anchoring the individual in a continuous and comforting fabric of institutions that also enriches the larger community.

Cultural pluralism became a way "to legitimate the divided loyalties of the individual," historian William Toll has written, "the multiple lines of attachment for groups, and the benefits to American society that had many cultural standards upon which to draw." In wishing for the uprooted to be implanted in the New World without forsaking traditions, the philosopher "provided an essential argument by which American Jews could reasonably declare their position within American society," Irving Howe added. "They would accept its rules, its norms, and its obligations, but would retain their distinctive styles of culture. If they were to remain Jews at all, they really had no other choice." Complete absorption into gentile America was unrealistic and undesirable for the masses who lived in the milieu of *Yiddishkeit* anyway. Kallen had, by contrast, grown up in a home that spoke neither Yiddish nor Hebrew but German; as an Ivy League–educated rationalist and a cosmopolitan academic, he could articulate a rationale for communal loyalties that probably most other immigrants could feel only instinctively. They were mostly bound to one another and could not have assimilated if they had wanted to, or tried to; Kallen himself had options.

That sort of detachment enabled him to see what he and other immigrants were doing – and what they were resisting. The term *cultural pluralism* first appeared within the pages of a book in *Culture and Democracy*, and its publication date is hardly accidental. For the differences among Jewish thinkers pale in comparison to the hostility that nativism represented. The year 1924 was also when Congress passed the Johnson–Reed Act, which signaled that applicants who were not of Western European or British stock might not be capable of becoming authentic Americans. Quotas worked against Europeans from the southern rim and the eastern end of the continent; in vain did New York Socialist Meyer London point out to his fellow legislators that "to prevent immigration means to cripple the United States. Our most developed industrial States are those which have had the largest immigration. Our most backward States industrially and in the point of literacy are those which have had no immigration to speak of." In vain did

Zangwill mention that, under the "Nordic dispensation" animating immigration restriction, Jesus Christ would have been sent back at Ellis Island. In vain did Finley Peter Dunne mock nativism when his Irish bartender proclaimed: "As a pilgrim father that missed the first boats, I must raise me claryon voice again' the invasion iv this fair land be th' paupers an' arnychists iv effete Europe. Ye bet I must – because I'm here first"; indeed, Mr. Dooley "felt enough like a native born American to burn a witch." The challenge to the very texture of democracy that mass immigration posed in the first quarter of the century heightened the theoretical as well as the practical effort to promote assimilation and "Americanization."

In arguing for "a democracy of nationalities" encouraging "the enterprise of self-realization through the perfection of men according to their kind," Kallen rejected homogenization and subservience to what has been termed *de facto Anglo-Saxon particularism*. Because people have to interact with one another, he insisted, plurality is fundamental to the human estate, in which its voices had to aspire to harmony, not to unison. In defending minority rights, he offered tantalizingly few details in describing the political arrangements and processes that would sanction such growth and development. But what made Kallen's theory reverberant is that, amid the chauvinism and nativism that the Great War had intensified, he championed diversity rather than absorption, particularism rather than conformism. The right to be equal did not contradict the right to be different.

Although he dissociated himself from the "isolationist pluralist thinking that is indigenous to Europe," and although one scholar of Kallen's thought denied that it was intended to duplicate the separatist enclaves of the Hapsburg Empire, historian Philip Gleason has interpreted Kallen's version of "American nationality not as a distinctive something-in-itself, but as a collocation of autonomous ethnic nationalities, each of which had its own spiritual enclave, all somehow coexisting harmoniously within the political entity called the United States." Kallen came to realize that the construct of "a federation or commonwealth of national cultures" needed to be softened, if not abandoned. Social scientist Lawrence H. Fuchs has explained why: "Kallen at first did not understand the totally voluntary nature of ethnic-Americanism when he argued that it was necessary for the United States to become 'a federation or commonwealth of nationalities' in order to ensure cultural democracy. Such a federation was out of the question. If it had occurred, the very basis of American unity – equal rights of individuals – would have been vitiated for the more traditional approach of other nations to group pluralism in which the identity and rights of the individual are derived from his or her membership in a group. That Kallen did not grasp the essence of voluntary pluralism – no one used the phrase – as a diversity based on the free choice of individuals united by a common civic culture was hardly surprising, since it had never existed in his or any-one else's experience before." By 1924, Kallen's national ideal had become a "fellowship of freedom and cooperation," which sanctioned what Fuchs himself termed *voluntary pluralism*.

In the *Nation* articles, Kallen had not introduced the phrase; "cultural pluralism" showed up nine years later. Although *Culture and Democracy* is dedicated to Wendell, who had died in 1921, the phrase itself was born while Kallen was serving as a teaching assistant to Santayana in either 1906 or 1907. In conversation with one of the undergraduates, Alain Locke, Kallen apparently came up with the phrase. Locke soon became the nation's first black Rhodes Scholar, but other Americans attending Oxford did not invite him to Thanksgiving dinner so that Southern whites would not be insulted. Kallen was also studying at Oxford in the fall of 1907, and found the snub so unjust that he refused to attend the dinner. But his indignant letter to Wendell provoked a shocking reply: "My own sentiments concerning negroes are such that I always decline to meet with the best of them . . . at table. . . . It would be disastrous to them . . . to expose them in private life to such sentiments of repugnance as mine."

Kallen's gesture of solidarity with Locke lacked liberality, however; anti-racism did not spur the break with fellow whites "mean-spirited enough to draw the color-line." Kallen told Wendell of having "neither respect nor liking for [Locke's] race." But he was "a Harvard man and as such he has a definite claim on me"; the color that mattered most was crimson. "In the face of social ostracism at Oxford," Toll has noted, "Kallen and Locke discussed at length cultural pluralism as a philosophy on which the dignity of a pariah group might be based. When each man returned to America, he found his warmest support among journalists and cultural nationalists of his own ethnic group." Springing from the ugliness of prejudice, *Culture and Democracy* somehow projected an ideal of creative cooperation.

Living on for another half-century, Kallen was granted opportunities to modify and update his theory. In a vacuum-packed life, the New School teacher moved on to many other topics, without ever disavowing his for-mulation of cultural pluralism. But he did little to refine or advance it as a policy, or to sharpen his appreciation of the ethnic values most wor-thy of preservation. In a series of essays entitled *Cultural Pluralism and the American Idea* (1956), the author broadened the notion of diversity to counter "an ancient authoritarian monism of culture," and connected the value of heterogeneity to the heritage of universalist political ideas. Kallen showed less interest in amplifying the multi-ethnic ideal (to which he attached only modulations) than in finding common ideological ground upon which all his fellow citizens were standing in 1956. In extending his 1924 chapter on "A Meaning of Americanism," he thus tried to put the legitimation of diversity in the service of consensus.

In a genial exchange of letters with T. S. Eliot, the philosopher failed to meet the poet's objections that Jewish culture had to stem from religion instead of ethnicity, and that the American Idea was not distinguishable from the general secular legacy of the Enlightenment. Eliot was quite unpersuaded by the claim that the cultivation of a distinctive Jewish subculture (or that of "any other racial minority") was compatible with what Kallen termed the political "religion of America." Eliot tweaked him that such "a national religion" looked less like consensus than the repressive uniformity that risked duplicating one of the worst features of monotheism. Kallen's contribution to democratic thought had come to a sad end. In a decade when the momentum of ethnicity appeared spent and when diversity looked divisive, he seemed to have reversed the stance adopted three decades earlier – perhaps in an effort to exert a direct influence in intellectual life that *Culture and Democracy* had not quite achieved.

* * *

Certainly, back in "the tribal Twenties," the case for minority rights and interests had managed to gain little traction; virtual oblivion was the immediate fate inflicted on Kallen's articulation of the case for heterogeneity. In the year his book was published, not only did the Johnson–Reed Act become law, but the Democratic Party at its presidential nominating convention could not muster a majority to denounce by name the Ku Klux Klan. No wonder then that the KKK's Imperial Wizard graciously conceded that "Americanism" could be defined as "a thing of the spirit, a purpose and a point of view." As though nodding to Kallen, Dr. Hiram W. Evans added that "the Klansman believes in the greatest possible diversity and individualism within the limits of the American spirit." However, that spirit had to be consistent with "fundamental national unity," and because it "can only come through instinctive racial understanding," aliens had to be excluded from democracy. The United States was intended to be a limited partnership, in which white supremacy and the political subjugation of Catholics to Protestants had to be sustained. Writing in the year Zangwill died, Evans dismissed the "melting pot" as a failure because some folks – especially Italians and Eastern European Jews – were inassimilable.

With immigration quotas fully imposed in the year the stock market crashed, the crystallization of *e pluribus unum* became less urgent than remedies for the problem of economic desperation. Then the struggle against the Axis – the tyrannies that subscribed to ideals of racial and cultural homogeneity – required an upward reevaluation of Kallen's democratic pluralism. Admittedly, such overtures were spasmodic; even during World War II, the *annual* quota for Chinese seeking naturalization rose to only 105. But Franklin D. Roosevelt was explicit in voicing a nonbiological definition of American nationalism (a "matter of mind and heart" and "never was a matter of race or ancestry"), and more vaguely encouraged a sense that diversity made for a better America. The presumption that tolerance was indeed compatible with patriotism could be gleaned from the across-the-spectrum success of Earl Robinson's *Ballad for Americans*. So central to the Communists' Popular Front mentality that Paul Robeson himself introduced this cantata in 1939, it was sung a year later at the GOP's nominating convention. Another vindication of Kallen's faith came in 1944, when the Supreme Court ruled in *Baumgartner v. U.S.* (322 U.S. 665) that a pro-Nazi who had been naturalized twelve years earlier could not be deprived of his citizenship (or his civil liberties). The pledge of allegiance was held to be political and juridical, but other sorts of loyalties need not be renounced. The right to be different – even for naturalized citizens – was not supposed to be a footnote to the right to be equal. In effect, civic attachment was to the stars and stripes; the public culture could be a patchwork quilt.

In 1952 (the year both Dewey and Santayana died), the National Council of Churches of Christ announced that cultural pluralism "envisages an overall unity based not only on common interests, but also a shared respect for the authentic inner life of individual groups – social, ethnic or religious." In echoing Kallen's case (without invoking his name), the National Council averred that "cultural pluralism, to be sure, defines not only an ideal but a continuing problem, since the shifting balance of forces in our society occasions recurring threats, now to the unity of the whole, now to the integrity of the parts. But cultural pluralism, as a national or a world ideal, has the merit of recognizing the necessity of maintaining a wholesome tension between unity and diversity." No wonder then that, in 1956, an astute scholar of ethnicity like Nathan Glazer could tell Kallen how "enormously stimulating" *Culture and Democracy* remained, "by far the best [book] that exists on the question of the impact of immigrant groups on

American culture." Glazer "was amazed to discover how much that I and others had thought and written about this matter had been written by you a long time ago. It is a book that repays re-reading greatly, and I have found very little in this area that does."

Exactly three decades after *Culture and Democracy* appeared, Ellis Island – the site, the portal that symbolized the transatlantic transplantation – was shut down, as though confirming the waning of ethnicity. In the 1950s, diversity was held to take the form of piety instead, and the first major restatement of pluralist social thought since *Culture and Democracy* was aptly offered by a Jewish theologian. Will Herberg assumed the task of balancing the general with the particular by popularizing the thesis of a "triple melting pot," in which the citizenry is not sorted out into the 106 categories that the *Harvard Encyclopedia of American Ethnic Groups* (1980) counted a generation later. Instead, the key affiliations consist of three forms of religious expression, which may be the only vestiges of Old World traditions left. With *Protestant-Catholic-Jew* (1955), Herberg became the most influential single revisionist of the legacy of cultural pluralism.

He advanced no special claim for the irrevocable identity of grandparents. Instead, he insisted that "the newcomer is expected to change many things about him as he becomes American – nationality, language, culture." But "he is *not* expected to change . . . his religion." This astounding claim is manifestly untrue, either normatively or descriptively. Herberg's error may have stemmed from his attempt to extrapolate from the peculiar fate of his fellow Jews to a larger pattern, which Gleason emphasized did not work for Roman Catholics. Nor did it even apply to Jews, whose ethnic allegiance ran deeper than their piety; only about half of them even then belonged to a synagogue. But by defining this 3 percent of the population – a demographic blip – as a religious group rather than as an ethnic minority, *Protestant-Catholic-Jew* made Jewry co-equal with the huge Protestant and Catholic denominations, a majestic one third of the makers of "the Judeo-Christian tradition." Herberg's "triple melting pot" thus did for his "co-religionists" what the United Nations did for Taiwan in calling it "China" and giving it a permanent seat on the Security Council. He heightened the visibility of the Jews but did not satisfactorily illuminate their status. The transformation of Kallen's ethnic pluralism into religious pluralism in the 1950s was misleading and too partial, and thus proved unsuccessful. Denying the residual force of the claims of ancestral allegiance, Herberg did at least get right the latitudinarianism of public life, its tendency to reduce friction and to promote a faith in a common faith (which Kallen himself promoted in his restatement of cultural pluralism a year after the publication of *Protestant-Catholic-Jew*). Herberg had rationalized tenacious religious allegiance as somehow very American.

His diagnosis of religious diversity took for granted a consensus on national values; *e pluribus* had been invariably followed by *unum*. The hospitality of the dominant culture, which had been so emphatically shaped by Puritans and pragmatists (the legacy of Wendell and James, respectively), needed only to be encouraged and enhanced, since it was neither repressive nor univocal. The public culture, the American Way of Life, had become a common inheritance, a birthright that the progeny of virtually all the immigrants shared.

Exactly four decades after *Culture and Democracy* was published, a sociologist of Jewish origins, Milton M. Gordon, extended and modified Kallen's work on cultural pluralism. It was a "remarkable and germinal" concept, Gordon noted, but he added that Kallen's writings also suffered from "a general framework of rhetoric and philosophical analysis which has not pushed to the fore that kind of rigorous sociological inquiry which the crucial importance of the idea ultimately demands." Gordon argued instead that "structural pluralism" was "the major key to the understanding of . . . ethnic makeup" in America. He defined his own term as referring "to a national society in which various groups, each with a psychological sense of its own historical peoplehood, maintain some structural separation from each other in intimate primary group relationships and in certain aspects of institutional life and thus create the possibility of maintaining, also, some cultural patterns which are different from those of the 'host' society and of other racial and ethnic groups in the nation." The second proviso indicated Gordon's sense that "racial and ethnic pluralism can exist without a great deal of cultural diversity; it cannot exist at all, however, without structural separation." He considered "cultural pluralism" primarily a first-generation phenomenon, with "Anglo-conformity" dominant for their posterity. But Gordon conceded that the sovereignty of Marcus L. Hansen's famous law (i.e., the third generation remembering what the second generation tried to forget) might operate in the form of "symbolic elements of the ancestral tradition" and that non-Protestant religious expression perpetuating some kinds of differentiation.

In 1955, Herberg had mentioned race only in passing, though in retrospect it seemed especially bizarre to have lumped black Americans in a category that fails to distinguish them from other Christians – especially from other Protestants. Indifference to race has been increasingly understood to be a fatal defect not only of Herberg's thesis, which stressed religion, but also

Kallen's, which stressed ethnicity. In 1915 and 1924, the hyphenates whose status was dubious were whites. It should come as no surprise that cultural pluralism neglected and, therefore, excluded nonwhites. Although a progressive who detested racial as well as religious discrimination, Kallen gave no seats in his orchestra to the indigenous Indians or to Asian Americans. Nor did he defy the widespread denial of the value of black participation in the nation's culture – even during the Harlem Renaissance. Happily, *Cultural Pluralism and the American Idea* (1956) excised the assumptions of white cultural supremacy that had disfigured his 1924 thesis, without thereby damaging its logic. Such revision suggests that the merit of Kallen's work does not depend on the perceptual limitations of its author, any more than the argument for "certain inalienable rights" depends on *its* creator, whose observation in *Notes on the State of Virginia* (1787) that blacks belong to a rhythm nation has ironically been converted into recent claims for a special contribution to American culture.

Determinism constituted an inherent flaw that could not have been remedied without scrapping the theory of cultural pluralism entirely. Kallen was an essentialist; he assumed what Isaac Berkson called "the ineradicable and central influence of race" and ethnicity. "An Irishman is always an Irishman," Kallen had asserted in 1918, "a Jew is always a Jew. . . . Irishman and Jew are facts in nature." Genealogy is destiny. "A man may change his surroundings," the philosopher added, but "cannot change his past. That is inalterable." Even amid that fluid "association of citizens" that constitutes democracy in America, identity is presumably so rigid that Jews, for example, could not be Poles or Anglo-Saxons; for their descendants to find mates outside their own groups would not be exogamy but "miscegenation."

Yet, already by 1920, such hereditarian rigidity was under assault from anthropologists like the German-born Jew, Franz Boas, upon whom Berkson drew in his critique of Kallen's work. "Variability within one race and overlapping between races are so great that one can prophesy nothing with any degree of certainty" about an individual's endowment, Berkson noted. "No mutual exclusiveness in the original nature of Jew and non-Jew" can be detected. Kallen's claim that grandfathers cannot be changed Berkson dismissed as "a sophism," since the traditions and models that grandfathers represent can be repudiated and ignored, whereas intermarriage means that "any individual who marries outside of his group is thereby changing the ancestry of his children." While valuing Kallen's gallant opposition to "prevailing theories of assimilation," Berkson found "ethnic predestination" untenable as a theory (and undesirable as a policy).

Ethnic predestination could not be squared with growing evidence of acculturation and assimilation – the processes that Zangwill and Antin had encouraged and that Theodore Roosevelt and Woodrow Wilson had endorsed. The promise that fate need not be programmed at birth was often fulfilled, whatever the consequences for the cohesiveness of minority life; and the free institutions that attracted so many immigrants to the United States made determinism vulnerable. If one generation (say, the first) was assimilationist, the second generation might readily be assimilated, and the third generation could pick a preferred grandfather. Not only names and spouses and religions and residences could be switched. The miracles of medical surgery have also made it possible even to change sex. Race can be blurred and altered too; sometimes the color line could be crossed, as the anonymous narrator does in James Weldon Johnson's anonymously published novel, *The Autobiography of an Ex-Coloured Man* (1912). The "one-drop rule" made such crossings surreptitious and sometimes illegal, but its very existence suggested how mixed were the ancestries of even those who were excluded from the dream of amalgamation.

For over a century after slavery was abolished, Virginia was not yet (as its official state slogan proclaims) "for lovers." Interracial marriage was prohibited in the South (and some other states) until the Supreme Court, in a case aptly entitled *Loving v. Virginia* (1967), unanimously abolished such laws. The growth of racial egalitarianism and of tolerance has accelerated exogamy – and invalidated Kallen's version of cultural pluralism. By the end of the twentieth century, more than half of those whose national origins are from Europe were marrying someone from another ethnic or racial group. Among second-generation Asians and Hispanics, the proportion who wed outside their own group was a third or higher. "As this pattern continues," Glazer predicted, "the ethnicity of the children becomes even more vestigial and symbolic." The 1990 census counted about four million Americans who have parents of mixed races.

Because Kallen's version of cultural pluralism cannot be separated from his belief that primordial ties of ancestry supersede voluntary associations, the value of his theory is now dubious. American Jews, like other ethnic groups, will increasingly have to take their chances in an open society that has repudiated determinism. A question, therefore, lingers: Can the communal institutions and philanthropic agencies that were so painstakingly constructed over the course of a century still flourish?

15

WAGING THE COLD WAR IN THE THIRD WORLD: THE FOUNDATIONS AND THE CHALLENGES OF DEVELOPMENT

GARY R. HESS

It was a heady moment in the history of American philanthropic enterprise abroad. The Ford Foundation, emerging in 1951 as the wealthiest philanthropic foundation, was contemplating a major commitment of its resources to India. The foundation's president, Paul Hoffman, who had headed the Marshall Plan program of economic assistance to war-ravaged Europe, and a few other Ford officials had just returned from a mission to India where they had met with several leaders, most notably an enthusiastic Prime Minister Jawaharlal Nehru, who welcomed outside support in the effort to build his nation's economy. This was a formidable challenge, for India ranked among the poorest countries in the world. The most pressing need, Indian officials and outside observers generally agreed, was to break the cycle of rural poverty marked by increasing population, inequitable distribution of land, and low-yielding agricultural practices – problems dramatized in the low output of 1950–1951 that led to famine conditions. There was a model of rural improvement at hand. For the previous three years, a small group of Americans led by Albert Mayer had been working with Indian officials in a pilot project of rural development. Already, the Etawah Project, located in north-central India, was credited with increasing agricultural output and promoting social reform. Envisioning the Ford Foundation as the catalyst of such change throughout the country, Hoffman exclaimed: "There is no reason why all 500,000 of India's villages could not make a similar advance!"

To Hoffman and his colleagues, the Cold War necessitated this commitment to Indian development. The recent Communist victory in the Chinese Civil War taught the "lesson" that Communism thrived on social and economic disorder; the failure to address these problems had led to the "loss" of the world's most populous country and that mistake could not be repeated in the secondmost populated country. Hoffman remarked that "if in 1945 we had embarked on such a program [in China]... the end result would have been a China completely immunized against the appeal of the Communists. India, in my opinion, is today what China was in 1945."

The Ford Foundation quickly translated its aspirations into practice. By early 1952, it had committed $3.9 million to the establishment of village development projects and the training of village workers. Working closely with U.S. government agencies and the government of India, the foundation assumed an important role not only in promoting rural change, but also in influencing India's overall plan of economic development.

This Ford Foundation commitment to India was representative of the greatly enlarged role of American philanthropic enterprise in what were then labeled the "developing" countries – the areas that eventually became known as the Third World. Representing a continuation of the pre–World War II assumption of the universality of American values and institutions, as discussed by Emily Rosenberg (Chapter 11), these philanthropic activities were pursued with a sense of urgency driven by the imperatives of the Cold War. The underlying argument of this essay is that three foundations – Ford, Rockefeller, and Carnegie – as important partners of the American government in combating the appeal of Communism in the developing world, undertook imaginative and far-reaching initiatives, but the long-term impact of their programs depended on the extent to which they were integrated with the politics and culture of recipient countries.

* * *

Underlying the expansion was the convergence of three related factors: first, a dramatic increase in the resources of the major foundations for overseas work; second, the national Cold War commitment to combating the appeal of Communism by promoting orderly economic and social development; and third, the foreign policy elite's acceptance of the emerging behavioral sciences, especially in the field of economics, as vital to guiding orderly change.

While the major foundations still appropriated most of their funds to domestic programs, the international expenditures increased significantly. The most important factor in this growth was the transformation of the Ford Foundation from a modest local organization into the wealthiest of American philanthropies. In 1949, its board of trustees appointed a committee headed by Rowan Gaither to chart the foundation's future. The

Gaither Report called on the foundation to address conditions that threatened another world war by projecting the American model of democracy as the alternative to totalitarianism and alleviating the factors that gave rise to Communism. Thus, the Gaither Report suggested that a principal objective should be programs that would bring "the improvement of the standard of living and the economic status of peoples throughout the world." As it implemented the Gaither Report, the leadership of the Ford Foundation concentrated on the Middle East and Asia because those areas "consist[ed] of many newly emergent nations precariously situated along the periphery of the Soviet-Communism orbit."

Complementing Ford's newly defined emphasis, the Rockefeller Foundation was changing its international priorities. Rockefeller's pioneering work in medical education and public health was essentially taken over by international organizations, and the Communist victory in China severed the foundation's connection with its most notable overseas institution, the Peking Union Medical College. Rockefeller's leaders now saw the foundation challenged by the "successful [Communist] scheme for development," which necessitated contributing toward a "broader program of developing the resources, material and human, of the underdeveloped areas." Dean Rusk, who became president of the foundation in 1952 after a decade of military and diplomatic experience, most recently as Assistant Secretary of State for Far Eastern Affairs, shared that vision. Advising trustees that political and economic developments in Asia, Africa, the Middle East, and Latin America would determine much of the world's fate in the latter half of the century, he argued that the foundation "accept a responsibility for doing what it can to assist these countries to erect free societies, a task which is crucial to the purpose of the foundation itself." In 1955, the Rockefeller trustees approved Rusk's proposal for an Expanded Program of $5 million per year for five to ten years specifically for programs in developing countries, thus bringing the total Rockefeller overseas commitment to about $10 million per year.

Like their counterparts at the Ford and Rockefeller Foundations, the leadership of the Carnegie Corporation expanded that philanthropy's international commitments as part of the national imperative to counter the appeal of Communism. Restricted by its charter to working in British or formerly British territories, the Carnegie Corporation built upon its long-standing commitment to the development of education in Africa. Anticipating that decolonization in Africa would follow in the trail of the independence of Asian peoples, Carnegie officials foresaw that Africa would become a focus of the Cold War rivalry and that their programs could help "Africans in the rank and file ... understand the differences between Communism and democracy."

As the three major foundations expanded their Third World programs, they both fostered and drew on the expertise of the emerging behavioral sciences. Beginning in the 1920s, the Rockefeller Foundation had supported research in the social sciences with increasing attention to addressing problems that undermined social stability. After World War II, Ford and Carnegie joined with Rockefeller in underwriting what soon became the dominant trends in sociology, political science, and economics, each discipline contributing to a view of modernization that stressed economic growth, gradual social and political change, and democratic ideals and institutions. Foundation officials, policymakers in Washington, and mainstream academics – often overlapping groups – thus came to see the American experience as a model for Third World development.

Of particular importance in the emergence of developmental economics was the Massachusetts Institute of Technology's Center for International Studies (MIT-CIS). Begun in 1951 and generously supported by the Ford Foundation, MIT-CIS under the leadership of Max Millikan, who had earlier been the director of economic research at the Central Intelligence Agency (CIA), emphasized "the application of basic social science research to problems of U.S. policy in the current world struggle ... [with] the ultimate aim of ... the production of an alternative to Marxism." Walt W. Rostow, MIT-CIS's most renowned economist, addressed that challenge. His influential *The Stages of Economic Growth: A Non-Communist Manifesto*, published in 1960 and written during a leave funded by the Carnegie Corporation, provided the classic expression of the buoyant expectation that the Western experience provided a model for orderly economic growth and political change in the Third World. Economic development offered emerging peoples "a potentially constructive outlet for nationalism, a social solvent, a matrix for the development of new leadership, a means for generating ... confidence in the democratic process." For the United States, Third World development was key to winning the Cold War. If properly channeled by the West, it would yield "in two or three decades ... a preponderance of stable, effective, and democratic societies [which would] give the best promise of a favorable settlement of the Cold War and peaceful, progressive environment." He confidently asserted that the "tricks of growth are not all that difficult" – indeed, the "tricks" had already been perfected in the West.

Development thinking assumed the importance of education, embodied in "human-capital" theory. Investment in education brought a high rate of return, human-capital theory assumed, because it increased labor productivity, promoted technological innovation, and enhanced equality. Thus, support of education became an important aspect of Western involvement in the developing world.

Reflecting the convergence of the foundations' objectives with U.S. foreign policy, the foundations typically worked closely with U.S. government agencies at home and overseas. This interaction represented what Peter Hall (Chapter 17) describes as the foundations becoming "extensions of government itself" with relationships that became "routinized" on the institutional and individual levels. Officials moved between prominent positions in the foundations and the U.S. government. The previously noted governmental backgrounds of Hoffman and Rusk that preceded their presidencies of the Ford Foundation and Rockefeller Foundation, respectively, were part of a pattern. John Foster Dulles served as chairman of Rockefeller's Board of Trustees from 1950 to 1952, when President-elect Dwight D. Eisenhower named him Secretary of State. Eight years later, Rusk's tenure as Rockefeller's president ended when he became Secretary of State under John F. Kennedy. Rusk's colleague in the Kennedy and Lyndon B. Johnson administrations, McGeorge Bundy, left his position as special assistant to the President for national security affairs in 1966 to become president of the Ford Foundation. David Bell, vice president in charge of Ford's International Division, had previously been the director of the Agency for International Development (AID). John J. McCloy had been president of the World Bank and the U.S. High Commissioner for Germany prior to serving as chairman of the Ford board of trustees. The interaction of foundations and government in the field was commonplace as well. For instance, when the Rockefeller Foundation was exploring the possibilities of supporting a university in Chile in 1962, the enterprise was strongly supported by U.S. Ambassador Charles W. Cole, who had taken that post a year earlier after serving as a Rockefeller vice president. The leadership of the MIT-CIS further underscored the close connection of foundation enterprises with the U.S. government: Millikan came from the CIA and Rostow took a leave to join the Kennedy administration, first as Bundy's deputy, then becoming under Rusk director of the State Department's Policy Planning Council, and eventually succeeding Bundy as Johnson's national security adviser.

Functioning as a nonofficial extension of U.S. policy, the foundations enjoyed a prestige that gave them advantages over government programs and enabled them to undertake initiatives that were beyond the scope of official agencies. Their nongovernmental status and avowedly international and humanitarian character enabled them to project a liberal image as nonideological and responsive institutions. They were, of course, not dependent on the political processes that governed Congressional authorizations; a foundation board could earmark funds for a project that might have taken months, if ever, to get through Congress. Foundation officials frequently enjoyed a stature in recipient countries that was beyond the political capacity of their official counterparts. For instance, the heads of both the Ford and Rockefeller programs in India had access to high-level officials and influenced government policy in ways that would have been unthinkable for any American official. Also, at times of stress in U.S. relations with other governments, foundations were often able to continue their work without interruption and sometimes became the principal representative of U.S. interests.

This relatively benign role of the foundations enabled them to earn a reputation for accruing greater benefits from their expenditures than did the governmental programs. Foundation resources never approached those of bilateral and multilateral assistance programs. At the peak of foundation work in the Third World in the 1960s, Ford was devoting about $50 million annually to overseas programs, Rockefeller was spending about $10 million, and Carnegie about $1 million. At that time, U.S. government foreign assistance was approximately $2.5 billion annually.

As they waged the Cold War in the Third World, these major foundations gave priority to the training of elites who would provide leadership, management, and technical knowledge. The Rockefeller Foundation and Carnegie Corporation historic practice of concentrating resources in a few fields and then within a few institutions guided the foundations in the Cold War era. The foundations strengthened what were judged to be the best indigenous universities where they fostered the American models of university organization, curriculum, and scholarship. In these "lead universities," the foundations enhanced the resources and facilities of selected programs, supported visiting professorships of American scholars, and funded fellowships for faculty and students in the recipient countries to pursue advanced study in the United States. The foundations generally gave priority to the social sciences, especially economics; this led to substantial contributions to the establishment of a number of institutes of social science research. Ford also emphasized programs in public administration and

Rockefeller in the sciences and medicine, while Carnegie concentrated on teacher training.

Augmenting the approach of leading universities, the foundations influenced Third World development by supporting various efforts to increase agricultural production. This led to programs of technical assistance, research, community development, and agricultural education.

* * *

India's strategic importance focused attention on its chronic food shortages and attendant dependency on grain imports. Accordingly, both Rockefeller and Ford undertook major programs in that country that sought to transfer practices that had been successful in America. Working with government of India officials who shared the Rockefeller leadership's view that agricultural education had to be radically transformed from its Anglo-Indian theoretical tradition, the foundation supported the establishment of provincial agricultural universities modeled on the American land-grant system (each linked to a U.S. land-grant university) and, at the national level, on an advanced-degree program at the Indian Agricultural Research Institute (IARI). At the center of Rockefeller's activities was Ralph Cummings, who became Field Director in 1953 and remained in India for ten years, becoming a confidante of Indian officials. Besides directing the Rockefeller programs, he served as acting dean of the IARI Post-Graduate School and as chair of the Agricultural Universities Commission.

Dwarfing Rockefeller's expenditures if not its influence, the Ford Foundation's 1951 commitment to a national program of village development was based on the tradition of agricultural extension in the United States. Ford cooperated with official U.S. agencies and the government of India in the establishment of the Community Development Program and the National Extension Service. Douglas Ensminger, a leading authority on rural development, left the U.S. Department of Agriculture in 1952 to head the Ford Foundation programs in South Asia. He remained for nearly twenty years, becoming arguably the most influential American in the country. He established close working relationships with high-level Indian officials, including Prime Minister Nehru, and influenced the goals and priorities of the Planning Commission as it developed the series of Five-Year Plans. With Ensminger's prodding and the promise of Ford support, the Government of India in 1960 established the Intensive Agricultural District Program, which concentrated the resources and technology needed for increasing production in pilot projects throughout the country. The Ford Foundation's efforts in India extended beyond agriculture to include policy-oriented economic research, management training, and urban planning.

In neighboring Pakistan, the Ford Foundation's support of the Planning Commission from 1954 to 1965 illustrated the capacity of a foundation to act expeditiously and in a politically sensitive area. Pakistan's interest in securing advice on the complex issues of economic planning was an ideal foundation project, for in a nation where the American presence was already substantial, reliance on official advisors would have left Pakistan's leaders vulnerable to criticism of dependence on the United States. Ford put together an agreement that provided for its collaboration with the Harvard University Graduate School of Public Administration and the Pakistan Planning Commission to train economists, enhance governmental economic analysis, and prepare long-term plans.

The foundations' role enhanced the credibility of India's and Pakistan's planning. This contributed to the commitment of large-scale economic assistance to those countries through a South Asian Consortium of several governments and multilateral agencies.

The Ford Foundation's programs in Burma and Egypt further illustrated its capacity to undertake initiatives that served official U.S. interests. Burma requested assistance in building an international Buddhist university, but official agencies were not permitted to fund a religious institution. So Ford, which shared the State Department's position that the United States needed to cultivate the friendship of Burma's neutralist government, supported the establishment of the Institute of Buddhist Studies in 1953. When the Burmese government later that year rejected bilateral aid from the United States, the foundation became for the next two years the principal agency of American influence in the country, supporting various rural development, agricultural research, and public administration programs.

In Egypt, Ford played an even more significant role in compensating for strains in bilateral relations. The foundation began its Egyptian operations in 1952 with grants to a few established educational institutions. In an important initiative, it supported the establishment of the National Institute of Management Development, which introduced the case-study method to management training in the Third World; within a decade, it was recognized as the preeminent institution of its kind in Africa and the Middle East. Besides those conventional measures, Ford also confronted the problems resulting from Congressional hostility toward economic assistance to Egypt and Secretary of State John Foster Dulles's abrupt termination in 1956 of support for the Aswan High Dam project. The foundation compensated by aiding the Aswan Regional Development Agency (ARDA), which President Gamal Abdal Nasser established. When the progress of ARDA and other projects were threatened by the renewal of Egyptian-Israeli tensions in 1967 and as foreign agencies were leaving because of impending war, the Egyptian government requested that Ford personnel remain and continue their work. Ford carried out its Middle Eastern program with political sensitivity: to avoid criticism at home, it downplayed its commitment to ARDA and other development projects; to uphold its stature in Egypt and elsewhere in the Islamic Middle East, Ford also kept its assistance to Israel out of the spotlight.

* * *

Having launched their development efforts in South/Southeast Asia, the Middle East, and Latin America, by the end of the 1950s the foundations were drawn toward Africa where impending decolonization highlighted its strategic significance. With the independence of Ghana in 1957 marking the beginning of the end of the European empires, the Carnegie Corporation organized a conference the next year in White Sulphur Springs, West Virginia, that brought together representatives of Western institutions with interests in Africa, including the major foundations, bilateral and multilateral aid agencies, British and American universities, and commercial firms. The conference represented the assumption, in the words of one scholar, "of the common interests of the African states and the free-world nations" and resulted in the establishment of the Africa Liaison Committee, which coordinated proposals for higher education in Africa and led to several joint foundation activities. This attention to Africa paralleled and interacted with the civil rights movement, discussed in the following chapter by Claude A. Clegg. The international dimensions of racial discrimination added to Africa's significance in Cold War strategy. The prevalence of segregation, which became a prominent feature of Communist propaganda in the developing world, undermined America's stature. The foreign policy elite favored civil rights legislation as essential to reconciling American democratic principles and practice.

The Carnegie Corporation's objective of influencing teacher training of the African peoples emerging from British rule coincided with the interest of Columbia University's Teacher's College in expanding its international programs. Accordingly, in 1960 Carnegie gave the first of several

grants to Teacher's College for a cooperative program in teacher education. That same year, it sponsored conferences in London and Princeton
that brought together representatives of foundations and various British,
American, and African agencies. The Carnegie-Columbia collaboration
became an important vehicle of American influence. Teacher's College established the Afro-Anglo-American Program in Teacher Education, which
linked educational systems in the newly independent states in formerly
British Africa with American educational philosophy and practices.

Decolonization in Africa quickly took on early Cold War overtones in
the Congo where the approach of independence led to instability and
violence – a situation in which the Ford Foundation assumed responsibilities that reflected essential U.S. objectives. Anti-Belgian riots in Leopoldville
in 1959 touched off an extended crisis marked by tension and fighting among
various Congolese groups. Concerned by the Soviet Union's capacity to ex-
ploit the situation, the United States and its European allies feared that
independence would lead to civil war and an international crisis. Neither
the U.S. government nor UN agencies were in a position to act expeditiously. At the suggestion of the State Department, the Ford Foundation
responded quickly to a proposal that addressed one of the problems facing
an independent Congo: the lack of an educated elite. The National Institute
of Political Studies (NIPS), established with Ford support in Leopoldville
in 1960, met that need, as its students subsequently assumed high positions
in the independent Congo. The U.S. ambassador in Brussels wrote, "the
grant is a striking example of how a large foundation can act quickly in
an important critical case." In late 1960 Ford officials also received a proposal from the UN Civilian Mission in the Congo to establish a school
for training public administrators. Within a few weeks, the foundation underwrote the National School of Law and Administration (NSLA), which
began operations in early 1961. The school's four-year program provided
the training for a core of elite civil servants who, within a few years, held
important administrative and judicial positions throughout the country. In
1967, President Joseph Mobutu announced that NSLA would be responsible for all the training and development of the Congolese civil service. The
Ford Foundation thus prominently guided the development of the NIPS
and NSLA and, in turn, the political leadership of the independent Congo
committed to the imperatives of civil society.

* * *

The expanded efforts of the Ford, Rockefeller, and Carnegie Foundations
in Africa reflected their greater overseas ambitions as they defined their

missions for the "development decade" of the 1960s, which Western leaders viewed as the critical period in Cold War competition in the Third World. The confidence of the foundations' leadership that their programs had been uniquely successful led them to commit more resources and to envision bolder initiatives. *The Ford Foundation in the 1960s* updated the goals of the Gaither Report and gave greater emphasis to foundation initiatives and "action programs," which led to an increase an overseas funding from about $15 million a year during the 1950s to approximately $50 million annually from 1963 to 1970. Meanwhile, as they commemorated the foundation's fiftieth anniversary in 1963, the Rockefeller trustees broadened Third World objectives and restructured programs to address five problems: world hunger, overpopulation, university development, equal opportunity, and cultural development. Like Ford's plans for the 1960s, the Rockefeller program emphasized a "problem approach" and "action programs." George Harrar, a Rockefeller vice president who had earlier headed the foundation's Mexican Agricultural Project, became president in 1961 and provided strong leadership in this new emphasis. Winning the Cold War in the Third World remained the central objective, and new measures were necessary to counteract the tactics of the Communist bloc. Harrar wrote: "Competition with the Soviet Union is a game that has to be played on all squares of the board and with a mixed and highly flexible strategy."

The most significant expression of the Rockefeller Foundation's expanded commitment was the launching of the University Development Program (UDP). Approved by the foundation's trustees in December 1961 at Harrar's urging, UDP committed resources to building a wide range of disciplines in selected lead universities. Kenneth Thompson, a Rockefeller vice president, reflected that "institution-building is at the heart of the foundation's tradition." The rationale of university development was rooted in this tradition plus the belief that, for the developing countries, the missing factor was educated people or trained leadership. After review teams examined nineteen prospective universities, the foundation established six initial UDP centers in 1963: one in Latin America (University of Valle in Colombia); three in Africa (University of Ibadan in Nigeria, University of Khartoum, University of East Africa); and two in Asia (University of the Philippines and a consortium of three universities in Thailand). The selection process favored institutions that had received earlier Rockefeller funding; among the UDP centers, only the University of East Africa and its constituent institutions had not benefited from earlier support. Over the next decade, Rockefeller expanded the

UDP program with additional centers in Chile, Brazil, Zaire (Congo), and Indonesia.

In an especially ambitious initiative, the Rockefeller Foundation joined with the Ford Foundation and Carnegie Corporation in fostering the University of East Africa (UEA), which consolidated the programs of the national universities of Tanzania, Kenya, and Uganda. Although the leaders in the three countries preferred independent universities, the foundations – together with official U.S., British, and international agencies – used their leverage to press for the federated regional university. Rockefeller sponsored a conference at its Villa Serbelloni in Italy in 1963 where foundation, African, British, American, and international agency officials laid the groundwork for the UEA, which was formally established later that year. The Western agencies' objective was to avoid duplication of programs while maximizing Western influence in a critical region's university system. The foundations each pledged support to UEA's development, concentrating on areas of traditional interest: Africanization of the faculty (Rockefeller) and administrative staff (Ford), education (Carnegie), biological sciences (Rockefeller), and social science faculty and research (Ford and Rockefeller).

The orientation toward Africa in the 1960s encouraged the foundations to give greater attention to the humanities, which became increasingly regarded as a means of cultivating the national self-identities of Third World peoples. Colonial rule in Africa had been especially destructive of indigenous culture. Robert July, an Africanist, exhorted his Rockefeller Foundation colleagues that "spiritual needs . . . are relatively ignored in the welter of economic planning, political activity, and public-health programs. . . . There is an equal need for national philosophies to match economic change and social progress and to give them meaning and justification." "Cultural development" was thus seen as providing a bridge between traditional values and institutions and the changes brought by modernization. This meant cultivating the study of history – in July's words, "the past must be studied as it never has been in Africa . . . to show people what they have been, why they are as they are, and where they are going" – and supporting the creative works of dramatists, writers, and artists. Rockefeller undertook a range of activities that highlighted indigenous cultural traditions and reduced parochialism by increasing contacts among educated Africans. The UDP expanded humanities offerings, increased library holdings, and Africanized faculties. In addition, Rockefeller funded a number of special projects, including the establishment the University College Institute of African Studies in Ghana and the national archives in Nigeria.

Complementing Rockefeller's "cultural-development" efforts in Africa, the Carnegie Corporation's teacher education programs strengthened the study of African cultures. Expanding on programs that had been started in the 1920s, Carnegie also supported library development in a number of countries and research on the African past, including a grant to the University of Ibadan in 1956 for research on West African history.

* * *

The foundations' boldness in the "development decade" was especially evident in the Ford Foundation's initiatives in the politically sensitive area of population control. Despite the evidence, by 1950, that world population was doubling every forty years with important implications for development, political and foundation leaders generally avoided the issue. It remained principally a concern of research organizations and family-planning organizations linked together in the International Planned Parent Federation. The Roman Catholic Church's opposition to birth control kept the U.S. government from becoming involved in population issues. In the UN, advocates of family-planning programs encountered the opposition of predominantly Catholic countries and the Communist bloc.

An exception on the issue of population control was John D. Rockefeller III who, as early as 1946, sent a team of researchers to Asia to study the population problem. Despite his interest, the trustees of the Rockefeller Foundation regarded the area as too controversial and as a threat to the foundation's work in predominantly Catholic countries. In 1952, Rockefeller personally established the Population Council, which emphasized scientific research as a means of stimulating awareness of population issues and forcing assessment of policy options. It became the center of population work in the United States, supporting research and surveys, training demographers and biomedical scientists, and gradually moving into the design of family-planning programs. Besides Rockefeller's personal support, the Population Council received the bulk of its funds from the Ford Foundation (beginning in 1954) and the Rockefeller Foundation (beginning in 1958). The cautious support, especially of the Rockefeller Foundation, meant that the Population Council became, in the words of its official historian, "a retailer for wholesale interests that preferred not to have their own population programs."

By 1959, however, the Ford Foundation, with the surprising support of the board chairman, Henry Ford, moved to the forefront of the population issue. Abandoning its traditional reluctance to support medical research, Ford provided substantial grants for biomedical research related to fertility. In its most visible step, Ford also undertook extensive birth-control programs overseas. This initiative capitalized on the recognition by leaders in several Third World countries that population growth hindered development. Most notably, the governments of both India and Pakistan officially recognized the social and economic problems resulting from their spiraling birth rates. The Ford Foundation responded with grants, some of which went through the Population Council, which supported the establishment of family-planning research centers, clinics and educational programs, and training of family-planning personnel. In India, Ford built on the Population Council's Taiwan Project that provided the first field experiment of the intrauterine device (IUD) and undertook pilot projects to introduce that practice and a major educational program to promote the adoption of condoms. Overall, the Ford Foundation played a significant role in India's emergence as a center of contraceptive research and practice.

The Ford Foundation pattern of family planning in South Asia was adapted to other areas. Typically working with the Population Council, Ford undertook programs that responded to the interest of the governments of Tunisia, Egypt, and Morocco in demographic research and family planning. Given the opposition of the Roman Catholic Church, Latin American governments concentrated on research and training of medical personnel in reproductive problems, which led to Ford programs in Chile, Mexico, Argentina, Colombia, and Uruguay.

As the Ford Foundation undertook population initiatives, the Rockefeller Foundation substantially increased its support of population issues, mostly through the Population Council. The Carnegie Corporation, as well as a number of smaller foundations, also contributed to the work in this field. The impact of American philanthropies was substantial; in the mid-1960s, they were contributing about half of all the international spending on population programs.

By that time, the pioneering work of the Ford Foundation, Population Council and, less directly, the Rockefeller Foundation – building as it did on the interests of a number of Third World governments – contributed to a significant change in the politics of family planning. Opposition lessened, as media coverage of food shortages in the Third World highlighted overpopulation, and population problems came to be seen increasingly in the context of humanitarian, environmental, and feminist issues. In his 1965 State of the Union Address, President Lyndon Johnson termed over-population "humanity's greatest challenge" and he authorized AID to move into the family-planning field. With many Third World governments actively pursuing family planning, the United Nations General Assembly in 1966 included assistance in "training information and advisory services in the field of population" in the mandate of all UN agencies. Under Robert McNamara's leadership beginning in 1968, the World Bank also moved aggressively into the field.

* * *

The foundations' contribution to population issues in the late 1960s paralleled their other most significant impact on the Third World: the culmination of the Green Revolution. This had its origins in the Mexican Agricultural Project (MAP) that Rockefeller launched in 1943 under Harrar's direction. By 1950, Rockefeller and Mexican scientists had developed and introduced high-yield varieties (HYV) of food grains, which brought a dramatic increase in food production. Although MAP was subsequently criticized for imposing an American model of agricultural development on a different society and failing to benefit subsistence farmers, it also constituted an opportune blending of a foundation initiative with the interests of Mexican political and scientific leaders in addressing the country's chronic shortages of corn and wheat. The early MAP research attracted much international scientific interest, leading to the establishment during the early 1950s of Rockefeller agricultural projects in Colombia and Chile and a Central American regional program. By 1961, Rockefeller was cooperating with the ministries of agriculture and agricultural colleges in fifteen Latin American countries. MAP's influence on Mexican society justified such expansion; by that time, HYV of corn and wheat, developed by Rockefeller and Mexican scientists over two decades, had contributed to Mexico's self-sufficiency in food production and an increase in per-capita caloric consumption during a period when the population was growing by 50 percent. Harrar and his colleagues saw MAP as a model for programs in agriculture in other developing areas. They envisioned further collaboration with Mexican scientists in research that would, in the words of Mexico's Secretary of Agriculture, contribute to the "struggle against poverty, misery, and hunger throughout the world." The Mexican government and the Rockefeller Foundation jointly established the International Center for

Corn and Wheat Improvement, which Mexico's president inaugurated with much fanfare in 1963.

That step reflected the Rockefeller Foundation's decision to take what was later termed the Green Revolution to the world. Rockefeller had established agricultural programs in India, Indonesia, and the Philippines, and was exploring opportunities in Africa. Increasingly, its activities concentrated on HYV grain research. With the help of the Ford Foundation, it launched in 1960 the International Rice Research Institute (IRRI) in the Philippines. Over the next decade, the Rockefeller Foundation joint programs with a number of countries led to the widespread cultivation of improved varieties of the cereals in the western hemisphere and large parts of Asia, the Middle East, Africa, and Europe.

Rockefeller's effort to carry the Green Revolution to India brought especially impressive results and illustrated the foundation's capacity to integrate its Indian Agricultural Program (IAP) with Indian interests and to draw on the results of research in other areas. Norman E. Borlaug, the Rockefeller scientist who had developed HYV of wheat in Mexico, toured India's agricultural regions in 1963, which led to Rockefeller's introduction of experimental varieties of wheat that had been tested in Mexico and rice that had been tested in Taiwan and at the IRRI. Ralph Cummings, Rockefeller's director in India, drew on his credibility with Indian leaders to gain their support for introducing the new varieties on an experimental basis. After further research improved their quality, HYV grains were widely adopted. This was an important contribution to India's eventual self-sufficiency in food production.

The much-heralded Green Revolution – a phrase coined in 1968 by a former AID official – promised to transform food production throughout the Third World. It brought Borlaug the Nobel Peace Prize in 1970.

* * *

The foundations' population and Green Revolution achievements occurred as the optimism of the "development decade" was giving way to disillusionment about the applicability of Western models and assistance programs. By the 1970s, the understanding between donor and recipient countries, which had been based on common assumptions about development, was eroding. Third World governments increasingly took a more reserved – if not suspicious – posture toward wealthy foreign institutions bearing supposed gifts and presuming knowledge of their problems. Meanwhile, radical critics challenged the underlying assumptions of development ideology; "dependency" thinking, which emerged among Latin American scholars, saw development as an enduring function of the expansion of capitalism and not as a first step in the process of economic growth.

In addition, political instability in some Third World countries and the disappointing performance of many developing economies challenged the assumptions of prevailing development thought, raising questions in the West about the value of assistance programs. Moreover, even where economic growth met expectations, it seemed to have little effect in addressing the problems of poverty. A World Bank report of 1970 concluded that the prevailing development doctrines concealed the imbalance between the "one third of the world . . . pulling steadily ahead, leaving the remainder of mankind in relative poverty, in many cases to live without clean water, education, basic medical facilities, or adequate housing." Reflecting the prevailing skepticism, Francis X. Sutton of the Ford Foundation observed that "there is growing doubt that we know what to do to bring about development. . . . We are less confident than we once were that the social sciences or tested practice offer ready means of dealing with [development]."

Accordingly, the American foreign-policy elite reoriented its development strategy to promote social-economic equality: "basic human needs." Responding to the "felt needs" of Third World peoples became the compelling priority of interaction with developing countries.

In a notable example of the new thinking, the Rockefeller Foundation modified the UDP – the centerpiece of its Third World activism. Dr. John H. Knowles, who succeeded Harrar as president in 1972, insisted that Rockefeller-supported universities overseas address social problems and policy issues. The UDP was thus renamed Education for Development (EFD) and the University Development Centers became Development Universities. Accordingly, programs moved beyond the conventional teaching and research functions, emphasizing internships, applied research, vocational training, and a range of outreach activities. In Thailand, for instance, Rockefeller joined with the three universities in the UDP/EFD consortium in launching the Maeklong Integrated Rural Development Project, an ambitious effort to provide health care, technical assistance, basic education, and agricultural extension services to a rural area west of Bangkok.

This rethinking of the foundations' Third World mission also elevated the significance of "cultural development," which came increasingly to be seen as an essential "human need" that would help to accommodate developing peoples to the challenge of modernization. The Ford Foundation had generally avoided support for cultural endeavors, but now undertook ambitious efforts in South and Southeast Asia. As one of its officials described the new mission: ". . . the past was [to be] no longer seen as a mere obstacle to modernization, but as a source of dignity and worth, to be explored and constructed in the present and carried forward proudly into the national future." Ford supported museological and historical conservation programs throughout the region, established a fellowship program for Southeast Asian archeologists at the University of Pennsylvania, funded training facilities at institutions like the National Museum in the Philippines and Indonesia's National Institute of Archeology, assisted the archeology department at Gajdah Mada University in Indonesia, fostered the establishment of the Council of Living Traditions in the Philippines, and initiated a program with the Press Foundation of Asia to train journalists in cultural reporting.

These programs took shape as the major foundations were reducing their overseas commitments. The reasons were varied: the war in Vietnam led to a certain disillusionment with foreign involvement and domestic problems highlighted by the urban turmoil and violence of the late 1960s demanded greater attention. The foundations terminated many of their Third World programs; either they had run their course (they were generally intended to be short term) or they did not seem worthy of further investment. With the reduction of American tensions with the Soviet Union and China during the 1980s, culminating in the end of the Cold War, the Third World was no longer considered an ideological battleground, but rather as part of an increasingly interdependent global system. Foundation activities over the last two decades of the twentieth century have shifted accordingly.

* * *

In retrospect, it can be said that the foundations achieved their basic Cold War – driven objectives in the Third World. Their programs contributed to the Western orientation of the preponderance of developing societies. Together with the U.S. government's Fulbright exchange program, the foundations provided educational opportunities that emphasized the American priorities of political stability, steady growth, and gradual social and economic change. Typically, members of Third World elites owed much of their education to American sources, beginning with American-supported universities at home and continuing with foundation or Fulbright-funded training at American universities. Study in the United States typically earned enhanced status at home and was a key to professional advancement. Through the emphasis of social science expertise, the foundations left behind a reliance, in particular, on Western-trained economists, who have played an important role in the leadership and bureaucracies of developing governments. As well, the Ford Foundation's heavy investment in public-administration programs influenced practices and policies in many countries. The Carnegie Corporation–Columbia University Teacher's College collaboration provided one of the most systematic programs of Americanization: personnel at educational institutes at universities in formerly British Africa were trained at Carnegie-funded universities, then typically went to Teacher's College for advanced degrees that conferred prestige and influence when they returned to their homelands.

Like other foreign-assistance efforts, the foundations had their most positive impact when their programs addressed the recipient's "felt needs," were mutually developed in ways that acknowledged the limitations of transferring Western practices, notions of civil society, and institutions, and were implemented in politically stable situations. These factors contributed to the particularly significant impact of the Ford Foundation and Rockefeller Foundation in India. Reviewing in the early 1970s their two decades of work in India, the foundations indeed engaged in self-congratulation. The Ford Foundation titled a study of the IADB *The Right Idea at the Right Time*. In 1972, Rockefeller judged its IAP sufficiently successful to close it after an expenditure of $8 million over twenty years. Harrar stated that programs should be ended "when our investment in money and manpower, etc. have been justified by demonstrable accomplishment"; in sum, he wanted Rockefeller to leave India as "winners." Subsequent scholarly analyses support these judgments. More basically, the HYV of grains took hold quickly in India because Rockefeller's IAP had built a scientific capacity to do adaptive research on food-grain technology, and Ford's IADB had developed a system for spreading the HYV throughout the country. Agricultural production in the IADB districts showed impressive gains. The foundations' impact can be traced to the genuine Indian interest in addressing its agricultural problems, the credibility of the foundations resulting from the quality of their leadership and technical personnel, and the close working relationship between Indians and Americans.

In many respects, however, the record of the foundations was disappointing. For instance, as early as 1977, the Ford Foundation reviewed administrative practices in recipient countries and questioned its investment in public administration. The Ford-funded programs were judged as failing to reach a significant portion of the civil services (a problem exacerbated by the mushrooming of bureaucracies throughout the Third World) and giving insufficient attention to the cultural impediments of exporting Western administrative methods.

As Ford's reservations about public administration suggested, the foundation programs risked cultivating Americanized leaders who viewed their nations' problems from a narrow perspective and lost identity with their own peoples and cultures. With respect to foundation programs in Africa, one critic observed in 1975 that "universities were capable of being at once mechanisms for political liberation and agencies of cultural dependency . . . [because] university graduates, precisely because they were the most deeply Westernized Africans, were the most culturally dependent." To the dismay of their American benefactors, these graduates often accommodated themselves to authoritarian governments that seemed to defy the imperatives of civil society.

Perhaps the most conspicuous failure of the foundations was the jointly fostered and funded UEA, which predictably suffered from national rivalries and the uneven development of the three constituent universities; it survived for only seven years before being disbanded in 1970. Foundation support continued for the separated universities and contributed to the University of Nairobi, Kenya, and the University of Dar es Salaam, Tanzania, but instability in Uganda led the foundations to withdraw from Makere University, which had been the strongest component of the UEA.

Beyond its involvement in UEA, Rockefeller's UDP-EFD program from 1961 until 1983, when it was phased out, repeatedly underlined the difficulties of building select universities. The identification of UDP-EFD universities, of course, triggered resentment from other institutions. Within the select universities, some disciplines benefited from Rockefeller support more than others. National politics in recipient countries affected UDP-EFD universities: Instability and unrest hampered and, at times, curtailed operations; government funding was subject to unexpected cuts. Moreover, the tendency of governments to establish more universities, often in response to regional pressures, reduced their financial support for and the potential national significance of the UDP-EFD universities. Political considerations in the selection of the UDP-EFD centers also affected their impact. Rockefeller occasionally launched programs more because of the strategic significance of the country than the viability and potential of its universities.

The UDP-EFD program had its most positive impact in countries where Rockefeller had been active earlier, political and educational leaders shared the Foundation's objectives, political stability (not necessarily based on democratic practices) prevailed, and American influence generally was strong. In Asia, UDP-EFD projects at the University of the Philippines and the Bangkok consortium (i.e., Kasetart, Mahidol, and Thamassat universities) in Thailand achieved the substance of their objectives, particularly in strengthening economics programs at both institutions, as well as agriculture in the Philippines and basic sciences in Thailand. In Africa, the UDP-EFD at the University of Ibadan in Nigeria was built on a strong base, earlier Rockefeller support, and cooperation with the Ford Foundation and the Carnegie Corporation. In Latin America, the UDP-EFD at the University of Valle promoted gains in the health sciences, engineering, and community health and rural development programs, although the objective of making Valle the nation's primary university was not realized.

Elsewhere, the UDP-EFD record was less impressive. A number of programs simply failed to reach their objectives; political unrest (as was the case at the University of Khartoum in Sudan and the Federal University of Bahia in Brazil) and ill-conceived or hastily established programs (at the University of Zaire and Gadjah Mada University in Indonesia) were the principal reasons. In two cases, programs were so poorly planned that they were abandoned at the exploratory stage; this occurred with a joint University of Chile–Catholic University program and at the Federal University of Minas Gerais in Brazil.

The balance sheet on the foundations' work in the Third World is one of a few significant accomplishments – notably on population issues, the Green Revolution, and the training of national leaders – and a number of disappointing projects. Many programs brought mixed results and others, perhaps especially in the cultural area, defy systematic evaluation. That the foundations contributed to change in the Third World over the last half-century is clear. Had foundation leaders in the 1950s and 1960s been able, however, to foresee the prevalence of poverty and social-economic inequality throughout the Third World at the beginning of the new millennium, they would hardly have been satisfied by the impact of their endeavors.

16

PHILANTHROPY, THE CIVIL RIGHTS MOVEMENT, AND THE POLITICS OF RACIAL REFORM

CLAUDE A. CLEGG III

April 16, 1968, was a pivotal day for race relations in Memphis, Tennessee. African American sanitation workers won a major victory against the city following a two-month strike, which had become a cause celebre for the then-fractured civil rights community. The strikers gained nearly everything they had asked for, including a pay raise and recognition of their union, Local 1733. City Hall even agreed to ban employment discrimination against black workers and to forgo dismissing individuals who had participated in the protest. In the larger macroeconomic picture, such labor victories would soon appear minuscule, dwarfed by the recession of the 1970s, with its stagflation and deficit spending. But on that particular spring day in Memphis, the nation watched high officials bow to garbagemen, who had united against their exploitation and triumphed.

The Memphis strike, while ultimately successful, was carried out at great cost and required an extraordinary commitment from the local community. The protest itself was triggered by the deaths of two black sanitation workers who, after being refused entry into a whites-only lounge, were accidentally crushed to death by their vehicle's trash compactor. Following the union vote supporting a strike on February 12, black Memphians, affected by the tragedy and sympathetic to the strikers, pledged as much as $100,000 to support the families of the protesters. Well wishes and charitable donations also came from outsiders. Walter Reuther, president of the Detroit-based United Automobile Workers union (UAW), conveyed well the empathy of laborers elsewhere by donating $25,000 to the cause. When Martin Luther King, Jr., the most prominent African American leader of the era, arrived in Memphis to champion the strikers' demands, the protest gained national attention, along with issues of race and class that it engendered. King may have best summarized the spirit of the strike and the outburst of compassion that it aroused during an April 3 sermon. "The question is not, 'If I stop to help this man in need, what will happen to me?' " he asserted. " 'If I do not stop to help the sanitation workers, what will happen to them?' That's the question." King's message was as prophetic as it was selfless; he was gunned down by an assassin the following day. Yet, his sacrifice, along with the charitable assistance of others, were the bricks and mortar of an idealistic age with multiple missions. These tumultuous events in Memphis were the concluding act of one of the greatest dramas in the history of American philanthropy and efforts to enhance national civilities.

Of all the events that have swept across the landscape of philanthropic reform in the twentieth century, the Civil Rights Movement has been the most transformative in regard to how Americans think about race and community. Spanning two decades (roughly 1950–1970), this movement employed a variety of tactics and principles – from Christian charity to civil disobedience – to dramatize the desire of African Americans to attain political enfranchisement and economic opportunities. Largely because it invoked traditional American ideals such as individual liberty and partici- patory democracy, the Civil Rights Movement inspired charitable and phil- anthropic impulses across racial, religious, regional, and class lines. Labor unions supported it morally and financially, as did churches, educational institutions, women's organizations, entertainers, and various nonprofit foundations. Most significantly, ordinary people of scarce means offered both personal and financial resources, and regularly risked life and limb to advance the cause.

The personal commitment and moral force behind the movement, along with the enhanced viability of black political power following World War II, gained it the attention of officials at all levels of government. The Demo- cratic Party, which dominated national politics during much of the 1960s, took particular interest in the civil rights struggle, drafting laws that banned discrimination in schools, the workplace, and the polling booth. The most idealistic and arguably the most calamitous part of the government's sup- port of the African American struggle for economic equality and oppor- tunity was Lyndon B. Johnson's Great Society agenda, especially its "War on Poverty." Stifled by the cost of the Vietnam conflict and the right- ward shift of American politics during the late 1960s, this exercise in state benevolence did produce fruits such as Medicare, Medicaid, job training, early-childhood education programs, and fair-housing legislation. But it also delineated very clearly – as did violent urban uprisings throughout the 1960s – the entrenched, systemic causes of poverty and frustration among African Americans, which could not be adequately addressed with limited social programs, antidiscrimination legislation, or even affirmative action.

This chapter focuses on a broad range of charitable and philanthropic institutional endeavors as they relate to the African American struggle for civil rights. Indeed, it merges individual charitable and collective institutional behaviors sometimes involving government as well as nonprofit organizations, under the term *philanthropy*. In the context of the Civil Rights Movement, philanthropy was a crucial part of the broad quest of African Americans for equality and inclusion, and it included governmental assistance in the pursuit of those goals. The efforts of blacks as individuals to aid and empower their own communities, organizations, and lives are, of course, central to this story about the enhancement of American society. Important too are the progressive interracial institutional arrangements that coalesced during the course of the struggle and in the face of sometimes ruthless opposition.

Nuances in charitable and philanthropic activities, most saliently revealed when assessing the motivations and political interests of donors and benefactors, must necessarily be considered within the context of social struggles such as the Civil Rights Movement. Although often motivated by a missionary fervor to realize liberal imaginings of the ideal society, gestures of sympathy and aid toward civil rights activists and organizations were not always selflessly disinterested in origin or purpose. Individual acts of benevolence carried varying moral weight and suggest both potentialities and boundaries. The range of possible motives behind such activities seems to refute any notions of an entirely idealistic philanthropy, untainted by political expediency, economic interests, or the social visions of both donor and recipient. In short, the Civil Rights Movement illuminated the formidable capacity of mass action, liberal idealism, and religious rhetoric to arouse an altruistic spirit among individual Americans and within their institutions. It unveiled, too, the limitations of philanthropy in a postwar capitalist society boldly challenged to countenance and redress its most enduring flaws: racial discrimination and inequality.

* * *

As with most social movements, the Civil Rights Movement and the charitable and philanthropic urges it inspired had antecedents that were the harbingers of the modern crusade against racial injustice. Over the past two centuries, there had actually been a number of civil rights campaigns aimed at acquiring citizenship and statutory equality for African Americans. One of the most notable was the abolitionist movement, discussed earlier in Wendy Gamber's chapter, which culminated with the Union victory in the Civil War and the liberation of black slaves. Subsequent federal benevolence – in the form of constitutional amendments that officially eradicated slavery, enfranchised black males, and codified equal rights for African Americans – revealed the possibilities of a new humanistic relationship between government and freed people. However, as Roy Finkenbine's chapter notes, the resurgence of white supremacist elements in the South and faltering political will regarding federal protection of black rights allowed state governments to subvert many of the gains made after emancipation. By the turn of the century, the reformist egalitarian ethos that the federal government had expressed earlier had waned. Illustratively, the U.S. Supreme Court, in its *Plessy v. Ferguson* decision (1896), completely capitulated to new Southern discriminatory laws, legally crystallizing the doctrine that "separate but equal" was adequate justification for racial segregation.

Emerging from both the reformist zeal of the Progressive era and the racial order affirmed in Plessy, the founding of the National Association for the Advancement of Colored People (NAACP) in 1909 signaled a convergence of charitable and philanthropic strivings among white social reformers and the civil rights agenda of W. E. B. Du Bois and other African Americans. Massive black migrations to northern and midwestern states encouraged the formation of a number of social welfare agencies, such as the National Urban League and African American branches of the YMCA and YWCA. Philanthropic and "uplift" work among black Americans was not confined to one shade of the political spectrum. The racial conservatism of Booker T. Washington, head of Tuskegee Institute in Alabama, enabled his "Tuskegee machine" to become a major conduit for white philanthropic contributions to the black community. His advocacy of industrial education and public acquiescence to segregation and black disfranchisement appealed to many white donors. Additionally, the Universal Negro Improvement Association (UNIA) of black nationalist Marcus Garvey succeeded where others failed by organizing the first all-black, mass-based organization. The UNIA did not only aim to economically and politically empower the African American community, but also to "redeem" Africa from European colonialism. Taken together, these groups constituted a modern iteration of nineteenth-century abolitionist activism and social reform, articulated through media and organizational techniques that presaged later developments.

The New Deal programs of Franklin D. Roosevelt's administration (1933–1945) engaged federal and state governments directly and substantially in relief work, although many of the reforms did not alleviate the plight of African American agricultural workers in the South. Important philanthropic work was still performed by black churches, but there were others who contributed considerable resources as well, from the Rosenwald Fund to the Communist Party. Following World War II, the national government – for the first time since Reconstruction – began to incrementally support legal equality and economic opportunity for African Americans. This development was greatly influenced by pressures from civil rights advocates, concern over the international image of the United States, and slowly shifting racial attitudes. The government's willingness – especially through the courts – to support antidiscrimination policies regarding defense industries, eliminate white primaries, and limit segregation of graduate schools was encouraging. However, including World War II veterans, most African Americans in the South still could not vote, serve on juries, or participate in public life. It was not until 1954, with the Supreme Court decision in the *Brown v. Board of Education* case, that segregation was outlawed in public schools. Only then did the federal government begin to commit itself in a substantial way to black equality, a necessary precondition for the successes of the Civil Rights Movement of the postwar era and the more general enlargement of American civil society.

Although the sweeping Brown decision was heralded by opponents of racial discrimination and segregation as a major civil rights victory, the modern Civil Rights Movement did not emerge full-blown from the halls of the Supreme Court, but instead from individual experiences in small communities. In these locales, ordinary people ignited the protest and activism that generated momentum for the struggle. Not surprisingly, these were also the people who sacrificed the most time, resources, and even physical safety for the advancement of the cause.

In Montgomery, Alabama, the arrest of a black seamstress named Rosa Parks for failing to relinquish her bus seat to a white patron, as the law required, energized a year-long boycott that ended in the desegregation of the bus system. Unlike previous protests of this type in other cities, the 1955–56 Montgomery boycott harnessed the power of the media to persuasively illustrate to the world the iniquities of Southern racism. Organized by a newly founded nonprofit collectivity, the Montgomery Improvement

Association (MIA), and led by a young Baptist minister, Martin Luther King, Jr., the boycott benefited from an outpouring of support from local groups, as well as outsiders.

Black churches were instrumental to the success of the boycott, for many of the mass meetings that inspired people to continue the protest took place there, as did much of the fund-raising. Donations from African American congregations in northern states also buttressed the treasury of the MIA, and with NAACP contributions, the MIA had received more than $4,000 from these sources by May 1956. The Women's Political Council (WPC), a group of professional black women who had been active for years in voter-registration activities in Montgomery, voiced its early support of the boycott. Having successfully pressed the city commission to hire four African American policemen in May 1954, these women were already known for their activism and helped mobilize other segments of the community. White labor and peace organizations, impressed by the nonviolent and honorable nature of the protest, sent funds, the UAW reportedly giving $35,000.

The mobilization of an entire community for bold action against racial discrimination set into motion social dynamics that reverberated throughout the country. Ordinary people, including ministers, seamstresses, domestic workers, and common laborers, stood together in Montgomery and won; the morality of their cause and its expression in dignified, nonviolent protest served as a model for African Americans elsewhere. In February 1960, when the sit-in movement was launched by four college students to desegregate a lunch counter in Greensboro, North Carolina, a similar wellspring of charity and conviction buoyed their protest. As other demonstrations were organized, clergymen, morticians, and business people offered to provide bail money for those arrested during protests. Outside of Greensboro's black community, news of the sit-in aroused humanitarian sentiments akin to the emotions stirred by the Montgomery boycott. "[I]n sitting down," asserted Frank Porter Graham, a former president of the University of North Carolina, the sit-in demonstrators "are standing up for the American dream." Expressing similar admiration, the North Carolina AFL-CIO passed a resolution supporting the protesters, and the North Carolina Council of Churches declared its approval of both the sit-ins and the "self-restraint under provocation" exhibited by the protesters.

Although an exemplary case, the well wishes and sacrifice occasioned by the Greensboro sit-ins were not unique. In countless communities caught in the wave of civil rights activism, progressive voices routinely chorused

against the shrill aspersions of segregationists, even when they were supported by local and state officials. For example, in 1960, in Orangeburg,
South Carolina, when hundreds of students were assailed with fire hoses
and tear gas and then arrested during a sit-in, the black community was
quick to offer assistance. After learning that more than $75,000 in bond
money was needed to free 388 students, sympathizers offered their homes
and other property, valued at approximately $100,000, as collateral to have
the students released. One of the most selfless (and dangerous) commitments to the civil rights struggle came from students in Nashville, who
volunteered to ride integrated buses through Southern states to test a federal ban on segregation in interstate transportation and ancillary facilities.
Several of the students composed wills before departing, but were resolute in their decision "because freedom was worth it." Nurtured by a
similar sense of mission, members of the Student Nonviolent Coordinating Committee (SNCC), a civil rights group organized in the wake of
the 1960 sit-ins, incessantly encouraged local people to act on their own
behalf.

While its presence was evident from the beginning, the role of the black
church in the Civil Rights Movement became more prominent after the
Montgomery bus boycott. In many ways, this development was inevitable,
despite the activities of secular, nonprofit civil rights organizations like
SNCC and the NAACP. Dating back to the American Revolution, churches
were central institutions in African American communities. Shut out of
electoral politics and other avenues of empowerment, blacks turned to
churches for leadership as well as spiritual nourishment. In the context of
the Civil Rights Movement, churches were ideal for organizing protests,
fund-raising, disseminating information, and even fashioning an ideology
of liberation. Regardless of how poor or oppressed a community might
be, there was almost always a religious institution present that held regular
meetings, drew diverse people together, expressed concern for the well-
being of members, and encouraged voluntarism and benevolence. Many
communities, like Montgomery and Greensboro, contained several black
churches that produced talented civil rights leadership. Unlike most other
members of the community, ministerial spokesmen were not susceptible
to economic reprisal for their activism because their salaries were usually
derived from collections.

Given these factors, it is understandable how the black church became
the vehicle through which much of the Civil Rights Movement, especially
on the local level, was organized. Yet, the church still had to cope with

many of the problems common to other reformist, nonprofit organizations. Ideological tensions made cooperation between conservative clergy and liberal activists difficult in some locales, because the former was often reluctant to disturb long-standing social mores or arouse the wrath of the white community. Petty interdenominational disputes and doctrinal differences divided some religious communities; personality clashes and selfish ambitions plagued others. From the beginning, local churches, which often had members directly involved in civil rights protests, were more amenable to aiding the struggle than their national parent organizations, which tended to be sympathetic but aloof observers. Over time, however, the National Baptist Convention and other groups invested a substantial amount of their prestige and resources in the Civil Rights Movement, particularly once it seized center stage of the American political scene in 1963–1964. Despite the initial caution of national religious organizations, local black churches commonly participated in civil rights coalitions, as in the case of the United Defense League (UDL) of Baton Rouge, Louisiana. In preparation for a bus boycott in June 1953, the UDL brought together a half-dozen autonomous organizations and created a rich pool of leadership skills, which optimized efficiency and minimized factionalism. Across the country, vast networks of African American clergymen and congregants shared their experiences in the struggle, eventually constructing a national narrative centered on their faith and duty as Christians.

Generally, the white religious establishment was slow to openly embrace the Civil Rights Movement, particularly prior to the 1960s. Individual clergymen, whether ministers, priests, or rabbis, approved of both the noble goals and nonviolent methods of the movement; however, the overall response of white congregations, both local and national, was lukewarm at best. The National Council of Churches (NCC) typified the early reaction of white Christian organizations to the movement. In June 1952, the General Board of the NCC adopted a "Statement on the Churches and Segregation" in which it condemned racial discrimination and segregation as "diametrically opposed to what Christians believe about the worth of men. . . ." Numerous other resolutions were issued during the decade, one lauding the Brown decision, another praising President Eisenhower's forceful stand against school segregation in Little Rock, Arkansas, in 1957. But taken together, these benevolent measures were effete gestures that went largely unnoticed by those in the trenches of the civil rights struggle.

Once major demonstrations occurred in Birmingham, Alabama, and Washington, DC, in 1963, white religious groups immersed themselves in civil rights work, providing personnel and funding for a number of local and national efforts. In April 1964, the NCC, through its Commission on Religion and Race, issued a call for ministers and laypersons to travel to Mississippi and serve as counselors to civil rights activists. Almost three hundred people heeded the request, including representatives from all the major Protestant denominations, several rabbis, and a few Catholic priests. During their sojourn, the volunteers picketed courthouses, attempted to register voters, and provided instruction at "Freedom Schools and Centers." In a few cases, the depth of their commitment to this humanitarian endeavor was so evident that racists in some communities harassed and even physically assaulted counselors. Most of the volunteers stayed in Mississippi for short periods, and almost all had left by August. For many, this experience was spiritually regenerative, and one minister in particular later remarked that his "profession of faith" mandated that he venture to Mississippi and that "I could not in conscience do other than respond." In addition to those who traveled to Mississippi, other white Christian and Jewish groups concurrently pressured Congress to pass a civil rights bill under consideration. In one of the most creative protests, Protestant, Catholic, and Jewish seminarians held a vigil at the Lincoln Memorial for almost two months until the passage of the 1964 Civil Rights Act in July.

Intertwined with Judeo-Christian concepts of charity, benevolence, and selfless service to a just God was the principle of nonviolence, which was at the ideological core of the Civil Rights Movement. The effective practice of nonviolent protest in the face of savage repression aroused the sympathies of clergymen, politicians, and laypersons like no other American social movement in the twentieth century. Modeled after Gandhi's civil-disobedience campaigns against British colonial rule, nonviolent resistance was grounded in the notion of redemptive suffering. As explained by Martin Luther King, Jr., its most prominent American advocate in the United States:

> . . . nonviolent resistance does not seek to defeat or humiliate the opponent, but to win his friendship and understanding. The nonviolent resister must often express his protest through noncooperation or boycotts, but he realizes that noncooperation and boycotts are not an end themselves; they are merely means to awaken a sense of moral shame in the opponent. The end is redemption and reconciliation. The aftermath of nonviolence is the creation of the beloved community. . . .

For King and others, nonviolent resistance was profoundly moral and eminently philanthropic. Moreover, it was a formidable weapon against evil and injustice, because it elicited the most charitable qualities of the human spirit. Unlike violence, it was not destructive or vengeful; it transcended human nature and reached for higher principles. The power of the nonviolent resister was in his ability to repudiate oppression without resorting to and thus validating the methods of the oppressor. "By appealing to conscience and standing on the moral nature of human existence," SNCC activists proclaimed in 1960, "nonviolence nurtures the atmosphere in which reconciliation and justice become actual possibilities."

Despite its popularity, it would be incorrect to assume that nonviolence was adopted uncritically by the entire African American community as the proper response to racial discrimination, disfranchisement, and violence. In fact, the meaning and utility of this form of protest was constantly debated, even among those who employed it in civil rights demonstrations. King fully embraced the principle of nonviolence, but others – including many SNCC activists of the mid-1960s – came to view it as simply a tactical response to oppression, only as valuable as the results it produced. Black nationalist groups like the Nation of Islam roundly criticized nonviolent protest as cowardly and ill-advised in the face of vigilantism and state-sponsored barbarism. Deadly urban rebellions throughout the Kennedy and Johnson administrations graphically confirmed that many frustrated African Americans in economically depressed cities had never believed in the efficacy of nonviolent resistance. Despite these exceptions, peaceful protests were cornerstones of the Civil Rights Movement. Undoubtedly, the employment of civil disobedience made the struggle politically viable and was largely responsible for the effusion of financial contributions, volunteerism, and goodwill that sustained it.

If the African American church, the philosophy of nonviolence, and the conviction of thousands of ordinary folks constituted the soul of the Civil Rights Movement, philanthropic donations from a variety of supporters were its life's blood. Without funding, the civil rights cause would have stagnated in many locales. Everything from making phone calls and printing leaflets to transporting voter registrants and posting bail for imprisoned protesters required money. In addition to church collections, which raised impressive sums, the contributions of various nonprofit foundations greatly expanded the financial wherewithal of the movement. These contributions helped civil rights organizations to pay staff expenses, coordinate conferences and strategy sessions, and launch increasingly more ambitious projects.

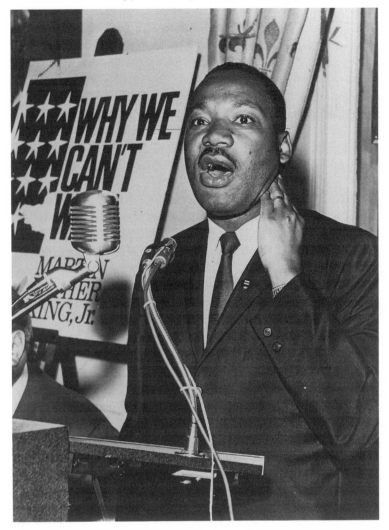

Martin Luther King, Jr., 1964 press conference on publication of *Why We Can't Want.* (Courtesy of Library of Congress.)

The Southern Christian Leadership Conference (SCLC), a ministerial nonprofit organization led by King, benefited handsomely from various foundations. For example, a grant from the Marshall Field Foundation helped the group to manage Citizenship Schools during the early 1960s.

These schools prepared local people for participation in civil rights activities and even provided basic lessons in reading and writings for the illiterate. In 1967, SCLC received an award of $230,000 from the Ford Foundation for its "Ministers Leadership Training Program," which was designed to produce leadership for the Poor People's Campaign of 1968. Along with these contributions, SCLC also won monies from the federal government for civil rights work, including more than $500,000 from the Office of Economic Opportunity, $109,000 from the Department of Education, and $61,000 from the Department of Labor. In essence, the linkage between government and SCLC nonprofit ventures was a strong one.

SCLC was not alone in regard to civil rights groups that secured funding from philanthropic donors. The Congress of Racial Equality (CORE), a more secular organization derived from the pacifist Fellowship of Reconciliation, drew substantial resources from white sympathizers across the country. The NAACP, though it had been forced to close its offices in Alabama, continued to garner a largess of donations from both African Americans and white liberals, especially in the North. In 1962, CORE allied itself with the NAACP, SCLC, SNCC, and the National Urban League to form the Council of Federated Organizations (COFO). This loose merger of civil rights groups, which was supposed to reduce duplication of efforts, attracted donations from a number of sources.

In the wake of the sit-ins and other campaigns, the Kennedy administration sought to steer the major civil rights organizations away from confrontational nonviolent protests and toward voter registration. The Freedom Rides and demonstrations in Albany, Georgia, in 1961 placed considerable pressure on the President to intervene in racially torn communities, a course of action that he believed would alienate Southern white voters. In lieu of taking a firm moral stand against ongoing segregation and discrimination – or simply providing federal protection for civil rights workers – the Kennedy administration, through Attorney General Robert Kennedy, helped coordinate foundation-based support for a voter-registration drive. A rather conservative approach to racial problems, this campaign was politically attractive to the cautious White House. It seemed to both address critics' charges of government indifference to civil rights issues and soothe white Southern fears regarding federal tampering with states' rights and traditions. On a practical level, garnering foundational support for administration initiatives (illustrated by Gary R. Hess's preceding chapter) could be easier to accomplish than successfully shepherding legislation through Congress. Foundations had helped American policymakers obtain strategic support among Third World countries floating between the polarities of the Cold War, and they could quickly be deployed to influence American policy at home. Suspicious of the Kennedys' motives, COFO agreed to embark on securing the franchise for black Southerners, most of whom were not allowed to vote. The offer of foundational monies, although tainted by politics, was simply too attractive to decline.

In early 1962, the Voter Education Project (VEP) was inaugurated. Its stated purpose was to study the causes of and suggest solutions to African American disfranchisement in the South. However, in practice, many VEP workers actually tried to register voters over the two-year life span of the project. The campaign was financed by the Taconic Foundation ($339,000), the Field Foundation ($225,000), and the Edgar Stern Family Fund ($219,000). Smaller contributions came from church groups, labor unions, and private individuals. By November 1964, when the VEP terminated, there were some notable gains: 38 percent of potential Southern black voters were now registered, up from 27 percent. Additionally, nonprofit civil rights groups themselves were enhanced, with SCLC and SNCC tripling their national staffs, and CORE's local branches increasing nearly twofold. Despite these figures, the VEP was not an unqualified success. The campaign was woefully underfunded, and the federal government made no real commitment to it in terms of finances or security arrangements for workers. Even the advances in voter registration were lopsided; most of the new voters lived in the upper South and urban areas. The pool of African American voters in Mississippi increased less than 2 percent, from 5.3 to 6.7 percent of the voting-age population. Finally, the COFO, which had been charged with spearheading the project, rarely worked as uniformly as planned. The major civil rights groups tended to function independently and in line with their individual agendas, with no singular focus on voter registration.

If the Kennedy-inspired VEP produced mixed results and was motivated in part by political expediency, the contributions of other public personalities to the civil rights struggle seemed more beneficent and sincere in contrast. During the summer of 1961, SNCC organized a seminar entitled "Understanding the Nature of Social Change" and invited a number of prominent academics and officials to participate. Among those attending were black scholars such as Kenneth Clark, E. Franklin Frazier, C. Eric Lincoln, and Rayford Logan. Such meetings helped the young activists to transform their unbounded idealism into a more sophisticated understanding of the "forces of the institutional world. . . ." In addition to distinguished academics, the Civil Rights Movement attracted the attention of a number of celebrities. Entertainers such as Nat King Cole, Sammy Davis, Jr., Floyd Patterson, and Marlon Brando donated significant amounts of money to SCLC. In an astounding fund-raising effort, singer-actor Harry Belafonte raised $50,000 during the 1963 Birmingham demonstrations to pay bail for detained protesters. In many instances, the commitment of these individuals was easily discernible, unobscured by any pretensions. "These people came, and they blended in," one participant in the Selma march of 1965 recalled. "They were so perfectly natural. . . . They tended to come down in almost awe of us. . . ."

Interestingly, the most extraordinary and meaningful sacrifices came from average people moved by the moral energies of the movement. There were local individuals such as Herman Bentley of Tuskegee, Alabama, who justified registering African Americans to vote in the 1940s "because of the Scripture I study. . . . I know I'm right because all people are created equal." Similarly, spurred by "a feeling of sickness inside of me that comes from a realization of the suffering of Negroes and the guilt of whites," Myra Ervin, an Iowan woman, encouraged her congressman to support civil right legislation to "make it possible for healing to begin." In Shreveport, Louisiana, African American teachers, fearful of employer reprisals, secretly supplied local civil rights workers "with stencils, pencils, paper, and money." In the wake of the Montgomery bus boycott, Martin Luther King, Jr. was approached by a middle-aged woman and told "My heart and pocketbook are at your disposal. . . ." These charitable expressions by people across the country were commonplace during the Civil Rights era. For each of those recounted here, there are hundreds of other instances of individual benevolence and sacrifice that have neither been recognized nor chronicled. In one of the more intriguing cases, an anonymous woman married to a Ku Klux Klansman occasionally telephoned the SNCC Mississippi office to inform activists of impending violence. It is unknown how many people she may have saved from injury or death. However, her timely warnings were not without risk to herself, for sometimes she concluded the calls suddenly, whispering, "I can't talk anymore; he's in the next room."

* * *

Although never entirely separable from nonprofit civil rights organizations, government support for the Civil Rights Movement was slow to manifest itself until after World War II. Successive administrations, particularly those of Franklin Roosevelt and Harry Truman, pushed for limited reforms in industrial employment and the military, but proposed no overall strategies for eliminating the racism and segregation that subjugated black communities. Furthermore, Congress exhibited little interest in civil rights matters and state governments, especially in the South, rarely took significant steps to improve race relations without being prodded by Washington. Ironically, it was the federal judiciary, which had earlier upheld segregation in the *Plessy* decision (1896), that led the governmental assault on racial inequality.

In addition to outlawing segregation in public education, the ruling in *Brown v. Board of Education* (1954) was redemptive for the Supreme Court. It reversed *Plessy* as it related to state school systems and, for the first time since Reconstruction, committed the national government to recognizing and protecting the rights of African Americans. Even the unembellished language of the decision seemed morally reflective, for it strongly suggested that the Court was not simply preoccupied with legalism, but instead endorsed a broader social ideal and a deep sense of civility. Illustratively, the verdict held that:

To separate [minority children] from others of similar age and qualifications solely because of their race generates a feeling of inferiority as to their status in the community that may affect their hearts and minds in a way unlikely ever to be undone....

We conclude that in the field of public education, the doctrine of "separate but equal" has no place. Separate educational facilities are inherently unequal.

Of the three branches of government, the Supreme Court most consistently supported the rights of black people. When the Civil Rights Movement dissipated, the Supreme Court still routinely sided with African American plaintiffs, as in the *Griggs v. Duke Power Company* decision of 1971. In this case, the Court ruled that individuals need not prove discriminatory intent on the part of an employer. If company policies produced racial disparities in pay, promotions, or workplace climate in general, then the employer could be found liable for racial discrimination in a court of law. While *Griggs* was not as monumental as *Brown*, it revealed a Supreme Court still endeavoring to undo persistent racial inequities.

Although it often appeared otherwise, the Supreme Court did not work in a vacuum when it came to crafting federal statutes regarding race relations. As early as 1941, President Roosevelt – prompted by a threatened march on Washington by civil rights advocates – issued Executive Order 8802, which established the watchdog Fair Employment Practices

Commission. Similarly, President Eisenhower convinced Congress to pass a largely symbolic civil rights act in 1957, creating a Commission on Civil Rights to investigate voting-rights violations. These measures notwithstanding, there was no substantial presidential action against racial segregation and disfranchisement until the 1960s. Only confrontational demonstrations and a looming racial crisis seemed to focus White House attention on civil rights issues.

This observation is quite applicable to John F. Kennedy's administration. During his three years in office, the President was only halfheartedly concerned with civil rights. Although black voters had made his 1960 victory possible, Kennedy did little to accelerate school desegregation and failed to effectively utilize the Federal Bureau of Investigation in civil rights investigations. Even more dismaying to activists, the President appointed at least five segregationists to the federal judiciary and grossly neglected the VEP. In a sense, Kennedy viewed African Americans as another special-interest group, like organized labor or a foreign lobby, and was thus less likely to observe their demands through moral lenses than through the prism of politics.

Despite these shortcomings, Kennedy's record on racial matters was not without bright spots. The administration often moved quickly against some forms of workplace discrimination, especially in government agencies. Executive Order 10925 facilitated the monitoring of contractors in an effort to eliminate racial bias in hiring. Still, Kennedy did not begin to seriously contemplate any major civil rights legislation until widely televised violence against Birmingham demonstrators forced him to intervene in 1963. Only then did the President publicly characterize the civil rights struggle as "a moral issue" in behalf of a fuller civil society and lend the authority of his office to the cause. "[T]he time has come for this nation to fulfill its promise," Kennedy announced to Congress in June. The country has to "make a commitment it has not fully made in this century to the proposition that race has no place in American life or law." Although Kennedy would be assassinated in November before any comprehensive legislation was passed, his rhetoric did set a tone for his vice president and successor, Lyndon B. Johnson, and the nation.

Compared to previous administrations, President Johnson was proactive on civil rights issues. Lingering political pressure from a massive biracial March on Washington in August 1963 certainly prodded him, as did racist terrorism against black children in Alabama and student volunteers in the Mississippi "Freedom Summer" project. Yet, unlike his immediate predecessors, Johnson appeared to grasp the moral legitimacy of the Civil Rights Movement and its significance to America's future. Partially due to his influence, Congress passed an omnibus Civil Rights Act in July 1964. Among other things, it banned discrimination in public accommodations, provided federal assistance for school desegregation lawsuits, and established the Equal Employment Opportunity Commission (EEOC) to fight bias in the workplace. The following year, graphic police brutality against civil rights protesters in Selma, Alabama, encouraged the enactment of the Voting Rights Bill, which effectively guaranteed the right to vote for all Americans. In a March address before Congress, President Johnson captured the new spirit of governmental philanthropy, declaring that the Civil Rights Movement "must be our cause too." In one of the more eloquent speeches of the period, he asserted that "it's not just Negroes, but really it's all of us who must overcome the crippling legacy of bigotry and injustice. And we shall overcome."

Beyond the powerful symbolism of a President publicly endorsing the civil rights cause, a fundamental shift in state policy toward the struggle had occurred by 1965. No longer was the Supreme Court the only major official ally of African Americans. Now, the Executive Branch and the Congress began to fully accept their responsibility for ensuring the rights of all citizens. The Civil Rights Act of 1964 was the fulfillment of the promise of the *Brown* decision, labeling as constitutionally and ethically wrong the use of race to justify privilege or disadvantage. As well, the Voting Rights Act of 1965 gave black Americans a new electoral voice and nullified the political subterfuges that Southern state governments had used for decades to silence them. Above all, these encompassing pieces of legislation transformed the Civil Rights Movement. It became more than a black cause: racial integration was the new social vision of the federal government. Private and government philanthropy had merged for a public good.

For the Johnson administration, grand civil rights achievements were a prelude to even grander social initiatives. Beyond helping African Americans attain a better quality of citizenship, the President also hoped to relieve the distressing economic situation that faced millions of Americans across the country. As part of his Great Society agenda, Johnson initiated a "War on Poverty," which called for a fuller elaboration of the welfare state established by Franklin Roosevelt's New Deal programs. Significantly, economists and government officials who sculpted the program exhibited innovative thinking in regard to poverty. Their approach was novel

Vice President Hubert Humphrey with Martin Luther King, Jr. and Coretta Scott King and Harlem, December 1964. (Courtesy of Library of Congress.)

in its optimistic reliance on modern social science for solutions, as opposed to the traditional conception of poverty as an irresolvable moral dilemma.

To the architects of the War on Poverty, the existence of poor people was less a result of their own personal deficiencies – redressible through social work and private charity – than a systemic problem requiring changes in economic policy. Further, through enacting legislation that confronted "root causes," poverty could conceivably be eradicated once and for all. It was important to factor the poor themselves into the solution, even to empower them with the resources necessary to act on their own behalf. Community groups and institutions, according to Johnson and his planners, were to supplant bureaucratic structures, allowing for more creative and efficient applications of federal funds to local problems. Philanthropic assistance to poor Americans was held as a legitimate, indeed a philanthropic, state obligation, but recipients were envisioned as playing a role in the improvement of their own lives.

Initially, the War on Poverty appeared to have enough momentum to have a considerable impact on the American poor. Between 1965 and 1967, Congress passed 181 bills requested by President Johnson, offering health care to the elderly and indigent, assistance to public education, monies for community development and transit systems, and aid to poor residents of rental housing. The Economic Opportunity Act of 1964 created the Office of Economic Opportunity, which coordinated programs such as the Job Corps, the Neighborhood Youth Program, and work-study programs for college students. Ambitious and far-reaching, the War on Poverty was the most extraordinary expression of state philanthropy since the Great Depression, saving tens of thousands of senior citizens, single mothers, and unemployed people from the worst privations of penury. In an era of low inflation and soaring gross national product, the federal commitment to end poverty seemed more real than at any time in American history.

Unfortunately, the opportunities of the War on Poverty were lost on a tragic and costly military conflict in Southeast Asia, which diverted substantial funding away from domestic programs. Also, conservative critics inflicted serious damage on the political will of the supporters of the administration's initiatives, vocally opposing massive government expenditures to promote the commonweal. By the late 1960s, the Johnson administration, irreparably damaged by its failure to end the bloodletting in Vietnam, fell under the shadow of the resurgent Right. When Richard Nixon won the Presidency in 1968, the Great Society experiment had already withered, along with much of the idealism that produced it. Even private philanthropy (as shown by Peter D. Hall in the next chapter) came under fire, resulting in the 1969 Tax Reform Act, which sought to ensure the financial accountability and political disengagement of charitable organizations.

The War on Poverty ultimately failed, but not utterly so. The myriad of programs that comprised the effort had a notable impact on poor people. Remnants of its arsenal, such as Medicare and Medicaid, remain to this day, and the expectation that government assist the poor in some manner is arguably ingrained in the American psyche. However, the antipoverty crusade was doomed, for it pleased too few people in theory and practice. Shifting political winds, stirred by the Vietnam conflict and waning confidence in liberalism, created both the New Left and a reactionary backlash. Conservatives attacked the War on Poverty for its extravagance, and radicals castigated it as unimaginative and constricted by a blind faith in capitalism. Caught in the middle, Johnson's last year in office was spent almost entirely on the defensive, marked by a paranoia that affected both his judgment and convictions.

For African Americans, the President and his programs received mixed reviews. Undoubtedly, they had benefited from many of the initiatives, and Johnson's civil rights advocacy was unmatched by his predecessors. However, the fiery black insurrections that razed dozens of ghettoes in the wake of Martin Luther King, Jr.'s assassination in April 1968 strongly suggested that the War on Poverty had failed to sufficiently address the "root causes" of the despair that gripped these communities. If anything, it had simply raised expectations that could not be wholly satisfied. Ironically, the eulogy that King desired to be given at his funeral was fitting for both his contribution to the civil rights struggle and Johnson's antipoverty campaign. In a speech two months before his death, King declared:

I'd like somebody to mention that day that Martin Luther King, Jr., tried to give his life serving others. . . . I want you to be able to say that day that I did try to feed the hungry. And I want you to be able to say that day that I did try, in my life, to clothe those who were naked. . . . I want you to say that I tried to love and serve humanity.

In many ways, this memorial is appropriate for all of the individuals who gave their time, resources, and lives to make the Civil Rights Movement possible. It is a testament to a generation's attempt to reimagine its humanity.

* * *

A range of charitable and benevolent activities – charitable, nonprofit, and governmental – affected the course of the Civil Rights Movement, as well as the overarching morality that guided it. In many instances, individual sacrifice and good will at certain junctures were as critical to the movement's success as institutional contributions. This discussion hopefully raises several questions regarding how best to define and understand the term *philanthropy* within a specific social and historical framework. Although there are many possible lines of inquiry, several queries seem to implicitly flow from this study.

Regarding the meaning of philanthropy in a highly politicized context, the attempt by the Kennedy administration to control the militancy of activists with the promise of foundational funding is instructive. The attachment of political strings seems more manipulative than benevolent, and certainly discloses much about the administration's social vision and commitment to civil rights. But this episode also raises pertinent questions: Was the philanthropic benevolence of whites toward black Americans inextricably tied to the ways white moderates and liberals defined the "social good" and civil rights, and thus subversive of alternative strategies and visions that African American activists might have otherwise pursued? Also, does (and should) benevolent giving from one individual or group to another implicitly create a reciprocal relationship where the recipient becomes in some way obligated to the donor? In historical context, motives may ultimately matter less than ends, for registering blacks to vote through the VEP was arguably a humanitarian objective, albeit politically convenient for the Kennedy administration. Nonetheless, motivation is not simply an academic question; it goes to the heart of any definition of charity, philanthropy, or civility.

Other questions raised by the relationship between the civil rights struggle and philanthropy have to do with the government's role. For example, can state enforcement of existing laws and codified constitutional rights on behalf of African Americans – a primary demand of civil rights activists – be considered philanthropic? Moreover, insofar as democratic governments are representative of and financed by the citizenry, what distinguishes state-sponsored philanthropy (like the War on Poverty) from private benevolence simply coordinated and distributed under government auspices? Finally, with a view to the post-Civil Rights era, how have race relations; public-welfare programs; private benevolence; and notions of merit, social justice, and individual responsibility evolved since the 1960s? Hall's subsequent chapter is instructive.

To view philanthropy within the boundaries of the Civil Rights Movement reveals much about the struggle and the people who participated in it. But viewing it from this angle also adds complexity to the issues of charity, philanthropy, and general benevolence. The questions of why people became involved, who benefited, and in what ways are relevant to determining the moral quality of charitable and philanthropic acts. However, it is probably less important to search for philosophical truths or absolute answers to these kinds of questions than to be cognizant of the relationship between motives and ends and the broader societal implications. The larger lessons of civil rights efforts undoubtedly lie in the ways that they highlight nuances in the attitudes of people and institutions undergoing significant social change.

17

THE WELFARE STATE AND THE CAREERS OF PUBLIC AND PRIVATE INSTITUTIONS SINCE 1945

PETER D. HALL

One afternoon in the spring of 1974, Council on Foundations President Robert Goheen – having just read the press release announcing the formation of a blue-ribbon panel on philanthropy to be sponsored by the Department of Treasury and privately funded – dashed off a hasty note to a colleague. "Big problem!" Goheen wrote of the Commission on Private Philanthropy and Public Needs (soon to be better known as the Filer Commission):

> I am not at all sure that this committee with mostly lawyers and other highly institutionalized establishment types are the best qualified – without some leavening – to decide all of these issues important to others that approach this matter from a different perspective. Has charity become all law? Is it irrecoverably committed to lawyers instead of its traditional practitioners?

By the time "traditional practitioners" like Goheen began to lament the shift of philanthropic leadership into the hands of "lawyers and other highly institutionalized establishment types," the transformation of philanthropy into a quasi-governmental domain was already well underway. By the end of the century, as the federal government devolved its functions to states and localities – and they in turn shifted responsibilities to private sector actors – it would become increasingly difficult to discern where government ended and the once-private domain of philanthropy began.

* * *

The philanthropy of today is almost entirely the creation of the past fifty years. Estimated to number about 12,000 in 1940 and 50,000 in 1950, by the 1960s, more than 300,000 charitable tax-exempt entities had registered with the Internal Revenue Service (IRS). By the mid-1970s, this number had doubled. Today they number nearly a million and a half organizations.

To be sure, before 1940, there were tens of thousands of charitable trusts, voluntary associations, eleemosynary corporations, religious bodies, and other entities that would today be classified "nonprofit organizations." Few of them, however, were registered with the IRS, the federal regulatory body that, by designating certain organizations "charitable tax-exempt," relieved them of the burdens of federal, state, and local taxation and offered donors "deductibility" – opportunities to reduce or avoid their tax liabilities through gifts and bequests to charity. Although these tax privileges had been part of the Internal Revenue Code since 1917, before World War II, few Americans earned enough to be subject to income taxation and individual and corporate income tax rates were so low that there was little incentive for organizations to register for exempt status.

All this changed during the 1940s, as the government urgently sought new revenues first to sustain the war effort and later to maintain international peace and military preparedness. In 1942, Congress authorized a universal personal income tax based on withholding and enacted steeply progressive tax rates for individuals and corporations (under these, the higher a taxpayer's income, the greater the tax liability). These created powerful incentives for individuals and corporations to make deductible donations and for nonproprietary organizations dependent on such donations to register with the IRS as charitable tax-exempt organizations.

Although there is some evidence that older organizations – both proprietary and nonproprietary – changed ownership forms and sought exempt status under the federal tax code, studies of organizational populations suggest that the vast majority of the philanthropic and nonprofit entities established after the war were entirely new creations.

Other factors also encouraged the proliferation of exempt entities. Government-funded voucher systems, such as the GI Bill – which provided educational benefits to returning veterans – fueled the founding of new colleges and universities and the expansion of older ones. As America settled into its role as defender of the free world, federal subsidies to higher education came to include scholarships, capital financing and operating support for defense-related teaching and research, and powerful tax incentives to encourage private philanthropic giving. Health care, an industry dominated by government-run and proprietary hospitals before the war, became a predominantly nonprofit domain thanks to federal subsidies for the construction of "voluntary" hospitals; the growth of federally funded health-related research through the National Institutes of Health, the National Science Foundation, and other agencies; and the expansion of public (i.e., Social Security) and private social and health insurance. Before the war, only 25 percent of American hospitals were "voluntaries" (the rest were government-run or operated for profit); by 1960, two thirds had converted to nonprofit ownership. By the 1970s, the federal government had become the largest single source of direct and indirect revenues for nonprofits.

* * *

Curiously, neither average citizens nor policymakers fully understood how profoundly changes in tax policy would affect the architecture and dynamics of economic, political, and social institutions in the postwar years. This was due to a number of factors. First, the nature of the legislative process, especially the reconciliation of opposing interests in Congress and the Executive Branch, ensured that even if policies were based on ideologies or clearly articulated theories, they ultimately emerged in negotiated increments shaped by practical politics and administrative pragmatism.

Second, neither policymakers nor the public possessed capacity to see or understand large-scale institutional change (e.g., there are no reliable figures on the number of unemployed during the Great Depression of the 1930s because the government had no way of collecting this information). Although the federal government had, as early as the 1920s, begun systematically gathering economic and social statistics, the academic social sciences – on whom government depended for policy advice – lacked adequate methods for analyzing these data.

Third, American politicians and policymakers – those best positioned to use quantitative data to inform government action – still conceived of the complex interdependencies of government, business, and society in ways that owed more to the political and economic philosophies of the eighteenth and nineteenth centuries than to the dynamic realities of the twentieth.

Fourth, even as late as the 1940s, American government lacked the capacity to frame policy or track its implementation. The practice of budgeting federal expenditures dated only to 1912. The National Income Accounts – the statistical system that would enable government to envision the scope and scale of national economic activity – dated only to 1939. The establishment of government bodies to interpret and act on these data – the Council of Economic Advisors, the Congressional Budget Office, and related agencies – were not established until after the war. And even then, the lack of technologies that could integrate and analyze large bodies of economic and social data posed a formidable obstacle to their serving as knowledge that was "usable" in any meaningful sense. Comprehensive retrospective data would not become available until 1949, with the publication of the first edition of *Historical Statistics of the United States*.

Nowhere did these conceptual, methodological, and administrative deficits show themselves more powerfully than in the inability of legislators, policymakers, journalists, and academics to discern the character of the welfare state being created after the war.

Economic planners wrote confidently of the necessity for central planning to stabilize the economy, to promote planning, and to facilitate mobilization in the event of war – without more than a hazy understanding of the interrelationships of economy, polity, and society. Although tax policy was being used to stimulate and target private financial and philanthropic activity by the 1940s, there was no systematic assessment of the efficacy of these efforts until thirty years later. As journalist Henry Suhrke would put it after witnessing a series of ill-informed interchanges between a congressional committee and foundation leaders, "someone, somehow, must gather statistics so that we will have an idea of what is going on in the foundation world."

* * *

The unexpected consequences of postwar tax policies emerged early. Because the charitable-organization provisions of the Internal Revenue Code were so vaguely drawn and because the charitable domain (due to the small number of registered entities within) was so unregulated, wealthy individuals, estate planners, and corporations hardpressed by high taxes took advantage of every loophole the law allowed. Some business corporations established foundations, donated all their assets to them (reaping generous tax benefits by doing so), and then leased back the assets, which they operated as exempt enterprises. Others established foundations as holding companies to ensure insider control, to prevent unfriendly takeovers, or to avoid estate taxation. (The privately held Ford Motor Company, for example, passed on the death of its founder to his descendants without paying any inheritance taxes. This was accomplished by reorganizing the firm: voting stock was passed on to family members; a new class of nonvoting stock was donated to a foundation, relieving the estate of tax liability. When the nonvoting stock was sold in the open market, the proceeds made the Ford Foundation the wealthiest charitable grantmaker in the world!) In some instances, charitable corporations purchased control of businesses, for which they claimed tax exemption. (The acquisition of the world's largest pasta manufacturer by the New York University Law School was particularly controversial.) By 1947, Congress – as part of a comprehensive overhaul of tax policy – had begun holding hearings on the use and abuse of exempt entities.

Tax avoidance was not the only aspect of philanthropy attracting congressional attention in the late 1940s and early 1950s. McCarthyism emerged and the liberal political orientation of some foundations and other tax-exempt groups alarmed those concerned about subversive activities. (Accused spy Alger Hiss had been president of the Carnegie Endowment for International Peace, and other foundations were regarded as having been inappropriately enthusiastic about friendship with the Soviet Union, civil rights, economic justice, world peace, and other issues that conservatives regarded as "un-American.") By the early 1950s, congressional committees were holding hearings on the activities of "foundations and other tax-exempt entities."

Although driven in part by Cold War anxieties over domestic subversion, the committees also displayed genuine puzzlement and concern about the growing numbers and influence of "charitable" entities whose activities seemed to go well beyond any conventional conception of charitable, educational, or religious enterprise. Exempt enterprises were being established in great numbers and for novel purposes – but the only language and concepts available to describe the phenomenon were terms like *philanthropy* and *charity* – which, even at that early date, were inadequate descriptors of tax-exempt entities that increasingly were drawing their revenues from government grants and contracts and sales of services rather than from such traditional sources as donations and bequests.

Those within the world of philanthropy were no better equipped than those outside of it to grasp unfolding changes. When major foundations, responding to the pleas of F. Emerson Andrews (the Russell Sage Foundation executive who was at the time the most knowledgeable student of American philanthropy), convened a conference of scholars at Princeton to draft a research agenda for the study of this domain, they could come up with nothing better than the term *philanthropy* to encompass their range of interests.

In retrospect, it is difficult to understand how sophisticated scholars and executives of major organized charities could fail to notice the extent to which such things as multimillion-dollar grantmaking foundations and universities, the national religious denominations, and such new charitable vehicles as community chests and community foundations differed from the voluntary associations celebrated by de Tocqueville a century and a quarter earlier. Whereas their emphasis on the continuities between traditional forms of voluntarism and modern philanthropic enterprise may have been self-serving, it seems more likely that it was due to a failure of vision and a lack of reliable information. (It's worth keeping in mind that systematic compilations of foundations and their assets wouldn't begin until after the Princeton Conference, with the publication of the Foundation Directory in 1960 – and that the IRS would not begin gathering and publishing data on tax-exempt entities until the middle of the decade!)

To Congress's credit, its sustained effort to redraft the Internal Revenue Code in 1954 produced a well-conceived classification of types of organizations eligible for various kinds of exemption. The "501(c)s" – as they became known to tax lawyers – distinguished more than two dozen types of nonstock corporations, including cemetery companies, charities, clubs, co-operatives, labor unions, mutual savings banks and insurance companies, patriotic and veterans organizations, and political parties, each of which was to be accorded particular kinds of tax treatment. Entities representing themselves as charitable, educational, or religious were eligible to receive 501(c)(3) designation, which carried with it complete exemption from corporate income taxes and deductibility of all contributions.

Although an improvement on the Section 101 catchall charitable designation in older versions, the 1954 version of the code left the definition of key terms like *charitable* and *philanthropic* troublingly vague. With minimal reporting requirements and no firm standards governing such things as self-dealing, donor control, and payout requirements, ample opportunity remained for both abusing philanthropic entities and expanding the range of activities that were arguably covered by the term *charitable*.

* * *

If pundits, academics, and policymakers had trouble appreciating the impact of tax policy on philanthropy, they had even greater difficulty understanding the larger dimensions of the institutional transformation they had set in motion. Chief among these was the recasting of relationships between government and private-sector actors once the federal government began routinely exercising its new capacities to influence economic, political, and social life through taxing, spending, and budgeting.

Traditionally, political theory had conceived of the relation between government and the private sectors as oppositional, with expansion of government diminishing private initiative and vice versa. No one foresaw that once the government began using its economic power to favor certain kinds of activity through direct and indirect subsidies and differential tax and regulatory treatment, the relationship between government and private initiative would become increasingly synergistic – so that the increasing scope and scale of government stimulated corresponding increases in the scope and scale of private enterprises of every type.

Undoubtedly Congress – and most Americans – would have preferred to return to the pre-Depression/pre-war ways of governing. But America's new responsibilities as "Defender of the Free World" and "Arsenal of Democracy" not only required the maintenance of a costly international military presence, but also a stable domestic economy capable of mobilizing on a war footing at a moment's notice.

Reconciling this conflict of political nostalgia and unavoidable responsibilities produced a uniquely American type of welfare state. Unlike its European counterparts, which were based on vast centralized bureaucracies, the Americans – ever sensitive to deep-seated suspicion of Big Government – created a different type of welfare state that centralized certain activities (e.g., revenue gathering and policy-making) and decentralized others (e.g., implementation of social welfare and educational programs) to state, local, and private sector actors. This was accompanied by important changes in federal fiscal practices, in which budgeting and spending goals shifted from balancing revenues and expenditures to ensuring that they fulfilled strategic and policy objectives. As Carolyn Webber and Aaron Wildavsky described the shift, the process of budgeting became introspective rather than critical. The question of "How much?" was transmuted into "What for?"

Reorganized financial practices combined with federal economic activism produced new kinds of political relationships in which nonprofit organizations came to play increasingly important roles. With the virtually unlimited revenues available through universalized income taxation and deficit spending (indeed, the government's borrowing capacity itself became an important economic management tool), budgeting ceased to be a zero-sum game in which one agency's gain was another's loss. Despite increasingly sophisticated oversight capacities and the creation of new policy-making and monitoring bodies (e.g., the Council of Economic Advisors, the Office of Management and Budget), the budgetary process became less rather than more centralized. Because most federal policies were implemented not by the federal government itself but by an assortment of agencies that interfaced with states, localities, and private-sector actors that actually carried out these policies, each area of activity developed its own internal and external constituencies: agency officials pushing to expand their resources and prerogatives, congressional and other elected officials who stood to gain from spending and hiring by government agencies, and organized beneficiary groups – "special interests" – that lobbied Congress, contributed to electoral campaigns, mobilized voters, and sought to influence public opinion through advertising and journalism.

In addition to receiving direct and indirect subsidies, nonprofits played increasingly important roles in formulating and advocating for particular policies. As traditional understandings of philanthropy and charity became blurred by the proliferation of new nonprofit entities, advocacy activities that in the past would have been carried on through trade associations came to be the province of national mass membership associations with 501(c)(3) status (e.g., the National Audubon Society, the Sierra Club, and the American Association of Retired Persons). Charitable tax-exempt status not only cloaked the causes these entities promoted in an aura of disinterested public-servingness, but – because donations to them were deductible – also made them attractive to foundations, corporations, and individual donors large and small.

Although classed as membership organizations, these new entities little resembled the national associations of the pre-war decades (i.e., service clubs and fraternal, sororal, veterans, and patriotic groups). The postwar associations had no social dimension: members seldom if ever met face to face, individually or collectively. Membership became a political and financial act, not a social commitment.

In terms of its political role, the emergent charitable tax-exempt universe of the postwar era differed dramatically from its associational domain of earlier decades. In the past, when national associations, foundations, think tanks, and other philanthropically supported entities sought to influence government, they generally did so as outsiders. In the postwar decades, associations – now enjoying the benefits of charitable tax-exempt status – increasingly became – if not extensions of government itself – intrinsic parts of the organizational field of public decision-making. The relationship between the Brookings Institution and the government that produced the Social Security Act in the 1930s was exceptional. By the late 1950s, such relationships were becoming routinized not only on the institutional level (with government contracting with think tanks for all manner of policy and technical services), but also on the individual level (as professional careers moved individuals from universities to operating and grant-making foundations or business corporations to government agencies and congressional staffs – and sometimes to elective office).

* * *

The univeralization of income taxation was a necessary concommitant of the shift in the politics of budgeting and expenditure and the emergence of third-party government that so favored the growth of private giving and the proliferation of foundations and other exempt organizations. Although the income tax had been in place since 1916, few Americans earned enough to have to file returns or make payments to the federal government. Beginning in 1935, the burden of taxation became steadily more onerous. In that year, Congress made tax rates on income and inheritances steeply progressive – placing particular burdens on the wealthy. During the war, Congress universalized the income tax and the practice of withholding and added to corporate liability with a steep excess profits tax. Inevitably, Americans – individual and corporate, wealthy and middle class – became more tax sensitive and this sensitivity began to shape their patterns of charitable giving, estate planning, and other economic behaviors.

Whereas this had the desired effect of encouraging the growth in number and size of foundations and other tax-exempt entities, it also produced an unanticipated political backlash, as the public perceived the tax privileges of the wealthy and the growing wealth of foundations as unequitable. Public disquiet began to come to a head in the 1960s, thanks to congressional gadflies like Texas populist Wright Patman and Harvard professor Stanley Surrey, whom President Kennedy had appointed to head the tax section of the Department of Treasury.

In July 1959, after intense lobbying by the Rockefeller family, the Senate Finance Committee recommended expanding the unlimited charitable deduction provision of the tax code – an item that permitted individuals who gave a certain proportion of their incomes to exempt organizations to entirely avoid paying income taxes. An influential minority on the committee – which included senators Russell Long, Albert Gore, and Eugene McCarthy – issued a sharply worded dissent, charging that the proposal would dangerously erode the tax base by encouraging "a proliferation of foundations . . . established by individuals and families." Noting that 87 percent of the 13,000 foundations then in existence had been created since 1940 and that twelve hundred new ones were being created annually, the senators warned that "at present rates of establishment, substantial control of our economy may soon rest in the 'dead hands' of such organizations, endangering the free choices presented by the marketplace and by the democratic processes of a free government, free economy, and a free society."

What started as an effort to encourage giving by the wealthy soon spun out of control into a broader debate over whether private philanthropy was obsolete in an era when government had assumed primary responsibility for public welfare and whether, if permitted at all, should be limited only to gifts to organizations that could demonstrate broad public support.

Senatorial skepticism was soon joined by outcries from the House, where Representative Patman initiated a series of attacks on foundations that would continue through the decade. His speeches and the published reports of his Small Business Committee received wide press coverage. And public concern was further intensified by bestsellers like Ferdinand Lundberg's *The Rich and the Super-Rich (1969)*, which drew on Patman's findings.

In the face of rising congressional and public demands, the Department of Treasury in 1965 circulated a set of proposals recommending major changes in the rules governing foundations, including prohibitions on business dealings between donors and the foundations they established, limits on foundation control of businesses, restrictions on the deductibility of donor-controlled gifts, and regulation of the representation of donors and their families on foundation boards.

Regulatory enthusiasm fueled the emergence of self-awareness in the fragmented philanthropic domain. Earlier in the century, philanthropic and charitable activists, political reformers, and socially concerned academics had been closely linked through organizations such as the National Conference of Charities and Corrections and the National Civic Federation. But the expansion in the range of purposes of charitable organizations; the growing assumption of welfare responsiblities by government (especially after 1933); and the institutionalization of social work, public administration, and the academic professions – as well as the dying off of the founding generation of American philanthropists and charities leaders – had rendered encompassing networks of this kind obsolete. By the 1930s, academics, professionals, business executives, and charitable administrators organized into specialized associations that represented and articulated their particular interests.

Another factor in this was growing secularization and religious diversity: earlier philanthropic unity had been based on the Protestant beliefs shared by most charitable, educational, professional, organizational, and community leaders. By the 1920s, Protestantism had broken into conservative evangelical and liberal modernist factions. Because Jews and Catholics had been excluded from leadership in the charitable mainstream, they had created parallel philanthropic and charitable organizations. As universities and government became more secular, they attracted academic professionals and civil servants who were increasingly likely to view religion as a divisive and reactionary force.

Organized religion had its own reasons to disassociate itself from secular philanthropy and philanthropically supported institutions. In addition to significant philosophical differences over the nature and purposes of charity, religious bodies (some of which were themselves under attack for their political activities and financial practices) were endeavoring to evade the regulatory tidal wave engulfing exempt entities by the 1960s.

Under these circumstances, unity of purpose even among foundations and the major national charities would prove elusive. In a 1964 memorandum pondering the formation of "a possible national association of foundations," Rockefeller family associate Raymond Lamontagne doubted that the existing contenders for philanthropic leadership – the Foundation Library Center (which published *The Foundation Directory* and a magazine, *Foundation News*), the Council on Foundations (a national trade association that had recently changed its name from the National Council on Community Foundations), the National Charities Information Bureau (a kind of Better Business Bureau for nonprofit organizations and donors), the New York University Conference on Charitable Foundations, or the half dozen regional conferences of foundations – could ever be persuaded either to merge into a single entity or to recognize the "need for and advantages of such an association."

Despite halting institutionally based efforts to frame a common vision of philanthropy's mission and purposes, individuals were weaving networks of conversation and enquiry that would ultimately become the basis for a new understanding of the tax-exempt universe. The most important of these was the 501(c)(3) Group, a loose network of tax lawyers, trade association and foundation staff, and executives of national charities formed to exchange information about the technical dimensions of the tax code as it affected charitable tax-exempt organizations. When the regulatory winds increased in velocity after 1965, the Group began to concern itself with more substantive policy issues.

Pragmatic rather than ideological in orientation, members of the group tended to define issues in economic and legal terms rather than political ones – an approach not shared by the top leadership of grant-making foundations. Word of the group's activities became known to the staffers in the Rockefeller family office. There John D. Rockefeller III – the eldest of the Rockefeller brothers, who had embraced philanthropy as a career – had enlisted in his increasingly anxious search for concepts and organizational vehicles that might reunify the philanthropic community.

The absence of a unified and coherent understanding of contemporary philanthropy became embarassingly evident during congressional hearings on the 1969 Tax Reform Act, which proposed to incorporate many of the suggested reforms of the previous decade. The heads of the major foundations offered coordinated defenses of foundation autonomy, evoking hallowed traditions of American voluntarism and warning against the evils of "government control" and actions that would "discourage individual charitable giving." Their unyielding posture on the one hand and their inability to speak the new economistic language of public policy on the other won them few friends. In the end, Congress adopted tax reforms that restricted excess business holdings, regulated donor control, mandated payout levels, curtailed political advocacy, allocated tax privileges according to tests of public support, and required detailed annual filings of activities from all secular exempt entities with incomes over a certain level.

Ironically, no one in the late 1960s really grasped the changing nature of the eleemosynary universe. Neither the government's tax policymakers nor philanthropy's spokesmen understood the ways in which the peculiar features of America's allocative welfare state had tied government and private sectors together. Each persisted in seeing the other as an autonomous actor: philanthropy's defenders viewed it as endangered by the growth of Big Government; detractors saw it as a threat to economic and political democracy. Although aware of the growing number of exempt entities (thanks to the fact that the IRS had begun tabulating numbers of organizations registered as nonprofit), none comprehended the ways in which the accelerating pace of government expansion correlated with proliferating numbers of nonprofit organizations. Nor – because they didn't understand the differences between traditional donative voluntary associations and contemporary nonprofits (which were increasingly likely to be commercial enterprises supported by user fees and grants and contracts from public and private agencies) – did they intuit the ways in which one of the most significant expressions of the expansion of government was the dramatic growth of the nonprofit domain.

* * *

If passage of the Tax Reform Act of 1969 left most philanthropic leaders in a state of shock, it energized those who understood the urgent need to reexamine and reconceptualize charitable tax-exempt activity – the 501(c)(3) Group and John D. Rockefeller III and his associates.

Even before the ink was dry on the tax reform bill, the Rockefeller collectivity had convened a blue-ribbon commission on foundations and philanthropy, seeking to conduct a broad survey of philanthropic practices. This survey of the opinions and attitudes of foundation leaders proved to be a dead end as far as new ideas were concerned. Another seemingly unrelated Rockefeller initiative – a set of surveys of youth attitudes undertaken as Rockefeller struggled to understand the radical activism on America's campuses and in his own family circle – would prove to be far more productive. By the mid-1970s, he would begin to view grassroots social-change movements with their emphasis on giving and volunteering by citizens as comprising a "second American revolution" based on "private initiatives in the public interest." In doing so, he and his associates began to grasp the extent to which "philanthropy" involved not only giving by the wealthy and grant-making foundations, but also a vast universe of entities that were neither governmental nor profit-seeking.

The 501(c)(3) Group started from a very different set of concerns – primarily focused on tax and regulatory issues as viewed through the lenses of law and economics. Recognizing that any defense of philanthropy would have to be grounded in the new economistic language of public policy, they began reviewing the extant literature on tax policy and charitable giving. Considering it seriously flawed and hopelessly ambiguous, they (with secret funding from the Rockefeller family) commissioned Harvard economist Martin Feldstein, who had previously done insightful work on health economics, to conduct a new study on the question of how tax policy affected giving.

When word of Feldstein's findings, which powerfully affirmed the impacts of tax policy, reached the Rockefeller Family office, John D. Rockefeller III's associates went into action to make sure that their implications became as widely known as possible. Working quietly behind the scenes, they began lining up political support within the Department of Treasury and among key congressional tax policy staff for a "Commission on Private Philanthropy and Public Needs." When this was in place, they set about recruiting those who would serve on the commission, a staff, and the consultants and researchers who would give its activities substance.

The commission was chaired by John Filer, CEO of the Aetna Insurance Company, and included present and former university presidents (i.e., William Bowen of Princeton, Edwin Etherington of Wesleyan, and Elizabeth McCormack of Hunter), representatives of major tax-exempt industries (i.e., Bayard Ewing of United Way, Walter McNerney of the American Hospital Association, and Alan Pifer of the Carnegie Corporation), leading businessmen (i.e., Filer of Aetna, Walter Haas of Levi Straus, Ralph Lazarus of Federated Department Stores, and investment banker C. Douglas Dillon), as well as religious and political leaders (i.e., George Romney and Rev. Leon Sullivan). Carefully balanced politically, religiously, ethnically, and regionally, the only conspicuous omission from the group was foundation leaders. The composition of the group made clear the fact that "philanthropy" was actively being redefined to include donees as well as donors.

Despite the best efforts of Rockefeller and his staff, profound differences in the ways even leading Americans viewed philanthropy became evident early on. Sessions devoted to forging agreement on fundamental principles were stormy. When the Commission issued its recommendations in 1975 under the title *Giving in America: Toward a Stronger Voluntary Sector*, it was accompanied by vigorous dissents from commission members and researchers (which appeared as an appendix to the volume and, at greater length, in the first of the six volumes of research papers the commission would issue in 1977).

Whatever else the commission may have achieved, its single indisputable contribution was agreement on the notion that "philanthropy" was more than just the domain of donors; it was, rather, a "sector" with entities and activities consisting of those covered in Section 501(c)3 of the Internal Revenue Code (notably, it did not, as then defined, include religious bodies or unincorporated voluntary associations).

The commission's report concluded by suggesting the need for continuing study and discussion of the issues and, to this end, recommended the establishment by Congress of a "permanent national commission" – a quasigovernmental entity with "broad public membership" to gather information and shape regulatory policy toward the "nonprofit sector."

Had a Republican been elected to the presidency in 1976, such a body might have been established. But the Carter administration, deeply skeptical of the value of regulatory bodies in which the industries to be regulated were so well represented, declined to pursue the Filer Commission's recommendations. Although disappointed, Rockefeller and his allies were not discouraged. They began working toward the creation of a private organization that could serve as a "common meeting ground" for the diverse nonprofit domain, which could help make it more visible and could effectively represent its interests to Congress and the public. This organization – named Independent Sector (IS) – would be established in 1980.

For continuing research on philanthropy and what was variously called the "independent," "third," or "nonprofit sector," industry leaders turned to academia, hoping that judiciously distributed grants would stimulate useful – and, they hoped, friendly – scholarship. Yale's Program on Nonprofit Organizations, founded in 1978, initially served as both a research center and regranter of funds to scholars at other institutions. Eventually, this function would be assumed by IS's Research Committee, which facilitated the establishment of research centers and teaching programs in universities throughout the country.

Although industry-funded scholarship attracted the most attention, thanks to annual convenings of researchers and philanthropic executives hosted by IS, it had no monopoly on efforts to study philanthropy and related issues. An independent group, the Association for Voluntary Action Research (AVAS), which had been founded in 1972, continued to hold its annual research conferences and to publish what was then the only scholarly journal in the field, the *Journal of Voluntary Action Research*. In 1989, AVAS changed its name to Association for Research on Nonprofit Organizations and Voluntary Action (ARNOVA) and that of its journal to *Nonprofit & Voluntary Sector Quarterly*. In the 1990s, other scholarly and professional associations were established, including International Society for Third Sector Research (ISTR) and the Nonprofit Management Association, and new scholarly journals began to appear, including *Nonprofit Management and Leadership* and *Voluntas*.

* * *

The election of Ronald Reagan marked a major change in the political circumstances surrounding American philanthropy in terms of both its relationships to the major political interest groups and of its understanding of its role in the polity.

Through most of the twentieth century, the American Right had been unremittingly hostile to philanthropy and philanthropically supported organizations. In contrast, when Ronald Reagan declared his intention to slash government social spending, he justified it on grounds that doing so would empower citizens and private groups to meet community needs – which he believed they could do more efficiently, flexibly, and responsively than Big Government. Reagan's proposals proferred both opportunities and threats to the nonprofit sector.

Reagan's conservative rhetoric drew on traditional ideas about the intrinsic opposition of government and private action – and, to the extent that these were still widely embraced by the leaders of American foundations and charities – they were applauded. A measure of the President's friendliness to philanthropy – and of philanthropy's leadership to work with the new administration – was the fact that when the President appointed a Task Force on Private Sector Initiatives to stimulate higher levels of corporate giving, E. B. Knauft – John Filer's right-hand man at Aetna and at the Filer Commission – was selected to serve as its staff director.

On the donee side, there was considerably less enthusiasm for Reaganism. Not only would proposed reduced tax rates be likely to diminish incentives for giving, but major cuts in social expenditure also would cripple nonprofits that had become increasingly dependent on government grants and contracts. These included not only colleges and universities (for which federal funds constituted nearly a third of annual revenues) and human services agencies (for whom direct federal funding constituted nearly all of their revenues), but also virtually all tax-exempt enterprises except religious bodies, which had become to varying degrees dependent on federal largesse. (These fears would be substantiated by the work of Urban Institute researchers Lester Salamon and Alan Abramson. In a 1981 study funded by the 501(c)(3) Group, they provided a sweeping assessment of the likely impact of Reagan's budget proposals, which called attention to the extraordinary dependence of the "independent" sector on direct and indirect government subsidies.)

Relationships between left and right in the realm of philanthropy were not entirely untroubled, however. In the mid-1980s, conservatives in the Council on Foundations rebelled against the efforts of the trade association's liberal leadership to adopt a set of "principles and practices" for member organizations. These included positions that were anathema to the "New Right," including affirmative action, open decision-making, public reporting, and pluralistic leadership. Although the effort to lead conservative grantmakers out of the Council failed, the organization ultimately responded to such threats by moderating its outspoken liberalism.

Another right-left conflict arose in 1985 when San Francisco's Bay Area Community Foundation sought to modify the provisions of a trust that had been left in its care. The trust, consisting of stocks from the inheritance of the widow of an oil company executive, had been established for the benefit of the people of one of California's most wealthy counties. Originally valued at $7 million to $10 million, the oil crisis of the 1970s had driven their value up to $340 million. Believing that this far exceeded the needs of Orange County's residents, the foundation petitioned the probate court to redirect a portion of the funds to meet the needs of other more needy recipients in the Bay Area.

This seemingly straightforward case sparked a bitter national struggle between conservative and liberal philanthropic leaders and scholars, with the former accusing the latter of being "grave-robbing bastards" for trying to alter the donor's intentions on flimsy grounds, while the latter responded that devoting such vast resources to people who really didn't need them constituted "charitable waste." Underlying the sometimes vivid rhetoric were serious issues regarding the question of whether philanthropy was merely a way of enshrining private intentions without regard to public needs – or whether there was a "philanthropic standard" against which the purposes and activities of exempt entities should be measured.

Ultimately, as with the "Principles and Practices" battle in the Council on Foundations, this Buck Trust case was the product of the increasing diversity of the philanthropic universe. Before 1970, almost all large American foundations were located in and around New York and were closely associated with the white Anglo-Saxon Protestant "Eastern establishment" that identified itself with the liberal domestic policies of the New Deal and the internationalist foreign policies of the Truman and Eisenhower administrations.

The postwar decades produced a dramatic transformation in the composition of American elites. Catholics and Jews joined the ranks of the educated and wealthy from which they had been previously barred. The shift of economic power to the South and West in the decades following the war turned these regions into centers of political consequence, while creating huge new fortunes. Many of the newly wealthy embraced conservative political and social agendas.

Although initially resistant to using nonprofit vehicles for advancing their social and political agendas, the crushing defeat of conservative Republican candidate Barry Goldwater in 1964 underscored the limitations of political campaigns – no matter how well financed – as means of influencing public opinion. Recognizing this, wealthy conservatives endeavored to create a conservative counter-establishment and policy elite. By the 1980s, large conservative independent and corporate foundations like Lilly, Pew, Olin, and Smith-Richardson were demanding a voice in shaping the national philanthropic agenda. In the meantime, conservative think tanks – the Heritage Foundation, the Hoover Institution, and the American Enterprise and Cato Institutes – began to serve as policy counterparts to such venerable liberal centers as the Brookings Institute and the Twentieth Century Fund.

* * *

The increasing political diversity of the foundation world precluded national philanthropic organizations like the Council on Foundations and IS from taking a unified stand against the Reagan administration's policies. Its ambivalence would deepen when Reagan's successor, George Bush, kicked off his 1988 presidential campaign with a speech proclaiming a vision of a nation illuminated by "a thousand points of light" representing the voluntary efforts of communities to assist their needy.

The success of conservative revolution moved the Democratic Party to the right. Hoping to woo back the blue-collar and white Southern voters who had abandoned their traditional allegiances to support Reagan – as well as the growing cohorts of right-leaning suburbanites – the party nominated Arkansas governor Bill Clinton, a Southern centrist who embraced a variety of conservative causes, including welfare and education reform, and who spoke eloquently of the importance of philanthropy and voluntarism in American life.

Although the postwar American welfare state was devolutionary and privatizing from its inception (witness the growth of the nonprofit sector after 1950), the terms *devolution* and *privatization* were seldom used before the mid-1980s – and when they were employed before 1992, they were almost invariably associated with Republican rather than Democratic policies and programs. But if the political right supplied the rhetoric for efforts to down-size government, liberals and progressives could take credit for actually implementing large-scale privatization, first through local nonprofit organizations – many of them faith-based – subsidized by Lyndon Johnson's War on Poverty, and later through deinstitutionalization of the mentally disabled and the subsequent creation of a vast system of community-based treatment and care provided by nonprofits operating under contract with state and local governments.

In fact, both left and right among the maturing Baby Boomers, who were taking their places as leaders by the last quarter of the century, shared an aversion to institutional bigness – the legacy of having undergone their formative political experiences during the tumultuous 1960s. Both conservative Christians who felt that federal government policies on school prayer, affirmative action, and civil and reproductive rights and pot-smoking, commune-dwelling draft resisters could easily agree on the evils of big government and the need to build a new social order more oriented to the individual than to the large institution. Even Boomer business people partook of this anti-institutionalist spirit, preferring the risks and rewards of entrepreneurship over the security of careers in large corporations.

Not surprisingly, philanthropy offered both left and right gratifying opportunities for translating private values into public ones without the onus of compromise and accommodation required by political and governmental processes. Writing in 1989, management guru Peter Drucker accurately captured the ethos of participation in the "counterculture of the third sector" when he described how the "nonprofit organizations of the so-called third sector" had become "creators of new bonds of community" for members of a generation that had abandoned "the political culture of mainstream society," where "individuals, no matter how well-educated, how successful, how achieving, or how wealthy" could "only vote and pay taxes . . . only react . . . only be passive." In Drucker's view, philanthropy offered members of the "knowledge class" expressive arenas in which individuals could exercise influence, discharge responsibilities, and make decisions in ways more suited to the desire for self-actualization that was replacing the traditional liberal ethos of service.

Although the continuing shift of education, health, and human services responsibilities from public to nonprofit and for-profit agencies during the 1990s altered the architecture of government, it did not involve significant changes in either the scope or scale of government. The federal government continued to be the chief source of public policy (although it left many of the details of implementation to the states) and revenue (nondefense discretionary spending – a significant proportion of which went to nonprofits – actually increased by 25 percent between 1985 and 1995, a period of supposed government retrenchment, continuing a long-term trend dating back to the 1950s).

* * *

Were Robert Goheen's fears about the impact of efforts by "lawyers and other highly institutionalized establishment types" to reform philanthropy borne out by the events of subsequent decades? In some ways, they were. In significant respects, philanthropy in the second half of the twentieth century did become "all law":

- The reconceptualization of philanthropy as the "nonprofit sector" made it coextensive with the range of entities covered by Section 501(c)(3) of the Internal Revenue Code.
- Efforts to comply with federal regulations and to engage in self-policing to prevent further episodes of regulatory enthusiasm fueled the professionalization of management in a domain that had traditionally been the preserve of volunteers.
- Increasing government subsidy of nonprofit activity, especially in health and human services, reduced the significance of traditional sources of income, especially donations.
- Legal reforms, especially the states' adoption of the American Bar Association's Model Nonstock Corporation Statute, which distinguishes between business and charity, encouraged entrepreneurial management practices and increased commercial activities by charitable corporations.
- Devolution and privatization, by encouraging government contracting with nonprofits, helped to erode the boundaries between government and once-philanthropic enterprises.

However, counterbalancing these changes were others that in significant ways reaffirmed traditional aspects of philanthropy:

- The creation of huge new fortunes in the last twenty years of the century shifted the balance of power in organized philanthropy from philanthropic institutions to the wealthy.
- The defeat of efforts to impose a "philanthropic standard," in freeing the wealthy from dependence on professional advisors and managers, encouraged philanthropic innovation and experimentation.
- The expectation of an extraordinarily large intergenerational transfer of wealth from the "Baby Boom" generation to their descendants renewed

attention to the potential importance of donative financing of nonprofit organizations and activities.

- Increasing values-driven philanthropy by members of evangelical religious groups diminished the significance of tax-based incentives for giving.

At the end of the twentieth century, American philanthropy was dramatically different from what it had been fifty years earlier – but the difference consisted not only of the addition of new elements, but also the reaffirmation of older traditions and practicies. Perhaps the greatest ambiguity in all this change involved the altered nature of government itself: although "big government" of the traditional type is disappearing as it shifts responsibilities to states, localities, and private sectors, it remains far from clear whether moving the public-private boundary constitutes a diminution of government or a functional enlargement of its scale and scope.

EPILOGUE: THE EUROPEAN COMPARISON

WILLIAM B. COHEN

When the Frenchman Alexis de Tocqueville arrived in the United States in 1831, he determined to observe as much about American society as he could. In *Democracy in America*, published after his return to France, he wrote about various aspects of the United States that he had found striking. Among them was the proliferation of associations he had found in each state, city, town, and village addressing the various needs of the citizenry. In Europe, only the state and its agencies, he argued, provided such services. His comparison between countries where the welfare of the citizenry was assured by voluntary groups with a Europe where the state fulfilled these functions was probably overdrawn for effect. Although in America the federal government was absent in the provision of services to its citizens, townships provided a number of services. In Europe, by contrast, local philanthropies were not totally absent either. But certainly it was true that in Europe, enjoying strong religious and state institutions built up for centuries, the welfare of its inhabitants was from early on far more dependent on state and church than was the case across the Atlantic.

As Louis Hartz suggested in his classic study, *The Liberal Tradition in America* (1955), feudalism in medieval Europe had established a strong sense of common responsibilities and institutions that provided at least a minimum of regard for the welfare of others. In contrast, in the New World, bereft of such traditions and institutions, society was seen as less responsible for the well-being of individuals, their fate depending on their own capacities. There are contrasts between the European and American experiences, but there are also parallels, reflecting how even in different environments charity could play analogous roles.

* * *

Charity and philanthropy provided a means to spread convictions, uphold existing institutions, and assert the bond between giver and receiver. In Christian Europe, the earliest examples of organized charity come from the era around the ninth century. Monasteries, in addition to being religious centers, were economic units, owning and exploiting vast tracts of farmland and vineyards. Until the rise of the state in the fifteenth and sixteenth centuries, they were the locus of much of European society. Monasteries provided aid to the homeless, the sick, and the pilgrims who often could not easily be distinguished from the vagabonds who haunted the roads and byways of the medieval countryside. Whereas monasteries played an important role in providing aid to the poor, the aid did not necessarily represent a large outlay for them.

In addition to tithes and the income from their economic activities, the Church received bequests from rich noblemen and the new class of merchants, providing daily provisions of food and drink, but also the founding of hospitals, which was the most common form of philanthropy in the Middle Ages. In the fourteenth century, Paris had sixty hospitals, Florence thirty, and Rome twenty-five. More than 10,000 hospitals existed in Europe at the end of the Middle Ages. These hospitals were not exclusively for the sick, but also were a refuge for the homeless, the aged, the orphans, the chronically ill, the handicapped, and others without the means to take care of themselves. Also, it was not uncommon for pilgrims and travelers to seek shelter in the hospitals. Large amounts of alms were also distributed. In 1355, a rich man in Lubeck provided in his will that alms be distributed to 19,000 people – that was for a population of approximately 23,000 thousand. The bequests to the church or monastic orders that administered aid to the poor often indicated that while taking care of the poor, the church would say mass for the donor's soul, usually joined in prayer by the recipients. In fact, to receive alms, the recipient was required to say prayers for the donor's soul. There was then an expected reciprocity between donor and recipient.

Some donations to the poor were individual, but more important were collective acts of charity, such as those exercised by guilds. Guilds regulated the trade for its members, provided occasion for conviviality, and in many cases in addition to supplying a form of insurance for the here and now by its mutual-aid provisions, also rendered for the hereafter, by giving to the poor – the moral credit flowing automatically to all its members. Northern and central Italy were particularly prosperous in the fifteenth and sixteenth centuries; there, confraternities, or brotherhoods, based on professional membership or in other cases, operating as neighborhood associations, provided aid to the needy. The confraternities were associations that operated as mutual-aid societies, helping each other when sick or unemployed, but they also were spiritual mutual-aid societies. They emphasized piety and pious living and by the good works they performed, won – it was assumed – for its members a common store of merit gaining them divine favor.

The confraternities provided dowries for poor girls, helped finance large civic and religious celebrations, gave alms to the poor, founded hospitals, and built lodging for the poor. At times, they could really make a difference in the lives of the indigent: The brotherhood of San Michele in Florence provided meals three or four times a week for 5,000–7,000 paupers.

The poor person was central to the Christian. He was Christ incarnate. If the poor were welcomed into heaven, the rich man faced more obstacles. Had Jesus not said it was easier for a camel to pass through a needle's eye than for the rich man to gain entry into heaven? Good deeds and charity to the poor, however, it was assumed, assured eternal life. One of the apocryphal books of the Bible, Ecclesiasticus, which was often approvingly quoted, claimed "almsgiving atones for sin." In a twelfth-century testament setting up foundations, a donor indicated his intent: "for the salvation of my soul and the souls of my ancestors and successors." The poor were the means through which the rest of society might gain salvation. St. Eligius declared, "God could have made all men rich, but He wanted there to be poor people in His world, that the rich might be able to redeem their sins." These ideas persisted for centuries; a sixteenth-century merchant in Antwerp who had endowed a hospital carved a plaque on its walls: "Heaven can be won with the strength of the sword, or bought with the power of gold." The rich needed the poor as a means to win paradise, while the poor relied on the generosity of the wealthy to survive. A symbiotic relationship between rich and poor provided for the cohesion of society.

Poverty was a blessing appearing to promise eternal life in the next world. The Franciscans and Dominicans in the thirteenth century celebrated poverty, living on the alms they gathered and being close to the poor, preaching to them and taking care of them. They were a model and a mirror of the values of medieval Europeans.

The saintliness of the poor and the admiration of them withered by the mid-fourteenth century. Europe was hit in the 1340s by the Black Death, which decimated the population by maybe as much as a third. Several results flowed from this catastrophe. The disease was seen as hitting the poor particularly hard, so the poor came to be regarded as diseased and a menace to the safety of others. There was also a labor shortage and anxiety among authorities in towns and in the country that there would not be enough workers available. Third, the Black Death created havoc in the lives of people, leading to large migratory movements, which also unsettled the authorities. As a result, by the mid-fourteenth century, strictures developed against beggary and vagabondage and instead the merits of steady work were upheld.

The poor were no longer seen as blessed but rather as a scourge. In Nuremberg in 1370, begging in front of a church was forbidden. The poor were no longer seen as incarnating Christ. "The Romance of the Rose," which gained a widened audience after the mid-fourteenth century, spoke of the poor in derogatory terms, "Cursed be the hour when the poor was conceived. . . ."

Localities helped their own poor but showed no mercy to beggars from outside the town walls. In Nuremberg, beggars were required to register with the city and carry on them a medallion indicating they had done so. In another German city-Köln in 1403-authorities threatened to cut the ears off and even put to death foreign beggars plying their trade within city walls.

The church seemed unable to cope with the influx of beggars and vagrants into towns. The perceived threat to the social order led increasingly to governmental intervention, especially at the municipal level. Secular authorities cooperated with the Church. In the fourteenth century, municipalities such as Barcelona and Valencia paid subsidies to the Church to run hospitals. Alms boxes were set up in churches. Special poor taxes were raised in Sweden and in Paris. In Turin in Northern Italy, the rich were asked to contribute money to the city's charity fund and a list was made public of those giving to publicize their generosity, while shaming those who had refused.

In the sixteenth century, the increase in population led to its outstripping resources. Cities were growing: Amsterdam had 30,000 in 1530, 115,000 in 1630, and close to 200,000 by the end of the seventeenth century. Lyon's population tripled between 1500 and 1700 from 30,000 to 90,000. London was the largest city in the Western world, with four hundred thousand people by the mid-seventeenth century. The number of poor was on the increase in towns, where they were particularly visible. In Nuremberg in 1525, a third of the population was poor or living close to the poverty line. Unrest was widespread. In the 1530s in the Hapsburg empire, there were 4.5 uprisings a year; in 1529, the poor rioted in Lyon; in England, there were grain riots.

In such a situation, the secular authorities stepped in, taking over from the churches many responsibilities for the care of the poor. Municipalities also started controlling confraternity activities. Some confraternities spent the bulk of their resources on amusements; municipalities began controlling their activities, requiring them to spend on the poor. But there was also a symbiosis between government and these private groups, cities granting subsidies to confraternity charitable activities.

The best example of a civil authority taking responsibility for the welfare of the poor was in the Flemish city of Ypres in 1525. It forbad begging, consolidated charitable resources, and provided aid for those unable to work; the able-bodied were required to toil. Symptomatic of the new attitude and often guiding municipalities in their actions was the Spanish humanist Juan Luis Vives's essay, "De Subventione Pauperum" ("On the Subvention of Paupers") (1526), which held civil authorities responsible for poor relief because they had a duty to preserve public order. Failure to provide assistance could undermine the social order, for the poor "driven by their needs in some cases turn thieves." Children and the ill must be cared for, the able-bodied taught a trade. The poor who did not want to work but were able-bodied could not be allowed to starve but should work. Public works were started to employ the poor. In 1525, they were hired to repair the Paris city fortifications. In the face of catastrophes, municipalities stepped in and played a major role in trying to reduce their impact. When famine struck Turin in 1587, the city in forty days distributed 28,000 pounds of bread, representing a significant expenditure of funds – namely, double that of the city's total yearly budget. The granting of aid solidified the authority of city magistrates. It was common, especially in the Germanies in the sixteenth century, to distribute prints of city magistrates giving charity, underscoring their worthiness.

The new repressive policies against the poor provided cheap labor, forcing into the market the able-bodied and depressing wages, when in the 1540s the economy was expanding. Thus, these welfare measures were not only aimed at the poor, but also served employers' needs for cheap labor. A strong moral dimension was present in these welfare measures; the poor who visited pubs were dropped from the aid rolls. Private donors also often established moral criteria; for instance, the Venetian confraternities gave only to the "virtuous poor," excluding from alms prostitutes and thieves.

In city after city, there was a greater emphasis on differentiating between "the deserving" and "the undeserving poor." Typically, the former were children, the aged, the sick, and otherwise handicapped; the latter were the able-bodied. If widows or abandoned women had child-raising responsibilities, they usually were accounted as "deserving"; men in similar situations were not. The establishment of control over the poor was intended to wipe out poverty. Until recently, it was believed that the Protestant Reformation transformed the care of the poor. It was argued that the Reformation, with its insistence that spiritual salvation did not occur as a result of deeds but rather of faith, reduced the desirability to give to the poor out of hope for eternal life. Thus, it was argued, a harsh system of governmental control over the poor was imposed. But the more severe system had already begun to emerge after the Black Death – more than a century and a half before the Protestant Reformation – in what was still a Catholic Europe. The charitable system established in Protestant-dominated cities beginning in the sixteenth century did not differ markedly from those existing in many Catholic cities at the time. The first wave of Europeans that came to the American colonies in the seventeenth century were English Puritans – a particularly severe branch of Protestantism. American historians believe that the Puritans' strictures against poverty were informed by their religious outlook. Whereas by the seventeenth century most West Europeans, Puritan or Catholic, differed in their attitudes only by degrees – the Puritans were harsher and less sympathetic to the plight of the poor. As Amanda Porterfield makes clear (Chapter 2), it was this English minority that much influenced attitudes toward caring for the well-being of the poor in the American colonies.

* * *

In Europe, much of the aid to the poor was urban-centered. The masses of the poor were easily visible in the urban setting; therefore, providing them with help seemed more urgent. Also capable of forming large unruly crowds, they were seen as a menace to public order. Therefore, most of the welfare services were available in cities. That in turn meant that the rural poor often went to the city in search of alms and the institutional care available. We know far less about the care of the rural poor who, until the end of the nineteenth century, comprised the majority of the needy.

Wealthy landlords and even fairly modest farmers fed passing vagabonds and left parts of their crops for the benefit of scavengers. From the early Middle Ages on, there are also examples of lords of the manor extending loans to nearby peasants, allowing them in harsh years when they had consumed all their grain to acquire seed to plant for the next harvest. Some landowners set up funds in their wills to help with seed money. In some societies, there were formal arrangements for the care of the poor; for instance, in Iceland, the communal authorities assigned the poor to a family, the length of stay being proportionate to the host farmer's wealth. Throughout Europe, most villages owned commons – common land that the poor had access to for grazing or collecting kindling wood. In England, the poor law of 1601 provided care for the poor both in cities and the countryside. England's law was the most comprehensive care system at the time. Each parish was responsible for its poor, providing food, clothing, medical care, and even funeral costs for the "deserving poor." The able-bodied poor, deemed "unworthy," were consigned to workhouses, so that they might recognize the advantage of work over sloth. Institutionalizing the poor was not just a punishment; it was also intended as a form of "re-education," to make them appreciate the virtues of labor. Usually, however, the largest number of residents were the sick, the aged, and the infirm, who rarely could work.

State intervention was intended to make the care of the poor more efficient so as to eliminate poverty or at least reduce the threat the poor represented to the social order. Beginning in the sixteenth century, as territorial consolidation occurred, creating increasingly large territorial units such as Spain, England, or France, the state ruling these territories also became stronger. Monarchs increasingly asserted their authority. The rivalry of states for influence on the European continent necessitated the mobilization of various groups of society, including the poor. By being transformed into productive citizens, the poor could add to the wealth of the state by their labor and their ability to pay taxes. Harshness against the poor increased to force them into useful occupations. On the continent, the poor were confined; they were enclosed in hospitals (which contained not just the poor sick, but also the poor). The first incarceration of the poor occurred in Lyon in 1614. Enclosed, the inmates were to work, producing goods that could help pay for their care. Those refusing to work in the workhouses or hospitals were severely punished. In a workhouse in Amsterdam, recalcitrant workers were locked in the basement, which was gradually filled with water; the inmates who wanted to escape drowning had to exercise themselves constantly to activate the pumps. The severity of the enclosure was intended to make the inmates prefer any occupation but immurement in the hospital or workhouse. Also, the segregation of the destitute was intended to safeguard the rest of society from what was feared might be the bad example of sloth and lack of foresight.

The interest of the state shaped welfare policies. Already in the fifteenth century, the Venetian state stipulated that the almshouses provide aid only to those who promised to serve as galleymen in case of war. In Britain, a number of charities, including private ones, were intended to ensure the recruitment of sailors for the navy. In seventeenth-century Amsterdam, aid was provided for sailors and ship carpenters during the slack season in the winter, so they would be available for the rest of the year, assuring Amsterdam and Holland of its opulence and influence. Population was seen as a source of wealth and power in seventeenth-century Europe. In France, Louis XIV explained that the establishment of foundling homes would allow for population growth: "some could go for soldiers and serve in our armies, and others become labourers, or dwell in the colonies that we are establishing to benefit the trade of our realm."

As the state became more active beginning in the sixteenth century, private giving also increased. In England, philanthropy was part of the culture of the merchant class. By the sixteenth century, acts of charity were expected of individuals who wished to be included in this class and receive the respect it enjoyed. Collective acts, by which a number of individuals joined together in making sources available – such as the confraternity – or groupings of London merchants who by subscription provided funds for a given charitable project – such as building hospitals – was one of the most effective means of philanthropy. By the mid-seventeenth century, 72 percent of the English merchant class was giving to charity, most by subscriptions. There were also some individual acts of great import; for instance, the donation by Thomas Guy, who had made his millions printing the Bible: he gave 250,000 pounds. to found Guy's Hospital in London. The honor of having his name affixed to the largest of the capital's hospitals must have provided some sense of reward for his generosity.

Some gifts, both in England and elsewhere, were more self-serving. For instance, donors to hospitals would specify that a certain number of beds would be reserved for them, members of their family, and/or their do-mestics. In Siena in northern Italy, by the mid-seventeenth century, most private bequests were for donors' own servants rather than unknown poor. Thus, philanthropy was exercised as a form of clientalism. By providing the assurance of care for family members and domestics, the donor secured the well-being of those he cared for, but also asserted his authority as head of family and employer.

Donors competed with each other to see who would be regarded as most generous. They built sumptuous hospitals with imposing facades and impressive stairways, advertising their wealth, power, and charitable spirit. Class respectability also played a role in fueling private charity. Formerly rich and powerful families who had fallen on hard times, the "shamefaced poor," could draw on funds provided by donors anxious to ensure that class status was preserved. The Venetian patriciate provided large amounts of charity to its own who had fallen on bad times – far more, in fact, than their small number warranted. In later centuries, similar practices persisted; in Amsterdam in the first half of the nineteenth century, the "shamefaced poor" received three to six times more aid from charities than the average recipient. In England, analogous efforts were made to uphold the respectability of upper-class members of society who had fallen on hard times. There were, among others, the Society for Relief of Widows and Orphans of Medical Men in London and its Vicinity and the London Clergy Orphan Fund.

Although donors gave generously, they gave with an eye toward institutions enjoying public esteem, rather than necessarily those answering a particularly acute need at the time. Thus, donations were given more frequently to children's hospitals than to those treating venereal disease, although the latter would have met an urgent need at the time. Giving to the latter, it was feared, would encourage vice and debauchery and reflect poorly on the donor. There were fashions in donating. In England in the first half of the eighteenth century, it was in vogue to give to hospitals, in the second half it was not. Although there were few deaf people, it was popular to give to institutions for the deaf. Another object of giving considered highly worthy was the terminally ill. Yet, of course, such a donation made no difference to the ultimate outcome, while other forms of charity could change people's life courses such as nutrition for undernourished children or helping the unemployed find jobs. Children were always popular objects of charity. The aged, on the other hand, who were in serious need until state pensions were established in the twentieth century, rarely received private charities.

* * *

Religion had not lost its force. Many were still giving to charitable causes in the belief that such an act would guarantee them eternal life. In the sixteenth century, another dimension in religion explained the passion for carrying out good works. As a result of the Reformation, two major Christian denominations competed for members. By acts of charity, each side thought it could preserve its own members' loyalty and or win new ones. In cities such as Nîmes in Southern France or Brussels in the Low Countries, where there were both Protestant and Catholic populations, each side aggressively provided aid in a battle for members. In Holland, a nation divided between Protestants and Catholics, both groups vied for souls by their welfare activities. Within Protestantism, there was also competition. For instance, in England the official Anglican Church and the Protestant groups not recognizing its authority, Dissenters and Quakers, launched rival programs to aid the poor. In the nineteenth century, with the development of anticlericalism in Catholic countries, the rivalry for influence between secular and religiously affiliated charitable groups fueled some of the charitable activities, as each side tried to outdo the other in founding schools, child-care centers, and programs of assistance to the poor. Some of these types of religious conflicts also explain American charitable activities, as shown in the chapters by Amanda Porterfield (Chapter 2), Wendy Gamber (Chapter 6), and Mary Oates (Chapter 13).

In terms of personal acts of charity, religion continued to be important all over Europe, as in the United States, in motivating generosity to the poor. In many Protestant countries, evangelicalism – that emphasized the individual's personal responsibility for his faith rather than tradition and sacraments – was a strong force in creating a culture of giving. Evangelicals, when rich, thought of their wealth as a stewardship; to be worthy of it, they displayed responsibility for the well-being of their fellow human beings. Evangelicals fueled reform movements in England such as the Antislavery Society, the Association for the Improvement of Female Prisoners, the Charity School Movement, and many others. Many of the evangelical leaders were active in more than one society and gave generously to several of them. William Wilberforce, best known for his founding of the Antislavery Society, regularly gave away one quarter of his income to seventy different organizations. In England, Quakers – also strongly motivated by their faith – were active in many social causes. Some Quaker families were particularly generous donors, notably the Cadbury family, which became famous as chocolate manufacturers. Cadbury gave away most of his wealth to charitable causes; he bought a newspaper to publicize the lot of the poor and the need for social improvement. Evangelical fervor, important in English philanthropic activities, was crucial in U.S. philanthropy (see the chapters by Robert Gross (Chapter 1), Amanda Porterfield (Chapter 2), and Wendy Gamber (Chapter 6)).

On the continent, Catholicism – in reaction to the inroads of secularism during the Enlightenment and the anticlericalism unleashed by the French Revolution – experienced a renewal of faith. In many cases this renewal included concern for the poor. In 1830s France, Fréderic Ozanam created the Society Saint Vincent de Paul, an order devoted to serving the poor. A traditional Catholic, Ozanam was concerned about the drift of the French working class into irreligion and by his fear of a coming conflict between rich and poor. The personal piety of many prominent Catholic families made them emphasize giving; in France, in Catholic cities such as Lyon and Lille, the entrepreneurial class was known for its philanthropic activities. Although philanthropy was closely linked to religious piety in areas like eastern and northern France, it was not the case in Brittany – an area of great piety but with a weak tradition of giving.

The papacy at the end of the nineteenth century provided a strong impetus for social action to alleviate the conditions of the poor. Pope Leo XIII, in his encyclical "Rerum Novarum" (of new things) – the most significant statement by the Vatican on social issues – decried the misery of the urban proletariate and the increased class animosities developing between poor and rich. The duty of Christians, the Pope reminded his followers, was to carry out social justice; workers should be protected from exploitation: "It is shameful and inhuman to treat men as chattels to make money." Employers should provide fair wages and decent working conditions and the state should intervene on behalf of the workers to see that accomplished. Leo XIII's encyclical reflected earlier social Catholic thinking and also inspired its growth. Social Catholicism flourished in France, Belgium, Germany, Italy, and Spain. Clerics and lay people militated for an improvement in the lot of workers through movements such as the Democratic Christian movement in France, the Opera dei Congressi in Italy, the Catholic trade union movement in Germany, and the Workers' Circles in Spain. Such movements preceded by decades the lay activities of American Catholicism, such as the Catholic Worker Movement founded in 1934 (see Chapter 13).

Religious minorities in a number of countries played an active role in charity work. In France, Protestants – motivated by religious ideals close to those of the evangelicals in England – led philanthropic movements such as the Philanthropic Society, movements to abolish slavery and to reform prisons. French Protestants often were well connected to reform groups in

Britain, transmitting ideas and helping to establish institutions based on models from across the channel.

Jews were active in philanthropy, mostly providing charity for their core-ligonnaires. Such an act, *tsedaka* (justice-charity), represented a religious duty, but also was intended to improve the image held of Jews in most European societies. Antisemites often pointed to poorly dressed and housed Jews, living at the margins of society, as illustrating the degeneracy of all Jews. By improving the lot of poor Jews, philanthropists wanted to make them and Jews in general more acceptable. If the main Jewish philanthropy was aimed at fellow Jews, Jews were also active beyond their number in various charitable groups aimed at the society as a whole. By participating in charitable organizations, Jews had opportunities to mix with people of position whom they might not encounter under other circumstances. In Copenhagen, Flora Abrahamson, daughter of a Jewish merchant, through her many charitable activities won an entrée to Danish high society. For several generations, members of the prominent Jewish banking house, the Lazard brothers, sat on the board of the child welfare organization in Paris; this position confirmed them as members of the elite and won them social acceptance, which, as Jews, they usually would not have enjoyed. In Paris, 20 percent of the sponsors of the Society of Visitors, modeled on London's Charity Society Organization, were Jews. The society was organized in the 1890s when Jews were on the defensive because a Jewish military officer, Captain Alfred Dreyfus, was suspected (wrongly) of spying for Germany. Jews, engaging in charitable work, were particularly eager to display their patriotism and concern for national well-being. In a parallel development in the United States, Jewish charities gave priority to their coreligionnaires; but, in a desire to win acceptance also provided assistance to others (see Chapters 8 and 14 by Kathleen McCarthy and Stephen Whitfield).

Whereas religion still plays a role in acts of charity, a secular nonreligious concept of private giving developed in the eighteenth century. In France, the terms *"bienfaisance"* (beneficence) and *"philanthropy"* came into use, denoting a secular motivation for giving; *charity* was seen as religiously based. In England, words such as *benevolence, sensibility, humanitarianism,* and *philanthropy* became part of the language (see G. J. Barker-Benfield's Chapter 3). The men of the eighteenth-century Enlightenment, the philosophes, saw philanthropy as a natural phenomenon. All humans were capable of a desire to do good and alleviate the suffering of one's neighbors. Philanthropy was not for the philosophe an act intended to make the giver feel better, but rather to improve society as a whole. It was a social act.

Various social groups required philanthropy of its members; for instance, the freemasons. It was a prominent free mason who founded the Philanthropic Society in France in 1780. Its purpose, the society declared, was "to provide for the well-being of our fellow men, to spread happiness, diminish suffering." In many European countries, various societies were established to better the human condition. There were antislavery societies and societies advocating prison reform, special education for the blind and the deaf, and for the alleviation of the poor. As in America, many of the patrons behind these groups were active in several societies; there was often an interlocking directorship in the philanthropic world.

Philanthropists collected statistics and publicized the plight of various groups. Their work made public authorities aware of issues they had not addressed. As a result, in the first decades of the nineteenth century, many governments ended the slave trade, abolished slavery, and instituted new kinds of prisons and methods of caring for the blind, the deaf, and the poor.

The eighteenth century considered humans to be affected by the environment they lived in. Therefore, the poor were regarded as less personally blameworthy for their situation and rather the product of society. Society was seen as responsible. The early eighteenth-century philosophe Montesquieu declared that "the state owes all citizens an assured subsistence." Later in the century, the French statesman Jacques Necker spoke of the need for state intervention to reduce the suffering of the poor, carrying out "the duties of society as a whole toward the unfortunate." And not only Enlightenment ideas, but even new religious movements in the eighteenth century made the same point. In England, Methodism removed the strictures against the poor. John Wesley, the founder of Methodism, declared "The Poor are the Christians." It was, he declared "wickedly devilishly false" to charge that poverty was due to idleness.

The French Revolution of 1789 inaugurated the first regime in Europe to propound the complete eradication of poverty. To be secure from want was a basic human right, "where there exists a class of men without subsistence, there exists a violation of the rights of humanity." François Rochefoulcauld-Liancourt, the leading member of the Revolutionary Assembly working on the problems of the poor, declared in 1790, "Every man has a right to subsistence. The duty of society therefore is to seek to prevent misfortune, to relieve it, to offer work to those who need it in order to live, to force them if they refuse to work, and finally to assist without work those whose age or infirmity deprive them of the ability to work." The Revolutionary

Assembly was strongly motivated by the eighteenth-century ideals of humanitarianism; the state's activities were to be the charitable impulse carried on collectively. While the Revolution proclaimed lofty goals, it relegated the implementation to municipalities. With limited funds, however, only the largest cities could provide any aid, and at that, it was rather modest in nature, of little value for the needy. Yet, the goal enunciated by the Revolutionary Assembly, the obligation of the state to provide for the well-being of its citizens, marked an important turning point – one that would be realized in the post–World War II era when so many European states established the welfare state. If the French and American Revolutions had a lot in common in their fight against tyranny and support for human liberty, none of the leaders of the American Revolution advocated that the state intervene to alleviate poverty. The John Adams depicted by Robert Gross (Chapter 1) provides a telling contrast with Rochefoulcauld-Liancour.

* * *

In Europe, there was often interaction between private and public spheres in providing aid for the poor, and it is impossible to separate the two. Emperor Napoleon granted state subsidies to the private Maternal Aid Society so it could help would-be mothers in distress. French municipalities appointed bureaus of beneficence to dispense aid to the poor. The bureaus were appointed from among prominent private citizens who disbursed funds that came from both the city coffers and private donations and foundations. The income from Lyon's private foundations devoted to care of the poor was so large that the city welfare office, which had access to those funds, ran its operations without any municipal funding. Within the city, many private charities received municipal subsidies to carry out their activities. Independent self-help groups, such as the mutual-aid societies with hundreds of thousands of members, received from time to time major subsidies from the central government in Paris. Usually, government orphanages, hospitals, schools, and welfare offices were staffed by religious brothers and nuns who worked for no remuneration, or at most a very modest one. The service of religious orders represented in Catholic countries a major form of philanthropy. The many government institutions could not have operated without their services.

In Britain, one can find similar examples of the interaction of private charitable institutions and the state. Parish funds set aside to administer the poor law were often allocated to private charities helping the poor. And the poor law administrators were private individuals volunteering their services. In the nineteenth century, private charitable groups established reformatories; after 1854, the British government sent juvenile offenders to these schools, subsidized by the exchequer. Most of the English schools were so-called charity schools, established by private bequests and privately administered. But after 1872, the British government became more intrusive and started regulating them. When at the beginning of the twentieth century, the British state funded insurance provisions, in many cases trade unions and friendly societies were often charged with administering those funds.

There were differences between states in the provisions they made for the poor. In England from 1601 on, the poor had access to aid, but not education; it was the late nineteenth century before education was freely available to all. In Prussia and France, free education provided by the state or local government was furnished much earlier, but poor relief came later. In some cases, activities that in most countries were considered among the duties of the state, were in private hands. In Britain, the Royal National Life Boat Institute, performing a similar function as the coast guard in the United States, was privately funded; in continental European countries, as in America, it was state-funded.

In times of emergencies, different institutions jointly tried to resolve problems. In the 1840s, when want and hunger swept Europe, one third of the extra aid doled out in Holland came from foundations, one third from individual donors, and the remaining third from municipalities (the central government contributed but 1 to 2 percent). In the same crisis in the late 1840s, the city council of Lyon launched a public fund drive to help support the large number of unemployed; the money it disbursed came from its own treasury, but also from countless donors from within the city and across the nation. It would be impossible to untangle private from public in most European welfare activities, for often the central government and the municipalities joined with churches, confraternities, and other private donors to combat poverty.

These patterns of state-private interaction to secure the public weal were by no means limited to Europe. As many of the authors in our book show, there were times, places, and causes when both sectors actively cooperated in the United States. Robert Gross reveals that to be the case in New York in the colonial era, Kathleen McCarthy in the eighteenth century, Roy Finkenbine during Reconstruction, Claude Clegg for the same period and again in the 1960s in regard to the struggle for racial equality, Stephen Warren in regard to Native Americans in the first half of the nineteenth century, and Mary Oates in showing the Catholic Church and the federal government jointly addressing social issues. On the whole, however, this cooperation historically was probably more sporadic and less frequent than it was in Europe.

The evidence is mixed as to whether, when state activities expanded, it discouraged voluntary giving, or the other way around – whether when private giving was up, it discouraged state support. No such clear relationship existed. Charitable activity generally increased in the eighteenth century, when the state came to expand its services, and that continued to be the case in the nineteenth century – an era when the state became even more powerful and philanthropic activities more ubiquitous. However, it was not true in all cases. In France, for instance, there was in the eighteenth century a decline in private giving, while in Italy it remained high, and in Britain it increased significantly. In the following century in all three countries, both public and private expenditures went up; the nineteenth century was an era of unprecedented wealth leading to greater state income and generous outpourings of philanthropy. Yet, the two did not maintain an even pace. Public disbursements toward the end of the century expanded even faster than the private. The private sector's growth was smaller than the public's; the resources the modern state had available to it outstripped what private giving could supply. For the United States, private activity often, compensated for the weak limited intervention of the state (see Chapters 4, 6, and 7 by McGarvie, Gamber, and Finkenbine). Yet, we also have examples of tremendous spurts of private charity when the states' outlays increased; for instance, during the Depression in the 1930s, as David Hammack shows, and overall since the 1960s, both private and public spending on the public weal have increased – although, as in Europe, the private sector represents a modest amount compared to the resources expended by states and by the federal government.

* * *

Beginning in the eighteenth century, privately sponsored charity was favored over that of the state. Liberal economic theory upheld the principle of *laissez-faire*; the economy, it was believed, was self-regulating. By the law of supply and demand, the needs of society would be taken care of. Many liberals (these are classical European liberals as compared to American liberals of the twentieth century, who had a different approach) opposed aid to the poor. The classical economist, Thomas Malthus, declared that "no person had any right on society for subsistence, if his labour will not purchase it." Providing aid to the poor would only worsen their lot, induce them to have more children, depress the labor market, and lead to greater poverty. The social uses of poverty were highlighted by the British economist, Arthur Young, who noted in 1781, "Every one but an idiot knows that the lower classes must be kept poor or they will never be industrious."

Whereas many liberals held on to ideas that conveniently protected their class interests, others appeared to be genuinely worried that state intervention on behalf of the poor would undermine the principles of economics. Many wealthy people believed, however, that by charity they could obviate the need for state intervention. Private intervention was also dictated by the need for class preservation. As one English Victorian argued, "We really can't quite button up our pockets . . . and say to the poor man, 'Starve, it serves you right.' If a pauper cannot but envy us, it is desirable that he should hate us as little as possible." Similarly, a prominent mid-nineteenth-century German liberal warned, "Hunger knows no laws, and no police, justice, or military is as powerful as a hungry crowd's call for bread. The result of widespread poverty is not just individual crime, but also revolutionary movements against the existing order. . . ." And in France, Baron Joseph de Gérando, considered one of the leading European experts on the problems of the poor, warned that the poor posed a threat "to peace, order, health, property"; if society wanted to protect itself, it had to provide some forms of assistance. Philanthropy could assuage class hatred and ensure class harmony; the mayor of Grenoble in 1860 noted that generous giving would lead "the most humble to ask themselves why they should have a social revolution in place of so much effort and devotion [by the rich]." Philanthropy as a means of social control, as Wendy Gamber (Chapter 6) and others remind us, was also a motivation in the United States.

Private giving could directly and immediately benefit the propertied classes. In the industrial English town of Huddersfield, some merchants who funded a dispensary explained their gift as being due to "the importance of the industrious poor to a mercantile District like this." Also, the dispensary ensured "the speedy return of the workman to his labour, diminishing the probable diminution of the loss of life."

There were innumerable motives for middle-class giving. The dispensing of charity was a social marker, a way of defining one's middle-class status, differentiating one from the poor. But it also provided propinquity to the aristocracy. In the nineteenth century, the aristocracy was generally aware of the need it had to display its usefulness to society; one way it did so was by being active in charitable organizations and even heading them. Compared to their number and probably even wealth, the aristocracy was overrepresented in charitable institutions. Membership in these societies gave the middle class the opportunity to mingle with the most prestigious members of society and, hopefully, have accrue to them some of the prestige of being able to rub shoulders with such worthy members. In France, the Philanthropic Society included dukes and princes of the royal house among its members; in Britain, royal princesses served as patrons to the Society Against the Cruelty of Animals. In Germany, Empress Victoria, Wilhelm II's spouse, presided over innumerable charitable activities.

Participation in philanthropic activity was prestigious and could provide a platform for political careers. In the French city of Lyon, nearly all mayors in the nineteenth century had, prior to winning the position of mayor, been members of the local bureau of benficence, the main city organ handing out welfare.

Involvement in philanthropic organizations compensated in countries like Germany for political powerlessness. Although the middle class had the vote (as all adult male Germans did after 1871), they had little influence on public affairs. If there was an elected parliament, government was not responsible to it but rather to the authoritarian Kaiser. Charitable endeavors provided an arena of action for the middle classes. They eagerly engaged in such activity to assert their abilities and right to participate in shaping civil society.

Charitable activity provided prestige and honors that many sought. Rather early on, charitable institutions found that publishing lists of donors encouraged further acts of generosity. Sometimes the wish for publicity favored donations to causes that were of less importance to the well-being of society. In France, donations to French scientific organizations were acknowledged in the national gazeteer, the *Journal Officiel*. As one critic pointed out, more worthy causes such as the mutual-aid societies could have used the funds, but because such donations did not win mention in the gazeteer, they more rarely were the object of philanthropy.

Donations might merit having one's name carved on an institution's walls, one's likeness reproduced in busts, and – if it was large and important enough – a statue in a city park or having a street named after one. When a doctor gave a large donation to the hospital in Nîmes, in southern France, his name was carved into a wall with that of other benefactors, thus "witnessing for eternity his sentiments of devotion and charity for the unfortunate." An observer of French philanthropy in the 1860s thought it was the desire to win favor in the eyes of our fellow humans and of God that propelled private giving: "One wants to leave behind something less perishable than oneself, a living witness which will plead among men for our memory and to God for our salvation." One might see parallel impulses motivating the large generous benefactors in America who affixed their names to some of the larger foundations (discussed by Sealander (Chapter 10), Rosenberg (Chapter 11) and Hess (Chapter 15).

* * *

An unprecedented amount of private giving occurred in the nineteenth century. It was, of course, as a result of the growth of industry and trade – an unprecedented era of wealth and well-being – but also of concentrated misery. Underlying philanthropic activity was an anxiety about the danger of increasing state intervention if the private sector did not meet the needs of the poor. Liberals sensed that the monied class could maintain its position only if it proved itself capable of diminishing the stresses of the capitalist system. In Paris, outlays of charity represented 20 percent of a bourgeois family's expenditures; in 1897, there were 2,700 different charitable organizations in the French capital. Many French provincial cities published volume-long guides to charitable institutions operating within its walls. Although there are no exact figures on charitable giving, contemporaries estimated that private aid to the poor equaled that provided by official municipal organs. In Marseille, there were 450 different private charitable institutions at the end of the nineteenth century – among them the Orphanage of the Sacred Heart, the Institution for Blind Youth, and a trade school for Jewish children.

The most ambitious charity network developed in Britain; except for expenditures on food, charitable giving represented the largest proportion of a British middle-class budget. In London alone, there were 600 charitable organizations by mid-century, and thousands half a century later. The annual income of these organizations from bequests and contributions was larger than the state budgets of many European states – by 1885, higher than the budgets of Sweden, Denmark, or Norway. The largest organized group was the Charity Society Organization (CSO), founded in 1869 and intended to combat poverty.

The CSO was based on a liberal premise that individuals, if given a little help, would be able to stand on their own feet and manage. But after a generation, the CSO members who had had an enormous faith in voluntarism came to understand the extent of poverty and its structural nature. The resources of private philanthropy, they came to realize, would never be sufficiently adequate to combat poverty.

Similar conclusions occurred in many areas of philanthropy. In the large cities of Europe that experienced massive immigration in the nineteenth century, slums grew at an alarming rate. Philanthropists in several countries pioneered efforts to provide cheap and adequate housing for workers. In England beginning in the 1840s, and in France forty years later, housing organizations raised money from local entrepreneurs with bonds yielding interest rates of 4 to 5 percent. They thus appeared to show that a profit, modest though it might be, was compatible with providing for the public good. But because these housing organizations were intended not to have any operating deficits, they could not take risks and would usually only accept as renters workers who earned steady and reasonably high wages. The poorest workers and certainly the unemployed and unemployable did not have access to this type of housing. Although the housing reformers made great efforts, they were totally inadequate in the face of the existing need. The number of units made available by the philanthropic housing societies in London in the thirty years following 1845 would have accommodated the growth of the city's population in six months! Some of the leaders of the housing movement recognized the magnitude of the problem and the incapacity of the private sector to resolve the housing crisis and appealed for state intervention.

In England, there was a thriving network of mutual-aid societies; with millions of members, they provided many services, including pensions. As a result of increasing longevity of its members toward the end of the nineteenth century, the mutual-aid societies faced a crisis – the income they had generated from their members was insufficient to cover the pension payments. The treasuries of the societies were headed toward bankruptcy; thus, state intervention in pensions became desirable. And the mutual-aid societies, which previously had prided themselves on workers' self-sufficiency, no longer opposed state action.

By the end of the century, however reluctantly, many of the most active members of various charitable groups realized that social problems were far too substantial to be resolved by private individuals and required state action. [Such a recognition seems to have occurred in the United States, as David Hammack (Chapter 12) reveals, during the Depression]. Nevertheless, the philanthropists and charity workers played a major role in identifying the issues the state needed to address. The problem of the urban housing supply had been identified by private philanthropists decades earlier. In a number of countries, philanthropists carried out extensive research on the situation of the poor. In Germany in the 1870s, the Social Policy Association, and in England Charles Booth in the following decade and Seebohm Rowntree at the turn of the century, and in France the Social Museum in the 1890s, provided stirring information on the poor. To some extent, at least, the publicity surrounding their reports led to the governmental decision to intervene more forcefully to combat poverty. One of the founders of the French Social Museum, Emile Cheysson, claimed in fact that the purpose of the "Museum" was to influence the legislators. He also noted that the nineteenth century merited the sobriquet the "century of social questions" – not because they were resolved, but for having posed the questions and clarified their extent.

The methods used by the private charitable groups to combat poverty also instructed the state, providing it with models. The Vincent de Saint Paul charities in France had in the 1830s visiting dames investigating applicants for aid, calling on them in their homes, seeing if they were worthy of aid, and offering advice on how better to manage their budgets. The COS supplied "friendly visitors" who performed chores similar to the ladies in France; they also proffered advice on childrearing and proper nutrition. The building societies sent visitors to collect rents and by giving practical advice, they attempted to ensure that the renters would remain or become self-sufficient and thus capable of paying their rent. In France, Germany, and Scandinavia, there were similar individuals who visited and advised the poor. They were the forerunners of a new profession, the social worker; and, as it had been in volunteer days, it was an essentially feminized profession. In Scandinavia, women volunteers served as deaconesses and in Catholic countries nuns tended the sick; deaconesses were the pioneers of nursing. In Britain, Florence Nightingale recruited middle-class volunteers to be nurses and so improved the image of nursing, which until the mid-nineteenth century had been considered a low unskilled occupation. Thanks to Nightingale's efforts, it came to be a respected profession – and in time would be state-funded.

* * *

Because women were not property owners, unless single or widowed, they were less philanthropic than men in the *ancien régime*. In Turin in Northern Italy in the seventeenth century, 22 percent of charitable gifts came from women. More than a third of the bequests were directed toward succoring women: defenseless unmarried young women, battered wives, and widows.

In France, the Maternal Society, founded in the late eighteenth century by noble women, provided aid for mothers or would-be mothers facing economic hardships. So many of the charitable activities of women, as in America (see Kathleen McCarthy, Chapter 8), were aimed at helping women in need.

Women were regarded as uniquely qualified to administer to the needs of the poor and the sick. The late-eighteenth-century French scientist, Cabanis, claimed that "Providence has called women in particular to help infants and indigent mothers, because their sensibility makes it easier for them to overcome the disgust surrounding the squalor of poverty." As G. J. Barker-Benfield argues, in Chapter 3, similar thoughts on the sensibility of women dominated Anglo-American thought beginning in the eighteenth century. Women themselves claimed that they had a special gift for charity work, a natural extension of their role as wife and mother; many Victorians called that gift "'social" or "civic maternalism."

In the nineteenth century, middle-class women were particularly active in charitable activities. The sexual division of labor increased in this era as middle-class men emphasized their role as breadwinners and women were relegated to a "separate sphere," the home. The one activity outside the home that was condoned and even celebrated was charitable works. Elizabeth Fry, Victorian prison reformer, urged women to play a role in society: "I rejoice to see the day in which so many women of every rank, instead of spending their time in trifling and unprofitable pursuits, are engaged in works of usefulness and charity." Fry and many of her fellow charity workers often provided services, particularly aimed at other women. Fry, for instance, worked with female prisoners. But women also served the community as a whole. In Scandinavia, countless women's groups ran soup kitchens, schools for the poor, orphanages, child care centers, and Bible and prohibition societies. In Norway, the Teetotaller's Society had 70,000 members in 1905. In Britain at the end of the nineteenth century, half a million women were working as volunteers in various charity activities. In these activities, women in Europe had worthy competitors across the Atlantic; women played a major role in the Benevolent Empire, as shown in the chapters by Amanda Porterfield, Wendy Gamber, and Kathleen McCarthy.

In Catholic countries, religious orders expanded their services to the sick and the poor. The papacy had favored cloistered existence for nuns, but in the 1840s, it increasingly allowed service-oriented religious orders. The nuns were active in teaching orders and provided care for the poor and sick. In the nineteenth century, the Sisters of Mercy, the Franciscan Sisters of the

Poor, the Sisters of St. Charles, the Daughters of Divine Providence, and the Sisters of Christian Instruction were but some of the new orders that were founded. These orders played a far greater role than male religious orders; in France, female orders were six times as large.

Although universal male suffrage was introduced in France in 1848, in England by increments in 1867 and 1884, and in Germany in 1871, women were excluded from the polity, not receiving the vote until decades later – in Britain and Germany after World War I and in France after World War II. Women were legally excluded from the polity, but they could significantly shape it by good works; charity provided a bridge between the home and the public arena of civil society. Charity work provided the means to prove women's ability to participate as public citizens. In Sweden, the social reformer Frederika Bremer believed that by social action, women could win recognition as citizens and the vote. In many of the Nordic societies, women's charitable groups, wanting to demonstrate female self-sufficiency, excluded males or had a quota as to how many men might be members. Many of the charitable associations women joined helped prepare them for public life; they might be regarded as "schools of democracy." Women, used to being relegated to the home, had to appear in public, speak in public, and organize and run societies that were often quite large. In England, the liberal reformer John Stuart Mill in 1861 pointed to the capacities women had displayed in charity work as proving them worthy of participating in government. Certainly, not all women active in charitable causes favored feminist causes; many opposed female suffrage. But they too had a strong desire to participate in shaping civil society, and this aspiration informed their charity work. As several of our authors reveal, in the United States charitable work was one of the important venues through which women shaped the American Republic and expected in return to be recognized as full citizens by gaining access to the ballot box.

* * *

In Europe, both public and private actions at the local and national level to alleviate social conditions were often inspired by experiments attempted elsewhere. Emulation and borrowing were frequent in the world of welfare and philanthropy. When the North Italian cities founded charity hospitals in the sixteenth century, they emulated those established in France a little earlier. Henry VII of England created the Savoy Hospital to look after the poor, choosing as his model the Santa Maria Nuova Hospital in Florence.

England in turn inspired others; the Scottish Poor Laws were copied after those of England, as was Amsterdam's workhouse. The sixteenth-century Spanish occupation of the low countries led to the emigration of thousands of Protestants who did not want to live under foreign and Catholic rule; they brought to their host countries new models for treating the poor. In London and Scandinavia, resident Dutchmen influenced the establishment of hospitals; the care of the poor in Denmark was patterned after that of Holland. In the eighteenth century, England looked for models for its hospitals to Paris, Lisbon, and Venice.

In France, many philanthropic organizations beginning in the eighteenth century patterned their existence after England's. The Philanthropic Society itself was modeled after that of Britain's, as was the Society of the Friends of Blacks after the Antislavery Society. So were countless societies to reform prisons, improve schools, and other worthy causes. In turn, France inspired reforms in other countries. An institution for juvenile delinquents, Mettray, became the focus of innumerable visits by foreign reformers and government.

In the 1870s, Scandinavia looked abroad for inspiration for many of its social policies. Programs of better housekeeping, intended to help the poor in Stockholm, was inspired by the example of the School of Cookery in London. The city's nurses' training program emulated that established by Florence Nightingale, and Stockholm's public-housing program was based on previous experiments in England and France. Copenhagen created welfare and milk programs for infants of the poor, inspired respectively by examples from Berlin and Paris.

As the wealthiest and most advanced industrial country in the world, Britain in the nineteenth century served more than any other nation as a model for foreign governments and private groups who wanted to improve the lot of the poor. But Britain was not beyond learning from others; in England in the 1870s, the government published a series on the *Poor Laws in Foreign Countries*. When at the beginning of the twentieth century, Lloyd George, the British Chancellor of the Exchequer, wanted to introduce a pension system, his office studied examples from Australia, Belgium, Germany, Italy, New Zealand, and Scandinavia. In 1909, Lloyd George visited Berlin to become personally acquainted with Germany's pension system.

Ideas on social improvement crossed the oceans. The English philanthropist Passmore Edwards, influenced by the Scotch-born American Andrew Carnegie, built public libraries in Britain – twenty-five in the

London area and Cornwell alone. In the years between the Civil War and World War II, American social reformers often looked to Europe for models of how to improve conditions at home. They studied social-welfare programs in Germany, public housing in Britain, adult education in Denmark, and farmer-help programs in Italy. Americans traveled to Europe, visited cities and farms, and tried to emulate the more successful programs they had surveyed, making them the basis of many of the social programs they implemented.

Nations borrowed ideas from each other and, to facilitate communication of ideas, representatives from many states gathered in international congresses. The International Congress on Public Assistance and Private Charity, meeting in Paris in 1900, drew 1,000 attendees. There were many other international groups concerned with public welfare, among them the International Committee on Social Insurance and the International Association on Unemployment.

Several charitable institutions had an international reach. Various European antislavery societies in the eighteenth and nineteenth centuries opposed slavery in the New World and in Africa. Other groups tried to spread Christianity. The London Missionary Society sent missionaries around the world. So did Catholic missionary orders, such as the French Fathers of the Holy Spirit and the White Fathers. Other organizations were purely humanitarian; although leprosy no longer existed in Europe, the National Leprosy Fund was established in London under the patronage of the Prince of Wales in 1889 to eradicate leprosy in Africa and Asia. Paralleling European philanthropy across the seas were American missionary societies beginning in the nineteenth century and foundations in the twentieth century that were active overseas in various endeavors, noted in the contributions of Porterfield, Rosenberg, and Hess.

The regulation of international relations also became an object of private philanthropic organizations. The Swiss Henry Dunant founded the International Red Cross in the 1860s, which provided relief to combatants in war; later, it became also a general relief organization. The Swedish industrialist and inventor of dynamite, Alfred Nobel, left his vast fortune to establish annual prizes "to those who, during the preceding year, shall have conferred the greatest benefit on mankind" in five human endeavors, including peace. The first award of the peace prize was made in 1901, jointly to Henri Dunant, founder of the Red Cross, and to the Frenchman Frédéric Passy, a leading pacifist and advocate of international arbitration.

In the field of peacemaking, Andrew Carnegie was, as Sealander shows, indefatigable.

* * *

Toward the end of the nineteenth century, government both at the local but particularly at the national level, increasingly intervened to alleviate the conditions of the poor. Domestic and international conditions, as well as a growing optimism about the human ability to transform and improve the environment, explain these developments. Industrialization and urbanization created large concentrations of poor that were seen as a threat to the social order. In March 1871, the Paris Commune, understood as a workers' revolution, erupted; in the process, 20,000 workers were slaughtered. Socialist movements burgeoned in many European countries. Violent strikes were common; anarchists, demanding social justice, assassinated heads of state, prime ministers, and many lesser government officials.

Conflict also was common on the international stage. In the last third of the nineteenth century, as competition between nation states heated up, they established large standing armies and unleashed an arms race. Statesmen faced the possibility of an armed conflict.

Governments had a strong sense of needing to appease the social conflict at home by improving the lot of the poor and strengthening their nations by effectively mobilizing the poor, so they would be willing and able to defend the nation in case of war. For both these reasons, the states concluded they needed a large, healthy, and reasonably satisfied population. Health and maternity care and pensions were adopted in France, Germany, and England at the turn of the twentieth century.

In the second half of the nineteenth century, the lot of many impoverished citizens improved. In the cities, slums were cleared and public-health measures eradicated scourges such as cholera. Wages improved, people had more to eat, and more were better clothed. Of course, there was a minority who suffered from the vagaries of the economy. While in the past, such a condition had been accepted as an example of the natural order of things, the increased well-being of the majority of the population made it less acceptable. The terrible poverty millions had lived in for centuries came to offend people. It was seen as an open indictment of society, a sign of incivility – and, possibly, it was remediable.

In the last few decades of the nineteenth century, there had been spectacular examples of peoples' abilities to transform nature and the human condition. Steamships and railroads conquered great distances; voyages, which in the past had taken weeks, now took but days. Mountain gorges were spanned and whole mountains removed if they were in the way. Machines made it possible for a handful of workers to produce what in an earlier day would have taken hundreds of laborers. Strides in medicine reduced smallpox, while progress in public health lessened the incidence of tuberculosis and typhoid. Such feats led to hopes that the application of "scientific" methods to poverty might also reduce or even abolish poverty. In these hopes, Europeans shared in common with Americans the faith in "scientific giving" that Sealander chronicles. The various schemes of visitors to the poor were impregnated with the hope that careful observation and supervision of the needy would resolve their problems. When private endeavors demonstrated their inadequacy, many thought the additional efforts of the growing state would – if not eliminate poverty – at least substantially reduce its incidence. The various state measures taken by European governments in the generation before World War I laid the foundations of the welfare state, which became common after World War II. Private charitable and philanthropic activities represented usually but a modest supplement to the massive resources that the welfare state could mobilize and disburse. Whereas in the past activities of the state on behalf of the poor could be regarded as an act of charity by the authorities, now welfare became part of citizenship; every needy citizen had a right to receive aid. Dwarfed by the state's activities, private charity and philanthropy lost their relative importance. And the state's activities on behalf of the poor were no longer viewed as charitable or philanthropic. An era had ended.

Over the centuries, Europeans had built up strong institutions, such as states and churches, that played an important role in providing for the public weal. When it became clear that the private sector could not alone provide for people's needs the state stepped in with relative ease. In 1883, the Conservative German Chancellor, Otto von Bismarck, provided state financed medical insurance for German workers; more than a hundred years later, America is still unwilling to provide similar services for its people. Even when the private sector does not provide the basic needs many Americans believe that all citizens should have, they are wary of calling upon the state. In that sense, Americans have remained heirs to the revolutionary leaders who believed that the best government is that which governs the least. Such ideas have a weak resonance in Europe.

A strong philanthropic tradition in Europe never negated the need for an active state. Especially with the growth of the state after the late nineteenth century, it seemed far more realistic to depend on it for one's well-being, rather than the various private charitable efforts. Although that was also the case in the United States, there much of the rhetoric belied this reality.

In the 1930s, with the adoption of the New Deal, it looked as if there were to be a convergence between the United States and Europe. Beginning in the 1890s until the 1930s, U.S. reformers looked to Europe for models of change; but as a result of the overwhelming global dominance their country had won after World War II, Americans ceased looking abroad for inspiration. Instead, they embraced a belief in American exceptionalism; many believed the private sector capable of resolving the very problems that in many cases unbridled capitalism had caused. Ignoring the much larger role the state occupied after the New Deal, many Americans continued to claim that a philanthropic impulse marked their countrymen and had the potential to resolve most of the problems they faced. Europeans had long since believed that charity and philanthropy were far too modest to address the array of issues confronting civil society.

SELECTED SOURCES AND SUGGESTIONS FOR FURTHER READINGS

The contributors to this book have drawn on and frequently contributed to the tremendous amount of recent scholarship addressing philanthropy in various academic disciplines. Much of this work, as will be evident, is in journal articles, book chapters, and dissertations. Complete texts devoted to a history of philanthropy are rare. One obvious exception is Robert H. Bremner, *American Philanthropy* (Chicago: University of Chicago Press, 1960, 1988). In addition, David C. Hammack, *The Making of the Non-profit Sector in the United States* (Bloomington: Indiana University Press, 1998) offers an extremely important historic collection of documents with excellent commentary. Good insights into the moral, psychological, and political influences on American philanthropy have been contributed by writers in other disciplines: Robert Coles, *The Call of Service: A Witness to Idealism* (Boston: Houghton Mifflin Co., 1993); and Robert N. Bellah, *Habits of the Heart: Individualism and Commitment in American Life* (New York: Harper and Row, 1985) are examples. Other monographs and collections of essays have attempted to address a more narrow scope of study in American philanthropy. For example, Dwight F. Burlingame, *The Responsibilities of Wealth* (Bloomington, IN: Indiana University Press, 1992), and Jesse Brundage Sears, *Philanthropy in the History of American Higher Education* (New Brunswick, NJ: Transaction Publishers, 1990). Most of the best work remains in academic publications directed to specific time periods, subject matters, and individuals.

CHAPTER 1: GIVING IN AMERICA: FROM CHARITY TO PHILANTHROPY

Two traditions of benevolence – charity and philanthropy – have given rise to separate traditions of scholarship. Historians of the one seldom notice the work of the other. The one exception is Daniel Boorstin, who argued long ago that the Old World heritage of charity gave way in the New World to the practice of philanthropy (*The Decline of Radicalism* [New York: Random House, 1969, Chapter 3]).

Boorstin notwithstanding, American benevolence owes its formative ideas and practices to English models, not only at the start of colonial settlement, but also through the eighteenth and early nineteenth centuries. The classic texts on the English tradition are W. K. Jordan, *Philanthropy in England, 1480–1660: A Study of the Changing Pattern of English Social Aspirations* (New York: Russell Sage Foundation, 1959); and David Owen, *English Philanthropy, 1660–1960* (Cambridge, MA: Belnap Press, 1964). Following the influential interpretation put forward in Max Weber's *The Protestant Ethic and the Spirit of Capitalism*, Jordan maintains that English Protestants broke dramatically with the Catholic resignation to the immutability of poverty and insisted that only the worthy poor deserved aid. That claim, endorsed by Stephen Innes in *Creating the Commonwealth: The Economic Culture of Puritan New England* (New York: W. W. Norton, 1995), is forcefully rebutted by Mordechai Feingold, "Philanthropy, Pomp, and Patronage: Historical Reflections upon the Endowment of Culture," *Daedalus* 116 (Winter 1987), 155–178. A more recent study of philanthropy in eighteenth-century England, Donna T. Andrew, *Philanthropy and Police: London Charity in the Eighteenth Century* (Princeton, NJ: Princeton University Press, 1989), is essential to understanding the ideas and practices that shaped the first ventures of Franklin and his contemporaries in British North America.

A broad view of American philanthropy in the nineteenth and twentieth centuries is set forth in Peter Dobkin Hall, *Inventing the Nonprofit Sector and Other Essays on Philanthropy, Voluntarism, and Nonprofit Organizations* (Baltimore and London: Johns Hopkins University Press, 1992). Thanks in good measure to Benjamin Franklin's initiative, Philadelphia was the center of philanthropy in the eighteenth century, and it continued to support important institutions in the new republic. Chapter 1 draws on Bruce Dorsey, "City of Brotherly Love: Religious Benevolence, Gender, and Reform in Philadelphia, 1780–1844" (Ph.D. dissertation, Brown University,

1993); see also Sydney V. James, *A People Among Peoples: Quaker Benevolence in Eighteenth-Century America* (Cambridge, MA: Harvard University Press, 1963). New England took the lead in benevolence during the generation following the American Revolution. The best study of this region is Conrad Edick Wright, *The Transformation of Charity in Pre-Revolutionary New England* (Boston: Northeastern University Press, 1992). New York City has been the subject of several interesting studies, including Carroll Smith-Rosenberg, *Religion and the Rise of the American City: The New York City Mission Movement, 1812–1870* (Ithaca, NY: Cornell University Press, 1971) and M. J. Heale, "From City Fathers to Social Critics: Humanitarianism and Government in New York, 1790–1860," *Journal of American History* 63:21–41 (1976). The culture of benevolence in the South has received far less attention. Particularly useful are Jane H. and William H. Pease, *The Web of Progress: Private Values and Public Styles in Boston and Charleston, 1828–1843* (New York: Oxford University Press, 1985) and Gail S. Murray, "Charity Within the Bounds of Race and Class: Female Benevolence in the Old South," *South Carolina Historical Magazine* 96:54–70 (1995).

The leading study of the almshouses, orphanages, penitentiaries, and reformatories of Jacksonian America is David J. Rothman, *Discovery of the Asylum* (Boston: Little Brown, 1971). The rise of the benevolent empire is traced by David Paul Nord, "Systematic Benevolence: Religious Publishing and the Marketplace in Early Nineteenth-Century America," in Leonard I. Sweet, ed., *Communication and Change in American Religious History* (Grand Rapids, MI: Eerdmans, 1993), 239–269. Finally, the study of women's history has produced important scholarship on both charity and philanthropy. See Lori D. Ginzberg, *Women and the Work of Benevolence: Morality, Politics, and Class in the Nineteenth-Century United States* (New Haven, CT: Yale University Press, 1990); Christine Stansell, *City of Women: Sex and Class in New York, 1789–1860* (New York: Knopf, 1986); and Suzanne Lebsock, *The Free Women of Petersburg: Status and Class in a Southern Town, 1784–1860* (New York: W. W. Norton, 1984).

CHAPTER 2: PROTESTANT MISSIONARIES: PIONEERS OF AMERICAN PHILANTHROPY

Any study of the role of Calvinist beliefs in the formation and fragmentation of New England communities should start with the works of Perry Miller. Perry Miller, *Orthodoxy in Massachusetts, 1630–1650* (Cambridge,

MA: Harvard University Press, 1933); _____, *The New England Mind: The Seventeenth Century* (New York: the Macmillan Co., 1939); _____, *The New England Mind: From Colony to Province* (Boston: Beacon Press, 1953). Much of the subsequent histories have attempted to explain how social tensions and concerns limited the attainment or perpetuation of "Godly communities." Among them are Edmund S. Morgan, *Visible Saints: The History of a Puritan Idea* (New York: New York University Press, 1963); _____, *The Puritan Family* (New York: Harper and Row, 1966); Paul R. Lucas, *Valley of Discord* (Hanover, NH: University Press of New England, 1976); Joseph A. Conforti, *Samuel Hopkins and the New Divinity Movement* (Grand Rapids, MI: Christian University Press, 1981). Morgan's work should be contrasted with that of David Hall, who contends that the family constituted a strength of Puritanism and not a cause of its decline. David D. Hall, *Worlds of Wonder, Days of Judgment* (New York: Knopf, 1989).

More recent histories have recognized the roles of race and gender in colonial New England's social structures. John Demos, *A Little Commonwealth: Family Life in Plymouth Colony* (New York: Oxford University Press, 1971; orig. 1970); and Philip J. Greven, Jr., *Four Generations: Population, Land, and Family in Colonial Andover, Massachusetts* (Ithaca: Cornell University Press, 1970). Implicitly, these works have disputed Miller's methodology while nonetheless confirming his findings. Both Amanda Porterfield and Laurel Thatcher Ulrich confirm a decline in Puritan community values in the adoption of more capitalistic individualistic values. Porterfield finds a decline in female piety attributed to the rise of humanism in the late 1600s corresponding to a decline in women's social status. Amanda Porterfield, *Female Piety in Puritan New England* (New York: Oxford University Press, 1992). Ulrich contends that women's essential economic roles in early New England enhanced their community status. As capitalism changed women's roles, their status declined. Laurel Thatcher Ulrich, *Good Wives* (New York: Knopf, 1982). This "golden-age thesis" in women's history is seen as romantic and oversimplified by some. Mary Beth Norton, "The Evolution of White Women's Experience in Early America," *American Historical Review*, 89-3:593–619 (June, 1984).

Missionary efforts at home and abroad emanated from these Calvinist communities. For background in American Protestant missionary history, see William R. Hutchison, *Errand to the World: American Protestant Thought and Foreign Missions* (Chicago: University of Chicago Press, 1987); Amanda Porterfield, *Mary Lyon and the Mount Holyoke Missionaries* (New York: Oxford University Press, 1997); R. Pierce Beaver, *All Loves Excelling:*

American Protestant Women in World Mission (Grand Rapids: William B. Eerdmans, 1968); Clifton Jackson Phillips, *Protestant America and the Pagan World: The First Half Century of the American Board of Commissioners for Foreign Missions, 1810–1860* (Cambridge, MA: Harvard University Press, 1969); Joel A. Carpenter and Wilbert R. Schenk, eds., *Earthen Vessels: American Evangelicals and Foreign Missions, 1880–1980* (Grand Rapids: William B. Eerdmans, 1990); and Paul William Harris, *Missionaries, Martyrs, and Modernizers: Autobiography and Reform Thought in American Protestant Missions*, 2 vols. University of Michigan Ph.D. Dissertation, 1986.

For discussion of American Protestant missions abroad, see Sushil Madhava Pathak, *American Missionaries and Hinduism: A Study of Their Contacts from 1813 to 1910* (Delhi: Munshiram Monoharlal, 1967); Norman Etherington, *Preachers, Peasants, and Politics in Southeast Africa, 1835–1860: African Christian Communities in Natal, Pondoland, and Zululand* (London: Royal Historical Society, 1978); John K. Fairbank, ed., *The Missionary Enterprise in China and America* (Cambridge, MA: Harvard University Press, 1974); Jane Hunter, *The Gospel of Gentility: American Women Missionaries in Turn-of-the-Century China* (New Haven: Yale University Press, 1984); John Joseph, *The Nestorians and Their Muslim Neighbors: A Study of Western Influence on Their Relations* (Princeton: Princeton University Press, 1961); and George F. Kennan, *Foreign Policy and Christian Conscience* (Philadelphia: American Friends Service Committee, 1959).

CHAPTER 3: THE ORIGINS OF ANGLO-AMERICAN SENSIBILITY

This chapter, as well as *The Culture of Sensibility*, are conceptually indebted to Donald B. Meyer's seminal work, *Sex and Power: The Rise of Women in America, Russia, Sweden, and Italy* (Middletown, CT: Wesleyan University Press, 1987).

The best general account of sensibility in Britain is Barker-Benfield, *The Culture of Sensibility: Sex and Society in Eighteenth-Century Britain* (Chicago: University of Chicago Press, 1992), which draws on Paul Langford, *A Polite and Commercial People, England, 1727–1783* (Oxford: Clarendon Press, 1986). Janet Todd, *Sensibility: An Introduction* (New York: Methuen, 1986), is very helpful to students; see also, Chris Jones, *Radical Sensibility: Literature in the 1790s* (New York: Routledge, 1993). A valuable introduction to the history of sensibility in America is Norman Fiering,

"Irresistible Compassion: An Aspect of Eighteenth-Century Sympathy and Humanitarianism," *Journal of the History of Ideas*, 37 (1976). Gordon Wood, *The Radicalism of the American Revolution* (New York: Vintage Books, 1991) integrates the history of sensibility in America with the history of society and politics, as Langford does for British history. Regarding more specific issues addressed in this chapter, an old but useful biography is D. L. Howard, *John Howard: Prison Reformer* (New York: Archer House, 1958). The history of consumption in both Britain and America that best takes account of gender is Carole Shammas, *The Pre-Industrial Consumer in Britain and America* (Oxford: Clarendon, 1990). Colin Campbell, *The Romantic Ethic and the Spirit of Modern Consumerism* (Oxford: Basil Blackwell, 1987), complementary to Max Weber, *The Protestant Ethic and the Spirit of Capitalism, trans. Talcott Parsons* (New York: Schribner, 1958) explores the link between sensibility and consumerism. For the profound significance of sugar in the world of consumption and empire, see Sidney W. Mintz, *Sweetness and Power: The Place of Sugar in Modern History* (New York: Penguin, 1985). Helpful in understanding the changing psychology and environment of businessmen, as well as the extreme class differences manifest in cities, are Peter Barstow, *The English Urban Renaissance: Culture and Society in Britain 1660–1760* (Oxford: Oxford University Press, 1989); Carl Bridenbaugh, *Cities in Revolt: Urban Life in America* (New York: Oxford University Press, 1994); and Gary Nash, *The Urban Crucible: Social Change, Political Consciousness, and the Origins of the American Revolution* (Cambridge, MA: Harvard University Press, 1979). For the relevant history of British and American Quakers, see James Walvin, *The Quakers: Money and Morals* (London: John Murray, 1997); Jean R. Soderlund, *Quakers and Slavery: A Divided Spirit* (Princeton, NJ: Princeton University Press, 1988); and David Brion Davis, *The Problem of Slavery in Western Culture* (Ithaca, NY: Cornell University Press, 1966), which is a guide to antislavery thought in general. Essential to understanding antislavery and, implicitly, sensibility's role in it are Claire Midgley, *Women Against Slavery: The British Campaign, 1780–1870* (London; NY: Routledge, 1992); and (for America) Julie Roy Jeffrey, *The Great Silent Army of Abolitionism: Ordinary Women in the Antislavery Movement* (Chapel Hill, NC: University of North Carolina Press, 1998). For an introduction to the panoply of reforms in America, see Ronald G. Walters, *American Reformers, 1815–1860* (New York: Hill and Wang, 1978), and Myra C. Glenn, *Campaigns Against Corporal Punishment: Prisoners, Sailors, Women, and Children in Antebellum America* (Albany, NY:

State University of New York Press, 1986). For women in philanthropic re-form, in addition to the books by Midgley and Jeffrey, see F. K. Prochaska, *Women and Philanthropy in Nineteenth-Century England* (Oxford: Oxford University Press, 1980); and, for America, Lori D. Ginzberg, *Women in Antebellum Reform* (Wheeling, IL: Harlan Davidson, 2000). Introductions to captivity narratives include Kathryn Zabell Derounian-Stodola and James Arthur Levernier, *The Indian Captivity Narrative, 1550–1900* (New York: Twayne, 1993).

CHAPTER 4: THE *DARTMOUTH COLLEGE* CASE AND THE LEGAL DESIGN OF CIVIL SOCIETY

The argument provided in Chapter 4 is implicitly at odds with earlier work, which places the design of the legal model for corporate philanthropy at the close of the nineteenth century. Barry D. Karl and Stanley N. Katz, "The American Philanthropic Foundation and the Public Sphere, 1890–1930," *Minerva* 19:2 (Summer, 1981): 236–270. The argument that law imposed a model for the institutional design of the early republic is derived from the recent historiographic argument that law functions semiautonomously. This contention has been asserted in work analyzing private law cases that utilized a contract-law paradigm to reshape American society consistent with Republican ideals. Christopher Tomlins, *Law, Labor, and Ideology in the Early Republic* (New York: Cambridge University Press, 1993); Michael Grossberg, *Governing the Hearth: Law and Family in Nineteenth-Century America* (Chapel Hill: University of North Carolina Press, 1985); Mark Tushnet, *The American Law of Slavery, 1810–1860: Considerations of Humanity and Interest* (Princeton, NJ: Princeton University Press, 1981). Chapter 4 provides support for the argument that public-law cases during this era applied the same model. A longer version of this argument was published previously. Mark D. McGarvie, "Creating Roles for Religion and Philanthropy in a Secular Nation: The *Dartmouth College* Case and the Design of Civil Society in the Early Republic," *The Journal of College and University Law*, 25-3 (Winter, 1999): 527–568. This argument owes a tremendous debt to the works of Sidney E. Mead, particularly his, *The Lively Experiment: The Shaping of Christianity in America* (New York: Harper and Row, 1963). It is also a legal history compliment to the works in intellectual history asserting the "republican synthesis." In particular, see Joyce Appleby, *Capitalism and a New Social Order: The Republican Vision of the 1790s* (New York: New York University Press, 1984); Gordon S. Wood, *The Radicalism of the American Revolution* (New York: Alfred A. Knopf, 1992). These authors contend that a liberal republicanism, rooted in Jeffersonian individualism and capitalism, determined the structure of American society in the early republic. Significant challenges to this prevailing school of thought have recently been raised by Barry Alan Shain, *The Myth of American Individualism: The Protestant Origins of American Political Thought* (Princeton, NJ: Princeton University Press, 1994); and William J. Novak, *The Peoples' Welfare: Law and Regulation in Nineteenth-Century America* (Chapel Hill: University of North Carolina Press, 1996). Also supportive of the presence of an alternative worldview among American laborers and its influence on private collective action is Franklin Folsom, *Impatient Armies of the Poor: The Collective Action of the Unemployed, 1808–1941* (Niwot, CO: University Press of Colorado, 1991).

Much has been written about the *Dartmouth College* case. See Maurice G. Baxter, *Daniel Webster and the Supreme Court* (Amherst, MA: University of Amherst Press, 1966); Bruce A. Campbell, "John Marshall, the Virginia Political Economy, and the *Dartmouth College* Decision," 29 *American Journal of Legal History* 40 (1975); Stephen J. Novak, "The College in the *Dartmouth College* Case: A Reinterpretation," *New England Quarterly* 47:550 (1974); Eldon L. Johnson, "The *Dartmouth College* Case: The Neglected Educational Meaning," *Journal of the Early Republic* 3:45 (1983); John S. Whitehead, *The Separation of College and State: Columbia, Dartmouth, Harvard, and Yale, 1776–1876* (New Haven: Yale University Press, 1973).

For histories of philanthropy in the early republic, see Conrad Edick Wright, *The Transformation of Charity in Post-Revolutionary New England* (Boston: Northeastern University Press, 1992); Lori D. Ginsburg, *Women and the Work of Benevolence* (New Haven: Yale University Press, 1990); Barbara L. Bellows, *Benevolence Among Shareholders: Assisting the Poor in Charleston, 1670–1860* (Baton Rouge: Louisiana State University Press, 1993); Robert F. Dalzell, Jr., *Enterprising Elite: The Boston Associates and the World They Made* (New York: W. W. Norton, 1987). An interesting use of republican ideology as the motivation for military service as a form of philanthropic behavior is Ricardo Herrera, *Guarantors of Liberty and the Republic: The American Citizen As Soldier and the Military Ethos of Republicanism* (Ph.D. Dissertation, Marquette University, 1998) (under contract, Southern Illinois University Press).

CHAPTER 5: RETHINKING ASSIMILATION: AMERICAN INDIANS AND THE PRACTICE OF CHRISTIANITY, 1800–1861

For background on American policies toward American Indians between the turn of the nineteenth century and removal, see Francis Paul Prucha, *The Great Father: The United States Government and the American Indians* (Lincoln: University of Nebraska Press, 1984); Prucha, *American Indian Policy in the Formative Years* (Cambridge, MA: Harvard University Press, 1962); Reginald Horsman, *Expansion and American Indian Policy, 1783–1812* (East Lansing: Michigan State University Press, 1967); see also Ronald N. Satz, *American Indian Policy in the Jacksonian Era* (Lincoln: University of Nebraska Press, 1975). For the rich but troubling legal history of the Jacksonian era, see Charles Wilkinson, *American Indians, Time, and the Law: Historical Rights at the Bar of the Supreme Court* (New Haven: Yale University Press, 1987). Earlier studies on the age of Jefferson and philanthropy include Bernard Sheehan, *Seeds of Extinction: Jeffersonian Philanthropy and the American Indian* (New York: W. W. Norton & Company, 1973). For recent surveys of this period in American life, see Joyce Appleby, *Inheriting the Revolution: The First Generation of Americans* (Cambridge, MA: Harvard University Press, 2000). The best recent study of American racial attitudes and policies toward American Indians during this period is Anthony F. C. Wallace, *Jefferson and the Indians: The Tragic Fate of the First Americans* (Cambridge, MA: Harvard University Press, 1999). And for new perspectives on religion in American life, see David D. Hall, *Lived Religion in America: Toward a History of Practice* (Princeton, NJ: Princeton University Press, 1997).

For case studies of Indian-white relations east of the Mississippi River during the early republic, see *Native Americans and the Early Republic,* Frederick E. Hoxie, Ronald Hoffman, and Peter J. Albert, eds. (Charlottesville: University Press of Virginia, 1999); and *Contact Points: American Frontiers from the Mohawk Valley to the Mississippi, 1750–1830,* Andrew R. L. Cayton and Fredrika J. Teute, eds. (Chapel Hill: University of North Carolina Press, 1998). For a detailed history of the religious and material exchange between the Creeks and missionaries and agents, see Joel W. Martin, *Sacred Revolt: The Muskogees' Struggle for a New World* (Boston: Beacon, 1991). For studies on Jean Baptiste Richardville, see Bradley J. Birzer, "Entangling Empires, Fracturing Frontiers: Jean Baptiste Richardville and the Quest for Miami Autonomy, 1760–1841" (Ph.D. Dissertation,

Indiana University, 1998); Stewart Rafert, *The Miami Indians of Indiana: A Persistent People, 1654–1994* (Indianapolis: Indiana Historical Society, 1996).

The history of Indians and missions has been largely defined by the issues outlined in Robert F. Berkhofer, Jr., *Salvation and the Savage: An Analysis of Protestant Missions and the American Indian Response, 1787–1862* (Lexington: University of Kentucky Press, 1965). See also R. Pierce Beaver, *Church, State, and the American Indians: Two and a Half Centuries of Partnership Between Protestant Churches and Government* (St. Louis: Concordia, 1966); more recent studies by the late William G. McLoughlin have set the debates in this field. See William G. McLoughlin, *Cherokees and Missionaries, 1789–1839* (Norman: University of Oklahoma Press, 1994); and McLoughlin, *The Cherokees and Christianity, 1794–1870: Essays on Acculturation and Cultural Persistence*, Walter H. Conser, ed. (Athens: University of Georgia Press, 1994), and McLoughlin, *Champions of the Cherokees: Evan and John B. Jones* (Princeton, NJ: Princeton University Press, 1990).

Scholarly attention has begun to turn to the Indian experience after removal and the Indian response to missions. For a wide-ranging discussion of removal and its implications, see William G. McLoughlin, *After the Trail of Tears: The Cherokees' Struggle for Sovereignty, 1839–1880* (Chapel Hill: University of North Carolina Press, 1993). See also Michael D. Green, *The Politics of Indian Removal: Creek Government and Society* (Lincoln: University of Nebraska Press, 1982). For the best studies on Kenekuk, see Joseph B. Herring, *Kenekuk, The Kickapoo Prophet* (Lawrence: University Press of Kansas, 1988); and Herring, *The Enduring Indians of Kansas: A Century and a Half of Acculturation* (Lawrence: University Press of Kansas, 1990). Historian Rebecca Kugel has also led the way with two impressive articles on the Ojibwe response to missionaries, including "Religion Mixed with Politics: The 1836 Conversion of Mang'osid of Fond du Lac," *Ethnohistory* 37:2 (Spring 1990), and "Of Missionaries and Their Cattle: Ojibwa Perceptions of a Missionary as Evil Shaman," *Ethnohistory* 41:2 (Spring 1994). Her recent book, *To Be the Main Leaders of Our People: A History of Minnesota Ojibwe Politics, 1825–1898* (East Lansing: Michigan State University Press, 1998), also concentrates on this important time period in the development of modern tribes.

For studies on American Indians and gender, see Theda Perdue, *Cherokee Women: Gender and Culture Change, 1700–1835* (Lincoln: University of Nebraska Press, 1998); Mary Young, "The Cherokee Nation: Mirror of the Republic," *American Quarterly* 33 (Winter 1981); Carol Devens, *Countering Colonization: Native American Women and Great Lakes Missions,*

1630–1900 (Berkeley: University of California Press, 1992); and Karen Anderson, *Chain Her by One Foot, The Subjugation of Women in Seventeenth-Century New France* (London: Routledge, 1991).

CHAPTER 6: ANTEBELLUM REFORM: SALVATION, SELF-CONTROL, AND SOCIAL TRANSFORMATION

The best general study of antebellum reform remains Ronald G. Walters, *American Reformers, 1815–1860* (New York: Hill and Wang, 1978). Nancy A. Hewitt, *Women's Activism and Social Change: Rochester, New York, 1822–1872* (Ithaca, New York: Cornell University Press, 1984) and Lori D. Ginzberg, *Women and the Work of Benevolence: Morality, Politics, and Class in the Nineteenth-Century United States* (New Haven: Yale University Press, 1990) are excellent analyses of women's philanthropic activities. Charles Sellers's magisterial *The Market Revolution: Jacksonian America, 1815–1846* (New York: Oxford University Press, 1991) offers an interpretation of the relationship between reform and economic change. See David J. Rothman, *The Discovery of the Asylum: Social Order and Disorder in the New Republic* (Glenview, IL: Scott, Foresman, 1971) for an illuminating discussion of institutions. Louis J. Kern, *An Ordered Love: Sex Roles and Sexuality in Victorian Utopias* (Chapel Hill: University of North Carolina Press, 1981) examines utopian communities. Several studies deal with various aspects of the temperance movement; see especially W. J. Rohrbaugh, *The Alcoholic Republic: An American Tradition* (New York: Oxford University Press, 1979); Jed Dannenbaum, *Drink and Disorder: Temperance Reform in Cincinnati from the Washingtonian Revival to the WCTU* (Urbana: University of Illinois Press, 1984); and Ruth Alexander, "We Are Engaged as a Band of Sisters: Class and Domesticity in the Washingtonian Temperance Movement, 1840–1850," *Journal of American History*, 75 (1988). Herbert G. Gutman, "Work, Culture, and Society in Industrializing America, 1815–1919," *American Historical Review* 78 (June 1973); Paul E. Johnson, *A Shopkeeper's Millennium: Society and Revivals in Rochester, New York, 1815–1837* (New York: Hill and Wang, 1978); Paul Faler, *Mechanics and Manufacturers in the Early Industrial Revolution: Lynn, Massachusetts, 1780–1860* (Albany: State University of New York Press, 1981); and Bruce Laurie, *Working People of Philadelphia, 1800–1860* (Philadelphia: Temple University Press, 1980) discuss the impact of the temperance movement on workers.

Stephen Nissenbaum, *Sex, Diet, and Debility in Jacksonian America: Sylvester Graham and Health Reform* (Westport, CT: Greenwood Press, 1980) is a useful biography; on sexuality, see also G. J. Barker-Benfield, *The Horrors of the Half-Known Life: Male Attitudes Toward Women and Sexuality in Nineteenth-Century America* (New York: Routledge, 2000). On abolitionism, see Lawrence J. Friedman, *Gregarious Saints: Self and Community in American Abolitionism, 1830–1870* (New York: Cambridge University Press, 1982); Paul Goodman, *Of One Blood: Abolitionism and the Origins of Racial Equality* (Berkeley: University of California Press, 1998); and Julie Roy Jeffrey, *The Great Silent Army of Abolitionism: Ordinary Women in the Antislavery Movement* (Chapel Hill: University of North Carolina Press, 1998). George M. Frederickson, *The Inner Civil War: Northern Intellectuals and the Crisis of the Union* (1965), offers a trenchant analysis of the U.S. Sanitary Commission. See also John Higham, *From Boundlessness to Consolidation: The Transformation of American Culture, 1848–1860* (Ann Arbor, MI: William L. Clements Library, 1969), for a discussion of changes in the nature of reform in the 1850s.

CHAPTER 7: LAW, RECONSTRUCTION, AND AFRICAN AMERICAN EDUCATION IN POST-EMANCIPATION SOUTH

The era of Reconstruction has been the subject of extensive recent historical writing. Any investigation of this period must begin with Eric Foner, *Reconstruction: America's Unfinished Revolution, 1863–1877* (New York: Harper and Row, 1988). However, an excellent new work, Heather Cox Richardson, *The Death of Reconstruction: Race, Labor, and Politics in the Post-Civil War Work, 1861–1901* (Cambridge, MA: Harvard University Press, 2001), challenges some of Foner's conclusions while contending that Reconstruction died because of ideological change resulting from a decline in the free labor ideology with the growth of industrial wage labor. The social and cultural history of Reconstruction is well covered in John Hope Franklin, *Reconstruction After the Civil War* (Chicago: University of Chicago Press, 1961); Eric Anderson and Alfred A. Moss, Jr., eds., *The Facts of Reconstruction* (Baton Rouge: Louisiana State University Press, 1991); Richard Lowe, "The Freedmen's Bureau and Local Black Leadership," *Journal of American Studies* 80 (December 1993): 989–98; David C. Rankin, "The Origins of Black Leadership in New Orleans During Reconstruction," *Journal of Southern*

History 40 (August 1974): 417–440; and Leon Litwack, *Been in the Storm So Long: The Aftermath of Slavery* (New York: Alfred A. Knopf, 1979). For earlier examinations of the nation's abandonment of Reconstruction in the 1870s, see Mark W. Summers, *Railroads, Reconstruction, and the Gospel of Prosperity: Aid Under the Radical Republicans, 1865–1877* (Princeton, NJ: Princeton University Press, 1984); and Nina Silber, *The Romance of Reunion: Northerners and the South, 1865–1900* (Chapel Hill: University of North Carolina Press, 1993). The intellectual history of the era is wonderfully captured in George M. Fredrickson, *The Inner Civil War: Northern Intellectuals and the Crisis of Union* (New York: Harper and Row, 1965); David W. Blight, " 'For Something Beyond the Battlefield': Frederick Douglass and the Struggle for the Memory of the Civil War," *Journal of American History* 75 (March 1989): 1156–78. The legal history of Reconstruction is interpreted from two very different perspectives in Herman Belz, *Abraham Lincoln, Constitutionalism, and Equal Rights in the Civil War Era* (New York: Fordham University Press, 1998), and John Hope Franklin and Genna Rae McNeil, eds., *African Americans and the Living Constitution* (Washington, DC: Smithsonian Institution Press, 1995).

The context for early foundation philanthropy, the story of African American education in the post-emancipation South, is effectively presented in James D. Anderson, *The Education of Blacks in the South, 1860–1935* (Chapel Hill: University of North Carolina Press, 1988). The rise of the black industrial-education curriculum in African American schools and colleges is the subject of Donald Spivey, *Schooling for the New Slavery: Black Industrial Education, 1868–1915* (Westport, CT: Greenwood Press, 1978). For missionary philanthropy, see James M. McPherson, *The Abolitionist Legacy: From Reconstruction to the NAACP* (Princeton, NJ: Princeton University Press, 1975); and Ronald E. Butchart, *Northern Schools, Southern Blacks, and Reconstruction: Freedmen's Education, 1862–1875* (Westport, CT: Greenwood Press, 1980). The effort of the freedmen's community to support their own schools is told in Herbert G. Gutman, "Schools for Freedom: The Post-Emancipation Origins of Afro American Education," in *Power and Culture: Essays on the American Working Class* (New York: Pantheon Books, 1987), 260–97. For the sponsorship of schools and colleges by African American denominations, see Dwight O. Holmes, *The Evolution of the Negro College* (College Park, MD: McGrath Publishing Co., 1934).

There are few published historical studies of the Slater Fund, and the foundation officials who managed and distributed its endowment. Two very different perspectives are offered by Roy E. Finkenbine, " 'Our Little

Circle': Benevolent Reformers, the Slater Fund, and the Argument for Black Industrial Education, 1882–1908," *Hayes Historical Journal* 6 (Fall 1986): 6–22; and John E. Fisher, *The John F. Slater Fund: A Nineteenth-Century Affirmative Action for Negro Education* (Lanham, MD: University Press of America, 1986). For a useful analysis of the relative strengths and weaknesses of these works, see Leslie H. Fishel, Jr., "The John F. Slater Fund," *Hayes Historical Journal* 8 (Fall 1988): 47–51. Unpublished studies include John H. Butler, "An Historical Account of the John F. Slater Fund and the Anna T. Jeanes Foundation" (Ed.D. Dissertation, University of California, 1931); and Roy E. Finkenbine, "A Little Circle: White Philanthropists and Black Industrial Education in the Post-Bellum South" (Ph.D. Dissertation, Bowling Green State University, 1982). Louis D. Rubin, Jr., *Teach the Freeman: The Correspondence of Rutherford B. Hayes and the Slater Fund for Negro Education, 1881–1893*, 2 vols. (Baton Rouge: Louisiana State University Press, 1959) is an interesting documentary history of the fund's first decade. For the conflict with William Hooper Councill, see Robert G. Sherer, *Subordination or Liberation: The Development and Conflicting Theories of Black Education in Nineteenth-Century Alabama* (University, AL: University of Alabama Press, 1977).

There are several excellent studies of the other foundations at work in African American education in the post-emancipation South. Accounts of the Peabody Education Fund include Earle H. West, "The Peabody Fund and Negro Education, 1867–1880," *History of Education Quarterly* 6 (Summer 1966): 3–21; and William Preston Vaughn, *Schools for All: The Blacks and Public Education in the South, 1865–1877* (Lexington: University of Kentucky Press, 1974). For a recent work on the General Education Board and the foundations under its umbrella during the early twentieth century, see Eric Anderson and Alfred A. Moss, Jr., *Dangerous Donations: Northern Philanthropy and Southern Black Education, 1902–1930* (Columbia, MO: University of Missouri Press, 1999).

CHAPTER 8: WOMEN AND POLITICAL CULTURE

The colonial context for philanthropy is presented very well in Gary B. Nash, *The Urban Crucible: Social Change, Political Consciousness, and the Origins of the American Revolution* (Cambridge, MA: Harvard University

Press, 1979); Peter Dobkin Hall, *Inventing the Nonprofit Sector* (Baltimore: Johns Hopkins University Press, 1992); Raymond A. Mohl, *Poverty in New York, 1783–1825* (New York: Oxford University Press, 1971); and Rhys Isaac, *The Transformation of Virginia, 1740–1790* (New York: W. W. Norton, 1982).

The changing legal and social status of women in the early republic is available in Linda K. Kerber, *Women of the Republic: Intellect and Ideology in Revolutionary America* (Chapel Hill: University of North Carolina Press, 1980); Kathleen D. McCarthy, "Parallel Power Structures: Women and the Voluntary Sphere," in McCarthy, ed., *Lady Bountiful Revisited: Women, Philanthropy and Power* (New Brunswick, NJ: Rutgers University Press, 1990); Lori D. Ginzberg, *Women and the Work of Benevolence: Morality, Politics, and Class in the Nineteenth Century United States* (New Haven: Yale University Press, 1990).

On the issue of middle-class women and leisure, see Jeanne Boylston, *Home and Work: Housework, Wages, and the Ideology of Labor in the Early Republic* (New York: Oxford University Press, 1990); and Margaret Morris Haviland, "Beyond Women's Sphere: Young Quaker Women and the Veil of Charity in Philadelphia, 1790–1810," *William and Mary Quarterly* 3rd Series 51:3 (July, 1994): 419–446.

The Sanitary Commission is a topic that needs much more attention from historians. In *The Inner Civil War* (New York, 1965), George Fredrickson provides perhaps the best summary history of this semipublic and semiprivate organization. See also Charles J. Stille, *History of the United States Sanitary Commission: Being the General Report of Its Work During the War of Rebellion* (Philadelphia: J.B. Lippincott, 1866). For more on Sanitary Fairs, see Lori Ginzberg, *Women and the Work of Benevolence*; Chapter 5; and Jeanie Attie, *Patriotic Toil: Northern Women and the American Civil War* (Ithaca: Cornell University Press, 1998), Chapter 7. Women's roles in nonprofit income generation are discussed in Ginzberg; Kathleen D. McCarthy, *Women's Culture: American Philanthropy and Art, 1830–1930* (Chicago: University of Chicago Press, 1991), Chapter 3; and Kathleen Waters Sander, *The Business of Charity: The Woman's Exchange Movement, 1832–1900* (Urbana: University of Illinois Press, 1998).

To explore the historiographic debate concerning the social agency of the poor, see for example, Clifford S. Griffin, *Their Brothers' Keepers: Moral Stewardship in the United States, 1800–1865* (New York: H. Wolff, 1960); Christine Stansell, *City of Women: Sex and Class in New York, 1789–1860* (New York: Alfred A. Knopf, 1986). For a rebuttal to the social-control theory, see Lois W. Banner, "Religious Benevolence as Social Control: A Critique of an Interpretation," *Journal of American History* 60:24–41 (1973); Peregrine Horden and Richard Smith, *The Locus of Care: Families, Communities, Institutions, and the Provision of Welfare Since Antiquity* (London: Routledge, 1998); and Peter Mandler, ed., *The Uses of Charity: The Poor on Relief in the Nineteenth-Century Metropolis* (Philadelphia: University of Pennsylvania Press, 1990).

For the relationship between women's religion and their charitable activities, see Mary Ryan, *Cradle of the Middle Class: The Family in Oneida County, New York, 1790–1865* (New York: Cambridge University Press, 1981); Hasia Diner, *Erin's Daughters in America: Irish Immigrant Women in the Nineteenth Century* (Baltimore: Johns Hopkins University Press, 1983). Race and charity is discussed in Elizabeth Fox Genovese, *Within the Plantation Household: Black and White Women in the Old South* (Chapel Hill: University of North Carolina Press, 1988): 39–42. Southern women's charities are described in Cynthia A. Kierner, *Beyond the Household: Women's Place in the Early South, 1700–1835* (Ithaca: Cornell University Press, 1998); Suzanne Lebsock, *The Free Women of Petersburg: Status and Culture in a Southern Town, 1784–1860* (New York: W. W. Norton & Company, 1984); Elizabeth R. Varon, *We Mean to Be Counted: White Women and Politics in Antebellum Virginia* (Chapel Hill: University of North Carolina Press, 1998); Jane H. Pease and William H. Pease, *Ladies, Women, and Wenches: Choice and Constraint in Antebellum Charleston and Boston* (Chapel Hill: University of North Carolina Press, 1990); and Jean E. Friedman, *The Enclosed Garden: Women and Community in the Evangelical South, 1830–1900* (Chapel Hill: University of North Carolina Press, 1985); Anne Firor Scott, *Natural Allies: Women's Associations in American Society* (Urbana: University of Illinois Press, 1991): 69; Drew Gilpin Faust, *Mothers of Invention: Women of the Slaveholding South in the American Civil War* (Chapel Hill: University of North Carolina Press, 1996).

The classic statement on the issue of domesticity as a "double-edged sword" is Barbara Welter, "The Cult of True Womanhood: 1820–1860," *American Quarterly* 151–74 (1966). Her findings should be tempered by reading Lucien Pye and Sidney Verba, *Political Culture and Political Development* (Princeton, NJ: Princeton University Press, 1965); and Barbara Leslie Epstein, *The Politics of Domesticity: Women, Evangelism, and Temperance in Nineteenth-Century America* (Middletown, CT: Wesleyan University Press, 1981).

CHAPTER 9: FROM GIFT TO FOUNDATION: THE PHILANTHROPIC LIVES OF MRS. RUSSELL SAGE

This study of the philanthropy of Mrs. Russell Sage positions itself within and between several different scholarly literatures. The main historiographical current in women's history sweeps toward the Progressive era, when a few women were able to create and occupy, if only for a few years, certain policy-making beach heads such as the U.S. Children's Bureau. This literature tends to shy away from the use of the term *charity*, preferring *voluntarism* or *activism*, (charitable donations of time), and *investment* (charitable donations of money), or even calling both *politics*. Kathryn Kish Sklar, "Who Funded Hull House," in Kathleen D. McCarthy, ed., *Lady Bountiful Revisited: Women, Philanthropy, and Power* (New Brunswick, NJ: Rutgers University Press, 1990): 94–118; Kathryn Kish Sklar, *Florence Kelley and the Nation's Work* (New Haven: Yale University Press, 1997); Robyn Muncy, *Creating a Female Dominion in American Reform, 1890–1935* (New York: Oxford University Press, 1991).

Important studies of women's philanthropy are Kathleen D. McCarthy, *Noblesse Oblige: Charity and Cultural Philanthropy in Chicago, 1849–1929* (Chicago: University of Chicago Press, 1982), which usefully includes men's benevolent activities as well; and McCarthy, *Women's Culture: American Philanthropy and Art* (Chicago: University of Chicago Press, 1991). Kathleen Sander analyzes charity as "nonprofit entrepreneurship" in Sander, *The Business of Charity: The Woman's Exchange Movement, 1832–1900* (Chicago: University of Chicago Press, 1998).

Numerous studies document the activities of nineteenth-century women in reform, the voluntary associations of churchwomen, clubwomen, temperance, and antivice reformers, some of whom later graduated to suffrage and socialism. The focus is on how voluntary associations helped women emerge as players in public policy, expanding their own possibilities while helping others. Major studies are Lori Ginzberg, *Women and the Work of Benevolence: Morality, Politics, and Class in the Nineteenth-Century United States* (New Haven: Yale University Press, 1990); Barbara Leslie Epstein, *The Politics of Domesticity: Women, Evangelism, and Temperance in Nineteenth-Century America* (Middletown, CT: Wesleyan University Press, 1981); Ruth Bordin, *Woman and Temperance: The Quest for Power and Liberty* (Philadelphia: Temple University Press, 1981).

Christine Stansell, *City of Women: Sex and Class in New York, 1789–1870* (New York: Knopf, 1986) drew attention to class in women's history, and recent studies have continued to explore the ways that benevolent activities (reform, charity, and philanthropy) helped middle- and upper-class women make claims for equality relative to men of their class by emphasizing their superiority over racial and cultural inferiors. Nancy Hewitt, "Charity or Mutual Aid: Two Perspectives on Latin Women's Philanthropy in Tampa, Florida," in *Lady Bountiful Revisited*: 55–69; Karen Anderson, *Changing Woman: A History of Racial-Ethnic Women in Modern America* (New York: Oxford University Press, 1996); Louise Michele Newman, *White Women's Rights: The Racial Origins of Feminism in the United States* (New York: Oxford University Press, 1999).

It has been useful in writing this history to think about voluntarism in terms of the creation of new arenas, sometimes called new "action contexts." Kathleen D. McCarthy, "'Parallel Power Structures': Women and the Voluntary Sector," in McCarthy, *Lady Bountiful Revisited*: 1–35; and Seth Koven, "Borderlands: Women, Voluntary Action, and Child Welfare in Britain, 1840–1914," in *Mothers of a New World: Maternalist Politics and the Origins of Welfare States* (New York: Routledge, 1993): 94–135; Craig Calhoun, ed., *Habermas and the Public Sphere* (Cambridge, MA: MIT Press, 1997). Because nineteenth-century women were excluded from formal politics, the professions, and the universities, the voluntary association was, to quote Elisabeth S. Clemens, "almost the **only** place to get things done." Clemens, Review of Anne Firor Scott, *Natural Allies: Women's Associations in American History* (Urbana: University of Illinois Press, 1991), *American Journal of Sociology* 98 (November 1992): 687.

Space is also important to the literature of the nonprofit sector, conceptualized as an arena outside the state and the business corporation. Peter Dobkin Hall, *Inventing the Nonprofit Sector and Other Essays on Philanthropy, Voluntarism, and Nonprofit Organizations* (Baltimore: Johns Hopkins University Press, 1992). Interest in voluntary associations among nonprofits historians owes less to the work in women's history, cited previously, than to contemporary debates about "civil society." Peter Dobkin Hall usefully summarizes the issues in H-STATE@H-NET.MSU.EDU, April 10, 2001.

If the nonprofit literature deals with an absence (the absence of the state and the business corporation), foundation literature is the province of the political and institutional historian. Barry D. Karl and Stanley N. Katz, "The American Private Philanthropic Foundation and the Public Sphere,

1890–1930," *Minerva* 19 (1981): 236–70 is the benchmark study. The literature on foundations is usefully surveyed by Susan Kastan, "Bibliography: Recent Writings About Foundations in History," Ellen Condliffe Lagemann, ed., *Philanthropic Foundations: New Scholarship, New Possibilities* (Bloomington, IN: Indiana University Press, 1999): 377–403. Judith Sealander, *Private Wealth and Public Life: Foundation Philanthropy and the Reshaping of American Social Policy from the Progressive Era to the New Deal* (Baltimore: Johns Hopkins University Press, 1997), tackles several foundations and a number of policy areas with verve. On the Russell Sage Foundation, John Glenn, Lilian Brandt, and F. Emerson Andrews, *The Russell Sage Foundation* (New York: Russell Sage Foundation, 1947); David Hammack and Stanton Wheeler, *Social Science in the Making: Essays on the Russell Sage Foundation* (New York: Russell Sage Foundation 1994); Hammack, "Russell Sage Foundation," in Harold M. Keele and Joseph C. Kiger, eds., *The Greenwood Encyclopedia of American Institutions: Foundations* (Westport, CT: Greenwood Press, 1984): 373–380. Maurine Greenwald and Margo Anderson, eds., *Pittsburgh Surveyed: Social Science and Social Reform in the Early Twentieth Century* (Pittsburgh: University of Pittsburgh Press, 1996) provide a long-overdue look at the foundation's most important initiative. See also Martin Bulmer, Kevin Bales, and Kathryn Kish Sklar, eds., *The Social Survey in Historical Perspective, 1880–1940* (New York: Cambridge University Press, 1991).

The late nineteenth-century emergence of the social sciences first attracted the interest of historians of professions. New scholarly work sees science as a "legitimizing discourse" and approaches the history of the social sciences as a case study in the production and dissemination of knowledge ("social facts"). I have found particularly useful Helene Silverberg, ed., *Gender and American Social Science: The Formative Years* (Princeton, NJ: Princeton University Press, 1998); and Ellen Fitzpatrick, *Endless Crusade: Women Social Scientists and Progressive Reform* (New York: Oxford University Press, 1990). Alice O'Connor, *Poverty Knowledge: Social Science, Social Policy, and the Poor in Twentieth-Century U.S. History* (Princeton, NJ: Princeton University Press, 2001) achieves all that its title promises; moreover, O'Connor finally gives the Russell Sage Foundation its due.

Much of the interesting writing on gifts has been done by cultural anthropologists. Useful for the historian of philanthropy is Mary Douglas, "No Free Gifts," introduction to Marcel Mauss, *The Gift: The Form and Reason for Exchange in Archaic Societies* (1990). Less accessible though still stimulating are Lewis Hyde, *The Gift: Imagination and the Erotic Life of Property*

(New York: Random House, 1979); and Annette Weiner, *Inalienable Possessions: The Paradox of Keeping-While-Giving* (Berkeley: University of California Press, 1992).

Numerous studies map the Progressive Era attitudes to wealth and poverty, and hence to philanthropy. The best study of the COS is Dawn Greeley, "Beyond Benevolence: Gender, Class, and the Development of Scientific Charity in New York City, 1882–1935" (Ph.D. Dissertation, SUNY, Stony Brook, 1995). On the settlements, a revisionist study is Ruth Crocker, *Social Work and Social Order: The Settlement Movement in Two Industrial Cities, 1889–1930* (Urbana: University of Illinois Press, 1992). A provocative overview of the class relations underlying late nineteenth-century philanthropy is Amy Dru Stanley, "'Beggars Can't Be Choosers': Compulsion and Contract in Post-Bellum America," *Journal of American History* 78 (1992): 1265–1293. See also Jane Addams, "The Subtle Problems of Charity," *Atlantic Monthly*, 83 (1899): 163–178.

Excellent treatments of the New York scene that have helped me place Olivia Sage in context are Maureen E. Montgomery, *Displaying Women: Spectacles of Leisure in Edith Wharton's New York* (New York: Routledge, 1998); Frederick Cople Jaher, "Style and Status: High Society in Late Nineteenth-Century New York," in Jaher, ed., *The Rich, The Well-Born, and the Powerful: Elites and Upper Classes in History* (Urbana: University of Illinois Press, 1973): 259–284; David Hammack, *Power and Society: Greater New York at the Turn of the Century* (New York: Russell Sage Foundation, 1982; repr., Columbia University Press, 1987); and the brilliant and entertaining history by Edwin G. Burrows and Mike Wallace, *Gotham: A History of New York City, to 1898* (New York: Oxford University Press, 1999).

And what of Mrs. Sage? We have Irvin Wyllie, "Margaret Olivia Slocum Sage," in *Notable American Women,* ed. Edward T. James et al., 3 volumes, (Cambridge: Harvard University Press, 1971), 3: 222–223; and James Allen Smith and Melissa Smith, "Sage, Margaret Olivia Slocum," *American National Biography*, ed. John Garraty and Mark Carnes (New York: Oxford University Press, 1999), 19: 193–194; and by a contemporary, Arthur Huntington Gleason, "Mrs. Russell Sage and Her Interests," *The World's Work* 13 (November 1906). Mrs. Sage speaks for herself in M. Olivia Sage, "Opportunities and Responsibilities of Leisured Women," *North American Review* 181 (1905): 712–721; and "Mrs. Russell Sage on Marriage," *The Sunday Herald* (Syracuse), June 21, 1903, p. 29. See also Mary Jane Fairbanks, comp., *Emma Willard and Her Pupils, or Fifty Years of Troy Female Seminary, 1822–1872* (New York: Published by Mrs. Russell Sage, 1898). Sage's bequests are listed in "Mrs. Sage Leaves Millions to Charity," *New York Times,* November 14, 1918, p. 13. James A. Hijiya, "Four Ways of Looking at a Philanthropist: A Study of Robert Weeks de Forest," *Proceedings of the American Philosophical Society,* 124 (1980): 404–418 is excellent, while Paul Sarnoff, *Russell Sage, The Money King* (New York: Ivan Obolensky, 1964) offers a gossipy and unreliable portrait of the unphilanthropic Sage.

Finally, this essay draws on some of the author's previously published work including, "'I Only Ask You to Divide Your Fortune With Me': Begging Letters and the Transformation of Charity in Late Nineteenth-Century America," *Social Politics* 6 (Summer 1999): 131–160, and "From Widow's Mite to Widow's Might: The Philanthropy of Margaret Olivia Sage," *Journal of Presbyterian History* 74 (Winter 1996): 253–264.

CHAPTER 10: CURING EVILS AT THEIR SOURCE: THE ARRIVAL OF SCIENTIFIC GIVING

Numerous works have addressed the tremendous social change that occurred in the early twentieth century. The best general history remains Robert H. Wiebe, *The Search for Order* (New York: Hill and Wang, 1967). More specific subject areas are addressed in Steven Diner, *A Very Different Age: Americans of the Progressive Era* (New York: Hill and Wang, 1998); Daniel Rodgers, *Atlantic Crossings: Social Politics in a Progressive Age* (Cambridge, MA: Belnap Press, 1998); James Beniger, *The Control Revolution* (Cambridge, MA: Harvard University Press, 1986); Olivier Zunz, *Making America Corporate* (Chicago: University of Chicago Press, 1990); David Brody, *Workers in Industrial America* (New York: Oxford University Press, 1993); David Montgomery, *The Fall of the House of Labor: The Workplace, the State, and American Labor Activism, 1865–1925* (New York: Cambridge University Press, 1987); David Danbom, *Born in the Country: A History of Rural America* (Baltimore: Johns Hopkins University Press, 1995); Jack Temple Kirby, *The Countercultural South* (Athens, GA: University of Georgia Press, 1995); David Noble, *America by Design: Science, Technology, and the Rise of Corporate Capitalism* (New York: Oxford University Press, 1977); Morton Keller, *Regulating a New Society: Public Policy and Social Change in America, 1900–1933* (Cambridge, MA: Harvard University Press, 1994); William E. Leuchtenburg, *The Perils of Prosperity* (Chicago: University of Chicago Press, 1958).

The role of science in the rationalization and professionalization of American society is addressed in Dorothy Ross, *The Origins of American Social Science* (Cambridge: Cambridge University Press, 1991); Martin Bulmer, Kevin Bales, and Kathryn Kish Sklar, eds., *The Social Survey in Historical Perspective, 1880–1940* (Cambridge: Cambridge University Press, 1991); Thomas Haskell, *The Emergence of Professional Social Science: The American Social Science Association and the Nineteenth-Century Crisis of Authority* (Urbana: University of Illinois Press, 1977); Stephen Turner and Jonathan Turner, *The Impossible Science: An Institutional Analysis of American Sociology* (Newbury Park, CA: Sage Publications, 1990); Charles Rosenberg, *No Other Gods: On Science and American Social Thought* (Baltimore: Johns Hopkins University Press, 1976); Ellen Fitzpatrick, *Endless Crusade: Women Social Scientists and Progressive Reform in America, 1830–1930*, (New York: Oxford University Press, 1990); Donald Fisher, *Fundamental Development of Social Sciences: Rockefeller Philanthropy and the United States Social Science Research Council* (Ann Arbor: University of Michigan Press, 1993); Mark Smith, *Social Science in the Crucible: The American Debate over Objectivity and Purpose, 1918–1941* (Durham, NC: Duke University Press, 1994).

Discussions of early twentieth-century philanthropy frequently have been addressed in works focused on the intellectual disaffection of the era and calls for radical social reform. These works also offer the advantage of providing an international context for American attitudes. Particularly noteworthy are James T. Kloppenberg, *Uncertain Victory: Social Democracy and Progressivism in European and American Thought, 1870–1920* (New York: Oxford University Press, 1986), and Richard Hofstadter, *Social Darwinism in American Thought* (Boston: Beacon Press, 1944, 1992). Works addressing more specific people, programs, or policies include Judith Sealander, *Private Wealth and Public Life: Foundation Philanthropy and the Re-Shaping of American Social Policy from the Progressive Era Through the New Deal* (Baltimore: Johns Hopkins University Press, 1997); Olivier Zunz, *Why the American Century* (Chicago: University of Chicago Press, 1998); David C. Hammack and Stanton Wheeler, *Social Science in the Making: Essays on the Russell Sage Foundation* (New York: Russell Sage Foundation, 1994); Ellen Lagemann, *Private Power for the Public Good: A History of the Carnegie Foundation for the Advancement of Teaching* (Middletown, CT; Wesleyan University Press, 1983); Ellen Lagemann, *The Politics of Knowledge: The Carnegie Corporation, Philanthropy, and Public Policy* (Middletown, CT: Wesleyan University Press, 1989); John Ensor Harr and Peter Johnson, *The Rockefeller Century: Three Generations of America's Greatest Family* (New

York: Schribner, 1988); Ron Chernow, *Titan: The Life of John D. Rockefeller, Sr.* (New York: Random House, 1998); Donald Critchlow, *The Brookings Institution: Expertise and the Public Interest in a Democratic Society* (De Kalb, IL: Northern Illinois University Press, 1985); Kathleen McCarthy, *Noblesse Oblige: Charity and Cultural Philanthropy in Chicago, 1849–1929* (Chicago: Chicago University Press, 1982); Mary Deegan, *Jane Addams and the Men of the Chicago School, 1892–1918* (New Brunswick, NJ: Transaction Books, 1988); Estelle Freedman, *Maternal Justice: Miriam Van Waters and the Female Reform Tradition* (Chicago: Chicago University Press, 1996); Joseph Frazier Wall, *Andrew Carnegie* (New York: Oxford University Press, 1970). For autobiographies and insider accounts, see Andrew Carnegie, *The Autobiography of Andrew Carnegie* (Garden City, NY: Doubleday, Doran and Co., 1909); Frederick Gates, *Chapters in My Life* (New York: Free Press, 1977); Abraham Flexner, *I Remember* (New York: Simon and Schuster, 1940); John Glenn, Lilian Brandt, and F. Emerson Andrews, *The Russell Sage Foundation* (New York: Harper, 1947); Raymond Fosdick, *The Story of the Rockefeller Foundation* (New York: Harper, 1952); Abraham Flexner and Esther Bailey, *Funds and Foundations: Their Policies, Past and Present* (New York: Harper, 1952); Raymond Fosdick, *Adventure in Giving: The Story of the General Education Board* (New York: Harper and Row, 1962); and Clyde Kiser, *The Milbank Memorial Fund: Its Leaders and Its Work* (New York: The Fund, 1975).

CHAPTER 11: MISSIONS TO THE WORLD: PHILANTHROPY ABROAD

The most thorough information on international philanthropic efforts in the first half of the twentieth century is Merle Curti, *American Philanthropy Abroad* (New Brunswick, NJ: Rutgers University Press, 1963). For histories that develop a more interpretive context, see Emily S. Rosenberg, *Spreading the American Dream: American Economic and Cultural Expansion, 1890–1945* (New York: Hill and Wang, 1982), and Akira Iriye, *The Globalizing of America, 1913–1945* (Cambridge: University of Cambridge Press, 1993). Some broad surveys of the work of major foundations, from a generally positive perspective, include Waldemar A. Nielsen, *The Big Foundations* (New York: Columbia University Press, 1972), and Joseph C. Goulden, *The Money Givers* (New York: Random House, 1971). Edward H. Berman, *The Influence of the Carnegie, Ford, and Rockefeller Foundations on American*

Foreign Policy: The Ideology of Philanthropy (Albany: State University of New York Press, 1983) presents a more critical perspective.

William Hutchison, *Errand to the World: American Protestant Thought and Foreign Missions* (Chicago: University of Chicago Press, 1987) provides a useful introduction to the late-nineteenth-century missionary movement. Jane Hunter, *The Gospel of Gentility: American Women Missionaries in Turn-of-the-Century China* (New Haven, CT: Yale University Press, 1987), and Jon Thares Davidann, *A World of Crisis and Progress: The American YMCA in Japan* (Bethlehem, PA: Lehigh University Press, 1998) provide examples, in specific contexts, of the reciprocal impacts of cultural interchange.

Ian Tyrrell, *Woman's World/Woman's Empire: The Women's Christian Temperance Union in International Perspective* (Chapel Hill: University of North Carolina Press, 1991) is a thorough history of the WCTU and, along with the work by Hunter, provides insight into the gender dimensions of late-nineteenth-century philanthropic efforts.

Sylvia M. Jacobs, ed., *Black Americans and the Missionary Movement in Africa* (Westport, CT: Greenwood Press., 1982) and Walter L. Williams, *Black Americans and the Evangelization of Africa, 1877–1900* (Madison, WI: University of Wisconsin Press, 1982) both provide background on African American missionaries and teachers. See also James T. Campbell, *Songs of Zion: The African Methodist Episcopal Church in the United States and South Africa* (New York: Oxford University Press, 1995). On the Tuskegee movements in Africa, see Kenneth James King, *Pan-Africanism and Education: A Study of Race Philanthropy and Education in the Southern States of America and East Africa* (London, Oxford: Clarendon Press, 1971).

Landrum R. Bolling, with Craig Smith, *Private Foreign Aid: U.S. Philanthropy for Relief and Development* (Boulder, CO: Westview Press, 1982), presents a useful if uncritical overview of the development of international relief work, but Merle Curti's *American Philanthropy Abroad* (New Brunswick, NJ: Rutgers University Press, 1963) is the standard, authoritative examination.

On the Red Cross, see Curti, in Clyde E. Buckingham, *For Humanity's Sake: The Story of the Early Development of the League of Red Cross Societies* (Washington: Public Affairs Press, 1964), and essays in Paul Weindling, *International Health Organisations and Movements, 1918–1939* (Cambridge, England; New York: Cambridge University Press, 1995). All deal with both the internal and external politics of this important organization.

The Carnegie Endowment and its place in the larger history of U.S. peace movements is well described in David S. Patterson, *Toward a*

Warless World: The Travail of the American Peace Movement, 1887–1914 (Bloomington, IN: Indiana University Press, 1976). Carnegie Endowment for International Peace, *Carnegie Endowment for International Peace: Summary of Organization and Work, 1911–1941* (Washington, DC: The Endowment, 1941) provides the best overview of its activities and programs.

On the Rockefeller Foundation's medical efforts, in addition to works given previously, see Marcos Cueto, ed., *Missionaries of Science: The Rockefeller Foundation and Latin America* (Bloomington, IN: Indiana University Press, 1994) and Steven Palmer, "Central American Encounters with Rockefeller Public Health, 1914–1921," in Gilbert M. Joseph, Catherine C. LeGrand, and Ricardo D. Salvatore, eds., *Close Encounters of Empire: Writing the Cultural History of U.S.–Latin American Relations* (Durham, NC: Duke University Press, 1998). Both stress the way local health activists shaped foundation programs. On Ceylon (Sri Lanka), Soma Hewa, *Colonialism, Tropical Disease and Imperial Medicine: Rockefeller Philanthropy in Sri Lanka* (New York: University Press of America, 1995) provides an illuminating, often critical, perspective.

On Rockefeller-funded agricultural reformers, Randall S. Stross, *The Stubborn Earth: American Agriculturalists on Chinese Soil, 1898–1937* (Berkeley: University of California Press, 1986), and Mary Brown Bullock, *An American Transplant: The Rockefeller Foundation and Peking Union Medical College* (Berkeley: University of California Press, 1980), provide somewhat different perspectives on the PUMC. Bruce H. Jennings, *Foundations of International Agricultural Research: Science and Politics in Mexican Agriculture* (Boulder, CO: Westview Press, 1988) is an uncritical study of the origins in Mexico of the Green Revolution.

CHAPTER 12: FAILURE AND RESILIENCE: PUSHING THE LIMITS IN DEPRESSION AND WARTIME

For the best current set of historical data on American philanthropy and nonprofit organizations, as well as on unemployment, income, and other aspects of U.S. economic history, see the *Millennial Edition of Historical Statistics of the United States* (Cambridge University Press, forthcoming). For an impressive analysis of church membership, see Roger Finke and Rodney Stark, *The Churching of America 1776–1990: Winners and Losers in Our Religious Economy* (New Brunswick, NJ: Rutgers University Press, 1992).

Mark Gottlieb's *The Lives of University Hospitals of Cleveland* (Cleveland, OH: Wilson Street Press, 1991), details the Depression-era challenges faced by that institution. David L. Sills's classic on the March of Dimes is *The Volunteers: Means and Ends in a National Organization* (New York: Arno Press, 1957; reprint edition, 1980).

Accessible and influential accounts of the poor during the Depression include Arthur M. Schlesinger, Jr., *The Crisis of the Old Order* (Boston: Houghton Mifflin, 1957), and Jacqueline Jones, *The Dispossessed: America's Underclass from the Civil War to the Present* (New York: Basic Books, 1992). For telling detail, see Florence T. Waite, *A Warm Friend for the Spirit: A History of the Family Service Association of Cleveland and Its Forbears* (Cleveland Family Service Association, 1960); Nathaniel Burt, *Palaces for the People: A Social History of the American Art Museum* (Boston: Little Brown, 1977); Edward H. McKinley, *Marching to Glory: The History of the Salvation Army in the United States, 1880–1992* (Grand Rapids, MI: W.B. Eerdmans Publishing Company, 1995); Mary J. Oates, *The Catholic Philanthropic Tradition in America* (Bloomington: Indiana University Press, 1995); Dorothy M. Brown and Elizabeth McKeown, *The Poor Belong to Us: Catholic Charities and American Welfare* (Cambridge, MA: Harvard University Press, 1997); and James W. Sanders, *The Education of an Urban Minority: Catholics in Chicago, 1833–1965* (New York: Oxford University Press, 1977). The most useful general analysis of New Deal policy remains Ellis W. Hawley, *The New Deal and the Problem of Monopoly: A Study in Economic Ambivalence* (New York: Fordham University Press, 1995). Guy Alchon's *The Invisible Hand of Planning: Capitalism, Social Science, and the State in the 1920s* (Princeton, NJ: Princeton University Press, 1985) is provocative. Lizabeth Cohen attributes more to mutual-benefit organizations in *Making a New Deal: Industrial Workers in Chicago, 1919–1939* (New York: Cambridge University Press, 1990) than does Daniel T. Rodgers in *Atlantic Crossings: Social Politics in a Progressive Age* (Cambridge, MA: Belnap Press, 1998). Historians of the New Deal and the American state continue to neglect the central role of philanthropy and nonprofit organizations in shaping federal activity.

On foundations, health care, and higher education, see Merle Curti and Roderick Nash, *Philanthropy in the Shaping of American Higher Education* (New Brunswick, NJ: Rutgers University Press, 1965); Ellen Condliffe Lagemann, *Private Power for the Public Good: A History of the Carnegie Foundation for the Advancement of Teaching* (Middletown, CT: Wesleyan University Press; Scranton, PA; distributed by Harper and Row, 1983); Steven C. Wheatley, *The Politics of Philanthropy: Abraham Flexner and*

Medical Education (Madison, WI: University of Wisconsin Press, 1988); David C. Hammack and Stanton Wheeler, *Social Science in the Making: Essays on the Russell Sage Foundation, 1907–1972* (New York: Russell Sage Foundation, 1994); Rosemary Stevens, *American Medicine and the Public Interest: A History of Specialization* (Berkeley: University of California Press, 1998); and Terry Boychuk, *The Making and Meaning of Hospital Policy in the United States and Canada* (Ann Arbor: University of Michigan Press, 1999). On history museums, see essays by Michael Wallace and others in Susan Porter Benson, Stephen Brier, and Roy Rosenzweig, *Presenting the Past: Essays on History and the Public* (Philadelphia: Temple University Press, 1986).

An exceptional account of the American Jewish response to the Holocaust is Lucien Lazare, *Rescue as Resistance: How Jewish Organizations Fought the Holocaust in France* (New York: Columbia University Press, 1996). Leon Shapiro, *The History of ORT: A Jewish Movement for Social Change* (New York: Schocken Books, 1980), provides telling detail. Histories of U.S. international relations continue to neglect the important stories of missions, Protestant outreach, Catholic charity, and other international religious ties.

In writing this essay, I have drawn on the manuscript records of the Russell Sage Foundation, the Community Service Society of New York, the Regional Planning Association of New York and Survey Associates, Inc., and The Survey in the Rockefeller Archive Center, Columbia University, Cornell University, the University of Minnesota, and Smith College; on records of Cleveland nonprofits in the Western Reserve Historical Society; and on my oral history interview with Jean Gottman in the Oral History Office at the Columbia University Library. I have also drawn on manuscript and other records of the American Association of Fund-Raising Counsel and The American City Bureau held in the Joseph and Matthew Payton Philanthropic Studies Library of the Indiana University/Purdue University at Indianapolis University Library. For other sources, see David C. Hammack, *Making the Nonprofit Sector in the United States: A Reader* (Bloomington, IN: Indiana University Press, 1998).

CHAPTER 13: FAITH AND GOOD WORKS: CATHOLIC GIVING AND TAKING

The only comprehensive exploration of American Catholic philanthropy from 1790 to the present remains Mary J. Oates, *The Catholic Philanthropic Tradition in America* (Bloomington: Indiana University Press, 1995). The effects of New Deal programs on the Catholic approach to charity are well developed in Dorothy M. Brown and Elizabeth McKeown, "The Poor Belong to Us": *Catholic Charities and American Welfare, 1870–1940* (Cambridge, MA: Harvard University Press, 1998). For more on the Catholic interpretation of stewardship, see Mary J. Oates, "Interpreting the Stewardship Mandate: A Historical Exploration of the American Catholic Experience," *New Theology Review* 9 (November 1996): 10–23.

Papal encyclical letters frequently address the religious call to give. Especially important since the 1930s are Pope Pius XII, "The Rights of Man," in V. Yzermans, ed., *The Major Addresses of Pope Pius XII* (St. Paul: North Central Publishing Co., 1961); and Pope John Paul II, *Centesimus Annus*, in David O'Brien and Thomas Shannon, eds., *Catholic Social Thought: The Documentary Heritage* (Maryknoll, NY: Orbis Books, 1995). Pastoral letters by the National Conference of Catholic Bishops have frequently focused on issues of charity and social justice. Especially valuable in this regard are "Economic Justice for All: Catholic Social Teaching and the U.S. Economy," *Origins* 16 (November 27, 1986): 409–55; and *Stewardship: A Disciple's Response* (Washington, DC: National Conference of Catholic Bishops, 1993). An excellent source for earlier episcopal letters is Hugh J. Nolan, ed., *Pastoral Letters of the U.S. Bishops*, 4 vols. (Washington, DC: National Conference of Catholic Bishops, 1984). Although the benevolent philosophy and works of religious sisterhoods have not received the attention from historians that they deserve, the scholarly literature on them is richer than that available on philanthropic laywomen. Two laywomen, Dorothy Day, founder of the Catholic Worker Movement, and Catherine DeHueck, founder of Friendship House, represent exceptions in this regard. Especially valuable are Dorothy Day, *House of Hospitality* (New York: Sheed and Ward, 1939); Dorothy Day, *Loaves and Fishes* (New York: Harper & Row, 1963); Dorothy Day, *On Pilgrimage* (Catholic Worker Books, 1948); and Catherine DeHueck, *Friendship House* (New York: Sheed and Ward, 1947). Marie de Lourdes Walsh, *The Sisters of Charity of New York, 1809–1959*, 3 vols. (New York: Fordham University Press, 1960), provides a good historical survey of the first charitable sisterhood in America. Two recent sociological studies of the waning of sisterhoods since the 1960s are Helen Ebaugh, *Organizational Decline in Catholic Religious Orders in the United States* (New Brunswick, NJ: Rutgers University Press, 1993); and Patricia Wittberg, *The Rise and Decline of Catholic Religious Orders: A Social Movement Perspective* (Albany: State University of New York Press, 1994).

Worthwhile analyses of general problems in church giving and charity organization include Donald P. Gavin, *The National Conference of Catholic Charities, 1910–1960* (Milwaukee: Bruce Press, 1962); *Toward a Renewed Catholic Charities Movement: A Study of the National Conference of Catholic Charities* (Washington, DC: National Conference of Catholic Charities, 1972); and Andrew Greeley and William McManus, *Catholic Contributions: Sociology and Policy* (Chicago: Thomas More Press, 1987). For more on the development of parochial schools, see Timothy Walch, *Parish School: American Catholic Parochial Education from Colonial Times to the Present* (New York: Crossroad Publishing Co., 1996).

Aspects of the influence of government and other extra-ecclesial funding in the context of religious philanthropy are discussed by Gene D. L. Jones, "The Chicago Catholic Charities, the Great Depression, and Public Monies," *Illinois Historical Journal* 83 (Spring 1990): 13–30; Richard J. Cushing, "The Survival of Our Private Charities," *Catholic Charities Review* 34 (April 1950): 86–91; and Matthew Ahmann, "Catholic Charities and Pluralism: Some Problems, Trends, and Opportunities," *Social Thought* 14 (Spring 1988): 4–12. A valuable sociological study comparing recent congregational giving in five Christian denominations, including the Catholic Church, is Dean R. Hoge, Charles Zech, Patrick McNamara, and Michael J. Donahue, *Money Matters: Personal Giving in American Churches* (Louisville: Westminster John Knox Press, 1996).

CHAPTER 14: IN DEFENSE OF DIVERSITY: JEWISH THOUGHT FROM ASSIMILATIONISM TO CULTURAL PLURALISM

This chapter is drawn from two of the author's previously published essays: the introduction to a reprint edition of Horace M. Kallen's 1924 volume, *Culture and Democracy in the United States* (New Brunswick, NJ: Transaction Books, 1998), as well as "The Smart Set: An Assessment of Jewish Culture," in *The Jews of Boston*, edited by Jonathan D. Sarna and Ellen Smith (Boston: Northeastern University Press and Combined Jewish Philanthropies of Greater Boston, 1995). On the key communal agency of roughly the second half of the twentieth century, see especially Marc Lee Raphael's *A History of the United Jewish Appeal, 1939–1982* (Chico, CA: Scholars Press, 1982). Abraham J. Karp covers much of the same terrain in

To Give Life: The UJA in the Shaping of the American Jewish Community (New York: Schocken, 1981). Why Jews give is treated in Jonathan Woocher's *Sacred Survival: The Civil Religion of American Jews* (Bloomington: Indiana University Press, 1986). See also Milton Goldin's earlier study, *Why They Give: American Jews and Their Philanthropies* (New York: Macmillan, 1976). This scholarly literature needs to be updated and extended. Two newspaper articles have also been informative: "Jewish Charities Raise Huge Sums in the U.S.," *Wall Street Journal*, March 31, 1983, pp. 1, 14; and "Foundations Gaining Lead in Underwriting Innovation," *Forward*, November 17, 1995, pp. 1, 8. The studies of ethnicity – in theory and practice – are voluminous. Among the most astute works in showing how the ideals of unity and multiplicity have somehow been reconciled are Lawrence H. Fuchs, *The American Kaleidoscope: Race, Ethnicity, and the Civic Culture* (Hanover, NH: University Press of New England, 1990); Philip Gleason, *Speaking of Diversity: Language and Ethnicity in Twentieth-Century America* (Baltimore: Johns Hopkins University Press, 1992); John Higham, *Send These to Me: Jews and Other Immigrants in Urban America* (New York: Atheneum, 1975); Michael Lind, *The Next American Nation: The New Nationalism and the Fourth American Revolution* (New York: Free Press, 1995); Arthur Mann, *The One and the Many: Reflections on the American Identity* (Chicago: University of Chicago Press, 1979); Werner Sollors, *Beyond Ethnicity: Consent and Descent in American Culture* (New York: Oxford University Press, 1986); and Michael Walzer, *What It Means to Be an American* (New York: Marsilio, 1992).

The secondary literature on Mary Antin is slim, but see the entry by Pamela S. Nadell in the first volume of *Jewish Women in America: An Historical Encyclopedia,* edited by Paula E. Hyman and Deborah Dash Moore (New York: Routledge, 1997). Check out also Joyce Antler's first chapter in her survey, *The Journey Home: Jewish Women and the American Century* (New York: Free Press, 1997). On the ideological tensions coursing through *The Melting-Pot* in particular, see Neil Larry Shumsky, "Zangwill's *The Melting Pot*: Ethnic Tensions on Stage," *American Quarterly*, 27 (March 1975), 29–41; Arthur Mann, "The Melting Pot," in *Uprooted Americans: Essays to Honor Oscar Handlin*, edited by Richard L. Bushman and others (Boston: Little, Brown, 1979); and David Biale, "The Melting Pot and Beyond," in a volume that he co-edited with Michael Galchinsky and Susannah Heschel, *Insider/Outsider: American Jews and Multiculturalism* (Berkeley: University of California Press, 1998). "The people's attorney" who became the first Jew to serve on the Supreme Court has inspired numerous studies. The turn to Zionism is explored in Allon Gal's *Brandeis of Boston* (Cambridge, MA: Harvard University Press, 1980). Sarah Schmidt has partly examined Kallen's career in *Prophet of American Zionism* (Brooklyn: Carlson, 1995). His cultural pluralism is the subject of Moses Rischin's essay, "The Jews and Pluralism: Toward an American Freedom Symphony," in *Jewish Life in America: Historical Perspectives*, ed. Gladys Rosen (New York: KTAV, 1978). William Toll's analysis of Kallen merits attention too, and appears as Chapter 3 of *Women, Men and Ethnicity: Essays on the Structure and Thought of American Jewry* (Lanham, MD: University Press of America, 1991). Given the relevance of the ideal of "cultural pluralism" to communal vigor and continuity, a serious and full-scale intellectual biography should be deemed exigent.

CHAPTER 15: WAGING THE COLD WAR IN THE THIRD WORLD: THE FOUNDATIONS AND THE CHALLENGES OF DEVELOPMENT

The most comprehensive overviews on foundation activities after World War II are Edward H. Berman, *The Influence of the Carnegie, Ford, and Rockefeller Foundations on American Foreign Policy: The Ideology of Philanthropy* (Albany, NY: State University of New York Press, 1983) and Robert F. Arnove, ed., *Philanthropy/and Cultural Imperialism: The Foundations at Home and Abroad* (Boston, MA: G. K. Hall, 1980).

For the development ideology that characterized the American approach to the Cold War on the Third World, see Robert Packenham, *Liberal America and the Third World: Political Development Ideas and Social Science* (Princeton, NJ: Princeton University Press, 1973); Walt W. Rostow, *Stages of Economic Growth: A Non-Communist Manifesto* (New York: Cambridge University Press, 1960); Robert Leonard, *To Advance Human Welfare: Economics and the Ford Foundation. 1950–1968* (Durham, NC: Center for the Study of Philanthropy and Voluntarism Institute of Policy Sciences and Public Affairs, Duke University, 1989).

Foundation programs are analyzed in the following works: James S. Coleman with David Court, *University Development in the Third World: The Experience of the Rockefeller Foundation* (New York: Pergamon Press, 1993); Kathleen D. McCarthy ed., *Philanthropy and Culture: The International Foundation Perspective* (Philadelphia: University of Pennsylvania Press, 1984); Soma Hewa and Philo Hove, eds. *Philanthropy and Cultural*

Context Western Philanthropy in South East and Southeast Asia in the Twen-tieth Century (Lanham, MD: University Press of America, 1997); Marcus Cueto, ed., *Missionaries of Science: The Rockefeller Foundation and Latin America* (Bloomington, IN: Indiana University Press, 1994); Kathleen D. McCarthy, "From Cold War to Cultural Development: The International Cultural Activities of the Ford Foundation, 1950–1980," *Daedalus,* 116 (1987): 93–117; Francis X. Sutton, "The Foundations and Governments of Developing Countries," *Studies in Comparative International Development,* 12 (1977): 94–119; Robert F. Arnove, "The Ford Foundation and 'Competence Building' Overseas: Assumptions, Approaches, and Outcomes," *Studies in Comparative International Development* 12 (1977): 100–126; Judith Nagelberg, "Promoting Population Policy: The Activities of the Rockefeller Foundation, the Ford Foundation, and the Population Council" (Ph.D. dissertation, Columbia University, 1985); Walter F. Ashley, "Philanthropy and Government: A Study of the Ford Foundation's Overseas Activities" (Ph.D. dissertation, New York University, 1970); George Rosen, *Western Economists and East Societies Agents of Change in South Asia, 1950–1970* (Baltimore, MD: Johns Hopkins University Press, 1985); L. A. Gordon, "Wealth Equals Wisdom? The Rockefeller and Ford Foundations in India," *Annals of the American Academy of Political and Social Science,* 554 (1997): 104–116; Uma Lele and Arthur A. Goldsmith, "The Development of National Agricultural Research Capacity: India's Experience with the Rockefeller Foundation and Its Significance for Africa," *Economic Development and Cultural Change,* 37 (1989): 305–343; Neil A. Patrick, *India's "Package Program" for Intensive Agriculture Development with Emphasis on Ford Foundation Participation* (New Delhi, 1972); Eugene Staples, *Forty Years: A Learning Curve – The Ford Foundation Programs in India, 1952–1992* (New Delhi: Ford Foundation, 1992); Anneliese Markus D. Kennedy, "The Office of Special Studies: A Study of the Joint Mexican Secretariat of Agriculture–Rockefeller Foundation Program in Agriculture, 1943–1963" (Ph.D. Dissertation, University of North Carolina at Chapel Hill, 1974).

CHAPTER 16: PHILANTHROPY, THE CIVIL RIGHTS MOVEMENT, AND THE POLITICS OF RACIAL REFORM

There is a voluminous body of literature on the Civil Rights Movement and its supporters. For general works, see Aldon D. Morris, *The Origins of the*

Civil Rights Movement (New York: The Free Press, 1984); Fred Powledge, *Free At Last? The Civil Rights Movement and the People Who Made It* (Boston: Little, Brown and Co., 1991); Harvard Sitkoff, *The Struggle for Black Equality, 1954–1980* (New York: Hill and Wang, 1981); and Henry Hampton and Steve Fayer, *Voices of Freedom: An Oral History of the Civil Rights Movement from the 1950s through the 1980s* (New York: Bantam Books, 1990). There are also several works on the civil rights struggle in various regions and locales. For the movement in the Deep South, see Howell Raines, *My Soul Is Rested: The Story of the Civil Rights Movement in the Deep South* (New York: Penguin Books, 1988). A thorough case study of a Deep South city is Robert J. Norrell's *Reaping the Whirlwind: The Civil Rights Movement in Tuskegee* (New York: Vintage Books, 1985). William Chafe's *Civilities and Civil Rights* (New York: Oxford University Press, 1981) looks at the Civil Rights Movement as it unfolded in Greensboro, North Carolina.

Many of the studies of civil rights leadership focus on Martin Luther King, Jr., and among the best works are David Garrow, *Bearing the Cross: Martin Luther King, Jr., and the Southern Christian Leadership Conference* (New York: Vintage Book, 1988); Taylor Branch's *Parting the Waters* and *Pillar of Fire* (New York: Simon & Schuster, 1988 and 1998, respectively); and Adam Fairclough, *To Redeem the Soul of America: The Southern Christian Leadership Conference and Martin Luther King, Jr.* (Athens: University of Georgia Press, 1987). For a representative sampling of King's speeches and writings, see James M. Washington, ed., *The Essential Writings and Speeches of Martin Luther King, Jr.* (New York: Harper Collins, 1986). The standard work on the Student Nonviolent Coordinating Committee is Clayborne Carson's *In Struggle: SNCC and the Black Awakening of the 1960s* (Cambridge, MA: Harvard University Press, 1996).

There are a number of accounts of the federal government's role in facilitating (and hindering) the success of the movement. Among the most useful are Kenneth O'Reilly, *Nixon's Piano: Presidents and Racial Politics from Washington to Clinton* (New York: The Free Press, 1995) and Victor S. Navasky, *Kennedy Justice* (New York: Atheneum, 1971). The Voter Education Project is discussed at length in Pat Watters and Reese Cleghorn, *Climbing Jacob's Ladder: The Arrival of Negroes in Southern Politics* (New York: Harcourt, Brace & World, 1967). J. Harvey Wilkinson III provides an insightful discussion of the judicial system's role in shaping civil-rights law in his *From Brown to Bakke: The Supreme Court and School Integration, 1954–1978* (New York: Oxford University Press, 1981). For the War on Poverty, see Donald T. Critchlow and Charles H. Parker, eds., *With Us Always: A History of Private Charity and Public Welfare* (Lanham, MD: Rowman & Littlefield Publishers, 1998) and Dona C. Hamilton and Charles V. Hamilton, *The Dual Agenda: Race and Social Welfare Policies of Civil Rights Organizations* (New York: Columbia University Press, 1997).

For the role of religious institutions in the Civil Rights Movement, see Gayraud S. Wilmore, *Black Religion and Black Radicalism* (Maryknoll, NY: Orbis Books, 1991). James L. Findlay, Jr., looks at the response of white Christians to the movement in *Church People in the Struggle: The National Council of Churches and the Black Freedom Movement, 1950–1970* (New York: Oxford University Press, 1993). Additionally, other works of interest include Vicki L. Crawford, Jacqueline A. Rouse, and Barbara Woods, eds., *Women in the Civil Rights Movement* (Bloomington: Indiana University Press, 1993); David Steigerwald, *The Sixties and the End of Modern America* (New York: St. Martin's Press, 1995); William H. Harris, *The Harder We Run: Black Workers Since the Civil War* (New York: Oxford University Press, 1982); and Lerone Bennett, Jr., *Before the Mayflower: A History of Black America* (New York: Penguin Books, 1988).

CHAPTER 17: THE WELFARE STATE AND THE CAREERS OF PUBLIC AND PRIVATE INSTITUTIONS SINCE 1945

The most comprehensive overview of the transformation of American philanthropy during the years 1940–1990 can be found in Peter Hall's *Inventing the Nonprofit Sector and Other Essays on Philanthropy, Voluntarism, and Nonprofit Organizations* (Baltimore: Johns Hopkins University Press, 1992). Carolyn Webber and Aaron Wildavksy's *History of Taxation and Expenditure in the Western World* (New York: Simon and Schuster, 1986) is the best available survey of the taxing, budgeting, and spending practices of the federal government in the postwar period. The ways in which government policies were implemented through the private sectors are admirably chronicled in Sanford M. Jacoby's *Modern Manors: Welfare Capitalism Since the New Deal* (Princeton, NJ: Princeton University Press, 1997) and Christopher Howard's *The Hidden Welfare State: Tax Expenditures and Social Policy in the United States* (Princeton, NJ: Princeton University Press, 1997).

Work on the evolution of the federal tax code includes John F. Witte's *The Politics and Development of the Federal Income Tax* (Madison, WI: University of Wisconsin Press, 1985), John D. Colombo and Mark Hall's *The Charitable Tax Exemption* (Boulder, CO: Westview Press, 1995), and Marion Fremont-Smith's *Foundations and Government: State and Federal Law and Supervision* (New York: Russell Sage Foundation, 1965). John G. Simon's "Tax Treatment of Nonprofit Organizations: A Review of Federal and State Policies," in W. W. Powell, *The Nonprofit Sector: A Research Handbook* (New Haven: Yale University Press, 1987) presents a fine overview of contemporary tax and regulatory issues as they affect philanthropy.

An extended account of the issues relating to the politics of philanthropy during the 1980s as manifested in the *Buck Trust* case can be found in the *University of San Francisco Law Review* 21(4) (Summer 1987).

Studies of devolution and privatization as they affect philanthropy and nonprofits include Lester M. Salamon's *Partners in Public Service: Government–Nonprofit Relations in the Modern Welfare State* (Baltimore, MD: Johns Hopkins University Press, 1995), Steven Rathgeb Smith and Michael Lipsky's *Nonprofits for Hire: The Welfare State in the Age of Contracting* (Cambridge, MA: Harvard University Press, 1993), Kirsten Gronbjerg's *Understanding Nonprofit Funding: Managing Revenues in Social Service and Community Development Organizations* (San Francisco: Jossey-Boss, 1993), and Elizabeth T. Boris and C. Eugene Steurle (eds.), *Nonprofits and Government: Collaboration and Conflict* (Washington, DC: Urban Institute Press, 1999).

The best accounts of the conservative revolution are Kirkpatrick Sale's *Power Shift: The Rise of the Southern Rim and Its Challenge to the Eastern Establishment* (New York: Random House, 1975) and Godfrey Hodgson's *The World Turned Right Side Up: A History of the Conservative Ascendancy in America* (Boston: Houghton Mifflin, 1996). James A. Smith's *The Idea Brokers: Think Tanks and the Rise of the Policy Elite* (New York: The Free Press, 1991) describes the role of these unique institutions and their political significance.

The current struggle to shape the direction of philanthropy are documented in Charles Clotfelter and Thomas Ehrlich (eds.), *Philanthropy and the Nonprofit Sector* (Bloomington, IN: Indiana University Press, 1999), which offers the views of philanthropic liberals, and two publications by the conservatively tilted National Commission on Philanthropy and Civic Renewal: *Giving Better, Giving Smarter: The Report of the Commission on Philanthropy and Civic Renewal* (Washington, DC: National Commission on Philanthropy and Civic Renewal, 1997); and John W. Barry and Bruno V. Manno (eds.), *Giving Better, Giving Smarter: Working Papers of the National Commission on Philanthropy and Civic Renewal* (Washington, DC: The Commission, 1997).

EPILOGUE: THE EUROPEAN COMPARISON

For a survey of the conditions of Europe's poor, a fine introduction is provided in Bronislaw Geremek, *Poverty – A History*, Agniedka Kolakowska, translator (1994).

The best overall survey of the poor and the attempts to aid them in the early modern era can be found in the two-volume work edited by Thomas Riis, *Aspects of Poverty in Early Modern Europe*, vols. 1–2 (1981–1986). Welfare practices in Protestant countries are described in Ole Peter Grell and Andrew Cunningham (eds.), *Health Care and Poor Relief in Protestant Europe, 1500–1700* (1997).

Broad opportunities for comparisons across nations and periods exist in various important collection of essays, among the most recent being Jonathan Barry and Colin Jones, eds., *Medicine and Charity Before the Welfare State* (1991); Hugh Cunningham and Joanna Innes, eds., *Charity, Philanthropy, and Reform* (1998); Peter Mandler, ed., *The Uses of Charity* (1990); Margaret Pelling and Richard M. Smith, *Life, Death, and the Elderly – Historical Perspectives* (1991); Stuart Woolf, ed., *The Poor in Western Europe in the Eighteenth and Nineteenth Centuries* (1986).

The particular role of gender in welfare measures and charity are deftly handled in two books: Gisela Bock and Pat Thane, eds., *Maternity and Gender Policies* (1991) and Birgitta Jordansson and Tienne Vammen, *Charitable Women, Philanthropic Welfare, 1780–1930* (1998).

There are few systematic studies of private philanthropy over any length of time. The only ones in English are on English philanthropy: David Owen, *English Philanthropy, 1660–1960* (1964), and F. K. Prochaska, "Philanthropy," in F. M. L. Thompson, ed., *Cambridge Social History of Britain, 1750–1950*, vol. 3 (1990).

England was the nation with the broadest provision of aid for the poor from early on. A strong and rich literature exists on the English poor law and its functioning: Lynn Hollen Lees, *The Solidarities of Strangers – The English*

Poor Laws and the People, 1700–1948 (1998); Michael E. Rose, *The Relief of Poverty, 1834–1914* (1972); and Peter Wood, *Poverty and the Workhouse in Victorian Britain* (1991).

The continuous interaction of reformers in Western Europe and the United States in the nineteenth and twentieth centuries is masterfully studied in Daniel T. Rodgers, *Atlantic Crossings – Social Politics in a Progressive Age* (1998).

AUTHOR PROFILES

EDITORS

LAWRENCE J. FRIEDMAN, Ph.D., UCLA

A professor of history and philanthropic studies at Indiana University, Larry has published numerous essays in academic journals and five other books addressing a broad range of subjects in American intellectual and cultural history, his most recent being *Identity's Architect: A Biography of Erik Erikson* (New York: Scribner, 1999). He has received several NEH research fellowships and has won several book prizes. Larry was a postdoctoral Fellow at the Menninger Foundation Interdisciplinary Studies Program in 1981 and was awarded the Fulbright Distinguished Chair to Germany for 2001–2002. His current project addresses the motivations and thoughts of intellectual emigres and their flight from the Holocaust.

MARK D. McGARVIE, Ph.D., INDIANA UNIVERSITY; J. D. MARQUETTE UNIVERSITY

Mark taught legal history and legal research and writing at SUNY at Buffalo School of Law during the 1999–2000 and 2000–2001 academic years. Since the fall of 2001, he has been a Golieb Fellow in Legal History at NYU School of Law. Mark has published several articles in law reviews and academic journals. His 2000 dissertation, "One Nation Under Law: America's Early National Struggles to Separate Church and State," addresses the intellectual and legal history of disestablishment. He is currently working on a biography of St. George Tucker, jurist and legal scholar in early nineteenth-century Virginia. Prior to pursuing an academic career, Mark practiced labor and employment law.

CHAPTER CONTRIBUTORS

G. J. BARKER-BENFIELD, Ph.D., UCLA

Ben is a Professor of History at SUNY at Albany. His book, *The Horrors of the Half-Known Life: Male Attitudes toward Women and Sexuality in Nineteenth-Century America* (New York: Harper & Row, 1976), was reissued with a new introduction in 2000, and *Portraits of American Women*, edited with Catherine Clinton (New York: St. Martin's Press, 1991) was reprinted in 1998. He published *The Culture of Sensibility: Sex and Society in Eighteenth-Century Britain* (Chicago: Chicago University Press, 1992). At present, he is writing on sensibility in America from the 1680s to the 1880s.

CLAUDE A. CLEGG, Ph.D., UNIVERSITY OF MICHIGAN

Claude teaches American History and the African diaspora at Indiana University. He is the author of *An Original Man: The Life and Times of Elijah Muhammad* (New York: St. Martin's Press, 1997). Claude has completed a book that examines the emigration of black North Carolinians to Liberia during the nineteenth century.

WILLIAM B. COHEN, Ph.D., STANFORD UNIVERSITY

Bill is a Professor of History at Indiana University and author of numerous scholarly essays and books on early modern Europe. He has received fellowships from the National Endowment of Humanities and the Fulbright Program. His latest book is *Urban Government and the Rise of the French City* (New York: St. Martin's Press, 1998).

RUTH CROCKER, Ph.D., PURDUE UNIVERSITY

Ruth has degrees from St. Anne's College, Oxford, and Purdue. She is currently Alumni Associate Professor at Auburn University, where she teaches History and Women's Studies. She has published *Social Work and Social Order: The Settlement Movement in Two Industrial Cities, 1890–1930* (Illinois,

1992). In 1992, she was an NEH Fellow at the University of Iowa. She is currently completing a biography of Mrs. Russell Sage.

ROY E. FINKENBINE, Ph.D., BOWLING GREEN STATE UNIVERSITY

Roy is associate professor of history and Director of the Black Abolitionist Archives at the University of Detroit Mercy. His major publications include the five-volume *Black Abolitionist Papers 1830–1865* (1985–1992), *Witness for Freedom: African American Voices on Race, Slavery, and Emancipation* (1993), and *Sources of the African-American Past* (New York: Longman, 1997).

WENDY GAMBER, Ph.D., BRANDEIS UNIVERSITY

Wendy is an associate professor of History at Indiana University and a former Associate Editor of the *Journal of American History*. She is the author of *The Female Economy: The Millinery and Dressmaking Trades, 1860–1930*, (University of Illinois Press, 1997). She is currently at work on *Houses, Not Homes: Boardinghouses in Nineteenth-Century America* (under contract, Johns Hopkins University Press).

ROBERT A. GROSS, Ph.D., COLUMBIA UNIVERSITY

Bob is the Forrest D. Murden Jr. Professor of History and American Studies at the College of William and Mary and Book Review Editor of the *William and Mary Quarterly*. His first book, *The Minutemen and Their World* (New York: Hill and Wang, 1976) won the prestigious Bancroft prize in American History. Since then, he has authored *Books and Libraries in Thoreau's Concord* (Worcester, MA: American Antiquarian Society, 1988) and edited *In Debt to Shays: The Bicentennial of an Agrarian Rebellion* (Charlottesville: University Press of Virginia, 1993). Bob focuses on American social and cultural history from 1750 to 1850. His interest in philanthropy studies grows out of his ongoing inquiry into the character of community in nineteenth-century New England. The product of that inquiry, *The Transcendentalists and Their World*, will be published by Hill & Wang in 2003.

PETER D. HALL, Ph.D., SUNY AT STONY BROOK

At Yale, Peter has long been a member of the program on nonprofit organizations. Recently, he was also Lecturer in Public Policy at the John

F. Kennedy School of Government, Harvard University. He is editor of the chapter on voluntary, nonprofit, and religious entities and activities for Millennial Edition of *Historical Statistics of the United States* (forthcoming from Cambridge) and author of a great many articles. He is also author of several books, including *Inventing the Nonprofit Sector and Other Essays on Philanthropy, Voluntarism, and Nonprofit Organizations* (Baltimore: Johns Hopkins University Press, 1992).

DAVID HAMMACK, Ph.D., COLUMBIA UNIVERSITY

David is Hiram C. Haydn Professor of History and Chair of the Educational Programs Committee of the Mandel Center for Nonprofit Organizations at Case Western Reserve University. He has degrees from Harvard, Reed College, and Columbia University, and has been a Resident Scholar at the Russell Sage Foundation, a Guggenheim Fellow, and a Visiting Scholar at the Program on Nonprofit Organizations at Yale. He edited and wrote extensive introductions for *Making the Nonprofit Sector in the United States: A Reader* (Indiana University Press, 1998); *Nonprofit Organizations in a Market Economy* (Jossey-Bass, 1993); and (with Stanton Wheeler) wrote *Social Science in the Making: Essays on the Russell Sage Foundation, 1907–1972* (Russell Sage Foundation, 1994). He also has published numerous articles in academic journals and several other books.

GARY HESS, Ph.D., UNIVERSITY OF VIRGINIA

Gary is Distinguished Research Professor of History at Bowling Green State University and was President of the Society for Historians of American Foreign Relations in 1991. His research has concentrated on U.S.–Asian relations and he has been a four-time Fulbright lecturer/scholar in India. His most recent book is *Presidential Decisions for War: Korea, Vietnam, the Persian Gulf* (Baltimore: Johns Hopkins University Press, 2001).

KATHLEEN McCARTHY, Ph.D., UNIVERSITY OF CHICAGO

Kathleen is Professor of History and Director of the Center for the Study of Philanthropy at The Graduate Center, City University of New York. She is the author of *Women's Culture: American Philanthropy and Art, 1830–1930* (Chicago: Chicago University Press, 1991, and co-winner of the ARNOVA Distinguished Book Award in 1994); *Noblesse Oblige: Charity and Cultural*

Philanthropy in Chicago, 1829–1929 (Chicago: Chicago University Press, 1980) and numerous articles and edited volumes, including "Women, Philanthropy, and Civil Society." She is currently completing a book on philanthropy and the rise of civil society in the United States from the eighteenth century to 1865.

MARY J. OATES, Ph.D., YALE UNIVERSITY

Mary is Research Professor of Economics at Regis College in Weston, Massachusetts, specializing in economics and American economic and religious history. Her latest book, *The Catholic Philanthropic Tradition in America*, was published by Indiana University Press in 1995. She has published numerous essays in academic journals. She is currently writing a book on American Catholic higher education for women since 1895.

AMANDA PORTERFIELD, Ph.D., STANFORD UNIVERSITY

Amanda has been President of the American Society of Church History. She is a Professor of Religious Studies at the University of Wyoming. She has authored numerous scholarly essays and several books, including *The Transformation of American Religion* (Oxford University Press, 2001), *American Religious History* (Blackwell Publications, 2001), *Mary Lyon and the Mount Holyoke Missionaries* (Oxford University Press, 1997), and *Female Piety in New England* (Oxford University Press, 1992).

EMILY S. ROSENBERG, Ph.D., SUNY AT STONY BROOK

Emily is DeWitt Wallace Professor of History at Macalester College, specializing in U.S. foreign relations in the twentieth century. She is the author of *Spreading the American Dream: American Economic and Cultural Expansion, 1890–1945* (New York: Hill and Wang, 1982) and *Financial Missionaries to the World: The Politics and Culture of Dollar Diplomacy, 1900–1930* (Cambridge, MA: Cambridge University Press, 1999), which won the Ferrell Senior Book award from the Society for Historians of American Foreign Relations in 2000. She has coauthored several textbooks, among them *In Our Times: America Since 1945* and *Liberty, Equality, Power: A History of the American People*, and written numerous articles on international finance, gender issues, and foreign relations. She has served on the board of the Organization of American Historians, on the board of editors of the

Journal of American History and *Diplomatic History*, and as president of the Society for Historians of American Foreign Relations.

JUDITH SEALANDER, Ph.D., DUKE UNIVERSITY

Judy is a Professor of History at Bowling Green State University. She has received research fellowships from, among others, the Rockefeller Foundation, National Endowment for the Humanities, Indiana University Center on Philanthropy, and Newberry Library. Her latest among numerous publications, *Private Wealth and Public Life: Foundation Philanthropy and the Re-Shaping of Social Policy, From Progressive Era to the New Deal* (Johns Hopkins University Press, 1997), won the Ohio Academy of History Book Prize. Her current project, *Reinventing Childhood: Twentieth-Century American State Regulation of Children's Work, Education, Health, and Welfare*, is due out shortly.

STEPHEN WARREN, Ph.D., INDIANA UNIVERSITY

Steve is an Assistant Professor of History at Augustana College. He previously held a similar position at Eastern Kentucky University. His areas of specialization include American Indian, Western, and Jacksonian history. He is currently finishing a book manuscript on the impact of removal and the reservation system on the Shawnee tribe.

STEPHEN J. WHITFIELD, Ph.D., BRANDEIS UNIVERSITY

Steve holds the Max Richter Chair in American Civilization at Brandeis University, where he has taught since 1972. Among his several books are *The Culture of the Cold War* (Baltimore: Johns Hopkins University Press, expanded edition, 1996) and *In Search of American Jewish Culture* (Hanover, NH: Brandeis University Press, 1999). He also served as a Visiting Professor at the Hebrew University of Jerusalem, at the Catholic University of Leuven in Belgium, and at the Sorbonne in Paris.

INDEX